STATISTICS FOR
SOCIAL SCIENCES

Bulk Sales

SAGE India offers special discounts
for purchase of books in bulk.
We also make available special imprints
and excerpts from our books on demand.

For orders and enquiries, write to us at

Marketing Department
SAGE Publications India Pvt Ltd
B1/I-1, Mohan Cooperative Industrial Area
Mathura Road, Post Bag 7
New Delhi 110044, India

E-mail us at **marketing@sagepub.in**

Get to know more about SAGE

Be invited to SAGE events, get on our mailing list.
Write today to **marketing@sagepub.in**

This book is also available as an e-book.

STATISTICS FOR SOCIAL SCIENCES

T. RAJARETNAM

 **SAGE**

www.sagepublications.com
Los Angeles • London • New Delhi • Singapore • Washington DC

SC

First published in 2016 by

 SAGE Publications India Pvt Ltd
B1/I-1 Mohan Cooperative Industrial Area
Mathura Road, New Delhi 110 044, India
www.sagepub.in

SAGE Publications Inc
2455 Teller Road
Thousand Oaks, California 91320, USA

SAGE Publications Ltd
1 Oliver's Yard, 55 City Road
London EC1Y 1SP, United Kingdom

SAGE Publications Asia-Pacific Pte Ltd
3 Church Street
#10-04 Samsung Hub
Singapore 049483

Published by Vivek Mehra for SAGE Publications India Pvt Ltd, typeset in Galliard BT 10/12pt by Zaza Eunice, Hosur, Tamil Nadu, India and printed at Saurabh Printers Pvt Ltd, Greater Noida.

Library of Congress Cataloging-in-Publication Data

Names: Rajaretnam, T., author.
Title: Statistics for social sciences / T. Rajaretnam.
Description: Thousand Oaks : SAGE Publications India Pvt. Inc, 2016. |
    Includes bibliographical references and index.
Identifiers: LCCN 2015039709| ISBN 9789351506553 (pbk. : alk. paper) |
    ISBN 9789351506560 (ebook) | ISBN 9789351506546 (epub)
Subjects: LCSH: Social sciences--Statistical methods. | Social
    sciences--Research--Methodology.
Classification: LCC HA29 .R235 2016 | DDC 519.5--dc23 LC record available at
    http://lccn.loc.gov/2015039709

ISBN: 978-93-515-0655-3 (PB)

The SAGE Team: N. Unni Nair, Alekha Chandra Jena, Anju Saxena and Ritu Chopra

3/17/17

Contents

List of Tables

List of Figures

List of Abbreviations

AIDS	Acquired immunodeficiency syndrome
ANOVA	Analysis of variance
BSS	Between sum of squares (in ANOVA)
CBR	Crude birth rate
CEB	Census enumeration block
CI	Confidence interval
CPR	Contraceptive prevalence rate
CV	Coefficient of variation
df	Degrees of freedom
DI	Dissimilarity index
ESS	Explained sum of squares (in regression)
Exp()	Exponent
GNI	Gross national income
HDI	Human development index
HIV	Human immunodeficiency virus
IHDI	Inequality-adjusted human development index
IMR	Infant mortality rate
IQR	Inter-quartile range
LHS	Left-hand side
ln(), Log()	Natural logarithm of
MCA	Multiple classification analysis
MESS	Mean explained sum of squares
MS	Microsoft
MUSS	Mean unexplained sum of squares
NA	Not applicable
NFHS	National Family Health Survey
NP	Non-parametric (test)
NSS	National Sample Survey
OLS	Ordinary least square
PPS	Probability proportional to size
PSU	Primary sampling unit
RHS	Right-hand side
SD	Standard deviation
SE	Standard error
Sig.	Significance level
SPSS	Statistical Package for Social Sciences
SRS	Simple Random Sampling

TSS	Total sum of squares (in ANOVA)
UNDP	United Nations Development Programme
USS	Unexplained sum of squares (in regression)
WSS	Within sum of squares (in ANOVA)

Preface

I am basically a statistician-turned demographer-cum-social scientist, engaged mainly in research activities in the broad areas of demography, public health, nutrition and livelihoods for the last 35 years. All these years my teaching activities were meagre and ever since I joined Tata Institute of Social Sciences, Mumbai, more than 7 years ago, I have been teaching basic but applied statistics to MA, MPhil and PhD students of different courses (Social Work, Development Studies, Women Studies, Habitat Studies, etc.) conducted by the Institute. Also, many students and researchers come to me seeking guidance in sampling and data analysis for their dissertation/research work.

During the course of my teaching and providing guidance, I found that the students were rather allergic to reading statistics books as they contain mainly equations and derivations and less of the description of applications. Nowadays, we have a number of software programs, such as Statistical Package for Social Sciences (SPSS), that perform the tedious and complex calculations but often users do not know when and how to apply a particular statistical method and how to interpret the results and draw inference. So, what is needed is an understanding of the techniques, their uses as to where and when to apply, how to interpret the results and draw appropriate inference. This book is written in that direction. In fact, this book is an amalgamation of my lecture notes on different chapters prepared over the years and updated from time to time.

In this book, I have avoided, as far as possible, the presentation of derivations but provided the explanation of what the methods/techniques are, when and where to apply them, what are the assumptions involved and how to interpret the results and draw inference. In addition, every technique is followed by examples with manual calculations, with MS Excel and/or with SPSS. The input and output formats of different statistical packages may differ but the contents would be largely the same, and so it would not be difficult for those who are conversant with other software packages to follow this book. With software packages, though users are not required to perform manual calculations, it is hoped that they can have a much better understanding of the techniques with the manual calculations presented in this book. From these angles, I consider this book a reference handbook and not a textbook. However, the presentation of some technical aspects (equations and derivations) is needed and I request the readers to cope with them or just skip them. I hope that social science students, teachers and researchers of various disciplines can better understand the techniques described in this book and apply them with ease.

T. Rajaretnam

Introduction to Statistics

THE MEANING OF STATISTICS

What Is Statistics?

Statistics is the science of collecting, summarising, analysing and interpreting *numerical* statement of facts (called *data*) about groups of people or objects (called *population*).

The statistical methods used to summarise and describe the data are often called *descriptive statistics*. The statistical methods used to draw inferences about population(s) based on samples drawn from them, as to, say, whether two populations are the same or differ with respect to some characteristic features of interest, are called *inferential statistics*. The descriptive and inferential statistical methods applied to any field of science are called *applied statistics*. A few examples of applied statistics are bio-statistics, business statistics, social statistics, econometrics, quality control and operations research. There is also a discipline called *mathematical statistics*, which is concerned with the theoretical development of statistical models, analytical methods and hypothesis testing procedures for specific situations and for complex relationships.

Applications of Statistics

Statistics is now applied in every sphere of human activity and is countless, and also the list is increasing day by day. A few of the commonly used applications of statistics are given below.

1. In health and medical science, statistical data and statistical techniques are used to study longevity, fertility, mortality, prevalence and incidence of diseases and so on.
2. In social science, statistical data and statistical methods are applied to understand people's knowledge and attitudes, levels of living and so on.
3. In business and industry, statistical techniques are applied to assess consumer preferences and pricing of goods, production optimisation and quality control.
4. In planning and programme development, statistical data and techniques are used to study the levels and pattern of development, regional and sectoral differences in development, and monitoring and evaluation of programmes, so that appropriate programmes could be developed or redesigned to achieve the desired goal for different regions.

Limitations of Statistics

Statistics has the following limitations:

1. Statistics deals with the aggregate of objects and not the individuals, and so it is suitable to infer about groups and not the individuals.
2. Statistical conclusions are true only on the average and not to every individual in the population. That is, statistical conclusions cannot be assumed to be true for each individual in

the population. For example, if the average depth of a river is 3 feet, it does not mean that one can cross the river just by walking through it because in some places the depth may be higher than the height of a person crossing it.

3.   Statistics cannot be expected to give solutions to problems. It only helps to analyse the problems. It is for the users to identify and devise appropriate strategies to solve the problems.

4.   Statistics is liable to be misused. Statistics is like clay and one can make a God or Devil as one pleases. For example, one may interpret a small difference as a serious problem, whereas others may dismiss it considering insignificant.

MEASUREMENT THEORY

Measurement theory deals with the classification or quantification (called *measurement*) of population units according to certain characteristics or attributes of interest. The way the measurements are made should be unique (unambiguous), valid (reasonable) and amenable for statistical treatment (analysis).

The measurement of an attribute of individuals or objects in a population is the process of assigning symbols, codes or numbers (called *values*) to them in such a way that the relationship of the values reflects the relationship of the individuals with respect to the attribute being measured. A particular way of assigning values to an attribute is called the *scale of measurement*.

For example, the height of a boy is 150 cm and that of a girl is 140 cm. Here, we have assigned the value (number) 150 for the height of the boy and the value 140 for the height of the girl, and we can relate them by saying that the boy is taller than the girl. Here, the assignment of the number is not arbitrary but based on standard measurement (centimetres) and the number is unique and valid. As the numbers are comparable (as mentioned above), the measurements are amenable for statistical treatment like deriving average height of boys and girls and hypothesis testing.

LEVELS OF MEASUREMENT

Levels of measurement refer to the types of relationships of the values (symbols, codes or numbers) assigned to attributes (variables). There are typically four levels of measurements, namely nominal, ordinal, interval and ratio measurements.

Nominal Measurement

In *nominal* measurement, the value (symbol, code or number) assigned to an attribute of individuals is only *symbolic*. Two individuals or members are assigned the same value if they possess the same (or same type of) attribute and are assigned different values if they possess different (or different types of) attributes. No ordering of the values is implied, that is, no value (so assigned) is said to be (or declared) better or higher than the other values.

For example, the sex of a person is assigned a value 1 if 'male' and a value 2 if 'female'. Although numerically 2 is greater than 1, there no such relationship or ordering is valid between a male and a female. That is, we cannot say that a female is greater (or better) than a male and vice versa. Because of the lack of ordering and since the values are not in a continuum scale, one cannot perform arithmetic operations, namely addition, subtraction, multiplication and division $(+, -, *, /)$ or logical operations $(>, <, =)$ on the data of nominal variables. That is, numerically $1+2=3$ but when we assign the code 1 for a male and 2 for a female, $(1+2)$ or for that matter (male+female) is meaningless.

However, nominal measurements are amenable for statistical treatment. For example, following the same coding system, we may count the number of males (code 1) and number of females (code 2) in a population and say that the population consisted of, say, 200 cases with code 1 and 150 cases with code 2, that is, the population consisted of 200 males and 150 females.

A few more examples of nominal variables are religion, caste or caste class, occupation and place of stay.

Ordinal Measurement

In *ordinal* measurement, the attributes are rank-ordered. For example, while measuring educational attainment, one may assign a value 0 for no education (or illiterate), 1 for primary education, 2 for secondary education and 3 for college/higher education. In this measure, a higher value means a higher level of education and so ordering is meaningful. That is, 2 is greater than 1 because secondary education is higher than primary education. But at the same time, the difference between 1 and 2 cannot be said to be the same as the difference between 0 and 1. That is, the difference between secondary education and primary education cannot be said to be the same as the difference between primary education and no education. As such, in ordinal measurement, the values are in some hierarchical order but not in a continuum scale and so one can perform logical operations (>, <, =) and not arithmetic operations (+, −, /, *). Please note that in nominal measurement, not even logical operation is valid.

Interval Measurement

In *interval* measurement, not only the ordering of values but also the interval (or distance) between values is meaningful. For example, in the measurement of temperature, the distance between 30 °C and 40 °C is the same as the distance between 70 °C and 80 °C (a difference of 10 °C). That is, the interval between two values is meaningful and interpretable. But at the same time, 80 °C is not twice hot as much as 40 °C. Similarly, we can measure 'years of schooling' of a person as, say, 10 years (secondary), 12 years (higher secondary) and 15 years (graduate degree). Suppose a person A has six years of schooling and another person B has 12 years of schooling, and we can say that person B has six more years of schooling than person A, but it is not appropriate to say that person B has double the schooling (education) of person A, or person B is twice better than person A in terms of schooling or education. So, with interval data, one can perform logical operations and also addition and subtraction, but at the same time, multiplication and division operations are not appropriate. Furthermore, a 'zero' measure is not a real '0' value or a starting point. That is, 'no' schooling is not 'zero' or 'nil' schooling and also 'zero' temperature is not 'nil' temperature but 'a level' of temperature.

Ratio Measurement

Finally, in *ratio* measurement, we can construct a meaningful ratio of two values. For example, weight is a ratio measurement (variable), in that a weight 80 kg is twice heavier as a weight 40 kg. In general, most 'count' variables are ratio measurements. For example, the number of students attending a special class in a day is a ratio measurement because if 10 students attend on Saturday and 20 students on Monday, then we can say that students attending special class on Monday is twice as many as that on Saturday. Also, a ratio measurement is an interval measurement that has a true zero point. For example, if no student attended the class, we can say that the number of students attended the class is '0' (zero). Similarly, income is a ratio measurement because an income

Figure 1.1 Schematic Presentation of the Measurement of Variables

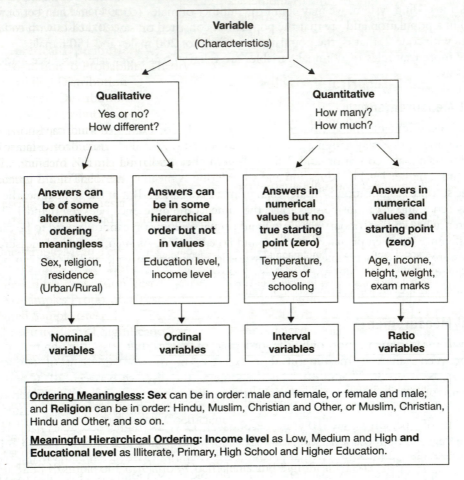

Ordering Meaningless: **Sex** can be in order: male and female, or female and male; and **Religion** can be in order: Hindu, Muslim, Christian and Other, or Muslim, Christian, Hindu and Other, and so on.

Meaningful Hierarchical Ordering: **Income level** as Low, Medium and High **and Educational level** as Illiterate, Primary, High School and Higher Education.

of ₹0 (zero) is truly 'no income'. For most statistical procedures, the distinction between interval and ratio measurements is not often recognised, and it is common to use the term 'interval' to refer to both interval and ratio variables. Occasionally, however, the distinction between interval and ratio scales is important.

A schematic presentation of the measurement of variables is presented in Figure 1.1.

STATISTICAL MEASUREMENT OF VARIABLES

Statistical Variable

A *statistical variable* or simply a *variable* is a characteristic feature of individuals in a population (or a sample), that differs or varies from one individual to another (e.g., sex, age, religion, etc. differ from one individual to another) and/or, for the same individual, from one point of time to another (e.g., age, weight, employment, income, etc. differ from time to time for the same individual).

Note: Characteristic features of individuals in a group that do not vary from one individual to another or from one point of time to another are 'not variables' for that group only. For example, in a group of mothers, sex is not a variable because all individuals in the group are females. Similarly, in a group of illiterate mothers, educational level is not a variable. In a group of children born in a particular year, age is not a variable.

Numerical and Categorical Variables

In statistics, variables are of two broad categories, namely numerical variables and categorical variables. *Numerical variables* are those variables that are measured in quantity or numerical values (e.g., age, height, number of children, income and so on). *Categorical variables* are those variables in which the individuals are classified or categorised into different groups (e.g., sex, occupation, religion, educational level). That is, numerical variables are *counts* or *quantities* possessed by individuals and categorical variables are *classification* or *categorisation* of individuals as belonging to one group or another. The interval and ratio variables are essentially numerical variables, and nominal and ordinal variables come under categorical variables in statistical analysis.

The difference between numerical and categorical variables is that numerical variables are amenable for statistical calculations such as mean, median, standard deviation and correlation, whereas categorical variables as such are not amenable for statistical measures but are amenable for distribution and tabulation. However, categorical variables can also be converted into a kind of numerical variables called dummy variables (discussed later in this chapter) and used in statistical calculations. In general, both numerical variables and categorical variables have statistical properties, but numerical variables have more statistical properties than categorical variables.

Continuous and Discrete Variables

The numerical variables are of two types, namely continuous variables and discrete variables. *Continuous variables* are those variables that take any value including fractional (decimal) values. For example, weight can take a value 5 kg, 5.2 kg, 5.23 kg and so on. On the other hand, *discrete variables* are those variables that take only selected values in a continuum or range (often integer values and not fractional values). The continuous variables are essentially interval and ratio variables, whereas discrete variables can be of any type, namely ratio, interval, ordinal and nominal variables.

For example, the number of children to a couple can be 0, 1, 2, 3 and so on; it cannot be 1.7 or 2.5. Please note that a variable is treated as a discrete variable based on the values it takes for an individual, and it is different from the average of values of a discrete variable. For example, the number of children to a couple is a discrete variable, but the average number of children per couple can take fractional/decimal values like 2.45. However, sometimes the difference between discrete and continuous variables is negligible. For example, the annual income of a family, measured in rupees, is expressed in integer numbers (discrete variable), but the values are usually very large, often in thousands, and the gap between two adjacent values, say 50,001 and 50,002, is practically negligible. Hence, the treatment of a variable as discrete or continuous is often a matter of convenience and is based on the magnitude and gap between the values the variable takes.

Types of Variables in SPSS

As this book makes use of Statistical Package for Social Sciences (SPSS) software for worked-out examples, it is important to note that SPSS considers numerical variables as 'scale' variable, and 'ordinal' and 'nominal' variables as two distinct types of variables in the same names. A truncated list of variables for a sample data as depicted in the 'variable view' window of SPSS is presented below. It can be seen that the last column indicates the variable's type. It is to be noted that SPSS automatically treats the variables as different types based on its own criteria, but sometimes the treatment is inappropriate, and, in this case, the user can change the type manually and often it is required.

11	CAge	Numeric	2	0	Age of child in months	None	None	5	≡ Right	◆ Scale
12	CSex	Numeric	1	0	Sex of child	{1, Male}...	9	7	≡ Right	♣ Nominal
13	OrdChild	Numeric	2	0	Birth order of child	None	99	7	≡ Right	◫ Ordinal

Independent and Dependent Variables

In general, hypotheses are stated to mean that a change in one or a few variables are set to bring about a corresponding change in another variable. In this format the 'a few variables' are called *independent variables* or *cause variables* and the 'another variable' is called the *dependent variable* or the *effect variable*. For example, in the hypothesis 'the better the education and the higher the income of parents, the better the growth (height) of their children', education and income of parents are independent variables and growth (height) of child is the dependent variable. It is because we have hypothesised (assumed) that the growth of children is depended on education and income of their parents.

That is, in a hypothesis the independent variable(s) influence(s) the dependent variable and not vice versa. That is, education and income of parents influence the growth of children and not the growth of children influence education and income of parents. But at the same time, the dependent variable in one hypothesis may be an independent variable in another hypothesis. That is, the growth of children (here, independent variable) influences their intelligence (dependent variable). Independent variables can be of any variable type, namely nominal, ordinal, discrete or continuous variables, but dependent variables are essentially ordinal, discrete or continuous variables, but rarely it can be nominal variables as well (influence of education on occupational pattern). (More on independent and dependent variables will be discussed in Chapter 11.)

Intervening or Control Variables

An intervening or control variable is a variable that alters the relationship between an independent variable and the dependent variable. That is, the intervening variable controls the effect of the independent variables on the dependent variable. For example, consider a study on the effect of education of women on the number of children born to them. In this, educated women may have a lesser number of children than illiterate women. But, at the same time, even among educated women, younger women may have a lesser number of children than older women. That is, all educated women may not have the same number of children. In other words, the age of a woman intervenes or controls or alters the relationship between the education of the woman and the number of children borne by her. So, when analysing the effect of education on the number of children of women, we need to control their age differences, and in this case the 'age of woman' acts as an intervening or control variable.

Please note that 'intervening' is somewhat or largely different from 'influencing' in that 'intervening' has a mandatory (positive or negative) effect as opposed to 'influencing' that may or may not have an effect (that is, optional effect). In other words, an intervening variable is an associate of the dependent variable and so in the analysis of finding the influence of independent variables on a dependent variable, there is a need to *control for* the effect of the intervening variable or variables.

Tips: Usually, dependent variables that change from time to time or season to season (time dependent) will have one or more intervening variables. Example: height, weight, children ever born, incidence of diseases.

Attribute or Code Variables

Ordinal and nominal variables are also called *attribute variables*. Usually, attributes are measured in terms of giving a numerical code (not in the meaning of the mathematical value) to categories of the attributes. For example, religion is classified in terms of numerical codes 1 = Hindu, 2 = Muslim, 3 = Christian, 4 = Sikh and so on. Please note that, here, 4 (Sikh) is not twice as much as 2 (Muslim). So, attributes are called code variables and not numerical variables.

In statistics, generally, attributes are also called variables, but attribute variables and numerical variables are treated differently in the analysis. So, one should be clear about the differences between attribute variables (or code variables) and real variables (or numerical variables) while applying statistical techniques.

A numerical variable can be converted into a code variable. For example, the variable 'age' can be converted into 'age groups', say, ages 0–4 as the age group 0–4, ages 5–9 as the age group 5–9, ages 10–14 as the age group 10–14 and so on. That is, 0–4, 5–9, 10–14 and so on are 'groups' and not 'values', and the groups may be given codes, say, 1 = (age 0–4), 2 = (age 5–9), 3 = (age 10–14), 4 = (age 15–19) and so on. Here, the number 4 (age 15–19) is not twice as much as 2 (age 5–9).

Dummy Variables

Similarly, but in a different way, an attribute variable can also be converted into a kind of (a set of) numerical variables, called *dummy variables*, by assigning a score 1 if a case possesses the particular attribute and 0 otherwise. Example: literacy status (literate or illiterate) of an individual can be coded as '1' if the person is a literate and '0' if illiterate. Now, the variable name needs to be slightly changed something like 'literate status' as we have given the value 1 if literate and 0 otherwise. Alternatively, depending on a specific need, the variable can also be defined as 'illiterate status' by giving the value '1' if illiterate and '0' if literate.

Please note that the variable 'literacy status' has two categories, namely literate and illiterate, or, in general, 'yes' and 'no' and so the variable is often called a 'binary variable' or 'dichotomous variable' (a binary variable is a variable that takes only two values). Furthermore, as the attributes are converted into a kind of numerical values, these binary variables are often called 'dummy variables'. Please note that the words 'dichotomous' and 'binary' mean 'two' and the word 'dummy' means 'not real' or 'indirect'.

While converting a binary variable into a dummy variable (value variable), we always assign the value '0' to one category and another value (usually '1') to the other category. The category that is assigned the value '0' is often called the 'reference category' and the other category is called the 'value category'. Please also note that the reference category should always take the value '0' and the value category usually takes the value '1', but it can also take other values, say, '100' if someone is interested in expressing it in terms of percentage. One may also choose any value, but the interpretation of results should be made accordingly. However, the code pattern 0 and 1 is often preferred as it has many statistical properties (see Chapter 5) and advantages (see Chapter 11).

Often code variables will have more than two categories, such as religion where, say, 1 = Hindu, 2 = Muslim, 3 = Christian and 4 = Sikh. In this case, it is not one dummy variable (as in the case of literacy status), but many dummy variables are to be created. The number of dummy variables that can be created is the number of categories in the variable. However, for the analysis purpose, it would be one less than the number of categories in the variable, and the last (left over) category is called the reference category (implied). Here, religion has 4 categories and so the number of dummy variables to be created is $4-1=3$, and each dummy variable will take a separate name. If we keep Sikh as the reference category, then the dummy variables are 'Hindu', 'Muslim' and 'Christian'. The variable 'Hindu' takes the value 1 if the individual is a Hindu and 0 otherwise. The variable 'Muslim' takes the value 1 if the individual is a Muslim and 0 otherwise. The variable 'Christian' takes the value 1 if the individual is a Christian and 0 otherwise. If all the three variables, namely Hindu, Muslim and Christian, take the value 0, then it means that the case is a Sikh and so there is no need to have an explicit variable for Sikh.

Please note that, although the fourth category 'Sikh' is not in the list of dummy variables, comparison and interpretation of results of each category are always made in comparison with the reference category, namely 'Sikh' (and hence called 'the reference category'). That is, the reference category is only hidden and not eliminated. So, the choice of the reference category is only a matter of convenience for comparative purposes and it will not change the ultimate results and conclusions in any way. The dummy variable concept is very useful in statistical analysis, specifically in multivariate analysis, of categorical variables.

An Example of Dummy Variable Coding

Let as assume that originally the variable 'religion' is coded as 1 if Hindu, 2 if Christian, 3 if Muslim and 4 if 'other religion'. As the variable 'religion' has four categories, we have to create $4-1=3$ dummy variables, and they are, to say, Christian, Muslim and Other with 'Hindu' as the reference category, as follows. However, for the purpose of demonstration of dummy variable coding, the category Hindu is also added in Table 1.1.

Hindu=1, if the person is a Hindu (original code 1), 0 otherwise
Christian=1, if the person is a Christian (original code 2), 0 otherwise
Muslim=1, if the person is a Muslim (original code 3), 0 otherwise
Other=1, if the person belongs to 'other religion' (original code 4), 0 otherwise

An example of dummy variable coding for six individuals is shown in Table 1.1.

Please note that for a categorical variable with dummy variables, for each individual, only one of the dummy variables will take the value 1 and all other dummy variables will take the value 0. That is, in each row, only one variable will take the value 1 and all other variables will take the value 0. For more details on applications of dummy variables, please refer to Chapters 5 and 11.

Table 1.1 Dummy Variables Coding Format

			Dummy Variables			
Person	Religion	Original Code	Hindu	Christian	Muslim	Other
1	Muslim	3	0	0	1	0
2	Other religion	4	0	0	0	1
3	Hindu	1	1	0	0	0
4	Christian	2	0	1	0	0
5	Hindu	1	1	0	0	0
6	Muslim	3	0	0	1	0

CHAPTER 2

Sampling Methods

SOME SAMPLING-RELATED TERMS AND DEFINITIONS

Population is a collection of all individuals or objects of a specified nature or characteristics in a well-defined area or territory. It is not restricted to human being alone; it may also refer to animals, plants and inanimate objects. When we undertake a study (complete enumeration or sample survey), the population under investigation is often called the *universe* of the study. The number of objects in the population may be finite (countable) or infinite (not countable). For example, the number of persons in a city, the number of patients who attended a clinic in one year, the number of mango trees in a grove and the number of cattle in a village are finite populations (may be large but countable), whereas the number of trees in a forest and the number of fishes in a sea are infinite populations (because practically not countable).

Census is the enumeration, investigation or study of all individuals (persons or objects) in a population. A sample is a finite subset of individuals (persons or objects) selected from the population. Usually, the term 'sample' is used when the units are selected by applying appropriate sampling procedure to represent the population. In such cases, a study of the sample units implies the study of the population as a whole. So, adopting appropriate sampling procedure is very important to draw a sample so that the sample adequately represents the population and the findings from the sample apply to the whole population.

Unit/individual is a member of (or an object in) the population or in a sample drawn from the population. A variable is a measure of some characteristic feature of the individuals in a population or a sample; for example, sex and weight are variables. Observations are individual members who are drawn from the population and measured or assessed with respect to a variable (characteristics). Population size (or simply population) is the number of individuals or units in the universe, and sample size is the number of individuals or units in a sample.

Unit of observation is the level at which information or data are obtained. Unit of enquiry is the level at which information is enquired and recorded. Unit of analysis is the level at which the information is analysed. For example, a mother is asked to report some particulars of her (say, age, education and occupation) and some particulars of each of her children (say, sex, date of birth and place of birth). Here, 'mother' is the unit of enquiry. Also 'mother' is the unit of observation/study for particulars of her (mother). While 'child' is the unit of observation/study for the particulars of children, again mother is the unit of enquiry. That is, the unit of enquiry may be the same or different from the unit of observation and also the unit of enquiry may be the same for many units of observations. If the data are analysed to obtain, say, the percentage of children enrolled in a school, then the unit of analysis is the child. On the other hand, if the data are analysed to obtain, say, the number of villages with at least 75 percent of children are enrolled in school, then the unit of analysis is the village.

A sample survey is the enumeration or investigation of a sample of units from a population to predict about the population. Sampling methods are the various procedures available to select a sample. A sample is said to be a random sample or probability sample if the selection was governed by the laws of chance, that is, each unit in the population is given some (not necessarily equal) opportunity of being selected. Sample size is the number of individuals or units in the sample.

A sampling unit is an individual or a group of individuals (or units) in a population (or, in a subset of population) that is clearly defined, identifiable, observable and convenient for enquiry. A sampling frame is a list (collection) of sampling units with their identification particulars (or map) that is used for the selection of sample units. As such, a sampling frame forms the basis for sample selection. A good sampling frame is one that contains all units of the population, clearly demarcated, up to date and free from omission and duplication of sampling units. For example, a family, a farm or a group of farms owned by a family, a village and so on are sampling units and the list of all such units in the population (say, in a district) is the sampling frame.

A sampling fraction (f) is the proportion of population units that is in the sample. It is the ratio of the sample size (n) to the population size (N). That is, $f=n/N$. A sampling interval is the interval between one sample unit and the next sample unit in the sampling frame. If the intervals are the same for all sample units, then the sampling interval (r) is the ratio of the population size (N) to the sample size (n). That is, $r=N/n$. The sampling interval applies mainly to systematic sampling methods.

Statistical data or simply data are the *numerical* statements of facts about a population or a sample. Primary data is the data that are directly observed or collected by an investigator (usually a researcher) or an agency as its first-hand experience. Secondary data are the data (raw data or tabulated data) that are used by a person or an agency other than the person or the agency that collected the data. That is, the primary data for one person/agency (who collected it) are the secondary data for another person or agency (when he/she/that uses the data).

Sample statistic or simply statistic refers to any statistical measure (for example, mean, median, standard deviation and correlation coefficient) that is *derived from a sample of observations* (usually to represent the population). Population parameter or simply parameter refers to any statistical measure (for example, mean, median, standard deviation and correlation coefficient) that is *derived from all observations in the population*. Please note that 'parameter' always refers to the population and 'statistic' always refers to the sample (drawn from the population).

Hypothesis is a statement of the nature of reality as perceived by the researcher that is subjected to verification (test) based on empirical (real or actual) data. A hypothesis is freely expressed in a statement usually as a relationship between two variables in a cause-and-effect manner. For example, a researcher may hypothesise that 'The intelligent quotient (IQ) level of children increases with the educational level of their parents'. In order to prove or disprove this hypothesis, the researcher would conduct a survey asking parents about their educational level and conducting a test to measure the IQ level of their children. The researcher will then analyse the data to see if there is any relationship between the IQ level of the children and the educational level of their parents. (More details in chapter on testing of hypothesis.)

A sampling error is the error arising while drawing inference about a population on the basis of a sample selected from it. It is the difference between an estimate (derived from a sample of observations drawn from the population) and the actual value (obtained through a population census). For example, the sampling error of mean refers to the difference between a sample mean and the population mean (assuming that the population mean is known). It is to be noted that the sampling error does not exist in complete enumeration (census). The sampling error can be estimated statistically based on the sample-based indices, on one hand, and population size, sample size and the sampling method followed in the selection of the sample, on the other. However, sampling error cannot be estimated for non-random or purposive samples. As such hypothesis testing does not apply to census and purposive samples.

The sampling error usually decreases with the increase in the sample size (see Figure 2.1). That is, other things being equal, the larger the sample size, the smaller the sampling error. However, as can be seen from the chart, after a certain level of sample size, any further increase in sample size will contribute only very little to the decrease in the sampling error. This shows that a minimum sample size is required to ensure a low level of sampling error and at the same time there is no need to increase the sample size beyond a particular level as it does not help much to reduce the sampling error but only will add to the cost of data collection. However, the minimum sample size required differs from population to population depending on the population size, sampling method and the variable(s) under investigation (explained later in this chapter).

A non-sampling error is the error arising at different stages of planning, training, data collection and data processing, and it includes the instructor bias, interviewer bias, non-response, coding and data entry errors, tabulation errors and the like. It applies to both complete enumeration and sample surveys, but it is likely to be less in sample surveys than in complete enumeration, as proper planning, better training of staff, close supervision, in-depth investigation and so on can be better ensured in sample surveys than in complete enumeration.

There are two types of non-sampling errors, namely the systematic error and the random or variable error. A systematic error is either due to the error in the tools used in the measurement of the units or due to the procedure followed in the investigation. For example, while taking weight of persons if the weighing machine is not zero-corrected, it makes a systematic error of lower or higher weight than the real weight for all cases measured using the machine. While estimating household income, if the income from certain sources is not considered, then we are systematically underestimating the total household income. A random or variable error is one that occurs at random. It is the inconsistency of responses or measurements produced by different investigators or due to external factors. An example of inconsistency between investigators is that different investigators asking questions or taking measurements in different ways resulting in different patterns of responses or measurements. External factors are such factors as the presence of outsiders

Figure 2.1   Relation between the Sampling Error and Sample Size

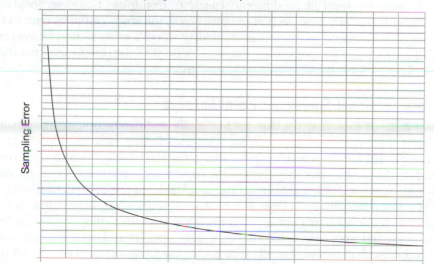

while seeking personal information about respondents, measuring weight whenever individuals are available either before or after heavy meals, with heavy or light dress and the like.

Both random and systematic errors have serious implications for the results of the survey; often the random errors are less serious for certain analyses, whereas systematic errors are less serious for certain other analyses. On average, the random errors in measurements tend to balance out, but systematic errors are more serious because they systematically either underestimate or overestimate the population parameters. On the other hand, systematic errors have less implication for differential analysis because all groups are on a common platform of under or overestimate so that the actual differences between the groups are less affected. Systematic errors can be identified and corrected using standards that match the real sample. Similarly, random errors can be minimised by following standard procedures, adequate training of investigators, better supervision and the like.

A standard error is the standard deviation of a sample 'statistic' derived from repeated samples (of same size) drawn from the same population. Please note that the sampling error and standard error are related aspects but are not the same. The standard error is the basis for determining the minimum sample size required for estimating a population parameter, for statistical investigation and for testing of hypothsis. The methods of determining the minimum sample size required for different types of investigation are presented later in this chapter.

TYPES OF SAMPLE SURVEYS

Cross-sectional Surveys

Cross-sectional surveys are carried out on a cross-section of the population units at one point of time. Please note that the cross-section means cutting across all sections of the population. For example, a cross-section of households implies a sample of households representing different religion, caste, landholding, income and the like from the population. Similarly, a cross-section of married women implies a sample of married women representing different age groups and different socio-economic groups in the community. Most of the one-time sample surveys fall in this category. Cross-sectional surveys are relatively quick, cheap and easy to carry out, and the data can be directly analysed especially for differential analysis. Examples of cross-sectional surveys are the study of food habits of a cross-section of households, the study of the income and expenditure pattern of a cross-section of workers in an industry (here a cross-section of workers implies workers of all cadres from labourers to executives as defined in the population) and the study of consumer preferences for select brands of consumer goods.

Repeat Cross-sectional Surveys or Panel Surveys

Repeat cross-sectional surveys are carried out repeatedly at different time points usually at fixed intervals of time, say, once a year or once in five years, by selecting each time separate sample units from the same population. In repeat surveys, usually, the survey design and the information collected are largely the same so that the results of the surveys are comparable for trend analysis. The National Sample Surveys (NSS) and National Family Health Surveys (NFHS) fall in this category.

A panel is a group of individuals or units who *share a common feature* or common characteristics, for example, households in a housing colony, households in a village or locality, employees of an organisation and so on. Here, the housing colony, locality and organisation are the shared features or common characteristics of all units. So, repeat cross-sectional surveys with the same or similar design and tools are also called the panel surveys.

Longitudinal or Cohort Surveys

A cohort is a group of individuals or units that had experienced an *event* during a short reference *period*, for example, children born during a particular year, students admitted to a college in a particular academic year, a group of employees recruited in an organisation in a particular year and so on. Please note that in a panel if we restrict the membership to a particular period, then the panel becomes a cohort (see in the following). As such, a cohort is a focused or restricted group and a panel is a broader group than a cohort.

A longitudinal survey is a repeated observation of a cohort or a panel of units over a long period of time (for years or even decades) usually at regular intervals. Longitudinal surveys are launched to obtain reliable information about events that are otherwise difficult to obtain retrospectively from cross-sectional surveys and/or to derive measures of incidence and/or prevalence of events over period, for example, monitoring height and weight of children, household survey of social and economic change, income and labour dynamics survey, youth development survey and so on that require assessments of the same group of individuals or households at regular intervals to obtain reliable and time-series information. However, the duration of assessment depends on the interest of investigation. The Sample Registration System of recording births and deaths in selected villages and urban units in different parts of India is a kind of longitudinal survey, with the panel being villages and urban units.

In longitudinal surveys, dropout for follow-up may threaten the validity of the results, especially when the dropout is substantial and group-selective. By group-selective, we mean that the dropout is substantially higher in one group (say Hindus) than in the other groups (say Muslims and Christians). Also, rapid changes in the socio-economic and environmental conditions during the observation period may also alter the behaviour of the people from time to time and, hence, the results for comparison between groups and over period.

Advantages of Sample Surveys

As against complete enumeration, sample surveys are less costly and less time consuming for both data collection and analysis. In sample surveys, the individuals can be examined in-depth and so data are more reliable and valid than complete enumeration. Furthermore, in sample surveys, more time can be spent with the individuals and so more information on a variety of subjects can be obtained. At the same time, sample surveys are subject to the sampling error. However, the total of sampling and non-sampling errors in sample surveys is usually much smaller than the non-sampling errors in complete enumeration. Thus, sample surveys have many advantages over complete enumeration.

Planning for a Survey

Planning a survey consists of the following steps:

1. State the problem encountered convincingly (if necessary, review literature, discuss with knowledgeable persons or conduct pilot survey).
2. Lay down the survey objectives precisely (it is not mere statements; it is rather what the survey is expected to reveal or throw open).
3. List the hypotheses to be tested, if any. More information on stating and testing hypothesis is given in Chapter 7.

4. Define the population to be studied in terms of geographic, demographic and other aspects. This is very important for a sample survey because the results of the sample survey are attributed to the population so defined.
5. Decide the questions to be asked and/or aspects to be examined, and it should be in line with the stated objectives and hypotheses of the study.
6. Place the questions in a questionnaire or schedule in an orderly manner and pre-test it with a few cases (not included in the sample) with respect to wordings, sequence of questions, reliability and validity of responses and the like.
7. Determine the number of units to be studied and the method of selection. The number of units to be studied depends on the objectives of the study, the indices to be estimated and the time and resources available for conducting the survey. More details are given in the 'Determination of Sample Size' section later in this chapter.
8. Decide on the sampling method(s) to be adopted. It should be based on the size of the population, distribution of the population (in geographical area and/or socio-economic pattern), availability of sampling frame at different levels and also the time and resources available for conducting the survey.
9. Draw the sample, recruit personnel for the survey, conduct appropriate training for them and deploy them for the field survey.
10. Conduct the fieldwork systematically as planned.

Random or Probability Sampling

There are broadly two types of sampling, namely random sampling and purposive sampling. Random sampling is the one in which each unit in the population has a chance (usually equal chance) of being included in the sample. In this method, no section of the population is excluded from the sample selection process (except in rare cases due to practical difficulties). Even if a sample is selected at random, it may not possess the characteristic features of the population if the selection procedure is not appropriate and/or the sample size is not adequate. A randomly selected sample by following the appropriate sampling procedure and with adequate sample size is often called a 'representative sample' if it reflects as closely as possible the relevant characteristics of the population under study. There are many random sampling methods and some of the common methods are described in the following sections. Similarly, there are also many non-random sampling methods and some of the common methods are described in the subsequent sections.

Simple Random Sampling Method

Simple random sampling (SRS) is the simplest of all random sampling methods. In the SRS method, the sample units are drawn (selected) from the population units one by one with equal probability (see Box 2.1) at each draw.

Box 2.1

The meaning of probability: Let the number of individuals/units (persons, items and so on) in the population is N (called the population size) and the number of units to be selected is n (called the sample size), then the chance (probability) of an individual being selected is n/N, that is, if $N = 100$, $n = 10$, then the chance (probability) of a unit being selected is $10/100 = 0.1$. Equal probability means that every individual in the population (here 100) will have equal chance (here 0.1 or 10 percent) of being selected.

There are three common methods of random sample selection methods, namely the lottery method, random number method and random number function method. The lottery method is simply writing down the names or serial numbers of all the units in the population, shuffling them and then drawing the required number of items one by one without showing preference to any item in the list. The random number method is one in which the random number table is used to draw the required number of items. A random number table is a set of random numbers that are randomly generated and arranged by experts and are made available in statistics textbooks and in the web (see Table C.1 in Appendix C). The random number method is used more often than the lottery method because the lottery method of writing down the names or serial numbers of all items and drawing the required number of units is often tedious, especially when the population size is large. The random number function method is the one in which random numbers are generated using the MS Excel 'Random' or 'Random between' functions, or using any other software that produces random numbers (the procedure is very easy and therefore has not been described here).

Merits and demerits: The merit of the SRS method is that it is very simple. The demerit is that the identity of each member of the population (sampling frame) is needed for sample selection, which is often difficult if the population is very large. Furthermore, if the population is very large and spread over a large area, the selected sample units may be scattered over the large area and studying (covering) the selected cases becomes difficult. At the same time, it is also likely that all subgroups of the population and geographical areas may not be adequately represented in the sample. Furthermore, if the sample size is large, the selection of sample units using the SRS technique with the lottery or random number method would be tedious. These demerits are clearly evident from the example given later in this chapter. So, the SRS method is rarely adopted in scientific surveys and if at all adopted it is only when the population size is small, say, less than 100 units or a few hundred units only.

Systematic Sampling Method

Systematic sampling is the method of selecting individuals at regular interval down the list (in the sampling frame), only the starting point being selected at random.

Selection procedure: Let N be the population size and n the sample size. For our exercise, let us assume that the population size N is 75 and the sample size n is 17. For systematic sampling, first arrange the N population units in some serial order (by area, by alphabetical order or by some characteristics feature). Second, calculate the sampling interval $(r)=N/n$ $(75/17=4.41)$. Please do not round the figure to the nearest integer as it will lead to the selection of deficit or excess sample cases (sometimes the last few units may not get a chance of being selected, or end up with selecting more than the required number of cases; it is not demonstrated here but the reader may try with some hypothetical numbers for N and n). Third, let R is r if r is an integer or R is the next integer from r (here $R=5$, the next integer as $r=4.41$), and from the first R units, select one unit at random, say, s, and it is the first selected unit. Let the selected unit in this case be $s=3$, that is, the third unit in the list is the first sample unit. Fourth, calculate $s+r$ and the unit having the rounded serial number is the second sample unit. In our example, $s+r=3+4.41=7.41=7$ (rounded) is the second sample unit. Next, calculate $s+2r$ and select the rounded serial number $(3+2*4.41=11.82=12)$. Continue the process $s+3r, s+4r, \ldots$ until n units are selected.

Note: There may be a possibility of the last calculated value (say V) greater than the population size N (if $s>r$, that is, when $s=5$ in our example). In this case, the last selected case is the case corresponding to $V-N$ (if $s=5$, then $V=5+16*4.41=75.56>75$, the round number is 76 and the selected case is $V-N=76-75=1$, the first case). Alternatively s can be a random number between 1 and N and when V exceeds N, follow the $V-N$ procedure. This procedure is often called the 'circular systematic sampling procedure'. The issues will be clear if one practises the exercise in different possible ways.

Merits and demerits: In systematic sampling, area/group representation is largely ensured if the population units are arranged accordingly. But, as in SRS, the identity of each member of the population is needed and the sample units may be scattered and so coverage would be difficult. Further, once the first unit is selected (at random), all other units are automatically fixed. So, the selected units will be changed depending on the serial ordering of the population units. Usually, the systematic sampling method is applied at the last stage (sometimes even at the intermediate stage) of the multi-stage sampling method (being discussed later in this chapter).

Probability Proportionate to Size Sampling Method

Probability proportional to size (PPS) sampling is a sampling technique in which the probability of selecting a sample unit (e.g., village, zone, district and health centre) is proportional to the size of its population size (e.g., number of persons, households, staff, patients and so on). It gives a random and representative sample. It is to be noted that, for applying the PPS method, the population size (e.g., number of persons, households, staff, patients and so on) of each unit should be known as it forms part of the sample selection process.

Usually, the PPS sampling method is applied at the intermediate stage in a multi-state sample selection process. For applying the PPS sampling method, we need to have the size of each sampling unit in the population. Suppose we want to select 10 villages from a district and then select 20 households from each selected village. Here, PPS sampling applies to selecting 10 villages from the long list of villages in the district.

We know that in a district there are villages with tens of households, hundreds of households and even thousands of households. If we apply SRS, we may end up with selecting all or most (selected) villages being small sized or large sized, making the sample selection biased towards the characteristic features of the selected type of villages. For PPS sampling, first, arrange the villages in some order (alphabetic, block-wise, literacy level-wise and so on) and obtain the cumulative number of households (population units) corresponding to each village. Then apply the systematic sampling procedure to the cumulative number of households of the villages. The resulting sample is the PPS sample.

It is clear from the description of the PPS sampling method that the probability of selecting a small-sized village is small (less) and the probability of selecting a large-sized village is large (high) because larger units have a higher chance and smaller units have a lesser chance of being selected. Once the intermediate units (here villages) are selected, a pre-determined number of ultimate units (say households) are selected from each of the selected intermediate sampling unit (village) irrespective of its population size so that the overall probability of selection of an individual (household) in the population remains the same. That is, in the intermediate stage, smaller units get a lesser chance and larger units get a higher chance of being selected, but in the next stage, among the selected units, the individuals in larger units get a lesser chance and the individuals in smaller units get a higher chance of being selected, so that, overall, in the population as a whole, the individuals (say households) have equal or almost equal probability of being selected.

Merits and demerits: PPS sampling is most useful when the sampling units vary considerably in size. This method is adopted when the sampling process involves two or more stages and is used in the intermediate stages of sampling. The demerit is that the size of each unit in the population is required to be known.

Note: In order to ensure the representation of sampling units of all sizes and from different areas and different sections of the society, the sampling units are arranged according to their sizes/area and cumulative frequencies are obtained before applying PPS sampling.

Stratified Sampling

Stratified sampling involves classifying the population units into a certain number of homogenous groups, called strata, and then selecting sample units independently from each stratum. The purpose of stratification is to ensure that the individuals within a stratum are as homogeneous or similar as possible, and the individuals in the different stratums (or strata) are as heterogeneous or dissimilar as possible. The strata should be mutually exclusive and collectively exhaustive. The classification of population units into homogenous groups is usually made according to one or more variables, called 'stratification variable(s)'. The stratification variable(s) should not be the dependent/important variables in the study, but should be closely related to them.

After stratification, the required number of sample units from each stratum is selected according to the SRS method or the systematic sampling method. The number of sample units to be selected from each stratum is usually in proportion to the size of the stratum and in this case no weighting of cases is required; otherwise, weighting is required (see the 'Sample and Population Weights' section later in this chapter). The stratification variables may be age, sex, geographical area, population size, educational level, development level and so on which are known to affect the variable(s) under investigation.

Example: Let the population units of 1,000 households are divided into two strata, say, slum households and residential households. Let the number of households in the slum area (say, stratum one) is 400 and the number of households in the residential area (say, stratum two) is 600. Let the number of sample households to be selected is 200. Then, under proportional allocation, the sample households to be selected from the slum area is $(400/1,000) * 200 = 80$ and from the residential area is $(600/1,000) * 200 = 120$. The total sample size is $80 + 120 = 200$.

Merits and demerits: The stratified sampling method increases efficiency per unit cost and so better estimate can be obtained with lesser sample size. It is possible to obtain estimates for sub-groups because a pre-determined number of units are selected from each stratum. The demerit is that the choice of the stratification variable should be appropriate and for which information is available.

Cluster Sampling

Cluster sampling is a sampling technique used when 'natural' grouping of units such as geographical divisions, slums, schools and hospitals exist in the population and the number of units is large. In this technique, the total population units are divided into the number of groups called *clusters* and the required number of clusters is selected according to a sampling method such as SRS, systematic sampling or PPS sampling method. In a one-stage cluster sampling method, all the units in the selected clusters are included in the sample and in a two-stage cluster sampling method only a proportion of units from each of the selected clusters are selected for inclusion in the sample. The clusters should be mutually exclusive and collectively exhaustive. The individuals within a cluster should be as homogeneous as possible and the clusters should be as heterogeneous as possible. The main purpose of using cluster sampling is that in some cases constructing a sampling frame that identifies every element in the population is impossible or too expensive and time consuming. However, in a two-stage cluster sampling method, a sampling frame is required only for the second stage of clusters selected in the first stage and that can be made relatively quickly and cheaper.

There are many differences between cluster sampling and stratified sampling. For cluster sampling, a population is divided into a number of (many) clusters, whereas for stratified sampling, a population is divided into a few strata only. In cluster sampling, the sample units are drawn from only a few of the many clusters in the population, whereas in stratified sampling, the sample units are drawn from each of the strata in the population. In stratified sampling, estimates can be made for each stratum in the population, whereas in cluster sampling, cluster-wise estimates are not possible. Usually, a stratification variable is a strict measure (scientifically derived index), whereas clustering can be made loosely (even based on personal judgement). The main objective of cluster sampling is to reduce cost by increasing sampling efficiency and it contrasts with stratified sampling where the main objective is to increase precision.

Merits and demerits: The cluster sampling method is convenient in cases where constructing a sampling frame is too expensive or impossible. Furthermore, it can be cheaper as the survey involves fewer travel expenses and administration costs. The demerit is that cluster sampling is associated with higher sampling error and also is difficult to measure. It is usually necessary to increase the total sample size to achieve the same precision as in SRS.

Multi-stage Sampling

Multi-stage sampling involves two or more stages in the sample selection process. That is, the (ultimate) sample units are obtained through a series of steps and in each step a sampling frame is obtained and the required sample units are selected by following an appropriate sampling procedure. The sampling frame, sampling units, number of sample units selected and the sampling method may differ from one stage to another.

For example, the selection of a representative sample of households from a district may be made in three stages. The first stage sampling unit may be a block and the sampling frame is a list of blocks in the district. From this list, a sample of blocks is obtained using cluster, stratified, systematic or probability proportionate to size sampling method. The second stage sampling unit may be a village in rural areas and a ward in urban areas, and a list of villages and a list of wards in the selected blocks are made. It is the sampling frame for the second stage sampling. From this list, a sample of villages and wards is obtained using PPS or the systematic sampling method. The third stage sampling units may be a household, and a list of households in the selected villages and wards is made to form the third stage sampling frame. From this list, a sample of households is obtained from each selected village/ward by following systematic or SRS method. Thus, the ultimate sample of households is drawn in three stages: a sample of blocks in the first stage, a sample of villages/wards from the selected blocks in the second stage and a sample of households from the selected villages/wards in the third stage.

Merits and demerits: Multi-stage sampling is preferred if the population is very large and vastly distributed such as a state or a country. In multi-stage sampling, although the sampling frame differs from one stage to another, the cost of obtaining the sampling frames is very less because they are simple and often readily available for use, probably except the last- stage sampling. A multi-stage sampling is more efficient than a single-stage sampling from the point of view of sampling variability, field operations and cost of conducting the survey.

SAMPLE SELECTION: A PRACTICAL EXAMPLE

In Table 2.1, a list of 50 villages with the number of households and contraceptive prevalence rate (CPR, the percentage of women of reproductive age 15–44 using a contraceptive method) is given. Draw a simple random sample, a systematic sample, a PPS sample and a stratified sample of size 6 each.

In this example, the population size is $N=50$ and the sample size is $n=6$, that is, we have to select 6 villages from the list of 50 villages.

Drawing a Simple Random Sample

For simple random sample selection, we need only the first two columns, namely 'Sl No.' and 'Village', and the other two columns are not required. For the sample selection, go to a two or higher digit random number table, start at a random row and column location, read the random

Table 2.1 List of 50 Villages with the Number of Households (HHs) and Contraceptive Prevalence Rate (CPR)

Sl No.	Village	HHs	CPR	Sl No.	Village	HHs	CPR
1	Pudakalkatti	433	58.2	26	Mangalgatti	306	53.3
2	Kyarkop	421	49.4	27	Ramapur	287	50.2
3	Govankoppa	192	52.6	28	Nigadi	346	49.1
4	Belur	395	49.6	29	Karadiguda	720	51.4
5	Goutan Nagalavi	48	50.0	30	Salikinkoppa	208	51.4
6	Benkankatti	227	48.5	31	Station Nagalavi	22	54.5
7	T.R. Nagar	36	36.1	32	Lakmapur	321	54.5
8	Mandihal	257	57.2	33	Kottur	734	57.6
9	Managundi	579	47.0	34	Daddikamalapur	88	52.3
10	Narendra	1,507	53.6	35	Heggeri	63	46.0
11	Lalgatti	74	54.1	36	Dandikoppa	141	60.3
12	Bellikatti	222	47.3	37	Neeralakatti	221	52.9
13	Mugad	815	51.7	38	Amblikoppa	151	50.3
14	Naikanhulikatti	127	49.6	39	Nuggikeri	160	55.0
15	Veerapur	187	59.4	40	Kalkeri	269	49.8
16	Thimmapur	294	54.4	41	Baad	302	47.4
17	Shivalli	551	48.6	42	Maragadi	357	58.3
18	Kallapur	178	61.2	43	Mansur	471	45.6
19	Yerikoppa	236	54.2	44	Devarhubli	346	48.3
20	Kavalgeri	336	57.7	45	Hoswal	87	39.1
21	Dasankoppa	45	48.9	46	Yadawad	540	54.1
22	Devagiri	94	58.5	47	Somapur	223	59.2
23	Hallikeri	266	53.0	48	Varavi Nagalvi	133	49.6
24	Marewad	523	57.0	49	Holtikoti	160	48.8
25	Kanavi Honnapur	332	56.6	50	Chandanamatti	197	54.8
					Total	15,228	52.6

numbers appearing in line, note down the last two digits that are between 1 and 50, and then mark the population units having these serial numbers. If the serial number is already marked, discard that number. Continue the process until six villages are marked. These are the six selected sample units.

I am just starting from the fifth column of the fourth row and going downward in the random number table (see Table C.1 in Appendix C). I am considering the last two digits only as N (50) has 2 digits. The random numbers appearing in line are listed in Table 2.2 and the numbers that are between 1 and 50 are marked. The selected units are marked in the list of villages in Table 2.3.

Note: The demerits of SRS are evident from the selection. It is seen that all the 6 selected villages are from the first 25 villages, and there is no representation from the second half of the villages in the list. Even within the first-half of the villages, 3 out of 6 villages are between the serial numbers 21 and 25. Furthermore, 11 villages (or 22 percent) in the population are with each 200–299 households and 4 villages (or 8 percent) are with each more than 600 households, but there is no village in the sample representing these categories. Furthermore, only 19 villages (or 38 percent) in the population are with each less than 200 households, but the sample representation is 66.7 percent in this category. That is, the selected villages are relatively small-sized villages. As such, although procedure-wise the sample is a representative sample, practically it does not represent the population in many ways.

Drawing a Systematic Random Sample

Rearrange and serial order the villages according to some aspect or variable (optional). Here, the villages are rearranged in the ascending order of number of households in the villages (Table 2.6) and perform the selection process as detailed in Tables 2.4 and 2.5.

The selected villages (units) are marked in the list of villages (Table 2.6). It is seen that all the six selected villages are at equidistance and the sizes of the selected villages are also more or less proportional to the sizes of the villages in the population. That is, there is a good representation of small-, medium- and large-sized villages.

Table 2.2   Sample Selection Using the Simple Random Sampling (SRS) Method

Sl No.	Random Numbers in Line (See Random Number Table, Appendix C)	Last Two Digits of the Random Number	Selection
1	29,066	66	>50, discarded
2	62,509	09	Selected (1)
3	84,294	94	>50, discarded
4	23,577	77	>50, discarded
5	16,614	14	Selected (2)
6	60,022	22	Selected (3)
7	68,181	81	>50, discarded
8	83,025	25	Selected (4)
9	80,951	51	>50, discarded
10	14,714	14	Repetition, discarded
11	00,721	21	Selected (5)
12	97,803	03	Selected (6)

Table 2.3   List of Villages Selected as per the SRS Method

Sl No.	Village	HHs	CPR	Sl No.	Village	HHs	CPR
1	Pudakalkatti	433	58.2	26	Mangalgatti	306	53.3
2	Kyarkop	421	49.4	27	Ramapur	287	50.2
3	Govankoppa	192	52.6	28	Nigadi	346	49.1
4	Belur	395	49.6	29	Karadiguda	720	51.4
5	Goutan Nagalavi	48	50.0	30	Salikinkoppa	208	51.4
6	Benkankatti	227	48.5	31	Station Nagalavi	22	54.5
7	T.R. Nagar	36	36.1	32	Lakmapur	321	54.5
8	Mandihal	257	57.2	33	Kottur	734	57.6
9	Managundi	579	47.0	34	Daddikamalapur	88	52.3
10	Narendra	1,507	53.6	35	Heggeri	63	46.0
11	Lalgatti	74	54.1	36	Dandikoppa	141	60.3
12	Bellikatti	222	47.3	37	Neeralakatti	221	52.9
13	Mugad	815	51.7	38	Amblikoppa	151	50.3
14	Naikanhulikatti	127	49.6	39	Nuggikeri	160	55.0
15	Veerapur	187	59.4	40	Kalkeri	269	49.8
16	Thimmapur	294	54.4	41	Baad	302	47.4
17	Shivalli	551	48.6	42	Maragadi	357	58.3
18	Kallapur	178	61.2	43	Mansur	471	45.6
19	Yerikoppa	236	54.2	44	Devarhubli	346	48.3
20	Kavalgeri	336	57.7	45	Hoswal	87	39.1
21	Dasankoppa	45	48.9	46	Yadawad	540	54.1
22	Devagiri	94	58.5	47	Somapur	223	59.2
23	Hallikeri	266	53.0	48	Varavi Nagalvi	133	49.6
24	Marewad	523	57.0	49	Holtikoti	160	48.8
25	Kanavi Honnapur	332	56.6	50	Chandanamatti	197	54.8
					Total	15,228	52.6

Table 2.4   Sampling Interval and Random Start for Systematic Random Sampling

No. of villages (N)	50
No. of villages to be selected (n)	6
Sampling interval ($r=50/6$)	8.33
A random number between 1 and 9 is ($s=9$)	5

(The random number chosen is the fourth column of the fifth row, last digit)

Note: If desired, one can arrange (sort) the sampling units according to some characteristic feature, provided information is available and useful, and then serial order the units. Doing so will ensure the selection of units having different levels of the characteristic features. However, if the list is given separately for different subgroups, rearrangement of the units should be done within the subgroups only and not overall. Here, the villages are arranged according to the number of households in the villages. One may also arrange the villages by the contraceptive use level for which information is available.

Table 2.5 Drawing a Systematic Random Sample

Sl No.	Description	Formula	Calculation	Selected Villages
1	First selected village	s	$=5$	5
2	Second selected village	$s+r$	$=5+8.33=13.33$	13
3	Third selected village	$s+2*r$	$=5+2*8.33=21.67$	22
4	Fourth selected village	$s+3*r$	$=5+3*8.33=30.00$	30
5	Fifth selected village	$s+4*r$	$=5+4*8.33=38.33$	38
6	Sixth selected village	$s+5*r$	$=5+5*8.33=46.67$	47

Table 2.6 List of Villages with a Marking of the Villages Selected as per Systematic Sampling Method

Sl No.	Village	HHs	CPR	Sl No.	Village	HHs	CPR
1	Station Nagalavi	22	54.5	26	Mandihal	257	57.2
2	T.R. Nagar	36	36.1	27	Hallikeri	266	53
3	Dasankoppa	45	48.9	28	Kalkeri	269	49.8
4	Goutan Nagalavi	48	50	29	Ramapur	287	50.2
5	Heggeri	63	46	30	Thimmapur	294	54.4
6	Lalgatti	74	54.1	31	Baad	302	47.4
7	Hoswal	87	39.1	32	Mangalgatti	306	53.3
8	Daddikamalapur	88	52.3	33	Lakmapur	321	54.5
9	Devagiri	94	58.5	34	Kanavi Honnapur	332	56.6
10	Naikanhulikatti	127	49.6	35	Kavalgeri	336	57.7
11	Varavi Nagalvi	133	49.6	36	Nigadi	346	49.1
12	Dandikoppa	141	60.3	37	Devarhubli	346	48.3
13	Amblikoppa	151	50.3	38	Maragadi	357	58.3
14	Nuggikeri	160	55	39	Belur	395	49.6
15	Holtikoti	160	48.8	40	Kyarkop	421	49.4
16	Kallapur	178	61.2	41	Pudakalkatti	433	58.2
17	Veerapur	187	59.4	42	Mansur	471	45.6
18	Govankoppa	192	52.6	43	Marewad	523	57
19	Chandanamatti	197	54.8	44	Yadawad	540	54.1
20	Salikinkoppa	208	51.4	45	Shivalli	551	48.6
21	Neeralakatti	221	52.9	46	Managundi	579	47
22	Bellikatti	222	47.3	47	Karadiguda	720	51.4
23	Somapur	223	59.2	48	Kottur	734	57.6
24	Benkankatti	227	48.5	49	Mugad	815	51.7
25	Yerikoppa	236	54.2	50	Narendra	1,507	53.6

Drawing a PPS Sample

Rearrange and serial order the villages according to some aspect or variable, if desired (optional). Here, the villages are rearranged in the ascending order of number of households in the villages. The procedure of sample selection is described below. First, obtain the cumulative number of households for each village (as shown in Table 2.9). Second, derive the sampling interval $r=N/n$ and choose a random number between 1 and r (Table 2.7). Third, by applying the systematic random sampling method, select the samples based on cumulative households (Table 2.8).

Table 2.7 Sampling Interval and Random Start for PPS Sampling

Total cumulative households of all villages (N)	15,228
No. of villages to be selected (n)	6
Sampling interval ($r = N/n = 15,228/6$)	2,538
A random number (s) between 1 and 2,538 is	1,420

(Selection started downwards from the first column of the fourth row, last four digits)

Table 2.8 Drawing Systematic Random Sample in PPS Sampling

Sl No.	Description	Formula	Calculation	Selection
1	First selected village	s	$=1,420$	1,420
2	Second selected village	$s+r$	$=1,420+2,538$	3,958
3	Third selected village	$s+2*r$	$=1,420+2*2,538$	6,496
4	Fourth selected village	$s+3*r$	$=1,420+3*2,538$	9,034
5	Fifth selected village	$s+4*r$	$=1,420+4*2,538$	11,572
6	Sixth selected village	$s+5*r$	$=1,420+5*2,538$	14,110

Table 2.9 Villages Arranged in Ascending Order of Number of Households, Cumulative Number of Households and PPS Sample Marking

Sl No.	Village	HHs	Cu HHs	PPS Sample	Sl No.	Village	HHs	Cu HHs	PPS Sample
1	Station Nagalavi	22	22		26	Mandihal	257	3,777	
2	T.R. Nagar	36	58		27	Hallikeri	266	4,043	3,958
3	Dasankoppa	45	103		28	Kalkeri	269	4,312	
4	Goutan Nagalavi	48	151		29	Ramapur	287	4,599	
5	Heggeri	63	214		30	Thimmapur	294	4,893	
6	Lalgatti	74	288		31	Baad	302	5,195	
7	Hoswal	87	375		32	Mangalgatti	306	5,501	
8	Daddikamalapur	88	463		33	Lakmapur	321	5,822	
9	Devagiri	94	557		34	Kanavi Honnapur	332	6,154	
10	Naikanhulikatti	127	684		35	Kavalgeri	336	6,490	
11	Varavi Nagalvi	133	817		36	Devarhubli	346	6,836	6,496
12	Dandikoppa	141	958		37	Nigadi	346	7,182	
13	Amblikoppa	151	1,109		38	Maragadi	357	7,539	
14	Holtikoti	160	1,269		39	Belur	395	7,934	
15	Nuggikeri	160	1,429	1,420	40	Kyarkop	421	8,355	
16	Kallapur	178	1,607		41	Pudakalkatti	433	8,788	
17	Veerapur	187	1,794		42	Mansur	471	9,259	9,034
18	Govankoppa	192	1,986		43	Marewad	523	9,782	
19	Chandanamatti	197	2,183		44	Yadawad	540	10,322	
20	Salikinkoppa	208	2,391		45	Shivalli	551	10,873	
21	Neeralakatti	221	2,612		46	Managundi	579	11,452	
22	Bellikatti	222	2,834		47	Karadiguda	720	12,172	11,572
23	Somapur	223	3,057		48	Kottur	734	12,906	
24	Benkankatti	227	3,284		49	Mugad	815	13,721	
25	Yerikoppa	236	3,520		50	Narendra	1,507	15,228	14,110

The selected units are those villages corresponding to the cumulative number of households, given in Column 5 of Table 2.8, and are marked and shown in Table 2.9. For example, the first selected village is the one corresponding to the cumulative number of households 1,420. In Table 2.9, the village Nuggikeri (serial number 15) is in the range of the cumulative number of households 1,270–1,429, and the cumulative number 1,420 falls in this range. So the village Nuggikeri is the first selected village. Other villages are marked in the same way.

It is seen from Table 2.9 that there are nine villages in-between the first and second selected villages, whereas there is only six villages in-between the second and third selected villages, and the number reduces as the order of the selected village increases. It is clear that one small village represents many small villages, but one large village represents only a few large villages, that is, the larger the size of the village, the higher the chances of it being selected.

Note: It may be possible that at the bottom end of the list, a few consecutive units (here villages) may get selected. It may happen when the units are relatively very large, the numbers of population units are not many and sample size relative to the population size is large, or in any of these combinations. Sometimes it may also be possible that some villages may represent more than one sample unit. This may arise when the unit is larger than the sampling interval. In that case, we have to consider this unit as two-sample units (and not one unit) for the purpose of next stage sampling.

Drawing a Stratified Sample

In this example, the population size (N) is 50. Let the stratification variable be CPR and we make three strata. Let stratum 1 is the group of villages with a CPR less than 50.0, stratum 2 is the group of villages with a CPR ranging from 50.0 to 54.9 and stratum 3 is the group of villages with a CPR of 55 and more. (Note: If there is any standard range, use that, otherwise use any arbitrary range in such a way that each stratum will have more or less equal number of units, or at least adequate number of units.)

Sort the villages by the stratification variable and divide the villages into three groups based on the stratification variable, then serial order the villages within each group. Draw two villages from each stratum using SRS, systematic sampling or the probability proportionate to size sampling method (whichever is appropriate); in this example, the SRS method is used. The sample selection is depicted in Table 2.10. Please note that we have drawn two villages from each stratum irrespective of the number of villages and total households in the respective stratum, and so either we have to adjust the number of households being selected in the next stage or use 'weight' to make the estimates based on the sample to represent the population.

PURPOSIVE OR NON-RANDOM SAMPLING

In non-probability sampling, the sample units are selected usually on the basis of their accessibility, convenience, specific purpose or with personal judgment. In some surveys, the purpose of investigation is not to predict about the population but to have an understanding of what is happening or has happened in some sections of the population. Furthermore, the investigating agency may be bound by the constraints of time, money and workforce. Under these circumstances, it is almost impossible and also not necessary to select sample units at random from the population. In that way, it is permissible, desirable and useful to apply non-probability (non-random) sampling in some investigations.

Table 2.10 The List of Villages in Each Stratum and the Marking of the Selected Villages

Village (sorted)	CPR	Sl No.	S	Village (sorted)	CPR	Sl No.	S	Village (sorted)	CPR	Sl No.	S
Stratum 1				*Stratum 2*				*Stratum 3*			
T.R. Nagar	36.1	1		Goutan Nagalavi	50.0	1		Nuggikeri	55.0	1	5
Hoswal	39.1	2		Ramapur	50.2	2		Kanavi Hon	56.6	2	
Mansur	45.6	3		Amblikoppa	50.3	3		Marewad	57.0	3	
Heggeri	46.0	4		Salikinkoppa	51.4	4		Mandihal	57.2	4	
Managundi	47.0	5		Karadiguda	51.4	5	3	Kottur	57.6	5	
Bellikatti	47.3	6		Mugad	51.7	6		Kavalgeri	57.7	6	
Baad	47.4	7		Daddikamalapur	52.3	7		Pudakalkatti	58.2	7	
Devarhubli	48.3	8		Govankoppa	52.6	8		Maragadi	58.3	8	6
Benkankatti	48.5	9		Neeralakatti	52.9	9		Devagiri	58.5	9	
Shivalli	48.6	10		Hallikeri	53.0	10		Somapur	59.2	10	
Holtikoti	48.8	11		Mangalgatti	53.3	11	4	Veerapur	59.4	11	
Dasankoppa	48.9	12	1	Narendra	53.6	12		Dandikoppa	60.3	12	
Nigadi	49.1	13		Lalgatti	54.1	13		Kallapur	61.2	13	
Kyarkop	49.4	14		Yadawad	54.1	14					
Naikanhulikatti	49.6	15	2	Yerikoppa	54.2	15					
Varavi Nagalvi	49.6	16		Thimmapur	54.4	16					
Belur	49.6	17		Station Nagalavi	54.5	17					
Kalkeri	49.8	18		Lakmapur	54.5	18					
				Chandanamatti	54.8	19					

Non-probability sampling can produce better results or more insight into the nature of the problem (under investigation) at low cost and time as compared to probability sampling, but the findings or results cannot be generalised to the population at large. For example, let us assume that suicides are reported more often in some communities or areas than others, and we want to find out who is committing suicide and why. As suicide is a rare event, to conduct a sample survey, we need to select a large number of or thousands of households to identify a few cases of suicide and such an exercise would be prohibitive. Furthermore, our objective is not to estimate the incidence of suicide but to understand the reasons behind people committing suicide. So, it would be sufficient if we could identify a few cases of suicide and enquire about the circumstances leading to the suicide.

In probability or random sampling, we will be able to calculate the probability of getting a particular sample from the population, but in non-probability sampling, we will not be able to obtain the probability because in this method the sample units are selected *not at random* but *by choice*. Another limitation of non-probability sampling is that we cannot generalise the results to the whole population. On the basis of the non-probability sample, we may at best say that there are problems of minor or serious nature in some sections of the population, but we cannot say much about it: the extent of the problem, the extent of people affected by it, the variation in the problem between different sections of the population and so on. Furthermore, non-probability samples are not amenable for statistical tests of significance (hypothesis testing) and multivariate statistical analysis. However, simple statistical measures such as percentage, mean, median and so on may be obtained, but such measures neither reflect the level nor any differences between groups. For example, to know the people's interest in buying certain consumer goods, usually surveys are conducted in select middle-class localities in cities. If so, the findings of the study cannot be considered as the interest of the middle-class people of the city as a whole, but we can say that such an interest is prevailing in the middle-class population in the city. It is very important to keep these points in view while deciding on the sampling method.

Some of the advantages of purposive sampling methods are that they are cheaper, can be used when a proper sampling frame is not available, the population is so dispersed that even cluster sampling is difficult or not efficient, the purpose of investigation is exploratory in nature (like fact finding and hypothesis generation and not hypothesis testing) and so on.

It is important to note that purposive sampling is related to sample selection from a population and not to the choice of population or subpopulation for a study. Often social science students and researchers have confused on this point and say that they have chosen the study population purposively and so the sample drawn from it is purposive sampling. For example, restricting a study to a village or to a small area, or to a particular section of the society, say children, adolescents, Hindus, Muslims and so on is not purposive sampling, but selecting sample units for investigation purposively and not at random from the chosen population is called purposive sampling.

Another example is, let us assume that we want to conduct a sample survey in five cities in the Maharashtra state with a special interest on Mumbai city. If we select five cities randomly from among the cities in Maharashtra, Mumbai city may or may not find a place in the sample. But to satisfy our objectives, we need Mumbai city to be in the sample. So we include Mumbai city purposively (that is, by not going through the selection process) in the sample and select the remaining four cities from among the remaining cities in Maharashtra. So we have five cities (units) in the sample with Mumbai city included purposively. However, the selection of subsequent stage sample units, say, wards and then households, may be made according to the specified sampling procedure. In this case, although we have selected Mumbai city purposively, the ultimate sample units, say households, are selected at random (some units are from Mumbai city and the others are from the remaining four cities). Here, although Mumbai city is purposively included in the sample, the final sample (households) is made at random and so population estimation can be made and the statistical treatment of data is relevant. Please note that this kind of sampling is in a way stratified sampling in which Mumbai city forms one stratum and all other cities together form another stratum. So, purposive sampling in some stages, except in the last stage, can also yield an ultimate probability sample provided all units in the population are considered in the sampling process in one way or another.

Some of the non-probability or purposive sampling methods are snowball sampling, convenience sampling, quota sampling, area sampling, dimensional sampling, diversity sampling, expert sampling, judgment sampling, modal instance sampling, heterogeneity sampling and so on. However, a few of these methods that are often used in social science surveys are described briefly and presented in the following.

Snowball Sampling

Snowball sampling is a non-probability sampling method used when the events being studied are sensitive in nature and/or rare in the population. Examples of such sensitive/rare events are suicides, induced abortion, especially among unmarried girls, HIV/AIDS cases, families with a member in army service, families with a member in a Gulf country, disabled persons, experts in a specified field and so on. When the events are rare or sensitive, it is extremely difficult not only to have a representative sample of events, but also to have a list of all such cases in the population. Furthermore, preparing a sampling frame based on official records or from other sources is often difficult as information may not be available in records and even if available it may be incomplete, not up-to-date and/or address not clear. In these cases, it is very difficult to study a representative sample of cases.

In the snowball sampling method, first we identify a few cases with the required rare or sensitive characteristics (units), and then referring to these cases, we generate more and more cases until the required number of cases is reached. Although this technique can lower costs and reduce time, the sample cannot be said to be a representative sample because we do not know the extent of such cases in the population and/or the characteristics of the 'reached' cases may not be the same as that of the 'not-reached' cases in the population. As such a snowball sampling method is a non-probability sampling method but is often useful for studying rare and sensitive events occurring in populations.

In the snowball sampling method, two types of referrals are made.

One type of referral method is that the initially identified few cases may identify a few other cases they know. That is, one identified case is used to identify a few more cases. This type of referral applies to events such as disability, families with a member in a Gulf country and persons with HIV/AIDS because they are likely to know a few other persons as they often come into contact with them. The other type of referral method is the use of key informants who identify some cases they know or come across. For example, a family with a suicide case may or may not be aware of other families in which suicide occurred. But at the same time some key persons in the community like headman may be aware of some suicide deaths occurred in the community. Similarly, a woman who underwent induced abortion may not know other women in the community who underwent induced abortion, but a local health worker or traditional birth attendant may be aware of some cases. In general, one type of referral is some respondents referring to some more prospective respondents and the other type of referral is some key informants referring to some prospective respondents. In the former case, a respondent is also a key informant for some more cases and in the latter case a key informant is not a respondent at all.

While attempting to gather information about a limited number of rare units from a population, the snowball sampling method would increase the efficiency of the study. This is a cost-effective method because unlike other methods, in this method, the respondents themselves or key informants are used to identify more and more cases instead of a detailed community survey that is time consuming and incurs high cost. So, snowball sampling is good for locating persons or families with specified characteristics if they are few in number in a population. The preparation of a sampling frame is too costly and time consuming, and/or people generally do not come forward to reveal their identity or share information about them due to the sensitive nature of cases. The disadvantage of the snowball sampling method is that it is not a scientific method as it relies on referrals. As such the sample may produce varied and inaccurate results and also we cannot estimate the sampling error. In this method, much effort is required for the preliminary round that involves contacting people and identifying cases rather than that for the main round that consists in conducting investigations or interviews. The method heavily relies on the individual investigator's ability to network and find appropriate key informants.

Convenience Sampling

Convenience sampling is a method of intercepting or contacting anybody who comes on the way, who is believed to be a member of the study population and who is sought to respond/answer to the questions. In this method, the investigators may walk on the street, sit in a tea stall, stand in front of a school or a health centre and so on, and intercept randomly some members, customers and students as the case may be and interview them. If it is found during the course of the interview that the person is not a member with the required characteristics in the population, the interview with him/her is abandoned. The process is continued until the required number of individuals is interviewed. Since the sample units are chosen in a convenient way by the investigator, this method is called convenience sampling. This method has all the advantages and disadvantages of a non-probability sampling method.

Quota Sampling

Quota sampling is a method of stratified sampling in which the selection within a stratum is not made at random. The selection of respondents is normally left to the discretion of the investigators, and they need to cover a fixed number (quota) of units from the area or locations allocated to them. In this method, the population is first stratified into a number of strata or locations, and in each stratum the investigators move around and interview the fixed number of individuals as they come across. The investigators stop the interview once the quota allocated to them is completed. In this way, quota sampling is very similar to convenience sampling except for the initial stratification of the population. The quota allocated within each stratum may be a fixed number or proportional to the size of the stratum. Sometimes the quota may be fixed for each investigator and for each day and in this case the investigators may be asked to choose different locations each day or every few days. This method also has all the advantages and disadvantages of a non-probability sampling method.

Dimensional Sampling

An extension to quota sampling is dimensional sampling. In the quota sampling method, the population is first stratified into a number of strata or locations, and in each stratum the investigators move around and interview the fixed number of individuals. In dimensional sampling, according to some characteristics of the respondents, such as gender, age, income, residence and education, a fixed number of individuals is interviewed from each group as they come across. This ensures that there are sample of units from different sections or with different dimensions of the population characteristics.

Area Sampling

Area sampling is in a way multistage sampling in which maps rather than household or population lists/registers are used as the sampling frame. Although sample selection based on the list is more precise and appropriate, often such lists are not available and even if available, they are grossly inadequate, incomplete or not up to date, and, on the other hand, preparing a list is costly and time consuming. In area sampling, the area to be covered is divided into a number of smaller subareas like villages in rural areas and wards in urban areas using maps and from which a sample of subareas is selected at random using SRS or a systematic random sampling method. In the next stage, from these subareas, either a complete enumeration is made or a further subsample is selected as ultimate sampling units.

DETERMINATION OF SAMPLE SIZE

The sample size required for estimating a population parameter from a survey investigation is based primarily on two aspects. The first is the constraints in the *availability of resources* (persons, money, materials and time) that sets the upper limit for the sample size, that is, the more the resources available, the more the sample size one can afford. The second is the minimum *statistical significance desired* (how accurately the results from the sample survey should reflect the population and how much of confidence we should ensure in the results) that sets the lower limit. In general, the smaller the sample size, the lower the accuracy and confidence in the results obtained from the sample. So, a reasonable minimum sample size is required to ensure a minimum level of accuracy and confidence in the results. If the minimum level of accuracy and confidence are not ensured, any conclusion derived based on such a sample study would be meaningless and misleading. So, the sample size should be set in such a way that it will ensure a minimum level of accuracy and confidence, while at the same time not increasing exorbitantly the cost of the survey (in terms of persons, money, materials and time), that is, setting a sample size is simply weighing the cost of the survey on the one hand and the statistical significance of the results on the other.

Note: For understanding the following two subsections, one would require the knowledge of 'testing of hypothesis' described in Chapter 7 and so one may skip these sections for now and go directly to the 'Equations for Sample Size Estimation' section that follows next.

In a probability (or random) sample survey, it is possible to ensure a pre-specified margin of error (level of accuracy) in the results for a particular level of significance (confidence level or α level) by suitably fixing the sample size. The margin of error that is permissible in the estimate (called *permissible error*) is usually taken as the maximum difference between the estimate (based on the sample) and the parameter value (of the population) that can be tolerated. It is to be noted that the smaller the margin of error, the larger the sample size required (please see Figure 2.1). It is to be note that the sample statistic can be derived from the survey, whereas the population parameter is usually unknown but reasonably assumed based on the sample results. The margin of error can be set at 5 percent, 10 percent or even 20 percent (or correspondingly 0.05, 0.1 or 0.2) of the population parameter value, but often 5 percent and 10 percent are used.

While the margin of error refers to the difference between the parameter and statistic, the standard error refers to the variation in the statistic if repeated samples are drawn from the same population. Generally, for a given sample size, the smaller the variation in the sample statistic, the higher the confidence in the estimate of the parameter that is based on the sample statistic. The confidence level is often set at 90 percent, 95 percent or 99 percent, but often the value 95 percent is used. An α level (significance level) is just one minus the confidence level, that is, a 95 percent confidence is a 5 percent significance level or a 0.05 α level. As in the case of the margin of error, to ensure a larger confidence level, the sample size should be larger. We know that for a normal variate, a 95 percent confidence level corresponds to the Z value of 1.96. The Z value for the 99 percent confidence level is 2.58 and that for the 90 percent confidence level is 1.64.

Applying these principles, we determine the sample size, but as the purpose of investigation differs, the sample size required for that investigation also differs. That is, the sample size required is different for different purposes such as cross-tabulation, population estimation, estimation for subgroups of population, comparison between groups within a population, comparison of groups between populations and so on. Here, we attempt to estimate the sample size required for population estimation and cross-tabulation, and give some hints for the others. Even in population estimation, different parameters can be estimated such as proportion, mean, variance, correlation coefficient and so on, but often we would be interested in two measures, namely mean and proportion. The estimation of 'mean' applies to numerical (discrete and continuous) variables and that of 'proportion' applies to categorical (nominal and ordinal) variables.

Sample Size Required for Estimating the Mean

In the social science research, we often deal with large populations. So, sample selection applies to large (or infinite) populations (of, say, size $N=10,000$ and above). For a large sample, the standard normal variate of the sample mean $\bar{x}$ is

$$Z = \frac{(\bar{x} - \mu)}{\frac{\sigma}{\sqrt{n}}} \tag{2.1}$$

The sample size n required to estimate the population mean is, from Equation (2.1),

$$n = \frac{Z^2}{D^2} \frac{\sigma^2}{\mu^2} \quad \text{(or)} \quad n = \left(\frac{Z}{D}\right)^2 * \left(\frac{\sigma}{\mu}\right)^2 \quad \text{(or)} \quad n = \left(\frac{Z}{D}\right)^2 * (CV)^2 \tag{2.2}$$

where

$Z=1.96$ at the 5 percent level, 2.58 at the 1 percent level of significance (also called the α level).

μ and σ=the mean and SD in the population (to be assumed appropriately).

D=the degree of accuracy desired (also called the margin of error), usually set to 0.05 (5 percent) or 0.1 (10 percent).

$CV=\frac{\sigma}{\mu}$, the coefficient of variation of mean (to be assumed appropriately).

It is to be noted that, apart from the Z value that can be often set at 1.96 (at the 5 percent level of significance or 95 percent confidence level), we need to know or at least have some idea about the population mean and standard deviation. With this idea, we proceed to estimate the sample size as follows.

Let $d = (\bar{x} - \mu)$ is the permissible error in the estimate. As the parameter μ is an absolute quantity and its magnitude and unit vary from variable to variable, a common absolute fixed value would be misleading because the fixed d value will be relatively large for small values of μ and relatively small for large values of μ. For example, the margin of error value $d=5$ is very large when $\mu=10$ (so that $\bar{x}$ can vary from $10-5=5$ to $10+5=15$, on either side), but it is very small when $\mu=1,000$ (so that $\bar{x}$ can vary only from 995 to 1,005). So, it is preferable to express d in terms of D times the mean μ, that is, $d=\mu * D$. If D is expressed in terms of the percentage value (say 5 percent, that is, $D=0.05$), then $d = \frac{\mu * D}{100}$, that is, we may set D as 5 percent or 10 percent of mean μ and then convert D into d using the above identity while determining the sample size. Usually, D is set to 5 percent of μ, meaning that the permissible error is 5 percent of the mean (μ). It is equivalent to saying that the difference in the estimate of the population mean μ is in the range of $(\mu-0.05\mu)-(\mu+0.05\mu)$. For example, a 5 percent margin of error for $\mu=10$ is $d=10 * (5/100)=0.5$ (so that $\bar{x}$ can vary from 9.5 to 10.5) and for $\mu=1,000$ is $d=1,000 * (5/100)=50$ (so that $\bar{x}$ can vary from 950 to 1,050).

Sample Size Required for Estimating the Proportion

For a large sample, the standard normal variate of the sample proportion p is

$$Z = (p - P) / \sqrt{PQ / n} \tag{2.3}$$

where

Z=1.96 at the 5 percent level, 2.58 at the 1 percent level of significance.
p=the sample proportion.
P=the population proportion and $Q=1-P$.
n=the sample size.

Let $D=(p-P)$ is the permissible error in the estimate. As D is smaller for smaller values of P and larger for larger values of P, usually D is expressed as the percentage of P, that is, D is expressed as $D*P$ or simply DP. Now Equation (2.3) becomes

$$n = \frac{Z^2 P * Q}{(D*P)^2} \quad \text{(or)} \quad n = \left(\frac{Z}{D}\right)^2 * \frac{PQ}{P*P} \quad \text{(or)} \quad n = \left(\frac{Z}{D}\right)^2 * \frac{Q}{P} \tag{2.4}$$

$$n = \left(\frac{Z}{D}\right)^2 * \frac{PQ}{P*P}. \quad \text{It can also be written as} \quad n = \left(\frac{Z}{D}\right)^2 * (CV)^2$$

where

Z=1.96 at the 5 percent level, 2.58 at the 1 percent level of significance.
P=Expected proportion in the population (to be assumed), $Q=1-P$.
D=the degree of accuracy desired, usually set to 0.05 of 'P' $(0.05*P)$.
CV=SD/mean, in that SD^2=PQ and mean=P.

Note: For binary variables taking values 0 and 1, it can be shown that P is the mean, PQ is the variance, $\sqrt{PQ}$ is the standard deviation (SD) and $\sqrt{PQ}/P$ is the coefficient of variation (CV). As such $n = \left(\frac{Z}{D}\right)^2 * (CV)^2$ applies to both means and proportions.

Important points: The mathematical formula for the determination of the sample size for the estimation of the mean is $n = \left(\frac{Z}{D}\right)^2 * \sigma^2$ and for the estimation of the proportion is $n = \left(\frac{Z}{D}\right)^2 * PQ$ if we express Z in terms of the absolute value of $D=(\bar{x}-\mu)$ or $D=(p-P)$, as the case may be, and these formulae may be found in some statistical textbooks. Although it is correct, using these formulae require setting D differently for different levels of μ and P. But, for the formula given in this book (that is, Equations 2.2 and 2.4), the DP is standardised and the same value applies to any absolute values of μ and P.

Equations for Sample Size Estimation

From the above two sections, we have rewritten the formulae for the estimation of the sample size for the mean and proportion of populations.

The sample size n required to estimate the *population mean* is:

$$n = \frac{Z^2}{D^2} \frac{\sigma^2}{\mu^2} \quad \text{(or)} \quad n = \left(\frac{Z}{D}\right)^2 * \left(\frac{\sigma}{\mu}\right)^2 \quad \text{(or)} \quad n = \left(\frac{Z}{D}\right)^2 * (CV)^2$$

where

Z=1.96 at the 5 percent level, 2.58 at the 1 percent level of significance (also called the α level).

μ and σ=the mean and SD in the population, respectively (to be assumed appropriately).

D=the degree of accuracy desired (also called the margin of error), usually set to 0.05 (5 percent) or 0.1 (10 percent).

$CV = \dfrac{\sigma}{\mu}$, the coefficient of variation of mean (to be assumed appropriately).

The sample size n required to estimate the population proportion is as follows:

$$n = \frac{Z^2 P * Q}{(D * P)^2} \quad \text{(or)} \quad n = \left(\frac{Z}{D}\right)^2 * \frac{PQ}{P * P} \quad \text{(or)} \quad n = \left(\frac{Z}{D}\right)^2 * \frac{Q}{P}.$$

It can also be written as $n = \left(\dfrac{Z}{D}\right)^2 * (CV)^2$,

where

Z=1.96 at the 5 percent level, 2.58 at the 1 percent level of significance.

P=expected proportion in the population (to be assumed), $Q = 1 - P$.

D=the degree of accuracy desired, usually set to 0.05 of 'P' ($0.05 * P$).

CV=SD/mean, in that $SD^2 = PQ$ and mean$=P$.

Unit of Enquiry and Sample Size

The sample size n determined from the above equations is the minimum number of cases reqired for study, investigation or measurement (of variables). But often the unit of enquiry may be different from the unit of measurement. For example, the unit of measurement may be a child (say, born in the last five years), but the unit of enquiry may be the mother. Furthermore, we may not have the list of children or mothers in the population, but we may have the list of families/households in the population, and even if it is not available, a list of families or households can be easily made through a quick enumeration. But preparing a list of children or mothers requires additional enquiries. So, often it may be desirable to set the sample size in terms of the number of families/households that would give the required number of mothers/children for investigation.

Let n be the required sample size of, say, children (of age below 5 years) and let h be the number of households required to survey in order to get n children. Accordingly, the next step is to estimate the sample size in terms of the number of households h that would give the required number of children n. Let c be the number of children (of age below 5 years) per household; then $n = h * c$ or $h = n/c$. Please note that if $c = 1$ (that is one child per household), then $h = n$ (that is, the number of households to be selected is the same as the number of children to be studied). If $c > 1$, then $h < n$ and if $c < 1$, then $h > n$.

Subgroups and Sample Size

The sample size n or h as determined above is only to have an estimate of the mean or rate for the population as a whole. But in reality, we often need to have estimates for subgroups of the population, say, for urban and rural areas, males and females, and for religious groups and so on. In this case, the sample size determined as above is for each subgroup and the *minimum* sample size required for the whole population is $n * s$, where s is the number of subgroups. But still there is a catch in it. Actually, the sample size n is for the smallest subgroup, and for the larger subgroups, the sample size required is proportionately higher if proper sample weight is not used. Please note that if one restricts each subgroup to the minimum sample size of n irrespective of its population size, then the stratified random sampling method needs to be applied and for each stratum the sample size can be n, but in this case, the estimation of the index for the population as a whole (all subgroups combined) will require appropriate sampling weights (discussed later in this chapter).

Example 1: Determine the number of households (sample size) required to be surveyed to estimate the mean number of living children of couples of age 35–49 in a district called 'A'. The maximum permissible error should not exceed 10 percent at the 5 percent level of significance.

Based on the literature review, it is expected that the mean number of living children of couples of age 35–49 in district A is around 3.5 with an SD of 1.5, and the proportion of couples of age 35–49 per 100 households is 35. The estimation of the sample size proceeds as follows.

Given that the average number of living children per couple of age 35–49 is 3.5, the expected SD of living children is 1.5 and the permissible error $D=10$ percent, or 0.1. The value of Z at the 5 percent level of significance is 1.96. The number of couples required to be studied, n, is determined as follows:

$$n=(Z\sigma/D\mu)^2=\{(1.96*1.5)/(0.1*3.5)\}^2=71 \text{ couples of age 35–49.}$$

Usually, we select households instead of couples to conduct the survey, and interview all the couples (wives) in the age group of 35–49 in the selected households. The number of households required to get 71 couples (wives) in the age group of 35–49 is $(100/35)*71=202$. So, the minimum number of households required to be selected is 202.

Example 2: Determine the number of households required to be surveyed to estimate CPR (percentage of couples with wives in the age group of 15–44 using a contraceptive method) in a district. The maximum permissible error should not exceed 5 percent at the 5 percent level of significance. Previous surveys indicate that the CPR in the district is about 45 percent and there would be 0.98 couples per household.

The sample size is estimated as follows:

The expected CPR is 45 percent, or $P=45/100=0.45$, $Q=1-P=0.55$.
The expected number of couples per household is 0.98.
The permissible error $D=5$ percent or 0.05.
The value of Z at the 5 percent level of significance is 1.96.
The number of couples required to be studied is

$$n=(Z^2Q)/(D^2P)=(1.96*1.96*0.55)/(0.1*0.1*0.45)=470.$$

With 0.98 couples per household, the number of households to be selected worked out to be $470/0.98=479$. That is, the minimum number of households required to be studied to estimate CPR in the district is 479.

Example 3: Determine the number of households (sample size) required to be surveyed to estimate the infant mortality rate (IMR) in a district. In view of the large number of households required to estimate the IMR, a three-year reference period may be adopted. The maximum permissible error should not exceed 10 percent at the 5 percent level of significance. Based on the literature review, it is expected that the IMR in the district would be around 50 per 1,000 live births, the crude birth rate would be 25 per 1,000 population and the average household size (number of members per household) would be 5.2.

The calculation is as follows:

The expected IMR is 50 or $P=50/1,000=0.05$, $Q=1-P=0.95$.
The expected average household size is 5.2.
The expected CBR is 25/1,000 population.
The permissible error, $D=10$ percent or 0.1.
The value of Z at the 5 percent level of significance is 1.96.
The number of births required to estimate the IMR is as follows:

$$n=(Z^2Q)/(D^2P)=(1.96*1.96*0.95)/(0.1*0.1*0.05)=7,299 \text{ births.}$$

If we consider a three-year reference period for the occurrence of births, then, assuming that equal number of births will occur each year, we need to enumerate one-third of the 7,299 births per year, that is, 2,433 births per year.

In this way, for rare events, we can reduce the sample coverage by increasing the reference period if the occurrence (that is, incidence and not prevalence) of events is our concern. However, how long the reference period can be extended depends on the correct and complete enumeration of the events in the population. Sometimes other considerations such as changes in the size of base population and changes in the frequency of occurrence of events over period are also taken into account while deciding the reference period. In the case of birth and infant death though the rates are derived on annual basis, a three-year reference period for the enumeration of births and infant deaths can be considered reasonable.

Next, to enumerate 2,433 births per year, we need to survey a population of $(1,000/25)*2,433=97,320$. With an average household size of 5.2, this population accounts for $97,320/5.2=18,715$ households. That is, in this population, the number of households required to be enumerated is 18,715 to estimate the IMR based on the occurrence of births and infant deaths during a three-year reference period.

Note: A comparison of Examples 2 and 3 clearly shows that, although we set the permissible error at a higher level in Example 3 (10 percent) as compared to Example 2 (5 percent), the number of cases and households required to be surveyed is enormously higher for estimating the IMR (Example 3) than for estimating the CPR (Example 2). This is simply because the occurrence of births and more so infant deaths is not as frequent (25 live births per 1,000 population or about 200 households, and 50 infant deaths per 1,000 live births) as women using contraception (almost half of the couples use contraception at any point of time). This demonstrates that, the smaller the proportion (incident or prevalence) of events, the larger the sample size required for estimating the proportion. However, in the case of rare events like infant deaths, we often set a higher margin of permissible error (D) such as 10 percent, 15 percent or 20 percent. So, often, setting the sample size is a matter of convenience keeping in mind the incidence/prevalence of the event and the availability of resources.

Theoretically, in division, for a given numerator value, as the value of the denominator decreases, the value of the answer increases. Accordingly, it can be seen from the formula that, with Z and D remaining the same, as P decreases, Q ($=1-P$) increases, Q/P increases manifold and, hence, n also increases manifold.

Sample Size Required for Tabular Analysis

The sample size required for frequency and cross-tabulation analysis is often governed by the chi-square test of goodness of fit (to be discussed in Chapter 7). For the chi-square test to be valid, the total minimum frequency should be 50, and the minimum expected frequency in each cell should be 5. Accordingly, for the frequency distribution and/or cross-tabulation, the total frequency should be at least 50 and the cell frequency should be at least 5, since the percentage distribution based on less than 5 cases in any cell and 50 cases on the whole will be unstable. For more details, please see Chapter 3.

Sample Size Required for Frequency Distribution Analysis

Let A, B and C be the three key variables in the analysis. Let A_s is the proportion of cases to total cases in the smallest category of the frequency table for variable A, B_s is the proportion of cases to total cases in the smallest category of the frequency table for variable B and C_s is the proportion of cases to total cases in the smallest category of the frequency table for variable C.

Let $n_0 = 50$ (minimum overall sample size required).
Let $n_1 = 5/A_s$ (minimum sample size required as per variable A).
Let $n_2 = 5/B_s$ (minimum sample size required as per variable B).
Let $n_3 = 5/C_s$ (minimum sample size required as per variable C).
Minimum sample size required is the maximum of the above.

That is, $n = \max(n_0, n_1, n_2, n_3)$.

Example 4: In a study of children born during the last five years, the order of birth, education of mother and religion are important variables. The grouping of variables and the frequency distribution obtained from a large survey conducted in a wider area (including the study area) are given in Table 2.11 (Columns 1 and 2). We have to estimate the minimum sample size required for a sample survey for the analysis based on the simple frequency distribution.

For sample size estimation, we assume that the frequency distribution obtained from the larger survey will broadly apply to the study area. The minimum frequency cells are marked. The estimate of the minimum sample size and the expected frequencies are worked out in the table. The table is self-explanatory and so no detailed explanation is required. The estimate shows that the minimum sample size required is 282 or about 300.

For some variables in the analysis, some categories are important for investigation and other categories are less important. For example, with respect to birth order, our focus may be on birth orders 1–3. And in this case, birth orders 4 and above can be considered in one category instead of categories 4, 5 and 6+. In this case, the expected frequency in the birth order category 4+ is $8.4 + 3.3 + 1.8 = 13.5$ percent and the minimum sample size required for the analysis by birth order is $n_1 = 5/0.135 = 37$, and the minimum sample required for the analysis by any of the three variables is 182 (maximum of 50, 37, 131 and 182).

Similarly, with respect to religion, if we consider Jain as an insignificant category, then the category 'Maratha' becomes the significant category with the least frequency and the minimum sample required for the analysis by religion is $n_3 = 5/0.096 = 52$. So, the minimum sample size required for analysis by any of the three variables is 131 (maximum of 50, 37, 131 and 52). Likewise we can minimise the sample size by appropriately choosing the variables and categories but without compromising on the validity of the estimates, that is, in this case, the percentage distribution.

Sample Size Required for Two-way Cross-tabulation Analysis

Let A, B and C be the three key variables in the analysis and A be the dependent variable, and B and C are two independent variables, that is, in Table 2.12, birth order (A) is cross-classified by religion/caste (B) and also birth order (A) is cross-classified by the education of woman (C). Let

Table 2.11 Sample Size Determination for Frequency Distribution Analysis

(1) Important Variables	(2) Expected (%)	(3) Minimum Sample Size	(4) Estimated Frequency
Total	100.0	$n_0 = 50$	282
Order of birth			
1	32.5		92
2	33.0		93
3	21.1		60
4	8.4		24
5	3.3		9
6+	1.8	$n_1 = 5/0.018 = 282$	5
Education of woman			
Illiterate	50.9		144
1–4 std	7.3		20
5–7 std	22.4		63
8–10 std	15.6		44
11+ std	3.8	$n_2 = 5/0.038 = 131$	11
Religion and caste			
SC/ST	18.9		53
OBC	12.3		35
Lingayat	45.1		127
Maratha	9.6		27
Muslim	11.4		32
Jain	2.7	$n_3 = 5/0.027 = 182$	8
$n = \max(n_0, n_1, n_2, n_3)$		282	282

AB_s is the proportion of cases to total cases in the smallest category of the two-way cross-table of A by B. Let AC_s is the proportion of cases to total cases in the smallest category of the two-way cross-table of A by C. Then, it is to be noted that, although a cross-table of variables B by C is possible, it is not our interest as it does not involve the dependent variable (A). The minimum sample size required is estimated as follows:

Let $n_0 = 50$ (minimum overall sample size required).
Let $n_1 = 5/AB_s$ (minimum sample size required as per variable B).
Let $n_2 = 5/AC_s$ (minimum sample size required as per variable C).
Then the minimum sample size required is $n = \max(n_0, n_1, n_2)$.

Example 5: In a study of children born during the last five years, the order of birth, religion/caste and education of mother are important variables with the order of birth being a dependent variable and the other two variables independent variables. The grouping of variables and the cross-table percentage distribution of data obtained from a large survey conducted in a wider area (including the study area) are given below (except the last column). We have to estimate the minimum sample size required for the analysis based on the two-way cross-table distribution of the data.

While looking for the minimum frequency cell, we have to exclude the rows and columns corresponding to marginal totals (marked in Table 2.12). In the table, the minimum frequencies are 0.2 percent and 0.1 percent when the birth order of children are cross-classified by the religion/caste and education of woman, respectively, and the estimates of the minimum sample sizes are

Table 2.12   Sample Size Determination for Cross-tabulation Analysis

		Order of Birth (A)				
	Total	*1*	*2*	*3*	*4+*	*Sample Size*
Religion/caste (B)						
Total	100.0	32.5	33.0	21.1	13.4	
SC/ST	18.9	5.5	5.5	4.2	3.6	
OBC	12.3	4.3	3.5	2.7	1.7	
Lingayat	45.1	15.5	15.7	9.0	4.8	
Maratha	9.6	3.0	3.0	2.2	1.4	$5/(1.4/100)=357^*$
Muslim	11.4	3.1	4.2	2.4	1.7	
Jain	2.7	0.9	1.0	0.6	0.2	$5/(0.2/100)=2{,}500$
Education of woman (C)						
Total	100.0	32.5	33.0	21.1	13.4	
Illiterate	50.9	14.0	15.7	12.2	9.0	
1–4 std	7.3	2.4	2.6	1.5	0.7	$5/(0.7/100)=714^*$
5–7 std	22.4	8.5	7.9	3.7	2.4	
8–10 std	15.6	5.8	5.4	3.2	1.2	
11+ std	3.8	1.8	1.4	0.5	0.1	$5/(0.1/100)=5{,}000$
8+ std	19.4	7.6	6.8	3.7	1.3	

$n=\max(50, 357, 714)=714$

Note: *Compromise: Jain category excluded; 8–10 std and 11+ std combined.

2,500 and 5,000, respectively (the last column). Please note that a division by 100 is seen because the minimum frequencies are expressed in terms of percentage. If we treat the category 'Jain' as insignificant or unimportant category and combine the education categories 8–10 standard and 11+ standard as 8+ standard, then the minimum sample sizes reduce to 357 and 714, and the overall sample size required is 714 (the maximum of 50, 357 and 714). It is clear that while deciding on the minimum sample size based on tabular analysis, we need to set the number of categories of the variables to a minimum with appropriate grouping without compromising on the objectives of the study.

Note: It is seen from Tables 2.11 and 2.12 that as the order of cross-tabulation (one-way, two-way and so on) increases, the cell frequencies decease. Furthermore, if there are more key variables, then $n=\max (n_0, n_1, n_2, n_3,\ldots)$ also increases, that is, as the number of variables and the order of cross-tabulation increase, the sample size required for the tabular analysis also increases, and often the increase is manifold. So, the determination of the sample size is a matter of compromise and is often decided by individuals familiar with sampling and survey data analysis.

Some Important Points on Sample Size Estimation

The following are some important points related to sample size estimation:

1. The lower the value of D (permissible error), the higher the degree of accuracy and the larger the sample size required.
2. The lower the level of significance desired, the larger the sample size required.
3. The smaller the population proportion P (that is, rare event), the larger the sample size required for estimating population proportion.

4. In large populations (universes), the sample size required for population estimation is independent of the population size. For example, the minimum sample size required for population estimation is the same for a small state like Goa and also for a large state like Maharashtra.
5. If estimates are required for different sections of the population (say each district of a state), the minimum sample size applies to each section or region and the total minimum sample size required for the entire population (state) is the sum of sample sizes of all sections (districts).
6. If the sample sizes are not in proportion to the population sizes of each section of the universe, a case-weighting is required for the overall population estimation in order to adjust for the disproportionate sample sizes drawn from each section of the universe.

SUBSAMPLE

A subsample is a smaller sample that is selected from a previously drawn larger sample. The method adopted for the selection of a subsample may be the same as the sampling method adopted for the selection of the larger sample, or it may be different. In a multi-stage sampling for the larger sample, the subsample may contain samples from all intermediate sample units or only a subsample of the sample units. Often the purpose of the subsample is different and wider than that of the larger sample. For example, the larger sample may be for the purpose of understanding the socio-economic condition of the study population, whereas the purpose of the subsample is for assessing the nutritional status of children. As an assessment of nutritional status requires anthropometric equipment and trained nutrition investigators, it may not be possible to conduct the survey on a larger sample. The advantage of having a subsample instead of another independent sample is that one can relate the nutritional status of children with the socio-economic characteristics obtained from the corresponding households of the larger sample. In this way, the subsample has very important purposes in social science research.

Replacement Sample or Supplementary Sample: What Is It?

It is supposed that the replacement sample or supplementary sample is a small sample of observations kept as reserved for replacement in case some of the main sample cases could not be interviewed. During my service, I came across some (if not many) social science scientists following this procedure. But as far as I know, there is no such procedure available in statistics. In the recent years, I have searched many statistics books and also search on the web, but I did not come across any such procedure discussed.

There are sampling procedures called 'sampling with replacement' and 'sampling without replacement'. In social science research, we generally follow the latter one. Please note that sampling with replacement is a sampling method that is different from the replacement sample. If we use a replacement sample, then the final sample cannot be considered as a probability sample and so population estimates and hypothesis testing break down.

Let us see a small example. Let the population size be $N = 1,000$, the main sample size be $n = 100$ and the replacement sample be $r = 10$. First, we select 100 units from the 1,000 units using SRS, and the probability of selecting a unit for the main sample is $p_m = n/N = 100/1,000 = 0.1$. Next, let us select the replacement sample and the probability of selecting a replacement sample is $p_r = r/(N-n) = 10/(1,000-100) = 10/900 = 0.011$. It is clear that the two probabilities are different and, therefore, the two samples cannot be combined. Further, in the main sample, all the members are interviewed if they could be reached, that is, each member is interviewed independent of whether other members are interviewed or not. But in the replacement sample, members are interviewed sequentially one after another only when a member from the main sample could not be interviewed, that is, an interview with a member from the replacement sample is conditional upon a member from the main sample could be interviewed and so estimating the probability of interviewing a member from the replacement sample becomes complicated. Furthermore, it is not guaranteed that all the members of the replacement sample will be interviewed even if they are available for the interview, that is, in some cases, we may not require all the members in the replacement sample and, in some other cases, the replacement sample may not be sufficient, resulting in determining the ultimate probability of sampling almost impossible. So, sampling with the replacement sample cannot be considered as a probability sampling method and it automatically becomes a non-probability sampling.

I have demonstrated this only to advise the social scientists to refrain from adopting the unscientific concept of replacement sample. Instead, if the social scientists expect that there would be a non-coverage of sample cases due to some reasons such as rejection, not at home, temporary migration, ineligibility and the like, then they can very well increase the (main) sample size appropriately so that the interview/coverage of the minimum required sample size can be ensured. This requires the researcher to assess the possible extent of non-coverage in advance and decide on the sample size for selection accordingly. In this case, the non-covered cases are assumed to be randomly distributed, so that the interviewed cases remained selected at random with equal probability. However, it is to be kept in mind that the non-coverage should remain low, preferably below 10 percent, and it is distributed across all areas and all sections of the community; otherwise, the interviewed cases may not be considered as a representative sample of the population.

At the same time, replacement is permitted on rare situations and that even only at the last-stage sampling unit and not at ultimate sample households. For example, we have selected 100 villages from a state according to some sampling procedure. During a field survey, the field team found that a sample village was submerged in dam water, destroyed due to natural calamity, or land acquired for some road/factory construction, and the people are displaced. In such circumstances, a nearby village with the similar characteristics or a random sample of village is selected by the coordinator of the study (and not by the field team) as a replacement.

SAMPLE AND POPULATION WEIGHTS

Often large-scale surveys will have an objective to estimate parameters for subgroups of the population. For example, a state-level survey may desire to have estimates for rural and urban areas of the state. Similarly, an all India survey would like to have estimates for each state. Here, the states and rural–urban areas are subgroups. Furthermore, we may have some special interest on some subgroups that may require relatively larger sample units to be surveyed.

For any parameter estimation, we require a minimum sample size irrespective of the population size (in the case of large populations). So we have to fix a minimum sample size for each subgroup. If each subgroup has the same number of population units, then the equal sample size from each subgroup can be obtained, and it will serve the purpose for the analysis of the data. Usually, it is not the case and the subgroups differ in their sizes; often the group differences may be manifold. For example, for many states of India, the rural and urban distribution of the population is roughly in the ratio of 67 percent to 33 percent, or 2:1. Under the propositional sample allocation strategy, we have to fix an appropriate minimum sample size for the smallest subunit and proportionately increase the sample size for the larger units. By doing so, we may end up with a very large total sample size which is often too difficult to be surveyed. For example, assuming the rural and urban households in the ratio of 2:1, if we determine a minimum sample of 200 households for urban areas, then we need to select 400 households for rural areas, making the total sample size 600 households.

Alternatively, we may have the same minimum sample size for each subgroup irrespective of its population size, or a slightly higher sample size for larger units but not in proportion to their population sizes, so that the total sample size is restricted to a manageable level. In the above case, if we select 200+200=400 households, then we can get estimates for both the subgroups. But deriving estimates for the total population (urban and rural combined) would require some adjustments, called weighting, for the disproportionate sample sizes drawn from the two subgroups. To make the estimates representative to the total population, we can derive two types of weights. One, to estimate the total units in the population having a specified characteristic feature, we use a weight called population weight, and another, to derive rates (say mean and percentages), we use a weight called sample weight. The derivation of population and sample weights is illustrated in the following.

An example: Given in Table 2.13 (Columns 1, 2 and 4) is the stratum-wise number of population units and the number of sample units (sample size).

The steps involved in the calculation of population and sample weights are described below.

1. Tabulate population and sample units by the subgroup of the population. (The size may be in terms of households, persons, women and the like.) In this example, Columns 2 and 4 are the distributions of population and sample units by the states.
2. Obtain the percentage distributions of population and sample units by the subgroup. It is presented in Columns 3 and 5, respectively. If the samples are proportionately allocated (and covered), then Columns 3 and 5 should have the same values. If they differ, then it means that the sample coverage is disproportionate to the population sizes of the subgroups and need adjustments (weighting) for analysing the data.
3. The population weight is the ratio of the population size to the sample size in a subgroup. In our example, the 387 units covered from AP are to be considered as 15,146 units in the population, and this can be achieved by using the factor 15,146/387=39.137. It is the population weight for the subgroup AP, that is, 387 * 39.137=15,146. Likewise, we can do the calculation for the other subgroups.

Table 2.13 Calculation of Population and Sample Weights

	Population Units		Sample Units		Weight for	
State or Groups	Number	%	Number	%	Population	Sample
(1)	(2)	(3)	(4)	(5)	(6)=(2)/(4)	(7)=(3)/(5)
AP	15,146	34.05	387	23.82	39.1370	1.429737
KA	10,546	23.71	427	26.28	24.6979	0.902254
KE	6,368	14.32	283	17.42	22.5018	0.822026
TN	12,422	27.93	528	32.49	23.5265	0.859462
Total	44,482	100.00	1,625	100.00	–	–

4. The sample weight is the ratio of the percentage of the population size to the percentage of the sample size in the subgroups. In our example, 34.0 percent of population units are in AP, but the sample units are only 23.8 percent of the total sample size. So, we have to consider 23.8 percent of the total sample units in AP as 34.0 percent of population units. This can be achieved by using the factor $34.0/23.8 = 1.43$. Value 1.43 is the sample weight for the subgroup AP, that is, $23.8 * 1.43 = 34.0$. Likewise, we can do the calculation for the other subgroups.

5. The weights so derived will apply to each and every sample unit in the subgroup. Usually, the weight is added to the cases in the data file as a weight variable. In every statistical analysis including the tabulation of data, the weight is to be applied and all software programs have provision for that. That is, each case should be considered as its corresponding 'weight' number of cases to make the sample distribution of data representative to the population distribution.

6. As each case is replaced by its weight and summed to get the distribution of the sample units in the frequency distribution or index calculation, it is advisable to retain as many decimal places as possible in the weight variable (usually, 5–8 decimal places). To achieve this percentage, the distribution of the population and sample units (Columns 3 and 5) should also have as many decimal places as possible (in Table 2.13 only two decimal places are shown).

7. Once weight is applied in the frequency distribution or cross-tabulation of the data, the weighted cell frequencies are no longer integers, though we may round it to the nearest integer, and many software programs provide for decimal places for cell frequencies while outputting tables.

Check: The product of the population weight and the sample size of all subgroups should add to the total population size. Similarly, the product of the sample weight and the sample size of all subgroups should add to the total sample size.

Important: If a sample is drawn proportionately from each subgroup of a population, then the weight will be 1 for each subgroup. But if the sample is drawn disproportionately, then the weight will be greater than 1 for the subgroups with larger units (that is, if the sample-to-population ratio is smaller) and will be less than 1 for the subgroups with smaller units (that is, if the sample-to-population ratio is larger). For more reliable estimates of population parameters, it is very important to ensure that the weight for any subgroup is not too high, preferably not greater than 2.0, but it can be too low for some subgroups. It is because a large weight, say 5, means that the one sample unit from the subgroup is equivalent to five units in the population. Suppose, if a sample unit from the subgroup takes a very high or a very low value for a variable (say income) and it amounts to 5 units having that value in the population, then accordingly it will shift the estimates of the population to a very high or very low value than the real value. But at the same time, if the weight is very small, then many sample units is equivalent to one population unit and so its impact on the population estimates will be less. So, while allocating sample sizes to population subgroups utmost care should be taken to ensure that the sample units to population units for any one subgroup is not too small as compared to that for the other subgroups in the population.

SAMPLING DESIGN IN NFHS-3

In this section, an example of sample selection adopted in the NFHS that was conducted during 2005–06 (NFHS-3) is presented with a view to make the readers understand the process involved in the sample selection for a sample survey. It is to be noted that the survey is acclaimed as one of the most popular sample surveys conducted in India, and the findings of the survey are used widely both nationally and internationally.

Sample Design

The third National Family Health Survey, NFHS-3, was conducted during 2005–06 in all the states of India on a sample basis. In this survey, a large number of key indicators related to the socio-economic status of households, mother and child health, nutrition and family welfare aspects were estimated. As the NFHS-3 proposed the estimation of a large number of indices, an initial sample size of 4,000 ever-married women (EMWs) of the reproductive age of 15–49 for large states and that of 1,500 EMWs for small states were proposed. The sample size was increased for some states to provide estimates for HIV prevalence.

A uniform sample design was adopted in all the states. In each state, samples were drawn from both the urban and rural areas, more or less in proportion to the size of the state's urban and rural populations. The rural sample was selected in two stages. In the first stage, villages were selected with the PPS sampling method as primary sampling units (PSUs), and in the second stage a systematic random selection of households was drawn within each PSU. In urban areas, a three-stage procedure was followed. In the first stage, wards were selected with the help of the PPS sampling method. In the next stage, one census enumeration block (CEB, consisting of about 100–150 households) was randomly selected from each sample ward, which served as the PSU for the urban areas. In the final stage, households were randomly selected within each selected CEB.

Sample Selection

For the sample selection of PSUs in rural areas, the 2001 census list of villages served as the sampling frame. The list was stratified by a number of variables. The first level of stratification was geographic, with districts being subdivided into contiguous regions. Within each of these regions, villages were further stratified using selected variables from the following list: village size, percentage of males working in non-agricultural sector, percentage of population belonging to scheduled castes or scheduled tribes and female literacy. From this list, the required numbers of villages was selected with the PPS sampling method, and these villages served as the PSUs for rural areas. However, large sample villages (with more than a specified number of households, usually 500) were segmented (divided into a number of segments or parts with each segment having about 150–200 households), and two segments were selected randomly using the PPS method. Household listing in these villages was carried out only in the selected segments and not in the entire village.

For the sample selection of PSUs in urban areas, the procedure adopted for the first stage of the sample design was similar to the one followed in rural areas. The 2001 census list of wards was arranged according to districts, and within districts, on the basis of the level of female literacy, a sample of wards was selected systematically with PPS. Next, one CEB as a PSU was selected from each selected ward using the PPS method.

Households Selection

For the households selection, a mapping and household listing operation was carried out (that is, an enumeration of households was made) in each PSU (village or segments of village in rural areas and CEB in urban areas). The listing provided the necessary frame for selecting households. The household listing operation involved preparing an up-to-date notional and layout sketch map of each selected PSU, assigning serial numbers to structures, recording the addresses or location of these structures, classifying the structures as residential and non-residential and listing the names of the heads of the households (in residential structures) in the selected PSUs.

The households to be interviewed were selected with equal probability from the household list in each PSU using the systematic sampling procedure. The interval applied for the selection was determined to obtain a self-weighting sample of households within each domain. On average, 30 households were initially targeted for selection in each selected PSU. However, as the number of households in the sample villages varied widely, to avoid extreme variations in the workload of the field teams, a minimum of 15 and a maximum of 60 households limit were applied for the rural PSUs. Each survey team supervisor was provided with the original household listing, layout sketch map and the list of selected households for each PSU. All the selected households were contacted during the main survey and those who could be contacted were interviewed. No replacement was made if a selected household was absent during data collection. (*Note:* This point is very important as many researchers replace households arbitrarily or from a stand-by subsample, making the ultimate sample a non-probability sample.) However, during the survey operation, if it was found that a PSU (village/CEB) was inaccessible, non-traceable or submerged/demolished, a replacement PSU with similar characteristics from the neighbouring area was selected by the nodal agency and provided to the survey organisation. Please note that the replacement is made in the intermediate sample units and not in the ultimate sample of households or units, the replacement units are not selected and kept in advance but done when the situation warranted it, and the replacement is made at the organisation level and not at the field investigator level.

Sample Weights

NFHS-3 is designed for self-weighting at the domain level, that is, at the level of urban and rural areas of each state. This means that all households in the same domain will share a common household weight. The design weight is the inverse of the overall sampling fraction in each domain. The overall sampling fraction is the product of the selection probabilities at each sampling stage (two stages in rural areas and three stages in urban areas). The design weight was adjusted for household non-response in the calculation of the household sampling weight. The adjustments for non-response were done at the domain level in order to preserve the self-weighting nature of the sample within domains. The sampling weights were further normalised at the national level to obtain national standard weights and at the state level to obtain state standard weights. The national standard weights were normalised so that the total number of weighted cases equals the total number of unweighted cases at the national level. The state standard weights were calculated to ensure that the total number of weighted cases equals the total number of unweighted cases for each state.

(For more details, please refer to International Institute for Population Sciences [IIPS] and Macro International. 2007. *National Family Health Survey [NFHS-3], 2005–06: India: Volume I*. Mumbai: IIPS, pp. 11–15.)

Important Points to Note

First, the sample size is determined based on the parameters being estimated (that is, the indices being derived from the survey data) and not by the sheer population size of the universe (here, the states). Although even the major states differ widely in their population sizes, the base sample size is fixed at approximately 4,000 households for larger states and 1,500 households for smaller states. So, the sample size is determined based on the parameters being estimated (also the availability of resources) and not based on the size of the universe, but what is required is appropriately distributing the sample units within the universe (sample selection) to represent the universe.

Second, the sample design consisted of a multi-stage-cum-multi-method sampling procedure with a probability assigned to each sample unit at each stage. Usually, in large-scale surveys, it is the case, so that a limited sample size gets adequate representation in the larger population universe like the state.

Third, the sample households are selected from a list of all households in the PSUs (sampling frame) made through a household enumeration (listing). As the sampling frame is made through a household enumeration, it is up to date and free from omission and duplication (except for the fault of the house listers, if any).

Fourth, the supervisors (and interviewers) are supplied with the pre-selected list of households and they had no option to choose a household or to replace it. For a survey to be called a sample survey, in no case the interviewers should have the option to choose a household or a respondent. They only need to go with a list (of households) and interview them if found and report back if not found. They should not be given the freedom to select a case or replace it.

Fifth, if the researcher expects that there would be the non-coverage of sample units, then they can increase the sample size in advance rather than replacing sample units later. However, they should ensure that the non-coverage is not substantial, may be, not exceeding 10 percent. It is because a higher non-coverage often arises due to a relatively higher non-coverage in some sections than the other sections of the population and this will have implications for reliably estimating population parameters.

Sixth, if the sample units are drawn disproportionately and/or if the coverage of households is different in different PSUs, it is required to estimate sample weight and apply in the analysis of the data. Then only the indices derived from the data can be considered reliable estimates for the population/universe.

CHAPTER 3

Tabular Analysis of Data

In Chapter 1, we have seen different types of variables, namely nominal, ordinal, interval and ratio variables. We have also seen the way the variables are treated in the statistical analysis, such as numerical and categorical variables, dependent and independent variables, intervening and control variables and so on. Furthermore, you might have studied elsewhere as to how to conduct a survey and computerise the data. Here, we assume that we have conducted a survey and the data are entered into the computer in (or converted to) the Statistical Package for Social Sciences (SPSS) format.

It is to be noted that SPSS is often considered as the best user-friendly statistical software package for the social scientists and, hence, in this book most examples are demonstrated with the help of this software.

The next step is to summarise the data and apply statistical techniques to draw inferences about the population from which the sample is drawn. In statistical analysis, we make inferences about the population based on a random sample of units or observations drawn from it. One form of summarising the data is tabulation. A table is a systematic classification of the data according to one or more variables, and the classified data (called frequencies) are arranged in a set of rows and columns in such a way that one can easily understand the pattern in the data. The process of making a table including the related calculations is called the tabulation of data. In other words, tabulation is counting or categorising the individuals (or observations) in a dataset according to one or more characteristics of the individuals (variables).

Categorising the individuals according to the values of only one variable (characteristics) at a time is called *frequency distribution* (e.g., distributing households by religion, say Hindu, Muslim, Christian and 'Other'. Please note that, here, 'religion' is the characteristics or variable under study, and Hindu, Muslim, Christian and 'Other' are the different (exclusive and exhaustive) values or categories of the variable. Categorising the individuals according to the values of more than one variable at a time is called *cross-tabulation* or simply *tabulation* (e.g., distributing the total households first by residence [urban and rural residence], and then by the religion [within the urban and rural residence]). If two variables are involved in the categorisation, then it is called two-way (cross) tabulation (e.g., as above) and if three variables are involved, it is called three-way (cross) tabulation, for example, distributing individuals first by sex, and then within sex by religion and then within sex and religion by the educational level and so on.

RATES AND RATIOS

Ratio

A ratio is a comparison of two numbers by division. Let A and B be two numbers. Then the ratio of A to B is expressed as A/B (read as A by B), $A:B$ (read as A is to B) or A to B. Mathematically, a ratio is expressed as a fraction of the two numbers (A/B) and more specifically as decimals. For example, if $A = 6$ and $B = 10$, then the ratio of A to B is $6/10 = 0.6$, and the ratio of B to A is $10/6 = 1.67$.

Often a ratio is expressed per unit (1), per 100 or per 1,000 for the convenience of expression and understanding. Some popular ratios in social sciences are:

$$\text{Sex ratio} = \frac{\text{males}}{\text{females}} * 100 \quad \text{(in demographic literature)}$$

$$\text{Sex ratio} = \frac{\text{females}}{\text{males}} * 1,000 \quad \text{(in Indian census)}$$

$$\text{Dependency ratio} = \frac{\text{Number of persons in the age group of } 0-14 \text{ and } 60+}{\text{Number of persons in the age group of } 15-59} * 100$$

$$\text{School enrolment ratio} = \frac{\text{Number of students enrolled in schools in an area}}{\text{Number of schools-age of persons in the same area}} * 100$$

$$\text{Literacy rate} = \frac{\text{Number of literate persons}}{\text{Total persons (or population)}} * 100.$$

Rate

A rate is a special case of a ratio, in which the numerator is a subset of the denominator or the numerator is closely related to the denominator. In the case of the sex ratio, males and females are two distinct groups and, therefore, the sex ratio is a ratio. On the other hand, the literacy rate is not only a ratio but also a rate as literates (in the numerator) are part of the persons (in the denominator). Let us consider a group of, say 200 persons, of whom 120 are literates and others are illiterates. We can define the literacy rate as the number of literate persons per 100 persons in an area. In our exercise, the literacy rate is 120/200 * 100 = 60 percent. Here, 120 persons in the numerator are those who satisfied the condition 'literate' among the 200 persons in the denominator.

Note: All the rates are ratios but not all the ratios are rates.

Now, let us consider this example. A vehicle has run 100 km with 10 litres of diesel. Although diesel and distance are two distinct aspects, we relate them in terms of 'mileage' of the vehicle, that is, the number of kilometres the vehicle has run for 1 litre of diesel. We calculate the mileage as follows:

$$\text{Mileage} = \frac{\text{Number of kilometres the vehicle has run}}{\text{Number of litres of diesel consumed by the vehicle}} = \frac{100}{10} = 10.$$

That is, the mileage the vehicle gives is 10 km per litre of diesel. It is a ratio as well as a rate. Although diesel and kilometre are two distinct aspects, they are related to the vehicle's capacity to run and, therefore, it is a rate.

Now, let us consider the school enrolment ratio and the school attendance rate. The school enrolment ratio is the ratio of the number of students enrolled in schools located in an area divided by the number of school-age children in the same area. Here, the data of the number of children enrolled come from the official statistics or school records, and the number of school-age children in the area comes from survey statistics. As such, the numerator data cannot be said to have come from or part of the denominator data. That is why the school enrolment ratio is a ratio and not a rate. On the other hand, consider the school attendance rate that is defined as the number of children of a particular age group studying in an area out of the number of children in the corresponding age group in the same area. Here, both the numerator and denominator data are from the same source, and, therefore, the school attendance rate is a rate.

Proportion and Percentage

A *proportion* is a fractional share of an individual, a group or a category to all individuals, groups or categories, respectively, in the population, that is, a proportion is the ratio of the number of individuals in one group to the number of individuals in all groups in the population (or sample). The sum of the proportions for all categories in the data (population or sample) will add up to 1. A percentage is a 'proportion' expressed per 100 units. The sum of the percentages of all categories in the population will add up to 100. So, a percentage value is 100 times the corresponding proportion value. It is clear that the proportions and percentages are standardised measures (expressed per unit and per 100, respectively) and are used mainly to compare the categories across populations or subgroups of the same population.

Let a population (or sample) has three categories (groups), say A, B and C with the corresponding sizes (persons) X, Y and Z, so that the total population N is $X+Y+Z$. Let $N=300$, $X=80$, $Y=120$ and $Z=100$ so that $80+120+100=300$.
The proportions are calculated as follows:

The proportion of persons in category A is $(X/N)=(80/300)=0.267$.
The proportion of persons in category B is $(Y/N)=(120/300)=0.400$.
The proportion of persons in category C is $(Z/N)=(100/300)=0.333$.
The total proportion is $0.267+0.400+0.333=1$.

The percentages are calculated as follows:

The percent of persons in category A is $(X/N)*100=(80/300)*100=26.7$.
The percent of persons in category B is $(Y/N)*100=(120/300)*100=40.0$.
The percent of persons in category C is $(Z/N)*100=(100/300)*100=33.3$.
The total percentage is $26.7+40.0+33.3=100.0$.

For intermediate statistical analysis, mostly the proportion values are used rather than the percentage values as it is convenient for mathematical operations. However, the final results are often expressed in terms of percentages. Please note that in social science research, often percent values are used rather than proportion values, simply for the convenience, easy understanding and explanation.

FREQUENCY DISTRIBUTION

The frequency distribution is the distribution of population (or sample) units according to one characteristic feature (variable) of the population at a time. A frequency distribution is also called one-way tabulation. A frequency (distribution) table is a tabular representation of the number of individuals (cases or units) in different categories of a variable. It consists of minimum two columns in which the first (left) column lists the categories of the variable and the second (right) column lists the number of individuals in the corresponding categories. The number of individuals in each category is called the cell frequency and the sum of the frequencies of all cells is called the total frequency that is nothing but the total number of observations or individuals in the dataset. The cell frequencies can also be presented in a standardised form with the total frequency being considered as 100 and the individual cell frequencies are proportionally adjusted in such a way that the total adds up to 100. This is called the percentage distribution of observations, which is easier to understand and compare between groups.

The example given in the section 'Proportion and Percentage' can be put in a tabular form as shown in Table 3.1. It is clear from the table that the categories (Column 1) are A, B and C and

Table 3.1 Frequency Distribution

Category (1)	Frequency (2)	Proportion (3)	% (4)
A	80	0.267	26.7
B	120	0.400	40.0
C	100	0.333	33.3
Total	300	1.000	100.0

the corresponding frequencies (Column 2) are 80, 120 and 100. The arrangement of the numbers in this way is called the frequency distribution and each number is called the cell frequency. The frequency distribution in terms of proportion values (Column 3) is called 'proportions' or 'proportional' distribution, and the frequency distribution in terms of percent values (Column 4) is called the 'percentage' distribution. Please note that often the word 'percent' and not 'per cent' (two words) is used to qualify a value (e.g., 40 percent) and percentage is used in sentences without a value (e.g., the percentage distribution of households by religion).

In addition, the 'cumulative frequency' and the 'cumulative percent' are also often calculated and added to the table. They are important for understanding the pattern in the data. The cumulative frequency of a category is the sum of frequencies of all the categories including the current category. Similarly, the cumulative percent of a category is the sum of the percentage values of all the categories including the current category. For Table 3.1, the cumulative frequency and cumulative percent are calculated as follows:

The cumulative frequency for category A is 80=80.
The cumulative frequency for category B is 80+120=200.
The cumulative frequency for category C is 80+120+100 (or 200+100)=300.

The cumulative percent for category A is 26.7=26.7.
The cumulative percent for category B is 26.7+40.0=66.7.
The cumulative percent for category C is 66.7+33.3=100.0.

The cumulative frequency and the cumulative percent values can be added to the table in two additional columns as shown in Table 3.2 (NA denotes not applicable). The table containing the categories and frequencies (in any combination of proportions, percentages, cumulative frequency and cumulative percent) is called the frequency distribution table or simply the frequency table. The cumulative frequency, specifically the cumulative percent, helps to understand the pattern of the distribution of cases up to the current category. It is valid and meaningful for ordinal variables (including discrete and continuous variables converted into ordinal variables) and not for nominal variables.

An SPSS Example

To run 'frequencies' in SPSS, use the menu 'Analyze => Descriptive Statistics => Frequencies' and a window like the one shown in Figure 3.1 will open with the variables in the data file listed on the left-side box and an empty box labelled 'variable(s)' on the right. Now, click on the variable or variables for which frequencies are desired and then click the right arrow (located in-between the two boxes). The selected variables are now transferred to the 'Variable(s)' box (here 'anaemia level of child', an ordinal variable) and then click 'OK'. Now, the data are processed and a table as shown in Table 3.3 is produced with frequency (distribution), percentage, valid percentage and cumulative percentage for each category of the variable.

Table 3.2   Cumulative Frequency Distribution

Category	Frequency	Proportion	%	Cumulative Frequency	Cumulative %
A	80	0.267	26.7	80	26.7
B	120	0.400	40.0	200	66.7
C	100	0.333	33.3	300	100.0
Total	300	1.000	100.0	NA	NA

Figure 3.1   SPSS Menu for Frequencies

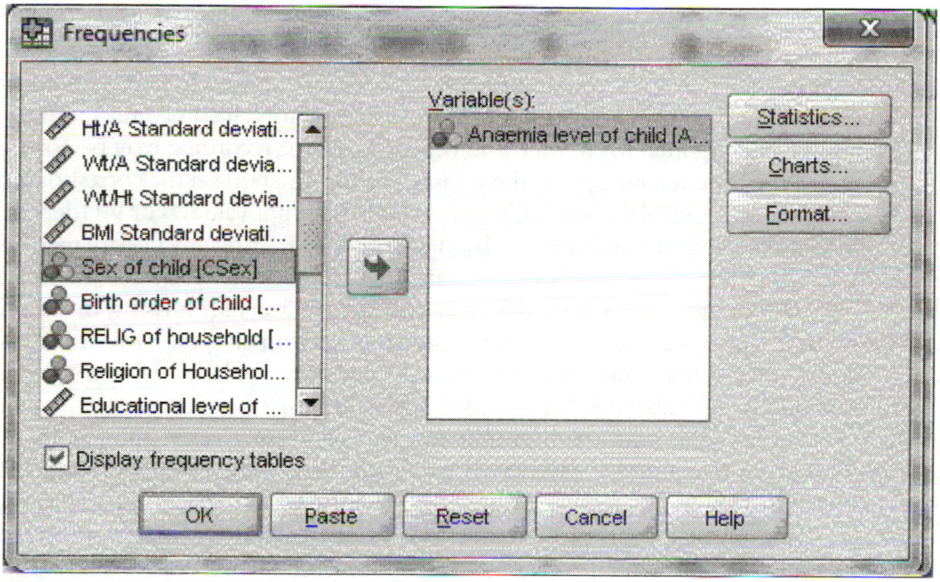

Table 3.3   First Example of SPSS Output on Frequencies

		Frequency	%	Valid %	Cumulative %
				Anaemia Level of Child	
Valid	Severe	10	1.0	1.5	1.5
	Moderate	114	11.5	17.6	19.2
	Mild	127	12.9	19.7	38.9
	Not anaemic	395	40.0	61.1	100.0
	Total	646	65.4	100.0	
Missing	9	236	23.9		
	System	106	10.7		
	Total	342	34.6		
Total		988	100.0		

It can be seen from the table that out of 988 children in the dataset, 10 children (1.0 percent) are severe anaemic ('%' column), 114 children (11.5 percent) are moderately anaemic, 127 children (12.9 percent) are mild anaemic and 395 (40.0 percent) are not anaemic (or normal). There are also 236 children (23.9 percent) for whom the information is *not available* (declared as 'missing' with code 9) and 106 children (10.7 percent) for whom the information or measurement is *not applicable* (declared as 'system' missing). Please note that the above statements based on the output table are correct, but drawing inferences based on the statements would be misleading until we read through the following few paragraphs, understand the problems and correct the statements accordingly.

In any survey, for some cases, some information may not be relevant (i.e., not applicable), and in the dataset, the cells corresponding to these variables are usually kept blank and SPSS treats these cells as 'system' missing. In our example (dataset), children below age 6 months are not measured anaemic status (i.e., the blood sample not drawn and the haemoglobin level not estimated), that is, the anaemia level is not applicable for them. These cases are treated as system missing cases by SPSS. Accordingly, the 106 cases corresponding to the category 'system' under 'missing' caption in the table are 'not applicable' cases.

Furthermore, it is usual that some respondents may not know or refuse to part with information on some variables (e.g., extramarital relationship, HIV/AIDS status, income and the like) or the investigators might have forgotten to record the information, or the recording may be not legible or the values are out of the expected range. For these cases, the information on the corresponding variables is treated as 'data not available' and usually given a code (and not value) 9 or 99 (depending on the number of digits allocated for that variable). In SPSS, we have to explicitly declare them as 'missing' (please refer to the SPSS manual for how to do it). In Table 3.3, the '236 cases' in the category '9' under 'missing' refer to such cases and in SPSS these cases are called 'user missing' or simply 'missing' cases. Please note that 'system missing' is different from 'user missing'; the former refers to the context in which the information is not applicable for a case, whereas the latter refers to the context in which the information is applicable but not recorded (either not asked, reported, coded or entered).

The problem of 'missing' is that, the more the number of missing cases, the less the number of valid cases for a given total number of cases. If we retain the missing category as one category, it reduces both the number and percentage distribution of the cases in each valid category, leading to drawing wrong or inappropriate inferences. In order to avoid this bias, we often exclude the missing cases and work out the percentage distribution for the total valid cases (for which the information is applicable and also available in the dataset). This is done with the assumption that the missing cases are randomly (uniformly) distributed in each subgroup of the population (though often it may not be true), so that the percentage distribution of valid cases is the same as the percentage distribution of all cases. Accordingly, excluding the 'user missing' and 'system missing' cases, the percentage distribution for the valid cases is presented in Column 4 in the table.

It is important to note that the terms 'system missing' and 'user missing' used in SPSS may be referred differently in different software programs, but their implications are the same. In any output table, if 'system missing' cases are included in the percentage distribution, then it should not be used and the percentage distribution should be reworked excluding the 'system missing' cases. Similarly, if 'user missing' cases are included in the percentage distribution, then ensure that the percentage of missing cases is negligible (say, below 5 percent) and, if large, then it is advisable to rework on the percentage distribution excluding the 'user missing' cases. At the same time, it should be kept in mind that, if the 'user missing' cases are relatively more in some categories than in the other categories, then the assumption that the missing cases are randomly distributed is invalid and biased. So if the missing cases are large or in substantial proportion (as shown in Table 3.3), care should be taken while drawing inferences based on the percentage distribution or even on the valid percentage distribution.

A modified and refined frequency table that may be presented in the report is shown in Table 3.4 (with a table footnote on the exclusion of missing cases). Often the cumulative percent is

Table 3.4   Number and Percentage Distribution of Children by the Anaemia Level

Anaemia Level	Frequency	%	Cumulative %
Severe	10	1.5	1.5
Moderate	114	17.6	19.1
Mild	127	19.7	38.8
Not anaemic	395	61.2	100.0
Total	646	100.0	NA

Note: Table excludes missing cases.

not included in the final table as one can easily make out from the percentage distribution if so desired. The advantage of the cumulative percent is that we can easily and directly say that as many as 39 percent of the children are anaemic and 19 percent are moderately or severely anaemic. On the other hand, just referring to a middle category and interpreting the percentage values may not be revealing much. For example, saying that 20 percent of the children are mild anaemic without referring to the 19 percent of the children who are more than mild anaemic does not mean much. So, whether the cumulative percent is added to the table or not, the interpretation of the table should refer to the related categories together.

Another example of the frequency distribution with a discrete variable (order of birth) based on SPSS is presented in Table 3.5. In this example, there are no missing cases and so the 'percentage' distribution and the 'valid percentage' distribution are the same. As such, the 'valid percentage' distribution can be dropped while presenting the table in the report. However, in this example, the 'cumulative percentage' distribution is valid and appropriate. The cumulative percentage distribution shows that as many as 82 percent of the children are second or lower order births and 93 percent are third or lower order births. On the other hand, only 18 (100−81.8=18.2=18) percent of the children are third and higher order births and just 7 percent are fourth and higher order births. Please note that while interpreting the figures in table, often the decimal values are corrected to the nearest whole number (and the decimal places are ignored) just for the convenience.

Frequency Distribution for Variables with Many Categories

For variables with many distinct values, be it nominal, ordinal, discrete or continuous variable, the frequency distribution will have many categories that will make it difficult to draw inferences based on the frequency table. So, it is always desirable to group the values to make the number of categories reasonably small.

In the case of nominal variables, very low frequency categories can be grouped together, provided these categories are not individually important in the investigation. For example, in the case of religion, Hindu, Muslim and Christian can be retained as individual categories, provided the frequencies in these groups are reasonably large, and other religious categories such as Sikh, Jain and Buddhist can be grouped together as a single category, say 'other religions', provided the individual category frequencies are small so that their combined frequency is reasonably large for analysis through the frequency table.

In the case of the ordinal, discrete and continuous variables, as the categories are in some ascending or descending order, we can group or regroup only the adjacent categories and not the categories randomly. In Table 3.5, the order of birth is a discrete variable, and the birth orders 4 and above are grouped as one category (4+). In Table 3.6, the distribution of children of age group 0–59 months is presented in the 6 months age group. In this table, the variable 'age of

Table 3.5   Second Example of SPSS Output on Frequencies

		Frequency	%	Valid %	Cumulative %
			Order of Birth		
Valid	1	480	48.6	48.6	48.6
	2	328	33.2	33.2	81.8
	3	112	11.3	11.3	93.1
	4+	68	6.9	6.9	100.0
	Total	988	100.0	100.0	

Table 3.6   Number and Percentage Distribution of Children by 6 Months Age Grouping

	Frequency	%	Valid %	Cumulative %
Valid 00–05	80	8.1	8.3	8.3
06–11	107	10.8	11.1	19.4
12–17	108	10.9	11.2	30.7
18–23	100	10.7	10.4	41.1
24–29	97	9.8	10.1	51.1
30–35	101	10.2	10.5	61.6
36–41	81	8.2	8.4	70.1
42–47	104	10.5	10.8	80.9
48–53	92	9.3	9.6	90.4
54–59	92	9.3	9.6	100.0
Total	962	97.4	100.0	
Missing system	26	2.6		
Total	988	100.0		

child' is a discrete variable with 60 distinct values. If we run frequencies for 'age of child' as it is (i.e., without grouping), we will have 60 categories and that will have little meaning for drawing inferences, besides lengthening the size of the frequency table. So, it is necessary to group the values into a few categories that will satisfy our analysis requirements.

Although there is no hard-and-fast rule for making categories, it would be reasonable if the age range is categorised as 0–5, 6–11, . . . , 54–59 months (i.e., 6 months or half-year age grouping, as shown in Table 3.6) or 0–11, 12–23, 24–35, 36–47 and 48–59 months (i.e., 12 months or one-year age grouping) that will satisfy many statistical analyses. Please note that age is defined as the completed number (integer number) of months/years lived and as such the fraction of the month/year remaining is discarded while calculating the age, that is, the age of a child who has completed 6 months and 23 days is 'age 6 months only' and not 7 months. If we use SPSS, we need to recode this variable, either as the same variable (in its own place) or as a different variable (retaining the 'age of child' variable as it is). Preferably, create a new variable for the modified codes (recoding procedure not discussed here, please refer to the SPSS manual), and then run frequencies for that variable. The SPSS output is shown in Table 3.6. From the table, it can be seen that around 10 percent of the children are in each 6 months age group, with a few exceptions. Specifically, the age group 0–5 months has recorded a relatively lesser proportion of 8.3 percent of children only. It may be due to the recent decline in fertility or the omission of relatively younger children than older children in the survey.

CROSS-TABULATION WITH TWO VARIABLES

Depending on the purpose or objectives of the study, often we have to examine the relationship between several variables at a time, so as to adequately describe the problem or to explore the possible relationships between the variables. This can be partly accomplished through the cross-tabulation analysis of the data. Cross-tabulation is the distribution of cases or observations according to two or more characteristic features (variables) of the observations. A general format of a two variables (two-way) cross-tabulation is given in Table 3.7.

That is, cross-tabulation with two variables (often called two-way cross-tabulation) consists of a series of rows and columns (see Table 3.7) in which the categories of one variable are listed on the row side and the categories of the other variable are listed on the column side. Usually, the first row and the first column will refer to the names of the row and column categories (often called 'value/code labels'); the last row and the last column will be the corresponding row and column total frequencies (often called 'marginal totals'), and the intermediate rows and columns will consist of the corresponding cell frequencies.

It is important to note that among the two variables, one should be the dependent (or study) variable and the other should be the independent (or control) variable (see Chapter 1 for dependent and independent variables). Often, the dependent variable is taken on the row side (frequencies of the categories of this variable are listed row-wise and so it is called the row variable) and the independent variable on the column side (frequencies of the categories of this variable are listed column-wise and so it is called the column variable). However, which variable should be the row variable and which should be the column variable is often the choice of the user and the requirements of the analysis.

An SPSS Example of Two-way Cross-tabulation

We have data on a sample of 988 children surveyed from the Goa state. Our problem is to investigate whether the anaemia level differs between male and female children. In this case, the 'anaemia level' is the dependent (or study) variable and 'sex of child' is the comparison (independent or control) variable.

To run cross-tabulation in SPSS, use the menu 'Analyze => Descriptive Statistics => Crosstabs' and a window like the one shown in Figure 3.2 will open with the variables in the data file listed on the left, and three empty boxes placed one below the other on the right. Now, transfer the variable 'Anaemia level of child' to the box labelled 'Row(s)' and 'Sex of child' to the box labelled 'Column(s)' and click 'OK'. Please note that the third box labelled 'Layer 1 of 1' is left blank, and it is for the use of three-way tabulation, discussed later in this chapter.

Table 3.7   Description of the Contents of the Table

	Column Variable				
Row Variable	Category 1	Category 2	Category 3	Etc.	Row Total
Category 1	x	x	x	Etc.	RT1
Category 2	x	x	x	Etc.	RT2
Category 3	x	x	x	Etc.	RT3
Etc.	Etc.	Etc.	Etc.	Etc.	Etc.
Column total	CT1	CT2	CT3	Etc.	Grand total

Figure 3.2 SPSS Menu for Crosstabs

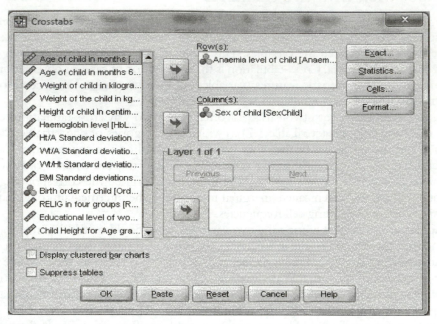

Table 3.8 SPSS Output for Crosstabs (Example 1)

Anaemia Level of Child * Sex of Child Cross-tabulation

Count

		Sex of Child		
		Male	*Female*	*Total*
Anaemia level of child	Severe	7	3	10
	Moderate	68	46	114
	Mild	63	64	127
	Not anaemic	196	199	395
	Total	334	312	646

The SPSS output is shown in Table 3.8. The top row is the table title, the next two rows and the left-most two columns consist of the labels of the variables and their categories, the last row and the last column give the respective row and column total frequencies (marginal totals) and the intermediate rows and columns give the corresponding cell frequencies.

In the table, the number of children who are not anaemic is 395 (the fourth row of the last column), the number of male children who are severely anaemic is 7 (the first row of first column) and the number of female children who are moderately anaemic is 46 (the second row of the second column). The column (marginal) totals are 334 males, 312 females and 646 total children (the number of children for whom the information on the anaemia level is available). Similarly, irrespective of the sex of the child, the row (marginal) totals are 10 severely anaemic children, 114 moderately anaemic children, 127 mildly anaemic children and 395 non-anaemic (normal) children.

As the column/row totals (or marginal totals) are different for different categories, we cannot directly compare the frequencies between the categories. For example, normal (not anaemic) children are 196 out of 334 male children, but 199 out of 312 female children. So, we need to standardise the frequencies in such a way that the data are directly comparable. The most common standardisation process in the tabular analysis is the percentage distribution of the frequencies.

Percentage Distribution in Cross-tabulation

Now, the question is: How to obtain the percentage distribution? There are three possible ways in which the percentage distribution can be obtained for a two-way cross-table. One, the row percentage distribution: the percentage distribution for each row by keeping the respective row total as 100. Two, the column percentage distribution: the percentage distribution for each column by keeping the respective column total as 100. Three, the total percentage distribution: the percentage distribution for all the cells in the table by keeping the overall (grand) total as 100. In SPSS, we can get any or all of these percentage distributions. For this, just click on the button labelled 'Cells…' in the 'Crosstabs…' window and a pop-up window will open and there under the panel 'Percentages', check the boxes named 'Row', 'Column' and/or 'Total' as desired. The SPSS output with the row and column percentages is given in Table 3.9.

In the table, the row-wise figures labelled '% within the anaemia level of child' is the row percentage distribution (note that the corresponding last column value is 100.0 percent) and the row-wise figures labelled '% within Sex of child' is the column percentage distribution (note that the corresponding last row value is 100.0 percent). Which percentage distribution is appropriate depends on the interest of our investigation. Usually, the percentage distribution is obtained for the dependent (study) variable for each category of the control variable. In our case, the dependent variable is the anaemia level and the control variable is the sex of the child, and, hence, the percentage distribution '% within Sex of child' is the appropriate one.

Not only SPSS but also most software programs print the percentage values one line below the cell frequencies (the cell frequency is called 'count' in SPSS) and not to the right (i.e., not

Table 3.9 SPSS Output for Crosstabs of a Two-way Table (Example 2)

*Anaemia Level of Child * Sex of Child Cross-tabulation*

| | | | Sex of Child | | |
			Male	Female	Total
Anaemia level of child	Severe	Count	7	3	10
		% within Anaemia level of child	70.0%	30.0%	100.0%
		% within Sex of child	2.1%	1.0%	1.5%
	Moderate	Count	68	46	114
		% within Anaemia level of child	59.6%	40.4%	100.0%
		% within Sex of child	20.4%	14.7%	17.6%
	Mild	Count	63	64	127
		% within Anaemia level of child	49.6%	50.4%	100.0%
		% within Sex of child	18.9%	20.5%	19.7%
	Not anaemic	Count	196	199	395
		% within Anaemia level of child	49.6%	50.4%	100.0%
		% within Sex of child	58.7%	63.8%	61.1%
	Total	Count	334	312	646
		% within Anaemia level of child	51.7%	48.3%	100.0%
		% within Sex of child	100.0%	100.0%	100.0%

Table 3.10 Number and Percentage Distribution of Children (0–59 Months) by the Anaemia Level, Classified by the Sex of Child

| Anaemia Level of Child | Sex of Child | | | | | |
| | Male | | Female | | Total | |
	Children	%	Children	%	Children	%
Severe	7	2.1	3	1.0	10	1.5
Moderate	68	20.4	46	14.7	114	17.6
Mild	63	18.9	64	20.5	127	19.7
Not anaemic	196	58.7	199	63.8	395	61.1
Total	334	100.0	312	100.0	646	100.0

column-wise), and the table does not look revealing. However, it is often desirable to have the number and percentage distributions on separate columns. So, we may use SPSS to obtain the frequency distribution only (i.e., without percentage values) and copy the table to an Excel sheet and work out the required percentages with appropriate formatting of the table as presented in Table 3.10. Is it not the table more compact and revealing?

Usually, the frequencies are presented as whole numbers and the percentage values are presented with one decimal place to make a clear distinction between them. However, while interpreting the percentage values in the table, often the values are rounded to the nearest whole number (decimal places are ignored for simplicity and easy understanding without loss of any significant information). For example, we may say that, among the male children, 59 percent are not anaemic, whereas among the female children, it is 64 percent.

Omitting the Number Distribution

As compared with the percentage distribution, the number distribution has a very less relevance for drawing inferences. But at the same time, it is important to have some knowledge of the number distribution, based on which the percentage distribution is made. This is because the larger the marginal total and cell frequencies, the better the stability of and confidence in the percentage distribution (explained below). So, the table can have detailed percentage values, but only the marginal total frequencies, that is, without the number distribution, as shown in Table 3.11. This format not only makes the table more compact, but also allows the variables with more column categories in the table, say up to 5–8 categories. It is to be noted that, although we have dropped the cell frequencies from the table, we can easily get them, if required, by simply multiplying the percentage values with the marginal total (e.g., $334 * 20.4/100 = 68.12 = 68$).

When the sample size or marginal totals or cell frequencies are small, the corresponding percentage values are not stable. That is, with small sample or cell size, even a small change in the number distribution will make a large difference in the percentage distribution. For example, on the one hand, consider a sample size of 10 cases. In this sample, if males and females are equally distributed (each 5 cases), the percentage distribution is 50 percent of males and 50 percent of females. By chance, if there is a difference of one case on either category (say 4 males and 6 females), the percentage distribution changes to 40 percent of males and 60 percent of females, that is, a difference of one case by chance has made a difference of 20 points in the percentage distribution. On the other hand, consider a sample of 100 cases and an equal distribution of 50 males and 50 females, or 50 percent of males and 50 percent of females. Here, by chance, a difference of

Table 3.11 Percentage Distribution of Children by the Anaemia Level, Classified by the Sex of Child

Anaemia Level	Male	Female	Total
Severe	2.1	1.0	1.5
Moderate	20.4	14.7	17.6
Mild	18.9	20.5	19.7
Not anaemic	58.7	63.8	61.1
Total (%)	100.0	100.0	100.0
Total (N)	334	312	646

one case or either category, say 49 males and 51 females, makes a difference of only two points in the percentage distribution. Hence, for an understanding of how stable the percentage distribution is, the marginal totals are often presented in the table along with the percentage distribution.

Independent Variable on Column Side

If there are many categories in the independent or control variable (e.g., the states of India), then the rows and columns can be swapped for convenience as shown in Table 3.12. In this case, the percentages are worked out row-wise and not column-wise. All these show that a two-way cross-table can be made in several ways depending on the nature of data, the number of cases and the importance of row and column figures for the purpose of investigation or to satisfy the objectives.

CROSS-TABULATION WITH THREE VARIABLES

If three variables are involved in cross-tabulation, then it is called three-way cross-tabulation. Among the three variables, one is the dependent variable, another one is the control variable and the third one is the independent variable. A three-way cross-tabulation is just an extension of a two-way cross-tabulation with the addition of one control variable. In a three-way cross-tabulation, the dependent variable and the independent variable are taken on the row and column sides, respectively (exactly as in the case of a two-way cross-tabulation), and the control variable is taken as the layer variable, that is, we see the effect of the independent variable on the dependent variable within each category of the control variable. Let us extend the example of a two-way cross-table, namely 'anaemia level by sex of child' to include religion. Here, our interest is to see the differences in the anaemia level by the religion of the mother. But we have already seen that the anaemia level differs by the sex of child. So, it is reasonable to analyse how religion affects the anaemic level among male and female children. It amounts to the three-way cross-tabulation of the anaemia level by the religion of the mother, classified by the sex of child.

To run three-way tabulation in SPSS, use the same menu 'Analyze => Descriptive Statistics => Crosstabs' and a window like the one shown in Figure 3.2 will pop-up. Now, transfer the variable 'Anaemia level of child' to the box labelled 'Row(s)', 'Religion of household' to the box labelled 'Column(s)' and 'Sex of child' to the box labelled 'Layer 1 of 1', and click 'OK'. The SPSS output is shown in Table 3.13.

It is clear that a three-way table is nothing but a set of two-way tables, one set for each category of the layer variable, that is, one for male and another for female children. Please note that some software programs give one more set (of a two-way table) for total (i.e., for male and female combined). In a three-way cross-tabulation, the percentage distribution is made for each layer of a two-way table in any combination of the three possible ways, namely row, column and total

Table 3.12 Percentage Distribution of Children by the Anaemia Level for Selected States of India

State	Anaemia Level				Children	
	Severe	Moderate	Mild	Not Anaemic	%	Number
Punjab	1.7	13.5	30.0	54.9	100.0	1,265
Haryana	2.3	23.4	38.3	36.0	100.0	1,220
Rajasthan	2.9	21.7	33.9	41.5	100.0	2,009
Uttar Pradesh	2.2	16.9	36.4	44.5	100.0	6,277
Bihar	1.3	18.8	51.7	28.2	100.0	2,231
West Bengal	1.1	16.7	48.0	34.2	100.0	2,294
Odisha	1.6	17.1	45.3	36.0	100.0	1,710
Chhattisgarh	1.4	17.0	40.2	41.3	100.0	1,573
Madhya Pradesh	1.1	16.1	41.8	41.1	100.0	3,006
Gujarat	2.8	18.7	39.1	39.4	100.0	1,537
Maharashtra	1.5	14.2	38.3	46.0	100.0	2,659
Andhra Pradesh	2.4	19.9	42.9	34.8	100.0	2,108
Karnataka	1.5	17.2	34.8	46.5	100.0	1,934
Tamil Nadu	1.4	13.3	41.0	44.2	100.0	1,686

Table 3.13 SPSS Output for Three-way Cross-tabulation

		Count					
			RELIG in Four Groups				
Sex of Child			Hindu	Muslim	Christian	Other	Total
Male	Anaemia level of child	Severe	5	1	1	0	7
		Moderate	43	15	9	0	67
		Mild	40	5	17	1	63
		Not anaemic	125	21	48	1	195
		Total	213	42	75	2	332
Female	Anaemia level of child	Severe	3	0	0	0	3
		Moderate	32	8	6	0	46
		Mild	44	5	15	0	64
		Not anaemic	126	18	54	1	199
		Total	205	31	75	1	312

percentages. However, it is advisable not to seek the percentage distribution in the SPSS output as the table will look clumsy, and it can be obtained later while making the final table in an Excel sheet. In three-way tables, often the number distribution is excluded from the final tables. As demonstrated above, not only the number distribution is less relevant for drawing inferences, but also it occupies an equal amount of additional pace in the already congested percentage distribution table.

The next table (Table 3.14a) is a revised format of Table 3.13 that gives the percentage distribution without the number distribution in a compact way. The table shows that between the three religious groups, namely Hindu, Muslim and Christian, anaemia is found more among the Muslim children (50 percent among males and 42 percent among females) and less among the Christian

Table 3.14a   Percentage Distribution of Children by the Anaemia Level, Classified by the Religion and Sex of Child

Sex of Child/ Anaemia Level	Religion of Household			
	Hindu	*Muslim*	*Christian*	*Total**
Male				
Severe	2.3	2.4	1.3	2.1
Moderate	20.2	35.7	12.0	20.2
Mild	18.8	11.9	22.7	19.0
Not anaemic	58.7	50.0	64.0	58.7
Total (%)	100.0	100.0	100.0	100.0
Total (*N*)	213	42	75	332
Female				
Severe	1.5	0.0	0.0	1.0
Moderate	15.6	25.8	8.0	14.7
Mild	21.5	16.1	20.0	20.5
Not anaemic	61.5	58.1	72.0	63.8
Total (%)	100.0	100.0	100.0	100.0
Total (*N*)	205	31	75	312

Note: * Includes three cases of other religions.

children (36 percent among males and 28 percent among females), whereas the Hindu children stood in-between (41 percent among males and 39 percent among females). The table also reveals that the anaemia level is uniformly higher among the male children than among the female children in all the three religious groups. This shows that sex differences in the anaemia level persist in all the three religious groups, but the differences are larger among the Muslim and Christian children than that among the Hindu children. To obtain 'percent anaemic', either we can add the percentage values for severe, moderate and mild anaemia categories ($2.4+35.7+11.9=50.0$ percent) or obtain 100 minus 'percent not anaemic' ($100.0-50.0=50.0$ percent).

In cross-tabulation, the cell frequencies deplete fast as the number of variables and/or categories of variables increases (compare cell frequencies in Tables 3.8 and 3.13). This is because, as the number of variables and/or categories increases, the number of cells in the table also increases in a geometric proportion, but the total number of cases or observations remains the same and is distributed in the increased number of cells. So, three-way and higher order tables should be attempted only when they are extremely required and the sample size is large enough to have minimum five cases in each cell. This is because the percent values based on the small cell frequencies are not stable and inferences drawn based on such percent values are not valid (discussed earlier). The minimum of five cases per cell is suggested based on the requirements for the chi-square test (χ^2 test) of significance (being discussed under 'testing of hypothesis'). At the same time, we can consider reducing (by regrouping or combining) the categories in such a way that the new set of categories satisfies the analysis requirements by decreasing the number of cells and increasing the cell frequencies. Accordingly, Table 3.14a is re-cast and presented in Table 3.14b by combining 'severe' and 'moderate' anaemia categories into one category, namely 'severe/moderate'.

Table 3.14b Percentage Distribution of Children by the Anaemia Level, Classified by the Religion and Sex of Child

Sex of Child/ Anaemia Level	Religion of Household			
	Hindu	Muslim	Christian	Total*
Male				
Severe/ moderate	22.5	38.1	13.3	22.3
Mild	18.8	11.9	22.7	19.0
Not anaemic	58.7	50.0	64.0	58.7
Total (%)	100.0	100.0	100.0	100.0
Total (N)	213	42	75	332
Female				
Severe/ moderate	17.1	25.8	8.0	15.7
Mild	21.5	16.1	20.0	20.5
Not anaemic	61.5	58.1	72.0	63.8
Total (%)	100.0	100.0	100.0	100.0
Total (N)	205	31	75	312

Note: * Includes three cases of other religions.

SOME SUGGESTED OPTIONS

Table Title and Caption

The title of a table usually consists two parts: the table number and the table caption. Some researchers may prefer to keep the table title out of the table (usually above the table), as in Table 3.7, while others prefer it to be the first row of the table. The general format of a table number is x.yz, where x is the chapter or section number, y is the table serial number within the chapter/section and z is the subtable in alphabetical order (if any). For example, look at Tables 3.14a and 3.14b. If there are no chapters and no subtables, then the table number can be 1, 2, 3 and so on without the chapter numbers. If there are only a few tables and they are spread over the report but located close to the text referring to the table values, then the table numbers may be omitted, provided there is no ambiguity in referring to the tables. The table caption should tell the contents of the table, namely what the cells contain (number or percent values), which variables are involved in the table, which area and time period it refers to and under what conditions the cells frequencies are generated; for examples, please see the tables presented earlier.

Important Points

In the case of the ordinal and interval variables, we need to express the categories or class intervals in ascending or descending order, and in the case of nominal variables, it may be according to the order of the importance of the categories or according to the smallest to largest frequencies or largest to smallest frequencies. The classes should be clearly defined, mutually exclusive (non-overlapping) and exhaustive (incorporate all possible answers). As far as possible, the class intervals should be of equal length, and open-ended classes should be avoided. However, at times, the beginning and ending classes may be of unequal length and/or open-ended. The number of classes should neither be too large nor too small, and empty and the low frequency classes should be avoided as far as possible. At the same time, ensure that each class has more or less equal frequencies, and the classes with too large and too small frequencies are avoided.

Simplified or Improved Tabulation Styles

In the following, a set of four two-way tables (Tables 3.15a–3.15d) for literacy of mother by religion to see how the percentage distributions can be obtained and presented are provided. Table 3.15a gives the number distribution. In Table 3.15b, we have obtained the column percentage distribution. It can be seen from the table that among the literate women, 64 percent are Hindus, 25 percent are Christians and just 11 percent are Muslims. So what? Are we going to change the religion status of the women to bridge the gap? No. Then what purpose does it serve? I have presented this table because I have come across people preparing tables of this type. Our purpose would be to find out in which religious group, the literacy level is higher and in which group it is lower so that the religious groups with a lower literacy level may be targeted for some special literacy campaign programmes to improve their literacy level in the near future. So, we need to get the percent distribution of literate and illiterate women by religion.

Now, let us work out the row percentage. It is given in Table 4.12c. It can be seen from the table that among Hindu women, 84 percent are literate, whereas among Muslim women, it is 80 percent and among Christian women it is as high as 93 percent. It implies that more efforts are needed to improve the literacy level of Muslim women and also that of Hindu women than that of Christian women. As shown in this table, the row percentage is more appropriate and is in order. In addition, it can also be seen that the percentage distribution does not mean the column percent only. Whether it should be the column percent or the row percent depends on the variables taken on the row and column sides and the purpose of investigation.

So far we have not said anything about illiterates. Do we need to make any statement about them? It is not necessary because once we say that 84 percent of the Hindu women are literate, it automatically means that the remaining 16 percent are illiterate. Then why should we keep it in the table when it fills up the space and makes the table clumsy? We can very well discard it, that is, we can discard the rows and columns that are less relevant for drawing inference and can easily be obtained from the other rows and columns. Let us see Table 3.15d. In this table, we have presented only two columns of data out of the six columns in Table 3.15c. With these two columns, we can describe the entire set of figures as in Table 3.15c and so Table 3.15d is preferred to Table 3.15c.

Percentages and Numbers in Parentheses

Tables 3.16a–3.16d give some formats for the presentation of numbers and percentages in a table. In Table 3.16a, the percentage figures are kept within parentheses, whereas in Table 3.16b, the frequencies are kept within parentheses. Table 3.16b is relatively a better way of presentation than that of Table 3.16a because we describe the table in terms of the percentage distribution rather than the number distribution. In Table 3.16c, the frequency figures are kept below the percentage values and in Table 3.16d, the numbers and percentages are presented in two separate blocks or layers.

The basic questions are: Why should we keep the numbers or percentages within parentheses? What is it that we are going to gain? Why not we keep them in two separate columns? To me there is no apparent gain or benefit in keeping the frequencies or percentage values within parentheses. Rather keeping them in two separate columns would be more revealing and reading the figures will be very easy. Furthermore, the position of the numbers and percentages in the table changes depending on the number of digits in the frequencies. Because of these limitations, it would be better if the table is presented as in Table 3.15d.

Table 3.15a Religion and Literacy Status of Mother

Religion	Literacy Status of Mother		Total
	Illiterate	Literate	
Hindu	100	542	642
Muslim	23	94	117
Christian	15	211	226
Total	138	847	985

Table 3.15b Religion and Literacy Status of Mother

Religion	Literacy Status of Mother					
	Illiterate		Literate		Total	
	No.	%	No.	%	No.	%
Hindu	100	72.5	542	64.0	642	65.2
Muslim	23	16.7	94	11.1	117	11.9
Christian	15	10.9	211	24.9	226	22.9
Total	138	100	847	100	985	100

Table 3.15c Religion and Literacy Status of Mother

Religion	Literacy Status of Mother					
	Illiterate		Literate		Total	
	No.	Row %	No.	Row %	No.	Row %
Hindu	100	15.6	542	84.4	642	100.0
Muslim	23	19.7	94	80.3	117	100.0
Christian	15	6.6	211	93.4	226	100.0
Total	138	14.0	847	86.0	985	100.0

Table 3.15d Literacy of Women by Religion

Religion	No. of Women	Percent Literate
Hindu	642	84.4
Muslim	117	80.3
Christian	226	93.4
Total	985	86.0

Table 3.16a Religion of Household and the Literacy Status of Mother

Religion	Literacy Status of Mother		
	Illiterate	*Literate*	*Total*
Hindu	100 (15.6)	542 (84.4)	642 (100.0)
Muslim	23 (19.7)	94 (80.3)	117 (100.0)
Christian	15 (6.6)	211 (93.4)	226 (100.0)
Total	138 (14.0)	847 (86.0)	985 (100.0)

Table 3.16b Religion of Household and the Literacy Status of Mother

Religion	Literacy Status of Mother		
	Illiterate	*Literate*	*Total*
Hindu	15.6 (100)	84.4 (542)	100.0 (642)
Muslim	19.7 (23)	80.3 (94)	100.0 (117)
Christian	6.6 (15)	93.4 (211)	100.0 (226)
Total	14.0 (138)	86.0 (847)	100.0 (985)

Table 3.16c Religion of Household and the Literacy Status of Mother

Religion	Literacy Status of Mother		
	Illiterate	*Literate*	*Total*
Hindu	15.6 (100)	84.4 (542)	100.0 (642)
Muslim	19.7 (23)	80.3 (94)	100.0 (117)
Christian	6.6 (15)	93.4 (211)	100.0 (226)
Total	14.0 (138)	86.0 (847)	100.0 (985)

Table 3.16d Religion of Household and the Literacy Status of Mother

Religion	Literacy Status of Mother		
	Illiterate	*Literate*	*Total*
Percent distribution			
Hindu	15.6	84.4	100.0
Muslim	19.7	80.3	100.0
Christian	6.6	93.4	100.0
Total	14.0	86.0	100.0
Number distribution			
Hindu	100	542	642
Muslim	23	94	117
Christian	15	211	226
Total	138	847	985

CHAPTER 4

Graphical Presentation of Data

The tabulated data are easier to read and understand than the individual observations (or raw data). Still a user needs some time to read and understand the tabulated data, especially when the categories are many. So, often, the tabulated data are presented in a graphical form as well for an easy and quick understanding of the pattern in the data. The purpose of the graphical presentation of data is to facilitate the reader to have a quick and first-hand observation of the pattern in the data just at the glance of the graph. Often, executives may not have much time to read through the entire table and text and make observations. Also, in conferences and meetings, participants would like to have the essence of the data and not the details, mainly for the sake of time and for the understanding of the participants of different disciplines. In such situations, graphical presentation comes handy as a visual aid to reveal the pattern in the data and to make quick inferences. The commonly used visual aids or graphical representations of data are pie charts, bar graphs, frequency polygons, frequency curves or line charts. For drawing charts, we use Excel rather than SPSS, because in Excel one can customise the charts freely, whereas in SPSS it is difficult.

PIE CHART

A pie chart (or pie graph) is a circular graph in which a circle is divided into pieces from its centre with each piece proportional to the number or percentage frequencies of the categories of the variable. A pie chart is particularly used to show the differences in the magnitude of the frequencies of *nominal variables* (sometimes ordinal variables also). Pie charts are not appropriate for numerical variables, but the numerical variables can be first converted into ordinal variables and then the pie chart can be applied. We can use either the number frequencies or percentage frequencies to draw a pie chart and both will be identical. The percentage distribution is used to draw the pie chart when the frequencies are large in size and when the relative distribution, and not the absolute distribution, is important. The pie chart will be better revealing only if the number of categories is small, say 3–5, and the proportion of cases (or percent of cases) in each category is reasonably large, that is, a pie chart is not much revealing if the percent values are close to zero in some categories and/or close to 100 in some (other) categories.

Table 4.1 gives the number and percentage distribution of households by religion for all India based on NFHS-3. Here, the number distribution is irrelevant as the religion-wise distribution of sample households does not reflect the total households in India. Also, the sample has missing cases and so we obtain the percentage distribution of households by religion for the valid cases to draw a pie chart.

To draw a pie chart in Excel, first select the data under the column 'Valid %', and then the corresponding labels under the column 'Religion'. Now, choose the menu 'Insert=> Pie' and click on the first or any item from the pop-up menu. Soon the chart is pasted on the Excel sheet as shown in Figure 4.1 (labels and formatting are added later). In Excel, many formatting options are available, but they are not discussed here.

Table 4.1   Number and Percentage Distribution of Households by Religion, NFHS-3, All India

Religion	Households	%	Valid %
Hindu	80,020	68.6	73.4
Muslim	13,354	11.4	12.3
Christian	10,042	8.6	9.2
Sikh	2,186	1.9	2.0
Buddhist	1,588	1.4	1.5
Others	1,822	1.6	1.7
Missing	7,640	6.5	NA
Total	116,652	100.0	100.0

Figure 4.1   Pie Chart for Religion, All India

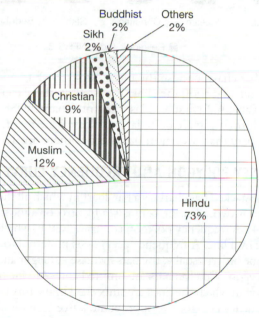

BAR CHART OR BAR GRAPH

A bar chart or a bar graph is a series of rectangular vertical bars drawn on the *x*-axis or horizontal bars drawn from the *y*-axis with each bar representing a category in the variable, and the height or the length of the bar is proportional to the number frequency or percent value of the category. The bars are of equal width and they are equidistant from each other. For nominal and ordinal variables with many categories, bar charts are preferred. Usually, vertical (or column) bar charts are preferred when the categories are a few, say 5–8, and horizontal (or row) bar charts are preferred when the categories are many, say more than 8 or 10.

To draw a vertical bar chart in Excel for Table 4.1, select the values under the column 'Valid %' and the corresponding labels under the column 'Religion', and then choose the menu 'Insert=>Column' and click on the first or any item from the pop-up menu, and soon the chart is pasted on the Excel sheet as shown in Figure 4.2 (labels and formatting are added later). Then format the chart as desired.

Figure 4.2   Vertical Bar Chart for Religion, All India

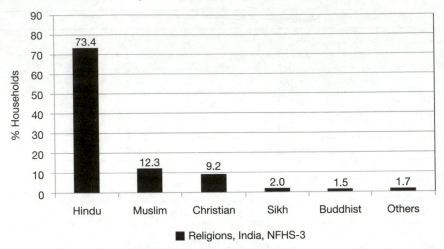

To draw a horizontal bar chart, choose the menu 'Insert => Bar' and click on the first or any item from the pop-up menu, and soon the chart is pasted on the Excel sheet. An example of the horizontal bar chart for Table 4.2 (first and last columns, namely 'State' and 'Mean') is shown in Figure 4.3 (labels and formatting are done later). Please note that for these data, a horizontal bar chart is more appropriate than a vertical bar chart as there are 13 states (categories).

HISTOGRAM, FREQUENCY POLYGON AND FREQUENCY CURVE

A *histogram* (also called the stacked bar chart) is a bar chart in which all the bars are stacked together, that is, the distance between two adjacent bars is set to zero or almost zero (see Figure 4.5 and compare it with Figure 4.4). A frequency polygon is a histogram in which the top of each set of two adjacent bars is connected by a line. A frequency polygon is preferred to a histogram when the categories are arranged in some order; usually, the bars increase in height and then decrease (see Figure 4.6). In the frequency polygon often the bars are omitted and only the line is retained. A *frequency curve* is a frequency polygon in which the lines are smoothed in the form of a curve (see Figure 4.7).

The histogram and frequency polygon are appropriate for ordinal variables (also discrete and continuous variables in the form of ordinal categories) with say 5–15 categories. However, for a frequency curve, the categories should be in numerical values and not just categories. As such a frequency curve is appropriate only for discrete and continuous variables with or without grouping. If grouping is made, then each class is to be of equal width and preferably the mid-point (value) of each class should be used as the categories. However, the end classes with very low frequencies may be treated as one class with appropriate or reasonable mid-point. Table 4.3 gives the percentage of males and females (ages 5 and above) engaged in economic activity (work participation rate) by age. For this dataset, we can draw the bar chart, histogram, frequency polygon and/or frequency curve as shown in Figures 4.4–4.7. Please note that the mid-point of age groups is shown in Table 4.3 for the purpose of the frequency curve in Figure 4.7. Also, Figure 4.8 shows the frequency polygon for the work participation rate for males and females to demonstrate how differential analyses can be performed with it.

Please note that the charts are made using Excel by choosing the menu 'Insert => Chart' and then selecting appropriate options. For Figure 4.4, select 'Column => Clustered Column' and for Figure 4.5 proceed further by right-clicking on the bars and selecting: 'Format Data Series => Series

Table 4.2 Percentage Distribution of Children Born in Last 3 Years by Order of Birth and Mean Order of the Births for Selected States of India

State	Total Children	Order of Birth of Child				Mean
		1	*2*	*3*	*4+*	
Tamil Nadu	1,735	42.0	37.5	13.8	6.6	1.89
Andhra Pradesh	2,292	38.0	37.1	14.1	10.7	2.04
Maharashtra	3,038	40.2	33.2	15.0	11.6	2.07
Punjab	1,307	39.1	32.0	17.1	11.8	2.09
Karnataka	2,188	37.1	33.7	16.0	13.1	2.16
West Bengal	2,368	38.5	30.8	14.6	16.0	2.27
Odisha	1,781	35.3	27.3	16.4	20.9	2.43
Gujarat	1,571	31.3	31.1	16.7	20.9	2.46
Haryana	1,256	32.8	30.8	15.3	21.1	2.54
Madhya Pradesh	3,016	29.1	26.3	16.8	27.8	2.78
Rajasthan	2,023	26.8	22.9	17.3	33.0	3.01
Bihar	2,320	24.2	21.1	16.7	38.0	3.26
Uttar Pradesh	7,051	23.2	22.0	16.7	38.1	3.26

Figure 4.3 Mean Order of Birth for Selected States of India

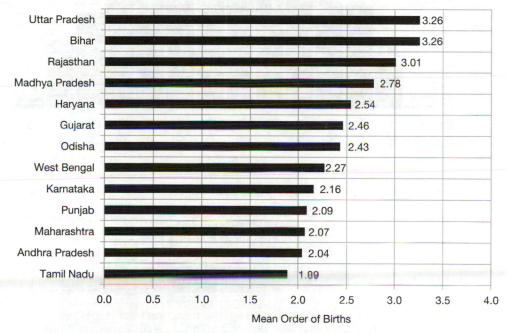

Options => Gap Width = zero' (or 10 percent for a gap like a line), and further selecting: 'Format Data Series => Border Colour = Solid line'. For Figure 4.6, select 'Line => Line with Markers' and for Figure 4.7 select 'Scatter => Scatter' with smooth Lines and Markers. It is to be noted that, for the line graph in Figure 4.6, add one more bar chart with the same values and then convert one as a line chart by right clicking on it and choosing 'change chart type'.

Figure 4.4 Bar Chart for Male Work Participation Rate by Age

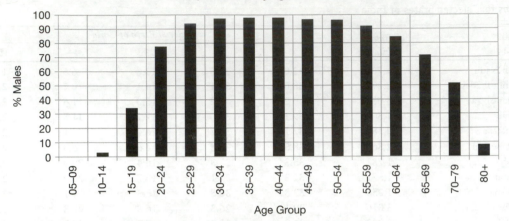

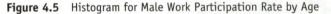

Figure 4.5 Histogram for Male Work Participation Rate by Age

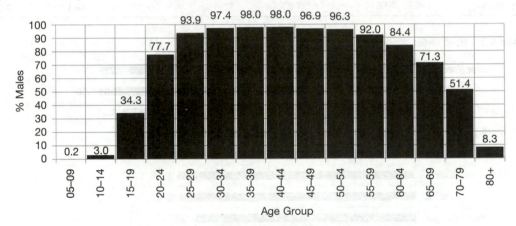

Figure 4.6 Frequency Polygon for Male Work Participation Rate by Age

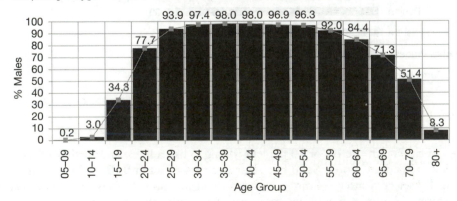

Table 4.3   Percentage of Males and Females (5+ Age Group) Engaged in Economic Activity by Age

Age Group	Age (Mid-point)	Male	Female
05–09	7.5	0.2	0.0
10–14	12.5	3.0	2.7
15–19	17.5	34.3	27.6
20–24	22.5	77.7	37.8
25–29	27.5	93.9	56.0
30–34	32.5	97.4	74.5
35–39	37.5	98.0	81.6
40–44	42.5	98.0	80.1
45–49	47.5	96.9	78.9
50–54	52.5	96.3	74.7
55–59	57.5	92.0	66.6
60–64	62.5	84.4	55.0
65–69	67.5	71.3	43.1
70–79	72.5	51.4	18.0
80+	77.5	8.3	0.6

Figure 4.7   Frequency Curve for Male Work Participation Rate by Age

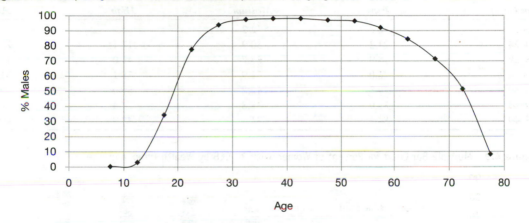

Note: The difference between a frequency polygon and a frequency curve is that in the former case the top of two adjacent bars is connected by a straight line, whereas in the latter case all these lines are adjusted in the form of a smooth curve.

CLUSTERED BAR CHART OR MULTIPLE BAR CHART

A chart with more than one set of staked bars is called a *clustered bar chart* or *multiple bar chart*. A multiple bar chart is often made for an index that is cross-classified with two variables. A frequency curve can also be made for the same. Table 4.4 gives the percent of women with three or more children ever born by the wealth index (as poor, medium and high) for women of different age groups.

To draw a multiple bar chart (Figure 4.9) select all the columns except the top row and choose 'Column => Clustered Column'. Rest is as usual.

Figure 4.8   Work Participation Rate by Age, Males and Females Compared

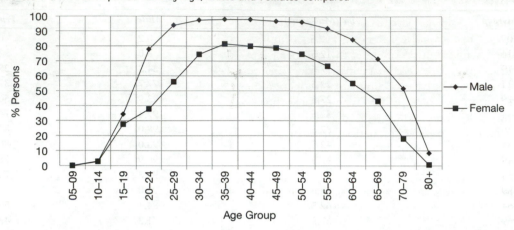

Table 4.4   Percent of Women with 3+ Children Ever Born (CEB) by Wealth Index Grade, Classified by the Age of Women

Age Group	Poor	Medium	High	All
15–19	0.8	2.2	0.7	2.0
20–24	21.2	30.9	17.1	25.9
25–29	58.9	53.7	45.0	47.8
30–34	75.0	51.9	58.1	51.6
35–39	79.5	42.8	59.0	49.1
40–44	83.0	35.8	54.4	44.4
45–49	83.4	31.4	48.9	40.0

Figure 4.9   Multiple Bar Chart for Percent of Women with 3+ CEB by Wealth Index and Age

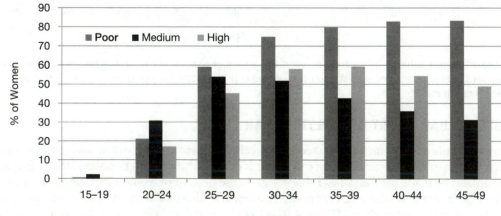

CUMULATIVE FREQUENCY CURVE OR OGIVE

A cumulative frequency curve or an ogive can be made for a frequency distribution as follows. For this, we consider Table 4.5. For drawing a cumulative frequency curve, first obtain the cumulative frequency distribution of either the number frequency or the percent values. In our exercise, we use the cumulative percentage distribution for the data presented in Table 4.5.

To draw an ogive or a cumulative frequency curve, first select the columns 'Children ever born' and 'Cumulative %' in Table 4.5 and choose the menu 'Insert => Chart => XY Scatter plot => Scatter with smooth lines and Markers' and the ogive chart is pasted on the Excel sheet (Figure 4.10).

A set of cumulative frequency curves or ogives can also be drawn for an index cross-classified by two variables. Table 4.6 gives cumulative mean children ever born by age of women for

Table 4.5 Percent and Cumulative Percentage Distribution of Women by CEB, All India, NFHS-3

Children Ever Born	Frequency	
	%	Cumulative %
0	32.0	32.0
1	12.2	44.2
2	19.7	63.9
3	15.0	78.9
4	9.3	88.1
5	5.3	93.5
6	3.0	96.5
7	1.6	98.2
8	0.9	99.1
9	0.5	99.6
10–16	0.4	100.0
Total	100.0	100.0

Figure 4.10 Cumulative Frequency Curve for Cumulative Percent of Women by Children Ever Born

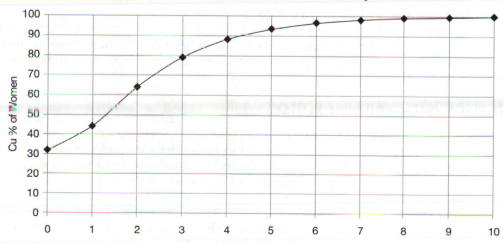

Table 4.6   Cumulative Mean Children Ever Born per Women by the Wealth Index, Classified by Age of Women

Age Group	Poor	Medium	High	All
15–19	0.22	0.13	0.05	0.11
20–24	1.52	1.07	0.63	0.93
25–29	2.88	2.32	1.57	2.05
30–34	3.76	3.10	2.25	2.81
35–39	4.31	3.72	2.75	3.34
40–44	4.71	4.05	3.08	3.65
45–49	4.92	4.32	3.43	3.92

Figure 4.11   Frequency Curves for Mean Children Ever Born by the Wealth Index and Age of Women

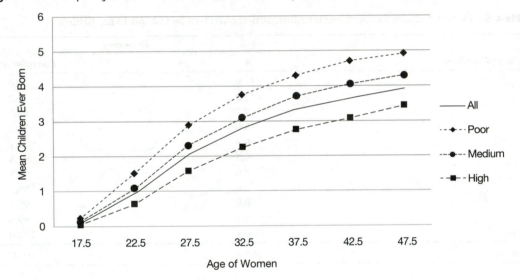

different categories of the wealth index (poor, medium and high). In this exercise, cumulative mean children ever born are used to draw frequency curves.

To draw cumulative frequency curves (Figure 4.11), select all the columns except the top row and choose 'Scatter => Scatter with smooth Lines'. The cumulative frequency curves are used to compare the patterns across different groups. From the chart, it is clear that the number of children ever born decreases as the wealth index level increases.

STEM PLOTS (STEM-AND-LEAF PLOTS)

A stem plot (stem-and-leaf plot) is a method of presenting a small dataset (say up to 50 data values of 2 or 3 digits). First, arrange the data values in the ascending order of their values and then divide each value into two parts, namely the 'stem' part consisting of the value excluding the last digit and the 'leaf' part representing the last digit only. In the next step, enter the stem values in an Excel sheet one below the other without repetition, and enter the leaf values one after another to the right of the corresponding stem values. The resultant shape of the presented values is the stem plot as shown in Table 4.8. Usually, the stem plot will look like a horizontal bar chart with the size (length) of the bar being the number of leaf values corresponding to the stem value.

One advantage of the stem-leaf plot over the bar chart is that in the stem-leaf plot we have the actual values besides the length of the bars representing the frequencies.

Draw a stem-leaf chart for the marks scored by 30 students in Basic Statistics.

46	50	52	46	30	32	34	25	18	41	43	59
66	69	71	65	54	55	58	54	20	40	61	63
8	15	35	5	78	82	83	74	24	100	60	17

To draw the stem-and-leaf plot, first reorder the values in the ascending order and then (as shown in Table 4.7) in an Excel sheet arrange the values 0–9 in the first row, 10–19 in the second row, 20–29 in the third row and so on. If there are no values for a row, here 90–99, leave it blank. Furthermore, for lesser digit numbers, add a zero before the values and treat them as string and not values for uniformity. In this example, the first row figures are 5 and 8 (single digits) and are written as 05 and 08. Now, add a column to the left and enter the number except the last digit (common digits) and then remove these digits from the values on the same row as shown in Table 4.8. This is the stem-and-leaf plot. Please note that in the table, the bordering is added (may be removed if desired) and formatted with necessary labelling.

Table 4.7   Arrangement of Values

05	08					
15	17	18				
20	24	25				
30	32	34	35			
40	41	43	46	46		
50	52	54	54	55	58	59
60	61	63	65	66	69	
71	74	78				
82	83					
100						

Table 4.8   Stem-and-leaf Plot

Stem	Leaf						
0	5	8					
1	5	7	8				
2	0	4	5				
3	0	2	4	5			
4	0	1	3	6	6		
5	0	2	4	4	5	8	9
6	0	1	3	5	6	9	
7	1	4	8				
8	2	3					
9							
10	0						

POPULATION PYRAMID

A graphical presentation of the values of the categories of a variable for two groups back to back is called a pyramid. As the graph often looks like a pyramid, this is called so. Often this pyramid is drawn to present and analyse the age–sex distribution of the population of a country or region, and is termed as a population pyramid. But now the application has been extended to other subjects as well.

A population pyramid is a graphical presentation of the age–sex distribution of the population of a country or a region. A population pyramid consists of two sets of back-to-back horizontal bar graphs built on the y-axis: one for males and the other for females. The bars are drawn for each 5-year age group, starting from the 0–4 age group, one over the other from the x-axis and the length of the bars proportional to the number or percentage of persons in the corresponding age group. The number of males and females may be shown as absolute numbers or as the percentage of the total male and total female population, respectively. Population pyramids are a useful tool for understanding the structure and composition of populations because they graphically portray many aspects, such as sex ratios and age structure. Pyramids also give an insight into the trends in population over time by their portrayal of the relative number of people in different age groups representing different age cohorts. The concept can also be extended to differential analysis of socio-economic data (presented later in this section).

Table 4.9 gives the percentage distribution of persons by sex and age (first three columns). The data are obtained from a sample survey of 7,000 households conducted in the Vidarbha region of Maharashtra state in 2009.

To construct a population pyramid with Excel, first we need to convert the absolute figures into the percentage distribution so that the figures are standardised to 100 for both males and females and in the table it is already done. Second, convert the male population data (percentage distribution) into negative numbers as in the column labelled 'Male' (it is made simply to drawing bars for males to the left of the y-axis). In the next step, block the data under the columns labelled 'Age group', 'Male' and 'Female' including the labels and choose the menu 'Insert=>Chart=>Bar=>Clustered Bar'. Soon a two-sided bar chart will be pasted on the Excel sheet as shown in Figure 4.12.

Table 4.9 Percentage Distribution of Persons by Sex and Age

Age Group	Male %	Female %	Male	Female
00–04	7.7	7.6	−7.7	7.6
05–09	8.2	8.1	−8.2	8.1
10–14	10.3	10.7	−10.3	10.7
15–19	10.3	10.3	−10.3	10.3
20–24	10.3	8.3	−10.3	8.3
25–29	8.0	8.3	−8.0	8.3
30–34	6.7	7.0	−6.7	7.0
35–39	7.0	7.3	−7.0	7.3
40–44	6.3	5.3	−6.3	5.3
45–49	5.2	6.3	−5.2	6.3
50–54	4.8	3.8	−4.8	3.8
55–59	3.6	3.5	−3.6	3.5
60–64	3.0	4.6	−3.0	4.6
65–69	3.9	4.3	−3.9	4.3
70–79	3.8	3.5	−3.8	3.5
80+	0.9	1.1	−0.9	1.1

Figure 4.12   A Two-sided Bar Chart Showing the Male Population Data on the Left to the *y*-axis, Whereas the Female Population Data on the Right

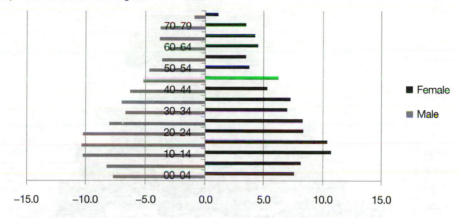

At this stage of the chart, the bars will be small in size, the left and right bars will not be on the same line for the same age group, there will be a gap between bars and the *y*-axis labels will be on the middle of the chart. We need to adjust or correct all these and also add labels as appropriate. We will do these one by one, that is, the rest of the exercise is simply a matter of formatting the chart, and a few of the important steps are explained below.

Step 1: Format the vertical axis. Move the cursor over the vertical axis (*y*-axis), right-click on it and choose 'Format Axis…' from the pop-up menu. We will see a dialogue box titled 'Format Axis' and in that under 'Pattern' (in older versions) or 'Axis Options' (in new versions) we need to set: Specify interval units = 1, Major tick mark type = None, Minor tick mark type = None and Tick mark labels = Low. This will move the *y*-axis scale values to the left of the chart area and also show all age groups.

Step 2: Format the horizontal axis. Move the cursor over the horizontal axis, right-click on it and choose 'Format Axis…' from the pop-up menu. We will see a dialogue box titled 'Format Axis' as above and in that choose 'Number' and select category = custom and type = 0;0. Also adjust the values of minimum, maximum, major unit appropriately. These will take care of the negative numbers and also show the *x*-axis values as desired.

Step 3: Adjust the bars. Move the cursor over to the bars, right-click on it and select 'Format Data Series…' from the pop-up menu. We will see a dialogue box titled 'Format Data Series' and in that choose 'Series Options' and adjust Overlap = 100, Gap width = 0 (or 5 percent for a line-like appearance between bars as in chart shown in Figure 4.13).

Step 4: Final formatting of the chart. Use the text box option to create labels for *x*-axis, *y*-axis, chart title and the bars. We can also colour the chart as desired. As this step is common to any chart, the procedure is obvious and hence not explained here in detail. After accomplishing the above steps, the chart will look like the one shown in Figure 4.13 and this is the population pyramid for the given age–sex data.

A few explanations based on the population pyramid are as follows. The population pyramid shows that the proportions of males and females in the 5-year age groups 0–4 and 5–9 are much lesser than that in the 5-year age groups 10–14, 15–19 and 20–24. Similarly, the 65+ age group population is also getting larger. These are indications for a recent decline in fertility and ageing of the population. The age distribution of the population does not show any marked differences by sex.

Figure 4.13 Population Pyramid, Vidarbha, Maharashtra, 2009

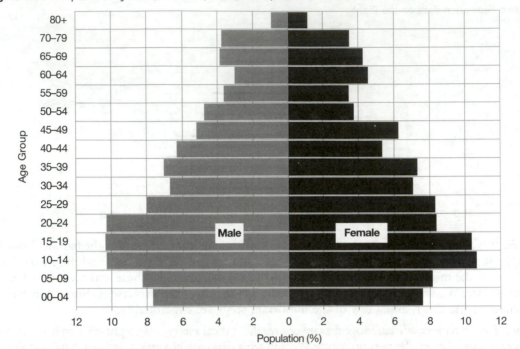

The population pyramid concept can be extended to analyse differentials in a study variable (say the literacy level) by a set of independent variables and compare the differentials between two groups (say males and females). Table 4.10 and Figure 4.14 give the percentage of males and females (age 15–59 years) literate by selected household characteristics, namely religion, caste class, type of house, electrification of house and landholding.

The chart clearly shows that the literacy level is much higher for males than that for females in all categories of the population. However, among males, the literacy level is slightly higher for Hindus than that for Muslims, but among females it is the same for both Hindus and Muslims, that is, with a few exceptions, the pattern of difference in literacy is more or less the same for both males and females belonging to the different sections of the population. See Chapter 13 for another example of the same.

BUILDING CHARTS WITH SPSS

We can also prepare charts using SPSS. For this, the unit level data are to be in the SPSS editor and the variables and categories are defined with appropriate labelling. Then use the menu 'Graphs' and choose one of the three options, namely 'Chart Builder', 'Graph-board Template Chooser' and 'Legacy Dialogs'. These options give a variety of graphs and are easy to obtain by choosing appropriate chart format and variables. The prime advantage of the charts in SPSS is its utility at the time of analysis of data. While analysing the data often we may need to know the pattern in the data before attempting specific procedure/analysis. At this stage, the SPSS chart builder comes handy to understand the pattern in the data instantly (see Chapter 11). At the same time, the SPSS gives only a limited opportunity to format the charts for the final presentation in the report. As such SPSS-based charts may be used for the preliminary analysis of the data, whereas Excel-based charts may be used in the final analysis of the data.

Table 4.10   Literacy Rate for Males and Females by Household Characteristics

Characteristics	Males	Females
Total	75.0	50.9
Religion		
Hindu	76.9	52.5
Muslim	71.7	53.1
Christian	82.7	69.0
Other	68.4	34.7
Caste class		
Scheduled caste	65.5	46.0
Scheduled tribe	73.6	47.8
Other backward class	76.5	52.5
General (Other)	85.9	64.3
Type of house		
RCC/Pucca	86.7	68.3
Semi Pucca	77.9	54.2
Kuchcha/Hut	69.8	43.4
House electrified?		
Yes	78.0	54.6
No	66.2	40.5

Figure 4.14   Literacy Level among Adult Males and Females by Household Characteristics

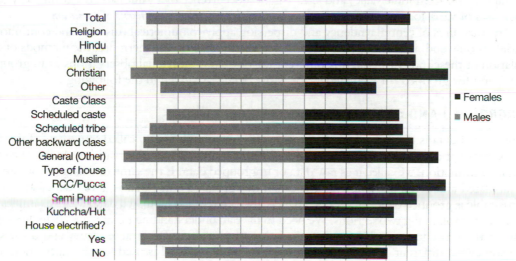

CHAPTER 5

Measures of Central Tendency and Dispersion

The frequency distribution gives a general idea about how the observations are distributed across different categories of a variable and further cross-tabulation provides how the observations are distributed across different categories of two or more variables. Although tabulation summarises the data to a great extent, the summarised data itself is often large, especially in the case of cross-tabulation involving variables with many categories. In addition, the graphical presentation of the data portrays a visual presentation of the distribution of observations, but it does not summarise the data further. As such, any statistical inferences made based on tabulated data are limited. So, often it is required to summarise the data still further into a few indices and to make inference based on their magnitudes. Usually, it is looked at in two ways.

First, by fixing a central point or a location at which the values of the variable tend to converge. There are different ways of fixing or measuring a central point and that are called *measures of central tendency*. Second, by measuring how much the values of the observations are dispersed or spread from the central point. These measures are called *measures of dispersion or variation*.

The commonly used measures of central tendency are *arithmetic mean* (or simply mean or average), *median* (middle value) and *mode* (highest occurrence of a value) and the commonly used measures of variation are *range, variance, standard deviation* and *coefficient of variation*.

The measures of central tendency and dispersion apply to numerical (discrete and continuous) variables only and not to code (ordinal and nominal) variables. Furthermore, the methods of calculation of these indices are slightly different for raw data (individual observations or ungrouped data) and for grouped (or tabulated) data. More details are given in the following.

UNGROUPED AND GROUPED DATA

Ungrouped data is the individual observations in a dataset. It is also called 'raw data'. Table 5.1 gives information on sex, age and education for nine individuals or observations. As it is the individual information, we called it as raw data or ungrouped data. If the same raw data (information) is tabulated and given in Table 5.2, it is called the 'grouped data', that is, a frequency table or a cross-table is grouped data. So, grouped data is also often called tabulated data. More examples are given in the following two sections. We need to have an understanding of ungrouped and grouped data as the procedures needed for the calculation of measures of central tendency and dispersion are somewhat different. However, if statistical software or Excel is used for the calculation, it is usually done with the raw data.

Note: The data we use in statistical software like SPSS is often the raw data (though sometimes grouped data are also used). However, it is important to know as to how raw and grouped data are dealt with in statistical computations.

Table 5.1   Ungrouped Data (Example)

Sl No.	Name	Sex	Age	Edu (Std)
1	Balu	M	25	5
2	Somu	M	20	7
3	Roja	F	23	3
4	Gupta	M	30	0
5	Remi	F	32	0
6	Kamu	F	27	10
7	Raj	M	34	8
8	Netu	F	28	2
9	Kemu	M	30	5

Table 5.2   Grouped Data

Variable	Frequency
Sex	
Male	5
Female	4
Age	
20–24	2
25–29	3
30–34	4
Education	
Nil (0)	2
1–5 std	4
5–10 std	3

ARITHMETIC MEAN

Arithmetic Mean for Ungrouped Data

The arithmetic mean (or simply mean or average) for ungrouped data is the sum of the values of all observations (of a numerical variable) divided by the number of observations.

Let $x_1, x_2, \ldots, x_n$ be the values of a variable, say X, of n observations; then the mean (of the variable X) is defined as

$$\text{Mean} = \frac{x_1 + x_2 + x_3 + \cdots + x_n}{n}.$$

Symbolically, the arithmetic mean (the above equation) is represented as

$$\bar{x} = \frac{1}{n} \sum_{i=1}^{n} x_i.$$

(The $\bar{x}$ is to be read as x bar, and the equation is read as x bar equals to 1 by n, with summation i equal to 1 to n, x_i.)

The equation is often written in a simplified manner without the summation subscript part as

$$\bar{x} = \frac{1}{n} \sum x_i.$$

Please note that in this format, the part $i=1$ to n is omitted only to mean that the summation is over all observations with respect to the variable.

Example 1: Mean for ungrouped data
Let $x_1=3, x_2=5, x_3=4$ and $x_n=x_4=6$; then

$$\text{Mean}=(x_1+x_2+x_3+x_4)/4$$
$$=(3+5+4+6)/4=4.5$$

Example 2: Mean for ungrouped data
The number of members in each of the sample of 12 families is given below. Find out the mean family size of the sample families.

Serial number	1	2	3	4	5	6	7	8	9	10	11	12
Family size	5	6	4	3	5	7	6	4	5	11	3	8

Summing the family size of 12 families and dividing the summed value by the number of observations, we obtain

Serial number	1	2	3	4	5	6	7	8	9	10	11	12	Sum	Mean=67/12=5.58
Family size	5	6	4	3	5	7	6	4	5	11	3	8	67	

That is, the mean family size is 5.58, and we may say that there are, on average, 5.58 members or nearly 5.6 members, in a family in the study population.

Arithmetic Mean for Grouped Data (Frequency Table)

Among n observations in a sample, let $x_1, x_2,..., x_r$ be the r different values or value ranges in a variable, say, X, and the values $x_1, x_2,..., x_r$ have repeatedly occurred $f_1, f_2,..., f_r$ times, respectively, that is, the value x_1 has occurred f_1 times, the value x_2 has occurred f_2 times and so on, and the value x_r has occurred f_r times. Now, $f_1 + f_2 +\cdots+ f_r = n$, the total number of observations and the arithmetic mean are

$$\bar{x} = \frac{f_1 x_1 + f_2 x_2 + f_3 x_3 +\cdots+ f_r x_r}{f_1+f_2+f_3+\cdots+f_r} \quad \text{or} \quad \bar{x} = \frac{f_1 x_1 + f_2 x_2 + f_3 x_3 +\cdots+ f_r x_r}{n}.$$

Symbolically,

$$\bar{x} = \frac{1}{n}\sum_{j=1}^{r} f_j x_j.$$

Note: The summation is from $j=1$ to r (r=number of groups) and not from $i=1$ to n (n=number of observations) as in the case of ungrouped data. The subscript j is chosen instead of i only to differentiate that here the subscript refers to groups (or classes) and not individual observations. Otherwise, it does not matter if we use the subscript i or j as long as we are clear that the summation is across the groups and not across the individual observations.

Example: The following table (Columns 1 and 2 only) gives the distribution of women by the 5-year age group. Find out the mean age of the women.
As the age groups are given in discrete class intervals and not the exact values, first we need to convert the class intervals into continuous class intervals as shown in Column 3, and then we obtain the mid-point of the age groups as shown in Column 4. It is to be noted that the age is

defined as the complete number of years lived and so the age group 15–19 implies 15 years 0 months to 19 years 11 months, and it can be written as 15–20 in a continuous class interval, and the mid-point is $(15+20)/2=17.5$ and not $(15+19)/2=17$. Please note that if the class intervals are made based on values that are corrected to the nearest whole number, we can obtain the mid-points directly as $(15+19)/2 = 17$. The row values of Columns 2 and 4 are then multiplied $(f_j * x_j)$ and entered in Column 5, and the sum of these values $(\Sigma_{j=1}^{r} f_j x_j)$ is presented down in the column $(=11{,}692.5)$. Now, calculate the arithmetic mean, which is the value divided by the number of observations $(11{,}692.5/383=30.5)$.

Merits and Demerits of the Arithmetic Mean

The arithmetic mean is a single value that summarises a set of (any number of, even thousands of) observations. As such the arithmetic mean is a simple index to summarise voluminous data. The merits of the arithmetic mean are that it is simple to calculate, based on all observations, easy to interpret and amenable for further statistical analysis. It is the most often used index in statistical applications. The demerits are that it is appropriate for numerical variables and not for code variables (ordinal and nominal variables). Furthermore, a few extreme values (called outliers) can change the mean value substantially. For example, the mean of the three values 3, 4 and 5 is 4 and that of the three values 3, 4 and 8 is 5, that is, the occurrence of a few extreme values can change the mean value substantially, resulting in inappropriate conclusions.

Combined or Weighted Mean

Let $\bar{x}_1$ (read as 'x one bar') be the mean of n_1 observations and $\bar{x}_2$ be the mean of n_2 observations; then their combined mean $\bar{x}$ is given by

$$\bar{x} = \frac{n_1 \bar{x}_1 + n_2 \bar{x}_2}{n_1 + n_2}.$$

Similarly, let $\bar{x}_1$ be the mean of one set of n_1 observations, $\bar{x}_2$ be the mean of another set of n_2 observations, $\bar{x}_3$ be the mean of another set of n_3 observations and so on, and finally $\bar{x}_r$ be the mean of n_r observations; then their combined mean $\bar{x}$ is given by

Table 5.3   Mean for the Frequency Distribution

Age Group	Number of Women	Age Group (in Continuous Class Intervals)	Mid-point of Age Groups	Age * Women
	f_j		x_j	$f_j * x_j$
(1)	(2)	(3)	(4)	(5)
15–19	59	15–20	17.5	1,032.5
20–24	72	20–25	22.5	1,620.0
25–29	65	25–30	27.5	1,787.5
30–34	59	30–35	32.5	1,917.5
35–39	53	35–40	37.5	1,987.5
40–44	43	40–45	42.5	1,827.5
45–49	32	45–50	47.5	1,520.0
Total	383	NA	NA	11,692.5

Mean = $11{,}692.5/383=30.5$

Table 5.4   Combined Mean of Many Groups

Groups	Cases	Group Mean	Total Children
i	n_i	$\bar{x}_i$	$n_i * \bar{x}_i$
1	200	2.34	468.0
2	300	3.01	903.0
3	250	1.99	497.5
4	520	2.22	1,154.4
5	120	2.54	304.8
Total	1,390	NA	3,327.7

Combined mean $= 3,327.7/1,390 = 2.394$

$$\bar{x} = \frac{n_1\bar{x}_1 + n_2\bar{x}_2 + n_3\bar{x}_3 + \cdots + n_r\bar{x}_r}{n_1 + n_2 + n_3 + \cdots + n_r}.$$

Symbolically,

$$\bar{x} = \frac{\sum n_j\bar{x}_j}{\sum n_j}.$$

Here, the group means are multiplied by their respective sample sizes, the multiplied values are summed and then the summed value is divided by the total number of observations in all the groups. As the group means are multiplied (weighted) by their respective sample sizes (frequencies), the combined mean is often called the weighted mean.

Note: Be aware of wrong use. Often people calculate the combined mean as $\bar{x} = \dfrac{\bar{x}_1 + \bar{x}_2}{2}$ and $\bar{x} = \dfrac{\bar{x}_1 + \bar{x}_2 + \bar{x}_3 + \cdots + \bar{x}_r}{r}$.

These formulae will give the correct result if and only if $n_1 = n_2 = n_3 = \cdots = n_r$ (obvious from the above equation) and for all other values the result would be wrong.

Example: The numbers of cases and their mean values for five sets of observations are given in Table 5.4. Find out their combined mean.

The required calculations and the combined mean value are shown in the same table, which need no explanation.

MEDIAN

When the observations are arranged according to their magnitude (values), the median is the value that divides the arranged observations into two equal halves. If all the observations are arranged in the ascending (or descending) order of the values of the variable, the median is the middle observation, that is, 50 percent of the values lie above the median value and the remaining 50 percent of the values lie below the median value. The median is often denoted by the symbol M_d.

Median for Ungrouped Data

If the number of observations is odd:
    Median=The value of the $\{(n+1)/2\}$th-ordered observation.

Example 1: The number of members in a sample of 11 families is given below. Find out the median.

Serial number	1	2	3	4	5	6	7	8	9	10	11
Family size	5	6	4	3	5	7	6	4	5	11 .	3

Step 1: Rearrange the values in ascending order

Family size	3	3	4	4	5	5	5	6	6	7	11

Step 2: Find out the $\{(n+1)/2\}$th value. It is $(11+1)=12/2=6$th value$=5$ (the grey cell in step 1).
$$\therefore \text{Median}=5.$$

If the number of observations is even:
Median=Average of the values of the $(n/2)$th and $\left(\dfrac{n}{2}+1\right)$th ordered observations.

   If the $(n/2)$th observation is x_1 and the next observation is x_2, then the median is $M_d = \dfrac{x_1+x_2}{2}$.

Be aware of wrong use:
Sometimes students calculate the median as $\dfrac{\left(\frac{n}{2}\right)+\left(\frac{n}{2}+1\right)}{2}$ or $\dfrac{\left(\frac{n}{2}\right)+\left(\frac{n+1}{2}\right)}{2}$; however, both are wrong. Please note that the median is not the order of the middle observation, but it is rather the value of the middle observation, that is, we need to identify the $(n/2)$th observation and take its value and not the number $(n/2)$ itself, for the calculation of the median.

Example 2: The number of members in a sample of 12 families is given below. Find out the median.

Serial number	1	2	3	4	5	6	7	8	9	10	11	12
Family size	5	6	4	3	5	7	6	4	5	11	3	8

Step 1: Rearrange the values in ascending order:

Family size	3	3	4	4	5	5	5	6	6	7	8	11

Step 2: Find out the $(n/2)$th and $\left(\dfrac{n}{2}+1\right)$th values.

   They are $(12/2)=6$th and $(6+1)=7$th values, that is, the values are 5 and 5.
$$\therefore \text{Median}=(5+5)/2=5.$$

Median for Grouped Data (Frequency Table)

First, convert the class intervals into continuous class intervals as in Column 3 of Table 5.5. Next, obtain the cumulative frequency distribution as in Column 4. Then, obtain the value $N/2$, where N is the total frequency. Now, identify and mark the class that corresponds to the cumulative frequency $N/2$; it is the median class. Then, calculate the median as follows.

   Let l be the lower limit of the median class (here, the median class is 25–30 and the lower limit of the median class is 25).
   Let c be the width of the median class (here 30–25=5).

Table 5.5 Median for the Frequency Distribution

Age Group (1)	Number of Women (2)	Age Group (in Continuous Class Intervals) (3)	Cumulative No. of Women (4)
15–19	59	15–20	59
20–24	72	20–25	131
25–29	65	25–30	196
30–34	59	30–35	255
35–39	53	35–40	308
40–44	43	40–45	351
45–49	32	45–50	383
Total	383	NA	NA

$N = 383$

$N/2 = 383/2 = 191.5$

Median class (corresponding to Cu frequency $N/2$) is 25–30

Lower limit of median class is 25

Median is $25 + ((191.5 - 131)/65) * 5 = 29.65$

Let f be the frequency in the median class (here 65).

Let g be the cumulative frequency of the class previous to the median class (here, the class previous to the median class is 20–25 and the corresponding cumulative frequency is 131).

Then, the median is calculated using the formula:

$$M_d = l + \left\{ \frac{(N/2) - g}{f} \right\} * c.$$

The calculations are made at the bottom of the table and the median is 29.65.

Note: In order for the dataset to have a median, there should be at least three distinct values (if ungrouped data) and at least three different classes (if grouped data). Furthermore, the median cannot be calculated if the first or last class interval has more than 50 percent of the total frequency or observations. In this case, we have to consider smaller class intervals and distribute the frequency. In general, the higher the number of classes (with lesser frequency per class), the more precise the median value.

Merits and Demerits of a Median

A median is not affected by extreme values. When extreme values are too large or too small, it heavily affects the mean but not the median. If the extreme classes are open-ended, median can still be calculated directly. However, for calculating the mean, the upper and lower limits should be known; else it is assumed and fixed at an arbitrary level. The demerit of a median is that it is not based on all observations and so is not amenable for further statistical analysis.

First and Third Quartiles

A median corresponds to the value of the 50th percentile of the *ordered* observations, or the value of the ordered middle observation. Like that, the first quartile corresponds to the 25th percentile, or the value of the observation that corresponds to the 1/4th of the ordered observations. Similarly, the third quartile corresponds to the 75th percentile, or the value of the observation that corresponds to the 3/4th of the ordered observations. The procedure for the calculation of the first and third quartiles is the same as that of the procedure for the calculation of the median, except for, in the case of grouped data, changing $N/2$ by $N/4$ for the first quartile and by $3N/4$ for the third quartile and accordingly changing the median class to the first quartile class and third quartile class, respectively.

MODE

A mode is the value that occurs most often in the data. The mode is often denoted by the symbol M_o.

Mode for Ungrouped Data

Example: The number of members in a sample of 12 families is given below. Find out mode.

Serial number	1	2	3	4	5	6	7	8	9	10	11	12
Family size	5	6	4	3	5	7	6	4	5	11	3	8

Step 1: Rearrange the values in ascending order

Family size	3	3	4	4	5	5	5	6	6	7	8	11

The value 5 occurred three times as compared to the values 3, 4 and 6 which occurred each two times, and the values 7, 8 and 11 which occurred each one time. So, the most frequently occurred value is 5, that is, mode=5.

Mode for Grouped Data (Frequency Table)

First, ensure that there is only one modal class and it is not the extreme (first or last) class, and if so, consider the redistribution of the data with shorter class intervals. Second, ensure that the class intervals are of equal length, especially the modal class and the preceding and succeeding classes. Third, if the class intervals are not continuous, convert the class intervals into continuous class intervals as in Column 3 in Table 5.6. Fourth, identify the modal class that corresponds to the maximum frequency. In our exercise, it is the class 20–25 that has the highest frequency of 72 (the next highest is 65 in the class interval 25–30). Then, calculate the mode as follows.

$$M_o = l + \frac{(f_m - f_p) * c}{(f_m - f_p) - (f_s - f_m)} = l + \frac{(f_m - f_p) * c}{2 * f_m - f_p - f_s}.$$

Let l be the lower limit of the modal class (here 20).
Let c be the width of the modal class (here 5).
Let f_m be the frequency in the modal class (here 72).
Let f_p be the frequency in the class preceding the modal class (here 59).
Let f_s be the frequency in the class succeeding the modal class (here 65).

The mode is calculated and presented at the bottom of the table.

Notes:

1. If the values are all different (that is, no two values are equal), then there is no mode.
2. If the number of values is large, then the mode is identified by constructing a frequency distribution of the data.

Table 5.6 Mode for the Frequency Distribution

Age Group (1)	Number of Women (2)	Age Group (in Continuous Class Intervals) (3)
15–19	59	15–20
20–24	72	20–25
25–29	65	25–30
30–34	59	30–35
35–39	53	35–40
40–44	43	40–45
45–49	32	45–50
Total	383	NA

$l=20$ and $c=5$

$f_m=72; f_p=59$ and $f_s=65$

Mode $=20+((72-59) * 5)/(2 * 72-59-65)=23.25$

3. Some frequency distributions may have two (or more) modes. If there are two modes, the data is said to be bimodal.

4. If there are more than one modal class, then mode is determined by the method of grouping the classes in different combinations (not discussed here).

5. If all values in the data occurred equally (no value occurred more frequently), then we say that the data has no mode. For example, the data values (5, 5, 5), (4, 5, 6, 7) and (4, 4, 5, 5, 6, 6) have no mode as there is no value that has occurred more frequently than the other values.

6. In order for a dataset to have a mode, there should be at least three distinct values (if ungrouped data) and at least three different classes (if grouped data), and one of the middle or intermediate values/classes should have a higher frequency than the preceding and succeeding values/classes. A mode does not exist if the first or last class has the highest frequency.

An SPSS Example of Deriving a Mean and a Median

To run a 'mean' (and for that matter, the measures of central tendency and dispersion) in SPSS, choose 'Analyze => Compare Means => Means'. A window like the one shown in Figure 5.1 will open with the variables in the data file listed on the left and two empty list boxes on the right, one below the other. Now, transfer the variable(s) for which the mean (or any measures of central tendency and dispersion) is required to the box labelled 'Dependent List' and transfer the group variable(s), if any, according to which the mean is to be obtained, to the box labelled 'Independent List' (optional). By default, SPSS will output the mean, number of cases and standard deviation (SD). If interested in the median and other indices, click on the 'Options' and choose the required indices. For this exercise, besides the default indices, only the 'Median' is chosen. Then click 'OK'. It is to be noted that SPSS produces the mode only for frequency tables under the menu 'Frequencies'.

For our exercise (NFHS data for Goa), we consider the weight of a child as a dependent variable and his/her age (in 6 months interval) as an independent variable. In the 'Options' window, we only choose the median. Now, the data are processed and the output is presented in Table 5.7.

Figure 5.1   SPSS Window for Means

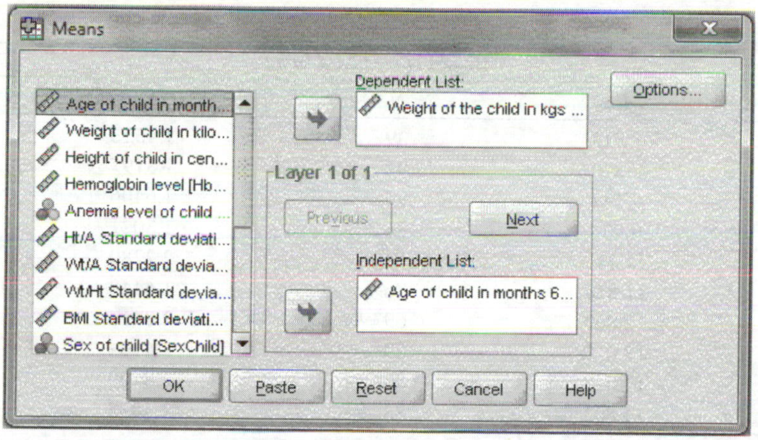

The table gives the 6-months age-wise number of children, mean weight (in kg), median weight (in kg) and SD of weight (SD is being discussed later in this chapter). The table output (format and meaning) is not described as it is self-explanatory.

Note: If the case-wise (ungrouped) data are the in MS Excel sheet, we can calculate the mean using the Excel function 'Average', the median using the function 'Median' and the mode using the function 'Mode'.

MEASURES OF DISPERSION

The different measures of central tendency are important depending on the specific nature of distribution of the data. These measures (averages) give us an idea about the convergence of observations about a central point. However, averages alone will not provide the complete picture of the distribution of the data. For example, consider three samples of three families each. Let the family sizes of the first sample be (5, 5, 5), the second sample be (4, 5, 6) and the third sample be (2, 5, 8). In all the three samples, the mean is 5 but the values are different. In the first sample, there is no variation in the family size of the three families, in the second sample, the family sizes are different but the variation is only one member on either side of the average and in the third sample, the variation is three members on either side of the average. So, in addition to the measures of central tendency, we need some measures to capture the variation in the data. The procedures that measure the variations in the data are called measures of variation or dispersion. Some of the common measures of variation are the range, inter-quartile range (IQR), variance, SD and coefficient of variation.

The Range

The range is the difference or distance between the two most extreme observations (the smallest and the largest values) in the data.

Let L be the lowest/smallest value and H be the highest/largest value in the sample of observations, then the range is $H-L$.

Note: The range is a crude measure of dispersion and is heavily affected by the extreme values, that is, even if only one value is too low or too high from all other values in the sample, the range will be too large.

Table 5.7   SPSS Output of Mean and Median Weight (kg) by the Age of Child (in Months)

| | Report | | | |
| | *Weight of the Child in kg* | | | |
Age Group	*Mean*	*N*	*Std. Deviation*	*Median*
00–05	5.813	39	1.4513	5.700
06–11	7.340	92	1.3197	7.300
12–17	9.142	96	1.6406	9.000
18–23	9.936	86	1.5021	9.750
24–29	11.226	84	2.2280	10.800
30–35	11.538	86	1.6448	11.500
36–41	12.809	69	2.3416	12.500
42–47	13.671	89	2.4104	13.300
48–53	14.046	85	2.8400	13.500
54–59	14.802	83	2.4878	14.600
Total	11.239	809	3.3263	11.200

Example: The number of members in a sample of 12 families is given below. Find out the range.

Serial number	1	2	3	4	5	6	7	8	9	10	11	12
Family size	5	6	4	3	5	7	6	4	5	11	3	8

The lowest value is $L=3$ and the highest value is $H=11$.
The range is $H-L=11-3=8$.

Inter-quartile Range

In the above sections, we have already studied the median and the range. When the observations are arranged in ascending order of their values, the range is the distance from the lowest to the highest values and the median is the middle value. If there are observations with extreme values (a few cases that are far away from the other observations), the range increases to that extent irrespective of the values of all other observations. To overcome this problem, we measure the 'IQR' that excludes the lowest 25 percent and the highest 25 percent of the cases and finds the range of the middle 50 percent of the cases only.

Let x be the variable and N be the total (cumulative) number of cases, and the observations are arranged in ascending order of their values or in class intervals. Now, divide the data into four equal parts (called quartiles). The value of x corresponding to the first one-fourth (1/4th) or 25th percentile of the cumulative number $(N/4)$ of observations is called the first quartile and is often denoted by the symbol Q_1. Similarly, the value of x corresponding to the three–fourths (3/4th) or 75th percentile of the cumulative number $(3*N/4)$ of observations is called the third quartile and is often denoted by the symbol Q_3. Needless to say that Q_2 is the middle value (corresponding to $N/2$) and it is nothing but the median. The calculations of Q_1 and Q_3 (first and third quartiles) are the same as the calculation of the median, with the only difference being that $N/2$ is to be replaced by $N/4$ and $3N/4$, respectively.

The IQR is defined as the distance from Q_1 to Q_3.
That is, $IQR=Q_3-Q_1$.

Variance

The variance is the sum of squares of the deviation of the individual observations from the overall mean value. There are two measures of variance: one for the population observations (called the *population variance* denoted by the symbol σ^2, read as sigma square) and the other for the sample observations (called the *sample variance* denoted by the symbol s^2, read as s-square).

Population Variance

The mathematical formula for the population variance is:

$$\sigma^2 = \frac{\sum(x_i - \bar{x})^2}{n},$$

where

Σ (sigma) stands for summation (different from σ),
x_i's are the individual values,
$\bar{x}$ is the mean and
n is the number of observations.

Applying simple arithmetic and summation rules, the equation can be re-written in a simplified form as follows:

$$\sigma^2 = \frac{1}{n}\sum x_i^2 - \bar{x}^2.$$

Caution: The Σ (summation) is for x_i^2 values only and not for $\bar{x}^2$ which is independent of the summation. Also, note that the division by n applies to the first term (summed values) only and not to $\bar{x}^2$.

Sample Variance

The mathematical equation of the sample variance is:

$$s^2 = \frac{\sum(x_i - \bar{x})^2}{n-1} \quad \text{or} \quad s^2 = \frac{1}{n-1}\left(\sum x_i^2 - n\bar{x}^2\right)$$

Important Notes

Please note the difference in the formula for the population variance and sample variance. For the sample variance, it is just the replacement of n by $(n-1)$ in the denominator. This is because for small samples, it is statistically proved that the sample mean ($\bar{x}$) is an 'unbiased estimate' of the population mean (μ) and the sample variance (s^2) is an 'unbiased estimate' of the population variance (σ^2). The statistical derivations are highly technical and are not required for us.

However, for large samples s^2 is almost equal to σ^2. For example, when $n=10$, $(1/n)=(1/10)=0.1$, $1/(n-1)=(1/9)=0.1111$ and the difference is 0.0111. When $n=200$, $(1/n)=(1/200)=0.005$, $1/(n-1)=(1/199)=0.005025$ and the difference is just 0.000025, that is, when the sample size is large, we can use the term $1/n$ instead of $1/(n-1)$ in the formula, that is, we can obtain σ^2 instead of s^2.

In social science investigations, normally, we will have samples much higher than the small sample size limit of 30 observations, and if so, for simplicity and for the ease of manual calculations, we may use the formula for σ^2 if the calculation is based on a reasonably large number of cases. Statistical software such as SPSS (including MS Excel) by default use s^2, which is applicable to σ^2 as well for large samples. Whatever may be the case, we can easily change from σ^2 to s^2 and vice versa, using the simple identity:

$$\sum(x_i - \bar{x})^2 = n\sigma^2 = (n-1)s^2.$$

That is, $n\sigma^2 = (n-1)s^2$ or $\sigma^2 = \dfrac{n-1}{n}s^2$ or $s^2 = \dfrac{n}{n-1}\sigma^2$.

So, we need to calculate either σ^2 or s^2 using the data and the other one, if needed, can be obtained using the above formula.

Standard Deviation

Population Standard Deviation

The mathematical formula for the population SD is just the square root of the population variance (σ^2). It is

$$\sigma = \sqrt{\frac{\sum(x_i - \bar{x})^2}{n}} \quad \text{or} \quad \sigma = \sqrt{\frac{1}{n}\sum x_i^2 - \bar{x}^2},$$

where
  σ (sigma) stands for the standard deviation,
  $\sqrt{}$ stands for the square root,
  Σ (sigma) stands for summation (different from σ),
  x_i's are the individual values,
  $\bar{x}$ is the mean and
  n is the number of observations.

Sample Standard Deviation

The mathematical formula for the sample SD is just the square root of the sample variance (s^2). It is

$$s = \sqrt{\frac{\sum(x_i - \bar{x})^2}{n-1}}$$

$$\text{or} \quad s = \sqrt{\frac{1}{n-1}\left(\sum x_i^2 - n\bar{x}^2\right)}.$$

Note: We can obtain s form σ and vice versa, and so there is no need to calculate both s and σ from the data itself. From the formulae for the population variance and sample variance, we obtain

$$\sum x_i^2 - n\bar{x}^2 = n\sigma^2 = (n-1)s^2$$

$$s = \sigma\sqrt{\frac{n}{n-1}} \quad \text{and} \quad \sigma = s\sqrt{\frac{n-1}{n}}.$$

Variance and Standard Deviation for Grouped Data

As in the case of the arithmetic mean for grouped data, the population and sample variances for grouped data are as follows:

$$\sigma^2 = \frac{\sum f_i (x_i - \bar{x})^2}{n} \quad \text{and} \quad s^2 = \frac{\sum f_i (x_i - \bar{x})^2}{n-1}.$$

Similarly, the population and sample SDs for grouped data are:

$$\sigma = \sqrt{\frac{1}{n} \sum f_j x_j^2 - \bar{x}^2} \quad \text{and} \quad s = \sqrt{\frac{1}{n-1} \left(\sum f_j x_j^2 - n\bar{x}^2 \right)},$$

where f_j is the frequency of occurrence of x_j in the dataset.

An Example of Calculation of Variance and Standard Deviation

Given here are two examples, one with ungrouped data and the other with grouped data, for the manual calculation of the variance and SD.

Example (Ungrouped Data): Table 5.8 contains the weight of 24 women. Find out the SD of the weight of women.

In Table 5.8, the columns 1, 2, 4 and 5 are the given data and the remaining (columns 3 and 6) are the calculations made from columns 2 and 5. The results (mean, population and sample variance and SDs) are presented in the table itself.

Example (Grouped Data): Table 5.9 shows the distribution of 1220 women by the number of children ever born to them. Find out the mean and SD of children ever born to the women.

In Table 5.9, the first three columns are the given data and the remaining columns are the calculations made from Columns 2 and 3. The results (mean, population and sample variance and SDs) are presented in the table itself.

Note: Please note that in the above two examples both population and sample variances (also SDs) are worked out for illustration only. In practice, we need to work out either one of them depending on whether the given data is a population or a sample.

If case-wise (ungrouped) data are in the MS Excel sheet, we can calculate the range using the Excel functions MIN (minimum) and MAX (Maximum), variance using the functions VAR (for sample) and VARP (for population), and SD using the functions STDEV (for sample) and STDEVP (for population).

An SPSS Example of Variance and Standard Deviation

To run variance and/or SD (or for that matter any measures of central tendency and dispersion) in SPSS, choose 'Analyze=>Compare Means=>Means' and follow the steps given in Figure 5.1 under measures of central tendency. The only addition is to choose the desired indices from the list of indices in the 'Options' list. A sample output with the SD is shown in Table 5.7.

Mean and Variance for Dummy Variables

So far we have used numerical variables to obtain the mean, variance and SD. How about categorical variables? We have already seen in Chapter 1 that categorical variables can also be converted into a kind of numerical variables called binary or dummy variables. The most common form of a dummy variable coding is 0 and 1.

Table 5.8 Example of Calculation of Variance and SD for Ungrouped Data

Item	Weight (kg)	Weight²	Item	Weight (kg)	Weight²
i	x	x^2	i	x	x^2
(1)	(2)	(3)	(4)	(5)	(6)
1	40	1,600	13	46	2,116
2	49	2,401	14	41	1,681
3	51	2,601	15	43	1,849
4	37	1,369	16	34	1,156
5	43	1,849	17	47	2,209
6	67	4,489	18	62	3,844
7	41	1,681	19	37	1,369
8	41	1,681	20	51	2,601
9	42	1,764	21	40	1,600
10	42	1,764	22	34	1,156
11	51	2,601	23	33	1,089
12	43	1,849	24	43	1,849
Sum				1,058	48,168

Population variance and standard deviation

Mean = 1058/24   44.083

Variance = (48,168/24) − 44.083 * 44.083   63.66

SD = $\sqrt{63.660}$ 7.979

Sample variance and standard deviation

Mean   44.083

Variance = (48,168 − 24 * 44.08 * 44.08)/23   66.428

SD = $\sqrt{66.428}$ 8.15

Note: $s = 8.150 > \sigma = 7.979$ because $n = 24$ is small.

Let us continue with an example. Let there be 10 persons and their literacy status is given in Columns 1 and 2 of Table 5.10. Let the dummy variable be x, taking the value 0 if illiterate and the value 1 if literate, and the coding is given in Column 3. Let us obtain the square of x that is presented in Column 4. The last row gives the values $n = 10$, sum of x, that is, $\Sigma x = 7$ and the sum of x^2, that is, $\Sigma x^2 = 7$.

Following the usual formula for the mean we obtain

$$\text{Mean } (\bar{x}) = \frac{x_1 + x_2 + x_3 + \cdots + x_n}{n} = \frac{7}{10} = 0.7.$$

In Chapter 3, we have seen that a proportion is calculated as the number of units (here persons) in one category to the total number of units. As there are seven literates among the 10 persons, the proportion literate (p) is $7/10 = 0.7$, that is, $\bar{x} = 0.7$ and $p = 0.7$. So, for a dummy variable, the mean is the proportion, that is, $\bar{x} = p$.

Similarly,

$$\sigma^2 = \frac{1}{n}\sum x_i^2 - \bar{x}^2 = \frac{7}{10} - 0.7^2 = 0.7 - 0.7^2 = 0.7 * (1 - 0.7) = 0.7 * 0.3 = 0.21.$$

Table 5.9   Example of Calculation of Variance and SD for Grouped Data

Serial Order	Children Ever Born	Number of Women	Total Children	NA
i	x_i	f_i	$f_i * x_i$	$f_i * x_i * x_i$
(1)	(2)	(3)	(4)	(5)
1	0	378	0	0
2	1	151	151	151
3	2	245	490	980
4	3	186	558	1,674
5	4	115	460	1,840
6	5	66	330	1,650
7	6	37	222	1,332
8	7	20	140	980
9	8	11	88	704
10	9	6	54	486
11	10	5	50	500
NA	NA	1,220	2,543	10,297

Population variance and standard deviation

Mean	$=2{,}543/1{,}220$	2.084
Intermediate step	$=(10{,}297/1{,}220)-(2.08 * 2.08)$	4.095
Standard deviation	$=\sqrt{4.095}$	2.024

Sample variance and standard deviation

Mean	$=2{,}543/1{,}220$	2.084
Intermediate step	$=(10{,}297-(1{,}220 * 2.08 * 2.08))/1219$	4.099
Standard deviation	$=\sqrt{4.099}$	2.025

Note: $\sigma=2.024$ and $s=2.025$ are almost equal because $n=1{,}220$ is large.

Furthermore, from the above example, we see that $\Sigma x^2 = \Sigma x = np = 7$. So, the population variance for a proportion can be written as

$$\sigma^2 = \frac{1}{n}\sum x_i^2 - \bar{x}^2 = \frac{1}{n}(np) - p^2 = p(1-p) = pq,$$

where $q = 1 - p$.

That is, $\sigma^2 = pq$.

For the given data, $\sigma^2 = pq = 0.7 * 0.3 = 0.21$, and it is the same as that we have obtained above.

We know that $n\sigma^2 = (n-1)s^2$ and so, $s^2 = \dfrac{n\sigma^2}{n-1} = \dfrac{npq}{n-1}$.

Thus, for dummy variables with coding 0 and 1, the following formulae for the mean, variance and SD will apply:

$$\bar{x} = p \qquad \sigma^2 = pq \qquad s^2 = \frac{npq}{n-1} \qquad \cdot = \sqrt{pq} \qquad s = \sqrt{\frac{npq}{n-1}}.$$

Table 5.10 Mean and SD for Dummy Variables

Person	Literacy	x	x^2
(1)	(2)	(3)	(4)
1	Literate	1	$1*1=1$
2	Illiterate	0	$0*0=0$
3	Literate	1	$1*1=1$
4	Literate	1	$1*1=1$
5	Illiterate	0	$0*0=0$
6	Literate	1	$1*1=1$
7	Literate	1	$1*1=1$
8	Illiterate	0	$0*0=0$
9	Literate	1	$1*1=1$
10	Literate	1	$1*1=1$
$n=10$	Total	7	7

Note: For dummy variables, the median, mode and range are *not* obtained as the variable takes only two values, 0 and 1. Furthermore, for dummy variables, the mean (or proportion) varies from 0 to 1. However, if the mean is 0 or 1, then the variable is constant and it is not amenable for any statistical analysis. So, in practice, p is >0 and <1, that is, $0<p<1$. Similarly, the variance is the maximum when $p=q=0.5$ and so the maximum variance is $p * q=0.5 * 0.5=0.25$. Hence, the variance varies from >0 to 0.25, that is, $0<\sigma^2 \le 0.25$.

The calculation of the mean, variance and SD for dummy variables using the SPSS and Excel is the same as that for numerical variables, and the only requirement is that the variable should be coded as 0 and 1.

Mean and SD for Dummy Variables with Three or More Categories

Let us continue with the categorical variable 'religion' that is used for demonstration in Chapter 1. In Table 5.11, religion is considered in four categories, namely Hindu, Christian, Muslim and Other. There are four dummy variables, namely Hindu, Christian, Muslim and Other, and the dummy variable coding is made for 15 observations. The mean, variance and SD are also obtained and presented in the last few rows of the table. It is clear from the table that the mean for Hindu is 0.333 and is equal to 1 minus the means of the other three dummy variables $(1-0.267-0.200-0.200=0.333)$. Similarly, the mean of Christian is equal to 1 minus the means of the other three dummy variables and so on. Hence, in multivariate analysis, we retain one category as the reference category and it may be any one category depending on convenience.

Coefficient of Variation (CV)

Coefficient of variation (CV) measures the relative or standardised variation in the population or sample observations with respect to the variable under consideration. In any dataset, the larger the values of the observations, the larger the mean we get, and generally, the SD will also be larger. So, we cannot directly compare the variation in two distributions (sets of observations) directly. For example, for the three values 3, 4, 5 (each value is one more than the previous value), the mean is 4 and the (population) SD is 0.82. At the same time, for the three values 39, 40, 41 (here also each value is one more than the previous value), the mean is as high as 40, but the (population) SD is still 0.82. Can we say that the variation of the two distributions is the

Table 5.11   Mean, Variance and SD for Categorical Variable (3+ Categories)

Serial Order	Religion	Original Variable	Dummy Variables			
			Hindu	*Christian*	*Muslim*	*Other*
1	Muslim	3	0	0	1	0
2	Other religion	4	0	0	0	1
3	Hindu	1	1	0	0	0
4	Christian	2	0	1	0	0
5	Hindu	1	1	0	0	0
6	Muslim	3	0	0	1	0
7	Christian	2	0	1	0	0
8	Hindu	2	0	1	0	0
9	Muslim	3	0	0	1	0
10	Other religion	4	0	0	0	1
11	Hindu	1	1	0	0	0
12	Hindu	1	1	0	0	0
13	Christian	2	0	1	0	0
14	Muslim	4	0	0	0	1
15	Hindu	1	1	0	0	0
$N=15$	Sum	NA	5	4	3	3
	Mean	NA	0.333	0.267	0.200	0.200
	Population variance	NA	0.222	0.196	0.160	0.160
	Sample variance	NA	0.238	0.210	0.171	0.171
	Population SD	NA	0.471	0.442	0.400	0.400
	Sample SD	NA	0.488	0.458	0.414	0.414

same? No. For example, the difference between the values 3 and 4 (i.e., 4−3=1) is 1/4=25 percent deviation from its mean, but the difference in the values 39 and 40 (i.e., 40−39=1) is just 1/40=2.5 percent deviation from its mean. So, we need an index to standardise the variation so as to compare the variation between populations or samples.

CV is an index that gives the standardised measure of the variation. It is nothing but expressing the SD per 100 mean (value) and is defined as

$$CV = \frac{SD}{Mean} * 100 \quad \text{or} \quad CV = \frac{\sigma}{\bar{x}}100 \quad \text{or} \quad CV = \frac{s}{\bar{x}}100.$$

Examples:
For the above ungrouped data, mean $\bar{x}=44.08$ and SD $\sigma=7.98$, and

$$CV = \frac{\sigma}{\bar{x}} * 100 = \frac{7.98}{44.08} * 100 = 18.1.$$

For the above grouped data, mean $\bar{x}=2.084$ and SD $\sigma=2.024$, and

$$CV = \frac{\sigma}{\bar{x}} * 100 = \frac{2.024}{2.084} * 100 = 97.1.$$

The runs scored by two cricket players, namely A and B, in a series of cricket matches was analysed and it was found that the mean number of runs scored were 43.2 and 39.6 per match with SDs 25.3 and 8.8, respectively. Examine the consistency performance of the two players.

From the mean runs scored by the two cricket players, we can say that player A is better than player B, as the mean runs scored per match by player A was higher at 43.2 as compared to 39.6 by player B. But at the same time, we see that the deviations in the runs scored by player B measured in terms of SD are only 8.8 as compared to 25.3 for player A. When the variation is compared in terms of the coefficient of variation (CV), we obtain

CV in the runs scored by player A = (25.3/43.2) * 100 = 58.6
CV in the runs scored by player B = (8.8/39.6) * 100 = 22.2

It is clear that, although the mean runs scored by player A is higher than the mean runs scored by player B, the variation in the runs scored by player A is much higher than the variation in the runs scored by player B. It means that, as compared to player A, player B is a more consistent player who can ensure a minimum number of runs if he enters the ground to play.

Notes:

1. We may use σ or s to derive the coefficient of variation depending on whether we are dealing with the population or sample. CV is often expressed in the percentage term.
2. The CV is independent of the unit of measurement and the number of observations and so it is directly comparable between groups.
3. The lower the value of the coefficient of variation, the greater the homogeneity or consistency of the observations, or the lesser the variability of the value of the members (or observations) within the group.

SKEWNESS AND KURTOSIS

The first step in most statistical analyses is to determine the *location* and *variability* of the given data and the second step is to understand the shape of the distribution so as to ensure that the data satisfy the required (fundamental) assumptions for the statistical application proposed. We have already learned the measures of central tendency and dispersion. Now, let us have a look at the visual display of the distribution of the data to understand the shape of the distribution of the data. The shape of the frequency distribution of the data in the form of a histogram (frequency polygon) or a frequency curve is looked at and also measured in two ways: first, skewness, the extent of symmetry or asymmetry of the shape of the diagram from a central point and, second, kurtosis, the peakedness or flatness of the curve or diagram. The frequency curve (or frequency polygon) may have a longer tail on one side (left or right) of the curve, that is, the curve is not symmetrical from its centre but stretched more on one side than the other. Skewness measures the extent of non-symmetrical nature of the distribution or curve. Next, the height of the curve around the centre may be too high (peaked) or too small (flat). Kurtosis measures the peakedness or flatness of the curve.

Before going into skewness and kurtosis, it would be desirable to have some idea about moments because they are used in the calculation of the indices determining skewness and kurtosis.

Moments

Let $x_1, x_2, \ldots, x_n$ be the values of a variable, say X, of n observations, then the rth moment of X about a point a is given by the following formula:

$$\mu_r' = \frac{1}{n}\sum(x_i - a)^r, \text{ where } \sum \text{ is summation over } i=1 \text{ to } n.$$

If we replace a by the mean $\bar{x}$, then μ'_r is called the *central moment about mean* or simply *central moment* and is denoted by the symbol μ_r, that is,

$$\mu_r = \frac{1}{n}\sum(x_i - \bar{x})^r$$

When $r=0$, the μ_r becomes $\quad \mu_0 = \frac{1}{n}\sum(x_i - \bar{x})^0 = \frac{1}{n}\sum 1 = \frac{1}{n}*n = 1$

When $r=1$, the μ_r becomes $\quad \mu_1 = \frac{1}{n}\sum(x_i - \bar{x})^1 = \frac{1}{n}\sum x_i - \frac{1}{n}n\bar{x} = 0$

When $r=2$, the μ_r becomes $\quad \mu_2 = \frac{1}{n}\sum(x_i - \bar{x})^2 = \sigma^2$

When $r=3$, the μ_r becomes $\quad \mu_3 = \frac{1}{n}\sum(x_i - \bar{x})^3$

When $r=4$, the μ_r becomes $\quad \mu_4 = \frac{1}{n}\sum(x_i - \bar{x})^4$ and so on.

It is clear from the above equations that the first central moment (about mean) is always zero and the second central moment is the variance. The second, third and fourth central moments will be used in the measurement of skewness and kurtosis and hence they are important here.

Skewness

Literally, skewness means the 'lack of symmetry'. The curve is skewed if (a) the curve is not symmetrical and has a longer tail on one side of the curve, (b) the mean, median and mode for the data are different (see Figure 5.2) and (c) the quartiles are not at equidistance from the median.

There are many measures of skewness using different combinations of the mean, median, mode and SD. The first to talk about skewness was Karl Pearson and he defined skewness as

$$S_k = \frac{\text{Mean} - \text{Mode}}{\text{Standard Deviation}}.$$

Figure 5.2 Skewness

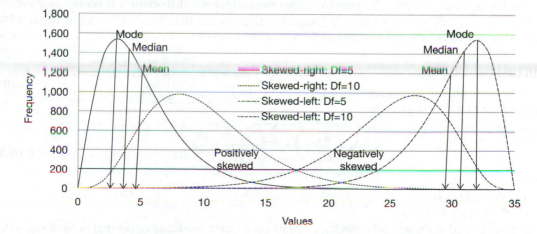

Figure 5.3 Kurtosis with Different Standard Deviations

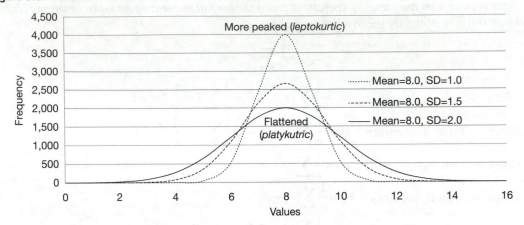

If the mode is not well defined, then using the median, $S_k = \dfrac{3(\text{Mean} - \text{Median})}{\text{Standard Deviation}}$ and this coefficient (of skewness) varies from –3 to +3.

The formula can be simplified as $S_k = \dfrac{\text{Mean} - \text{Median}}{\text{Standard Deviation}}$ (varies from –1 to +1).

A more mathematically well-defined skewness based on raw data is given by

$$S_k = \frac{\mu_3}{\sigma^3} = \frac{\sum (x_i - \bar{x})^3}{(n-1)s^3},$$

where
n is the sample size and
s is the sample SD.

Please note that for a frequency distribution, the part $\sum (x_i - \bar{x})^3$ is to be changed as $\sum f(x_i - \bar{x})^3$.

For all these measures, the value 0 means that the curve or distribution is symmetric or almost symmetric at mean, a value >0 (positive value) means that the distribution is positively skewed or skewed to the right and a value <0 (negative value) means that the distribution is negatively skewed or skewed to the left (see Figure 5.2).

Kurtosis

Kurtosis or 'convexity of curve' helps us to know the flatness or peakedness of the curve. The kurtosis for raw data is given by

$$S_k = \frac{\mu_4}{\sigma^4} - 3 = \frac{\sum (x_i - \bar{x})^4}{(n-1)s^4} - 3,$$

where
n is the sample size,
s is the sample SD and
the '–3' is used in the formula only for convenience to treat moderate or normal peakedness as 0.

Please note that for a frequency distribution, the part $\sum(x_i - \bar{x})^4$ is to be changed as $\sum f(x_i - \bar{x})^4$ and is also part of fourth central moment. For this measure, the value 0 means that the curve or distribution is moderate or normal (also called *mesokurtic*), a value >0 (positive value) means that the distribution is more peaked than normal (called *leptokurtic*) and a value <0 (negative value) means that the distribution is flattened than normal (called *platykutric*).

A Numerical Example

Table 5.12 gives the monthly per capita consumer expenditure (MPCE) for rural areas of Rajasthan and Maharashtra as per the National Sample Survey (NSS) round 61, year 2004–2005.

As the MPCE is given in class intervals, the frequencies are taken at the middle of their respective classes. It is to be noted that the frequencies are standardised to 1,000 persons (similar to percentage). Figure 5.4 provides the graphical depiction of the data. It is important to note that the x-axis should reflect the MPCE values in a continuum (distance proportionate to value) and not as a category (each category at equidistance). For this, we need to choose the graph/chart type 'Scatter with straight lines' or 'Scatter with smooth lines' with or without markers. On the other hand, if we choose 'Line' graph/chart type, we will get a wrong one because it will treat each class being located at equidistance. In this exercise, we have chosen 'Scatter with straight lines and markers' in the MS Excel. The skewness and kurtosis values presented at the bottom of the tables are as obtained from MS Excel (calculation in Table 5.13) and also obtained from the SPSS output.

Table 5.12 Monthly Per Capita Consumer Expenditure (MPCE) for Rural Areas of Rajasthan and Maharashtra as per NSS 2004–2005

MPCE Class (₹)	MPCE Mid-point	Rajasthan	Maharashtra
0–235	116.0	13	49
235–270	252.5	21	56
270–320	295.0	58	95
320–365	342.5	74	102
365–410	387.5	99	99
410–455	432.5	94	90
455–510	482.5	129	95
510–580	545.0	155	100
580–690	635.0	140	103
690–890	790.0	122	98
890–1,155	1,022.5	52	56
≥ 1,155	1,600.0	43	57
Total (per 10,000)		1,000	1,000
Calculated (from Table 5.13)			
Skewness		1.934	1.741
Kurtosis		4.479	3.097
SPSS output			
Skewness		1.937	1.743
Kurtosis		4.507	3.119

Figure 5.4   MPCE Rajasthan and Maharashtra (Rural) NSS 2005–2006

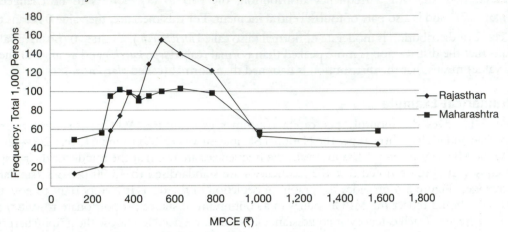

It is clear from Table 5.12 that the skewness and kurtosis values obtained from the calculation (using MS Excel) and that obtained from SPSS are almost the same. It is clear that the MPCE for rural areas of both Rajasthan and Maharashtra are positively skewed and the skewness is more for Rajasthan than for Maharashtra. Similarly, the kurtosis also shows that both the curves are peaked and the peakedness is substantially higher for Rajasthan than that for Maharashtra.

Note: Though a worked example for skewness and kurtosis is presented, it is not often used, but the eye view of the shape of the curve or polygon (see Chapter 4) is important in understanding the distribution. The shape of the curve or for that matter skewness and kurtosis is clearer when we talk about theoretical distributions under 'probability theory'.

Table 5.13   Calculation of Skewness and Kurtosis for Table 5.12

x	Freq (f)	D	fD	fD^2	fD^3	fD^4
Rajasthan						
116.0	13	−466.3	−6,061.3	2,826,063.9	−1,317,653,694.2	614,356,693,733.3
252.5	21	−329.8	−6,924.8	2,283,443.2	−752,966,549.2	248,291,096,084.1
295.0	58	−287.3	−16,660.5	4,785,745.3	−1,374,707,726.1	394,885,481,686.6
342.5	74	−239.8	−17,741.5	4,253,542.4	−1,019,788,909.1	244,494,900,861.7
387.5	99	−194.8	−19,280.3	3,754,848.0	−731,258,519.1	142,412,962,233.4
432.5	94	−149.8	−14,076.5	2,107,970.0	−315,669,554.2	47,271,673,580.1
482.5	129	−99.8	−12,867.8	1,283,570.9	−128,036,842.1	12,771,739,016.0
545.0	155	−37.3	−5,773.8	215,078.0	−8,011,761.6	298,442,125.4
635.0	140	52.7	7,384.9	389,551.4	20,548,639.7	1,083,930,471.4
790.0	122	207.7	25,345.4	5,265,502.3	1,093,905,465.8	227,258,313,571.6
1,022.5	52	440.2	22,893.0	10,078,620.4	4,437,107,572.9	1,953,434,390,399.9
1,600.0	43	1,017.7	43,763.2	44,540,003.9	45,330,566,723.9	46,135,161,617,980.5
Sum	1,000	−86.006	0.0	81,783,939.5	45,234,034,846.6	50,021,721,241,744.2
Mean/moments	582.3	−0.086	0.0	81,783.9	45,234,034.8	50,021,721,241.7
Skew/kurtosis					1.934	4.479

Maharashtra

116.0	49	−435.7	−21,349.0	9,301,633.8	−4,052,666,045.6	1,765,722,280,090.2
252.5	56	−299.2	−16,754.9	5,012,954.8	−1,499,845,992.3	448,744,921,829.9
295.0	95	−256.7	−24,385.9	6,259,721.9	−1,606,833,057.4	412,464,404,825.2
342.5	102	−209.2	−21,337.8	4,463,737.2	−933,787,044.6	195,342,647,008.4
387.5	99	−164.2	−16,255.2	2,669,007.3	−438,234,983.6	71,955,554,901.3
432.5	90	−119.2	−10,727.5	1,278,648.9	−152,407,273.1	18,166,032,507.7
482.5	95	−69.2	−6,573.4	454,841.9	−31,472,331.5	2,177,696,505.5
545.0	100	−6.7	−669.4	4,481.0	−29,995.6	200,790.3
635.0	103	83.3	8,580.5	714,808.6	59,547,847.9	4,960,693,020.5
790.0	98	238.3	23,354.0	5,565,395.5	1,326,267,131.5	316,057,415,044.5
1,022.5	56	470.8	26,365.1	12,412,864.2	5,844,050,951.8	2,751,414,252,404.0
1,600.0	57	1,048.3	59,753.4	62,639,891.8	65,665,774,381.1	68,837,825,278,308.9
Sum	1,000	280.672	0.0	110,777,986.9	64,180,363,588.6	74,824,831,377,236.3
Mean/moments	551.7	0.281	0.0	110,778.0	64,180,363.6	74,824,831,377.2
Skew/kurtosis					1.741	3.097

Notes: $D = x - \bar{x}$ (deviation from mean).
^ stands for exponent.
Mean/moment is divided by $n = 1,000$.

Theoretical Distributions

This chapter does not describe any statistical application that the social science students and researchers can use directly, but rather it gives an understanding that almost all statistical applications rest on probability theory. The data or observations we use in any statistical application, be it the simple frequency distribution, the derivation of mean and standard deviation or the advanced testing of hypothesis and regression analysis (discussed later in this book), are all assumed to have come from a population (universe), drawn at random by using an appropriate probability sampling method, and the distribution of the observations follows a specified pattern or shape. So, it is very essential for the social science students and researchers to understand what is probability and probability distribution, and how probability theory is the basis for sample selection, tabulation, derivation of indices, testing of hypothesis and advanced statistical analysis.

INTRODUCTION TO PROBABILITY THEORY

We often come across experiments or trials with two types of outcomes:

1. The outcome is expected (unique, certain and known). For example, if we throw a stone with initial velocity u and acceleration a, then the velocity v at time t is $v = u + at$ and it is certain, unique and known beforehand (i.e., before doing the experiment).
2. The outcome cannot be expected in advance, that is, we get a result but the result is not unique, not certain of which is the outcome and not known in advance. In other words, the result can be one of many possible outcomes and which one is the actual outcome will be known only after the experiment is performed. For example, if we toss a coin, the outcome may be head or tail (two possible outcomes) and which one is the outcome will be known only after the experiment (tossing a coin) is done.

The experiments of type (1) mentioned above are known as 'deterministic' or 'predictable' experiments, that is, a deterministic model is one which stipulates that the condition under which an experiment is performed determines the outcome of the experiment. On the other hand, there are experiments which do not follow the deterministic approach and are known as 'unpredictable' or 'probabilistic' experiments. A statistician is basically concerned with experiments of the second type, that is, drawing conclusions (or inferences) from experiments involving uncertainties or probabilities. For the conclusions and inferences to be reasonably accurate, an understanding of at least certain elements of probability theory is essential. Before we go into the probability theory, gaining an understanding of certain terms and concepts related to probability theory may be appropriate.

Sample Space

An *experiment* is a procedure that can be repeated any number of times (theoretically infinite number of times) and has a well-defined set of possible outcomes. *Sample space* is the set of all possible outcomes of an experiment. An *event* is a subset of the sample space of an experiment. For example, a coin tossing is an experiment as the coin can be tossed any number of times. A coin has two faces, namely, 'head' and 'tail' and are together called sample space. A sample space is usually denoted by the symbol 'S' and all the possible outcomes are listed one by one with each one separated by a comma. The whole set is kept within a set of two flower brackets, { }, that is, S = {Head, Tail} or S = {0, 1} by considering tail as 0 and head as 1. Similarly, in tossing two coins the sample space is S = {HH, TT, HT, TH}, where H represents head and T represents tail. In this sample space, some events are E1 = {HT}, E2 = {TH} and E3 = {HH}. In throwing a die, the sample space is S = {1, 2, 3, 4, 5, 6} and some events are E1 = {2}, E2 = {3} and E3 = {6}.

Basic Types of Events

Mutually exclusive events: These are the events that cannot occur simultaneously (i.e., cannot occur together). In tossing a coin, if the event 'head' occurs then the event 'tail' cannot occur in the same trial. However, 'tail' may occur in another trial. Similarly, in throwing a die, the events 1, 2, 3, 4, 5 and 6 are mutually exclusive.

Complementary events: If A is the occurrence of an event, then $\bar{A}$ (or) A' (Note: $\bar{A}$ is to be read as A-bar and A' is to be read as A-dash) is the non-occurrence of the event and the event $\bar{A}$ is called the complement of the event A. Any event A and its complementary event A' are mutually exclusive. For example, the events head and tail in a single toss of a coin are complementary events because if 'head' occurs, 'tail' cannot occur, and vice versa.

Independent events: Two or more events are said to be mutually independent events if the outcome of one event does not affect the outcome of the other event. They are the events that are not dependent on what occurred previously. Each toss of a coin is an independent event as the occurrence of head or tail in one toss is independent of the occurrence of head or tail in the previous toss. In tossing two dies, the occurrence of '4' in the second die is independent of the occurrence of '4' in the first die.

Conditional events: These are events that are dependent on what had occurred previously. For example, if four cards are drawn from a pack of 52 cards one by one, the chances of the fourth card being a 'Spade King' is dependent on the outcome of the first three cards in which 'Spade King' has not occurred.

Bernoulli Trials

A *Bernoulli trial* is an experiment with two possible random outcomes, usually termed as success and failure. Mathematically, success is being thought of as taking the value 1 and failure as taking the value 0. If p is the probability of success, then the expected value or the mean of such a random variable is p and its standard deviation is $\sqrt{p(1-p)}$ (already discussed in Chapter 5). Please note that the words 'success' and 'failure' are only labels for outcomes and it should not be construed in the literal meaning of success and failure of an experiment or exercise. A Bernoulli process consists of repeatedly performing the Bernoulli trial under identical conditions but in independent situation. The Bernoulli trials process is one of the important random processes in probability theory because of its wide applicability. It is named after James Bernoulli, the inventor of the process. Essentially, the process is a sequence of generic trials that satisfy the following assumptions:

1. Each trial has two possible outcomes, generically called success and failure, with values 1 and 0, respectively.

2. Each trial is performed under identical situations, that is, the equipment, environment and process of performing the experiment are the same for each trial.
3. The trials are independent, that is, the outcome of one trial has no influence on the outcome of any another trial in the experiment.
4. In each trial, the probability of success is p and the probability of failure is $q = 1 - p$, where p takes the value 1 if the outcome of a trial is a success and 0 if the outcome is a failure.

Thus, the Bernoulli trials process is characterised by a single parameter p. The most obvious example of Bernoulli trials is coin tossing, where success means head and failure means tail (or one can also term success means tail and failure means head). The parameter p is the probability of getting head. Bernoulli trials are also formed when we draw a sample from a dichotomous population. For example, the objects in the population could be coins with heads and tails occurring, persons of males and females being selected, and so on.

Definition of Probability

If a trial of an experiment results in n possible, exhaustive, mutually exclusive and equally likely ways and of which r ways are favourable to the happening of an event E, then the probability p of the event E is given by:

$$p = P(E) = \frac{Number\ of\ favourable\ ways}{Number\ of\ possible\ ways} = \frac{r}{n}$$

Please note that the word 'exhaustive' means all the possible ways of occurrence, 'mutually exclusive' means each outcome is distinctly different and no overlapping of outcomes, and 'equally likely' means each outcome has the same chance of occurring. In other words, the possible ways are the sample space discussed above.

For example, in throwing a die, the possible ways are $\{1, 2, 3, 4, 5, 6\}$ and so $n = 6$. If the event is the occurrence of 3 then $P(E)$ is $P(3)$. Here, the number of favourable ways is one, that is $\{3\}$ only, and so $r = 1$. Accordingly,

$$p = P(3) = \frac{Number\ of\ favourable\ ways}{Number\ of\ possible\ ways} = \frac{1}{6} = 0.1667$$

Similarly, in tossing a coin, the possible ways are $\{head, tail\}$, $n = 2$. If the event is the occurrence of 'head' then $P(E)$ is $P(head)$ and $r = 1$. So,

$$p = P(head) = \frac{Number\ of\ favourable\ ways}{Number\ of\ possible\ ways} = \frac{1}{2} = 0.5$$

Axioms

Let S be the sample space of a random experiment, and A, B, C, etc., are random events associated with the random experiment. The following axioms will apply. The axioms are also called Kolmogorov axioms, named after the famous Russian mathematician Andrey Kolmogorov.

Axiom 1: The probability of an event A is a non-negative real number, that is, the probability of the event A is $P(A) \geq 0$. Similarly, $P(B) \geq 0$, $P(C) \geq 0$, etc.

Axiom 2: The probability of a certain (sure) event in the sample space is 1. The certain event is the sample space S and its probability is 1, that is, $P(S) = 1$.

Axiom 3: The probability of two or more mutually exclusive events is the sum of the probabilities of the individual events, that is, For two events A and B, $P(A \cup B) = P(A) + P(B)$.

For many events A, B, C, etc., $P(A \cup B \cup C \cup \ldots) = P(A) + P(B) + P(B) + \cdots$

Properties of Probability

The various properties of probability are:

1. The probability of occurrence of an event must be a value between 0 and 1 (both inclusive), that is, $0 \leq P(E) \leq 1$. (From axiom 1)
2. The probability of an impossible event is 0, that is, $P(\text{impossible event}) = 0$.
3. The probability of an absolutely certain event is 1, that is, $P(\text{certain event}) = 1$. (From axiom 2)
4. If $p = P(E)$ is the probability of occurrence of an event then $q = P(\bar{E}) = 1 - p$ is the probability of non-occurrence of the event, that is, $p + q = 1$. In words, the sum of probabilities of occurrence and non-occurrence of an event is equal to 1.
5. The sum of probabilities of all possible mutually exclusive events will add to 1. For example, in throwing a die, the events $\{1, 2, 3, 4, 5, 6\}$ are mutually exclusive events and the probability of occurrence of each event is 1/6 and the total probability is $6 * (1/6) = 1$. (From axioms 2 and 3)

Additive Law or Addition Theorem of Probability

*If two or more events are mutually exclusive then the probability of occurrence of **any one** of them is equal to the sum of the probabilities of occurrence of the individual events.*

The case of two events: If two events are mutually exclusive, then the probability of occurrence of any one of them is the sum of the individual probabilities. If an experiment results in n possible, mutually exclusive and equally likely ways and of which m_1 ways are favourable to the happening of the event E_1, and m_2 ways are favourable to the happening of the event E_2 so that E_1 and E_2 are mutually exclusive, then the probability of occurrence of the event E_1 or E_2 is:

$$P(E_1 \text{ or } E_2) = P(E_1) + P(E_2) = \frac{m_1}{n} + \frac{m_2}{n} = \frac{m_1 + m_2}{n}.$$

The case of r events: Extending the law we can state that, if an experiment results in n possible, mutually exclusive and equally likely ways and, of which, $m_1, m_2, m_3, \ldots, m_r$ ways are favourable to the happening of the mutually exclusive events $E_1, E_2, E_3, \ldots, E_r$, respectively, then the probability of occurrence of any one of them is:

$$P(E_1 \text{ or } E_2 \text{ or } E_3 \text{ or} \ldots \text{or } E_r) = P(E_1) + P(E_2) + P(E_3) + \ldots + P(E_r)$$

$$= \frac{m_1}{n} + \frac{m_2}{n} + \frac{m_3}{n} + \ldots + \frac{m_r}{n}$$

$$= \frac{m_1 + m_2 + m_3 + \ldots + m_r}{n} = \frac{1}{n} \sum_{i=1}^{r} m_i.$$

Note: If $E_1, E_2, E_3, \ldots, E_r$ comprise all the possible mutually exclusive events then $m_1 + m_2 + m_3 + \cdots + m_r = n$ and the probability of occurrence of any one of them is 1.

Example: In a class of eight students with names A, B, C, D, E, F, G and H, what is the probability of selecting the student A or E?

Among the eight students (A, B, C, D, E, F, G and H) selecting one student is possible in eight ways, that is, either A, or B, or C, or D, or E, or F, or G, or H may be selected. Given all students have equal chance of being selected, the probability of selecting a student is $P(1 \text{ student}) = 1/8$. As such the probability of selecting A is $P(A) = 1/8$ and the probability of selecting E is $P(E) = 1/8$. Now selecting A or E is possible in two out of eight ways, that is, $P(A \text{ or } B) = 2/8$.

Alternatively, using the additive law we can get the probability as follows. As selection of A or B among the eight students is mutually exclusive, applying the additive law we get:

$$P(A \text{ or } B) = P(A) + P(B) = (1/8) + (1/8) = 2/8.$$

Multiplicative Law or Multiplication Theorem of Probability

If two or more events are independent then the probability of joint (simultaneous) occurrence of all of them is equal to the product of the probabilities of occurrence of the individual events.

The case of two events: If two events are independent, then the probability of simultaneous occurrence of both of them is the product of the individual probabilities. In an experiment if one trial results in n_1 possible, mutually exclusive and equally likely ways and of which m_1 ways are favourable to the happening of the event E_1 and in an another trial results in n_2 possible, mutually exclusive and equally likely ways and of which m_2 ways are favourable to the happening of the event E_2 so that E_1 and E_2 are independent, then the probability of joint occurrence of the events E_1 and E_2 is:

$$P(E_1 \text{ and } E_2) = P(E_1 E_2) = P(E_1) * P(E_2) = \frac{m_1}{n_1} * \frac{m_2}{n_2} = \frac{m_1 m_2}{n_1 n_2}.$$

The case of r events: Extending the law we can state that in an experiment if r trials result in, respectively, $n_1, n_2, n_3, \ldots, n_r$ possible, mutually exclusive and equally likely ways and, of which, $m_1, m_2, m_3, \ldots, m_r$ ways are favourable to the happening of the events $E_1, E_2, E_3, \ldots, E_r$, then the probability of occurrence of all of them together is:

$$P(E_1 E_2 E_3 \ldots E_r) = P(E_1) * P(E_2) * P(E_3) * \cdots * P(E_r)$$

$$= \frac{m_1}{n_1} * \frac{m_2}{n_2} * \frac{m_3}{n_3} * \ldots * \frac{m_r}{n_r} = \prod_{i=1}^{r} \frac{m_i}{n_i},$$

where $\prod$ (phi) stands for multiplication.

Example: In a class of five students, three are boys with names A, B and C, and the remaining two are girls with names X and Y. Given all students have equal chance, what is the probability of selecting the boy A and the girl X for a programme?

The possible combinations of one boy and one girl are {AX, AY, BX, BY, CX, CY} = 6 ways, and of which the desired combination AX occurs only once and, hence, the probability of selecting the boy A and the girl X is 1/6.

The same can be proved using the multiplicative law as follows.

The probability of selecting the boy A from among the three boys is $P(A) = 1/3$.
The probability of selecting the girl X from among the two girls is $P(X) = 1/2$.
As selecting a boy from among the boys and a girl from among the girls is independent, $P(A \text{ and } X) = P(A) * P(X) = (1/3) * (1/2) = 1/6$.

PROBABILITY DISTRIBUTION

Now let us do an exercise. A coin has two sides; head (H) and tail (T). If we toss two coins at a time, we get any one of the four combinations; head and head, head and tail, tail and head, and tail and tail. Symbolically, let these combinations be HH, HT, TH and TT. Next, let us see what are the chances of getting these combinations? There are four possible combinations and so the chance of getting HH is one out of the four combinations or possibilities with probability ¼. Similarly, the chance of getting HT, TH or TT is ¼. Symbolically:

(1) Probability (HH)=¼=0.25
(2) Probability (HT)=¼=0.25
(3) Probability (TH)=¼=0.25
(4) Probability (TT)=¼=0.25

The items (2) and (3) are the same if our interest is only combination and not permutation (order). So we can combine both the combinations as:

$$\text{Probability (HT or TH)}=¼+¼=2/4=½=0.5.$$

Let us say that our event (variable) is 'number of heads'. The different combinations are 0 heads, 1 head and 2 heads. Alternatively, the same can be defined in terms of 'number of tails' as two tails, one tail and 0 tails, respectively. Rewriting the probability in terms of number of heads, we get the following.

$$\text{Probability (0 heads)}=¼=0.25$$

$$\text{Probability (1 head)}=½=0.50$$

$$\text{Probability (2 heads)}=¼=0.25$$

This is called the *probability distribution* of getting 0, 1 and 2 heads in tossing two coins. Please note that the probabilities of all combinations add to 1.0.

Let us repeat the exercise 100 times. We will get the following distribution. Since each trial is independent, by applying multiplicative law of probability of independent events, we get:

Number of times 0 heads=probability (0 heads) * number of tosses.

That is,   Number of times 0 heads=0.25 * 100=25

Similarly,   Number of times 1 head=0.50 * 100=50

Number of times 2 heads=0.25 * 100=25

This is called expected or *theoretical distribution* of getting number of heads in tossing two coins 100 times. Please note that the total frequencies of all combinations add to the total number of tosses, that is, $25+50+25=100$. The event 'number of heads' in tossing two coins is a discrete variable (x) taking integer values 0, 1 and 2. The mean number of heads in tossing two coins is:

$$\bar{x} = \frac{\sum fx}{n} = \frac{25*0+50*1+25*2}{100} = \frac{0+50+50}{100} = 1,$$

where f stands for frequency and x stands for probability.

So, theoretically we should get a mean of one head if we toss two coins any number of times. Please note that we will get the same value if we use the probability value of tossing two coins once $\{(0.25 * 0+0.50 * 1+0.25 * 2)/1\}=1$, or 1,000 times $\{(250 * 0+500 * 1+250 * 2)/1,000\}=1$ and hence the use of the term 'any number of times'.

Now let us take two coins and practically conduct the tossing exercise for 100 times. Do we really get 25 times 0 heads (two tails), 50 times one head (one head and one tail), and the remaining 25 times two heads (0 tails)? The answer is 'likely' and not 'definitely' but we can say that it would be close to it. Let us assume that we have got the following distribution.

Number of times 0 heads = 21 times

Number of times one head = 46 times

Number of times two heads = 33 times

This is called empirical or *frequency distribution* of getting number of heads in tossing two coins. The mean number of heads is:

$$\bar{x} = \frac{\sum fx}{n} = \frac{22 * 0 + 46 * 1 + 32 * 2}{100} = \frac{0 + 46 + 64}{100} = \frac{110}{100} = 1.1.$$

Now we have two means, one is the theoretical mean and the other is the empirical mean. To distinguish the theoretical mean from the empirical mean, the theoretical mean (also called population mean) is often denoted by the symbol μ (read as *mu*) and the empirical mean (also called sample mean) is denoted by the symbol $\bar{x}$. In our exercise $\mu = 1.0$ and $\bar{x} = 1.1$. In general μ is the value that we get from the theoretical or population distribution and $\bar{x}$ is the value that we get from the sample distribution. Generally, if we repeat the exercise more and more number of times, we will tend to get $\bar{x} = 1.0$.

THEORETICAL DISTRIBUTIONS

What Is a Theoretical Distribution?

A distribution is the description of the 'shape' of the frequent distribution of a batch of measurements (observations). The characteristics of the distribution are often defined in terms of a few descriptors or indices derived from the batch of measurements and these indices are called 'parameters'. A generalised form of a distribution is called a theoretical distribution. A theoretical distribution can serve as the basis for standardised comparison of empirical distribution of observations and help us to test hypothesis and to estimate confidence intervals for inferential statistics. It also forms the basis for the application of appropriate statistical methods to empirical data.

BINOMIAL DISTRIBUTION

A random experiment is performed repeatedly a large number of times with each trail having two (binary) outcomes, say, 'success' for the occurrence of an event and 'failure' for the non-occurrence of an event. Let the number of trials be n, the probability of success be p and the probability of failure be $q = 1 - p$. The probability of r successes and $n - r$ failures in the n independent trials, according to the multiplicative law of probability, is given as follows.

One combination be {SSS ... r times, FFFF ... $n-r$ times} where S stands for a success and F stands for a failure. When $r = 0$, the combination is {FFF ... n times} and when $r = n$, the combination is {SSS ... n times} but when $r > 0$ and $r < n$ (i.e., $0 < r < n$), the combination is not one but many while taking into account the order of trails. For example, when $r = 1$ the combinations are (in the order of trials) {S, FFF ... $n-1$ times}, {F, S, FFF ... $n-2$ times}, etc., and there will be n ways. In general, the number of combinations of n things taken r at a time is:

$$\binom{n}{r} = \frac{n!}{r!(n-r)!}$$

(please see Appendix A at the end of this book for more details on permutations and combinations).

Of these, according to the multiplicative law, the probability of one combination of r successes and $n-r$ failures is:

$P(r$ successes and $n-r$ failures$) = [p * p * p \dots (r$ times$)] * [q * q * q \dots (n-r$ times$)]$

$$= p^r * q^{n-r}.$$

Hence, the probability of r successes in n trials in any order (i.e., for $\binom{n}{r}$ combinations), according to the additive law of probability, is

$$P(r \text{ success and } (n-r) \text{ failures}) = \binom{n}{r} p^r q^{n-r} \quad (\text{or}) \quad {}^nC_r\, p^r q^{n-r}.$$

The Binomial probability distribution is often expressed as

$$P(x = r) = P(r) = P(r; n, p) = P(n, p) = \binom{n}{r} p^r q^{n-r}.$$

Please note the different ways of expressing the binomial distribution. In the format $P(x=r)$, x is the variable and r is the event to occur, that is, among the many possible values of x, the value r is one. In the format $P(r)$, x is implicit and not written. In the format $P(r; n, p)$, x is implicit, r is the event, and n and p are parameters of the binomial distribution. In the format $P(n, p)$, both x and r are implicit and only the parameters are specified (it is the format often used in many statistical textbooks to refer theoretical distributions). Otherwise all the four formats mean the same.

The probability of number of successes and failures so obtained is called *binomial probability distribution*. The binomial distribution was first discovered by James Bernoulli in the year 1700 and published posthumously in 1713. The binomial probability distribution carries the name 'binomial' because it is based on *bi* (two) outcomes, namely, success and failure.

Properties of Binomial Distribution

A binomial probability distribution has the following properties:

1. The experiment consists of a number of (n) repeated trials.
2. Each trial has two possible outcomes termed success and failure, with probabilities p and q, respectively.
3. The number of successes r ($r=0, 1, 2,\dots, n$) is called a binomial random variable and $P(r)$ gives the probability of r successes in n trials.
4. Binomial distribution is a discrete probability distribution as the variable r takes only integer values (and not fractional values).
5. The mean value of the binomial distribution is the expected number of successes in n trials and is given by $E(r) = \mu = np$.
6. The variance of the binomial distribution is $V(r) - \sigma^2 = npq$.
7. In a binomial distribution, the parameters n and p are needed (required) and sufficient (enough) to determine the probability distribution.

Example: In an experiment, 10 coins are tossed simultaneously a number of times. Find out the probability of occurrence of 0, 1, 2,..., 10 heads assuming that the coins are unbiased and also biased in various degrees. Also plot the probabilities in a graph and analyse the pattern.

In this example, number of trials (coins) is $n = 10$ and the possible occurrence of number of heads is $r = 0, 1, 2,..., 10$. The probability of occurrence of a head in tossing a single unbiased coin is $p = 0.5$. If the coin is biased, the probability of occurrence of a head in tossing a coin (p) can be less than or greater than 0.5. Let us consider four different probabilities, say, 0.2, 0.3, 0.7 and 0.8.

The probabilities of occurrence of number of heads $r = 0, 1, 2,..., 10$ are given in Table 6.1 and Figure 6.1. It is to be noted that the probabilities can easily be obtained using the Excel function 'BINOMDIST(number_s, trials, probability_s, cumulative)'. In this function, number_s = r, trials = n, probability_s = p, cumulative = 1 (or TRUE) if cumulative probability is required and 0 if not required.

Table 6.1 Binomial Probability Distribution

$n =$	10	10	10	10	10
$p =$	0.2	0.3	0.5	0.7	0.8
r	$P(r)$	$P(r)$	$P(r)$	$P(r)$	$P(r)$
0	0.1074	0.0282	0.0010	0.0000	0.0000
1	0.2684	0.1211	0.0098	0.0001	0.0000
2	0.3020	0.2335	0.0439	0.0014	0.0001
3	0.2013	0.2668	0.1172	0.0090	0.0008
4	0.0881	0.2001	0.2051	0.0368	0.0055
5	0.0264	0.1029	0.2461	0.1029	0.0264
6	0.0055	0.0368	0.2051	0.2001	0.0881
7	0.0008	0.0090	0.1172	0.2668	0.2013
8	0.0001	0.0014	0.0439	0.2335	0.3020
9	0.0000	0.0001	0.0098	0.1211	0.2684
10	0.0000	0.0000	0.0010	0.0282	0.1074
Total	1.0000	1.0000	1.0000	1.0000	1.0000

Figure 6.1 Binomial Probability Distribution ($n = 10$)

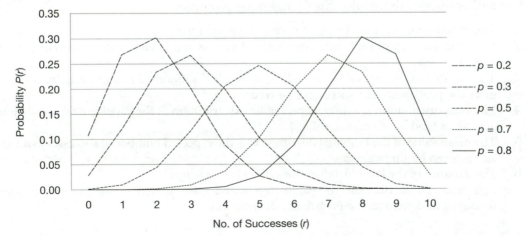

It is clear from Figure 6.1 that with $p=0.5$, the probability distribution is symmetric at $r=5$ (i.e., at half of n), for the values of $p<0.5$, the distribution is skewed to the right and for the values of $p>0.5$, the distribution is skewed to the left. It is to be noted that the probability distribution is the same for $p=0.2$ and $p=0.8$ ($0.8=1.0-0.2$) and for $p=0.3$ and $p=0.7$ ($0.7=1.0-0.3$) but the distribution is in the reverse direction ($r=10, 9, 8,\ldots, 1, 0$) and accordingly the chart is also reversed with the skewness towards left. This shows that the binomial distribution is the same for both p and q ($=1-p$).

POISSON DISTRIBUTION

In binomial distribution we have a sample of definite size n and we know the number of 'successes' and 'failures', that is the probability of success p. However, we come across situations where the sample size is very large or even indeterminate and the number of successes or failures is very small (i.e., p or q is close to 0). Examples of this situation are road accidents, maternal deaths, infant deaths, suicides, mental retardation, etc. In such cases, we are dealing with rare or isolated events in a continuum of space (say, area, distance or time). What we can do is divide the interval (time, distance, area, volume) into very small sections and calculate the mean number of occurrences in the interval. This gives rise to the Poisson distribution.

Poisson distribution (or Poisson law of small numbers) is a discrete probability distribution that expresses the probability of a given number of events occurring in a fixed interval (of time, distance, area, volume, etc.) if these events occur with a known average rate and independently of the time since the last event. In other words, Poisson distribution enables us to determine the probability of, say, r events to occur during a specified interval (of time, distance, area and volume) if the average occurrence, say, λ is known under the condition that the events are independent of the specified interval since the last event occurred. The distribution was first introduced by Siméon Denis Poisson and published with his probability theory in 1838.

If the expected number of occurrences in an interval is λ, then the probability that there are exactly r occurrences (r being a non-negative integer, i.e., $r=0, 1, 2,\ldots$) is equal to

$$P(x=r)=P(r)=P(r,\lambda)=\frac{\lambda^r e^\lambda}{r!},$$

where e is the base of the natural logarithm ($e=2.71828\ldots$), r is the number of occurrences of an event, $r!$ is the factorial of r, and λ is the expected number of occurrences during the given interval (a positive real number). For example, if an event occurs on average four times a minute, and one is interested in the probability of the event occurring r times in an interval of 10 minutes, one would use a Poisson distribution as the model with $\lambda=10*4=40$. The Poisson distribution is applied to systems with a large number of possible events (sample events), each of which is rare.

The Poisson distribution can be derived as a limiting case of the binomial distribution under the following conditions.

1. The number of trials, n, is indefinitely large, that is, $n\to\infty$ (to be read as, n tends to infinity).
2. The constant probability of success for each trial, p, is indefinitely small, that is, $p\to 0$.
3. So that, $np=\lambda$ (λ to be read as lambda) is a finite positive real number. Thus, $p=\lambda/n$ and $q=1-\lambda/n$.

Properties of Poisson Distribution

A Poisson probability distribution has the following properties:

1. Unlike Binomial distribution, Poisson distribution does do not occur as outcomes of a definite number of trials of an experiment but occurs at random points of time and space wherein our interest is in the number of occurrences and not in non-occurrences.
2. Poisson distribution is a discrete probability distribution as the numbers of occurrences are integer values (and not fractional values).
3. The mean value (mean number of occurrences) of the Poisson distribution is $\mu=\lambda$.
4. The variance of the Poisson distribution is $\sigma^2=\lambda$, that is, $\mu=\sigma^2=\lambda$. Thus, the number of outcomes fluctuates about its mean λ with a standard deviation $\sigma = \sqrt{\lambda}$. This fluctuation is often called *Poisson noise* or simply noise and it is commonly used in electronics.
5. The Poisson distribution may be applied in situations of occurrence of rare events such as death due to specific diseases, number of suicides in a specified area, number of air accidents, etc.

Example: The following table gives the number of road accidents per day during a one year period. Check if the data follows a Poisson distribution and if so, what is the expected distribution of accidents?

No. of accidents per day	0	1	2	3	4	5	6	Total
No. of days of accident	130	120	95	12	4	3	1	365

For the above frequency distribution, the mean $\mu=1.049$ and variance $\sigma^2=1.044$ (please apply mean and variance to the above distribution as demonstrated in Chapter 5 on central tendency and dispersion). It is clear that the mean and variance are close to each other (almost the same) with a percentage difference of $[100 * (1.049-1.44)/1.049] = 0.5$ percent (<1 percent) only. A Poisson distribution implies that its mean=variance=λ, that is, for a Poisson distribution its mean and variance are the same. In this example also the mean and variance are almost the same. So, it is appropriate to consider (assume) that the given distribution of accidents follows a Poisson distribution.

So, we can calculate Poisson probabilities and fit a probability model to the dataset and the output is given in Table 6.2. In the table, the columns r and f contain the given data. The column $P(r)$ gives Poisson probabilities based on the Excel function POISSON.DIST$(r, \lambda, FALSE)$, in which, r takes the values 0–6, $\lambda=\mu=1.049$ and 'FALSE' is an option to instruct the function

Table 6.2   Poisson Probabilities Exercise

No. of Accidents per Day	No. of Days of Accident	Probability of Event r	Expected Frequency
r	f	P(r)	N*P(r)
0	130	0.35	127.9
1	120	0.37	134.1
2	95	0.19	70.3
3	12	0.07	24.6
4	4	0.02	6.5
5	3	0.00	1.4
6	1	0.00	0.2
Total (N)	365	1.00	365.0

Figure 6.2   Observed and Expected Accidents in One Year

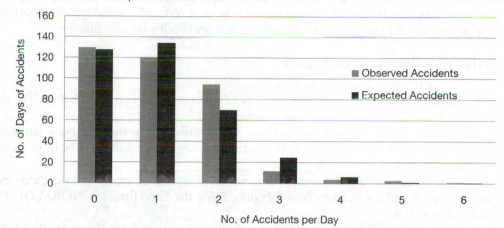

to output probability and not cumulative probability. Please note that the function name is POISSON in the older versions of the MS Excel program. The observed and expected number of days by the number of accidents per day is also given in Table 6.2 and Figure 6.2.

We can use chi-square goodness-of-fit test to test if the Poisson model is a significant (appropriate or adequate) fit to the given data, and it is covered in Chapter 7. But the real-life application is the other way round. For example, we have the data on road accidents for a number of years and it was found that the accident rate was substantially higher than the prescribed level. Please note that the accidents rate is the mean $\lambda = \mu$ (average road accidents per day) and is based on the experiences in the last few years. As the government considered that the accidents rate is substantial (or higher than the prescribed level), it took a number of steps (measures) to contain the accidents. After implementing the measures for the last one year or more, we have the data for the recent one year. Now our problem is to check if the accidents have significantly (or substantially) decreased due to the measures taken by the government. As accidents are rare events, we apply Poisson theory to obtain estimated accidents and use the chi-square test of significance to see if the accidents have significantly reduced after the implementation of the measures. For the test procedure, please see Chapter 7.

NORMAL DISTRIBUTION

Normal distribution is a continuous probability distribution with a bell-shaped curve and its tails stretch infinitely in both the directions. The distribution is symmetric on both sides from its mean (μ), its maximum frequency (height of the distribution or curve) is again at μ and its point of inflection is at its standard deviation (σ). A normal distribution is described by its mean (μ) and standard deviation (σ), and these two indices are the *parameters* of normal distribution and they define the normal distribution completely. As the normal distribution is bell-shaped at its mean, the mean, median and mode of a normal distribution coincide, that is, all have the same numerical value.

The normal distribution is described by the equation:

$$P(x) = f(x) = N(\mu, \sigma^2) = \frac{1}{\sigma\sqrt{2\pi}} e^{\left(\frac{(x-\mu)^2}{2\sigma^2}\right)}.$$

Please note that $f(x)$ is a general notation to refer to a function (equation), $P(x)$ is a general notation to refer to a probability distribution (function) and $N(\mu, \sigma^2)$ is the specific notation to refer to a normal distribution, more specifically, normal probability density function.

Properties of a Normal Distribution

The normal curve is symmetrical about its mean μ.

The vertical line from the mean divides the area of the curve into two equal halves. The total area of the curve is equal to 1 (the total sample space).

The normal curve is completely determined and also described by its mean and standard deviation, that is, in a normal distribution, only two parameters are required to describe it: its mean μ and its standard deviation σ.

The shape of the normal distribution for different combination of means and standard deviations ($\mu = 5$ and $\mu = 8$ and $\sigma = 1$ and $\sigma = 2$), as obtained using the Excel function 'NORM.DIST', is presented in Figure 6.3.

It is clear from Figure 6.3 that (a) the shape of all normal curves are symmetric from their respective means, (b) for a given SD, as the mean increases the curve only shifts to the right without changing its shape, (c) for a given mean, as the SD increases the shape of the curve flattens without changing its position, (d) though it appears that the curve touches the x-axis, in reality it never touches it (though its value tends to reach zero) and (e) for a given mean and SD, the normal distribution is uniquely determined.

In Figures 6.4 and 6.5, the mean – SD and mean + SD locations are marked. It can be shown by using the Excel function 'NORM.DIST' that the area of the normal curve from $(\mu - 1\sigma)$ to $(\mu + 1\sigma)$ is 68.3 percent of the total area, the area from $(\mu - 2\sigma)$ to $(\mu + 2\sigma)$ is 95.4 percent and the area from $(\mu - 3\sigma)$ to $(\mu + 3\sigma)$ is 99.7 percent. The calculations are presented in Table 6.3 and how to use the Excel function is described later in this chapter.

THE STANDARD NORMAL DISTRIBUTION

We have seen from the figures earlier that the shape of the normal curve is unaffected by its mean and the location of the curve is unaffected by its SD. We have also seen under Chapter 5 that the

Figure 6.3 Normal Distribution with Mean=5 and 8 and SD=1 and 2

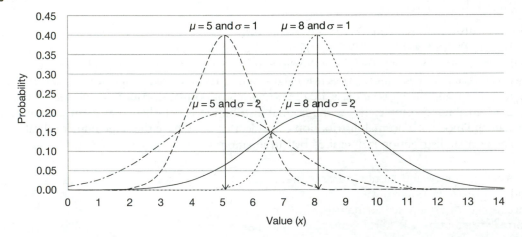

Figure 6.4   Normal Distribution with Mean=5 and SD=1

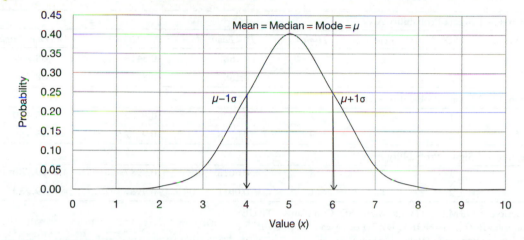

Figure 6.5   Normal Distribution with Mean=5 and SD=2

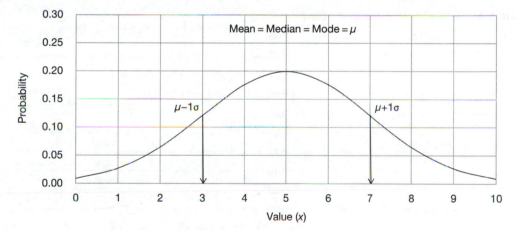

magnitude of the SD depends on the magnitude of the mean and that is why we have considered the index 'coefficient of variation'. So, for the application of the normal distribution under varying units of measurements, a standard format is of great help. Accordingly, a standard normal variate (variable) and a standard normal distribution can be defined if we create a new variable, say Z, from the original variable X using the mean and SD, namely, $Z = \dfrac{X - \mu}{\sigma}$ (called standard normal variate), and then the normal distribution becomes the standard normal distribution and its probability density function is:

$$f(z) = N(0,1) = \frac{1}{\sqrt{2\pi}} e^{\left(\frac{-z^2}{2}\right)}.$$

As such, for a standard normal distribution (see Figure 6.6), the mean is always zero ($\mu=0$) and standard deviation is always 1 ($\sigma=1$), and that is why the variable Z is called standard normal variate and the standard normal distribution is denoted as $N(0,1)$. It is clear that a standard normal distribution is free from unit of measurement, symmetric from the mean zero, takes values

Table 6.3 Normal Probability Calculation

Mean +/- 1 Sigma Probability Area						
Mean	*SD*	*Low*	*High*	*P(<Low)*	*P(<High)*	*%P(Low–High)*
5	1	4	6	0.1587	0.8413	**68.269**
5	2	3	7	0.1587	0.8413	**68.269**
Mean +/- 2 Sigma Probability Area						
5	1	3	7	0.0228	0.9772	**95.450**
5	2	1	9	0.0228	0.9772	**95.450**
Mean +/- 3 Sigma Probability Area						
5	1	2	8	0.0013	0.9987	**99.730**
5	2	-1	11	0.0013	0.9987	**99.730**

Function: NORM.DIST(Value, Mean, SD, Cumulative=TRUE)
Example: $P(<Low)$=NORM.DIST(Low, Mean, SD, TRUE)
$\%P(Low–High)=P(<High)–P(<Low)$

Figure 6.6 Standard Normal Probability Curve

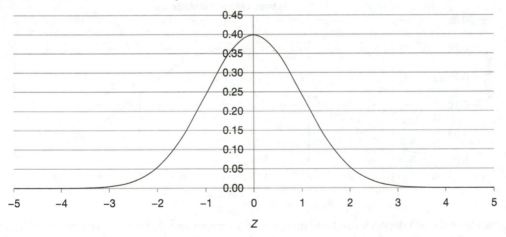

from $-\infty$ to $+\infty$ (minus infinity to plus infinity) and the area of the curve from -3 to $+3$ is 99.7 percent. In other words, according to the normal curve probability density function, 95 percent of the data will fall within 1.96 (or, approximately and conveniently 2) standard deviations (from the mean), and 99 percent of the data will fall within 2.58 standard deviations (from the mean). These are basic concepts used in hypothesis testing and determining confidence intervals discussed in Chapter 7. For a standard normal distribution, the values of skewness and kurtosis are zero.

CENTRAL LIMIT THEOREM

The central limit theorem states that given a distribution with mean μ and variance σ^2, the sampling distribution (see the next chapter for a description) of the means approaches a normal distribution with a mean (μ) and a variance σ^2/n, as the sample size n (of each sample) increases. It is important to note that according to the central limit theorem, the *sampling distribution of the mean* approaches a normal distribution as the sample size *n* increases, no matter what the shape of the original distribution is. In a sampling distribution, the number of samples is assumed to be infinite and for most distributions, a normal distribution is approached very quickly as *n* increases. In general, the central limit theorem implies that the distribution of an 'average' tends to be normal as the sample size increases even if the distribution from which the average computed is not a normal distribution.

Because of the properties of the central limit theorem, the normal distribution is often used to describe random variables, especially those having symmetrical, unimodal distributions. However, in many cases, the normal distribution is only a rough approximation of the actual distribution. For example, the income distribution of households is skewed with a few households having a very high income and many households having a small income. But we assume that the deviation is negligible or within acceptable limits, and allow one to solve problems by assuming a normal distribution.

Example: Based on a census conducted in a district, the average number of members per household is 5 with a standard deviation of 2. If you are conducting a sample survey in this district, what percentage of households do you expect will have three or less number of members and what percentage of households will have eight or more number of members, if the household size is assumed to be normally distributed?

Based on normal probability distribution, we have the *Z* table that gives the probability for a given value of *Z* and vice versa (presented at the end of this book, see Tables D.1 and D.2). Alternatively, we can also get the values using the Excel function 'NORM.DIST'. The procedure is explained here.

Normal Probability Calculation Using Excel Function

=NORM.DIST(

NORM.DIST(**x**, mean, standard_dev, cumulative)

Open MS Excel and type the function in a cell '=NORM.DIST ('and soon you will see the display as follows (it may differ from version to version). In the display enter the values, *x* means the value for which probability is required (here 3 in the first case), mean=5, standard_dev=2, cumulative=TRUE (because we want the probability from lowest to 3) and press enter. The value 0.158655 is pasted in the cell and it means that 15.86 (or 16) percent of the households are expected to have each three or less number of members per household. Similarly, NORM.DIST(7.99,5,2,TRUE)=0.932543 and the probability that the household size is 8 or more is 1−0.932543=0.067457 or 6.7 percent or nearly 7 percent. That is, about 16 percent of households are expected to have each three or less members per household and 7 percent of the households are expected to have each eight or more members per household.

Normal Probability Calculation Using Z Table

First, convert *X* values into *Z* values using the transformation $Z = \dfrac{X - \mu}{\sigma}$.

If X=3, then Z=(3−5)/2=−0.1 and CuProb(−0.1)=0.15866 (from *Z* table).

If X=7.99, then Z=(7.99−5)/2=1.495. The value 1.495 falls in-between 1.49 and 1.50 and so we will obtain the probabilities for these two values and take the average as the probability value for 1.495. CuProb(1.5)=0.93319 and CuProb(1.49)=0.93189 (from *Z* table) and CuProb(1.495)=(0.93319+0.93189)/2=0.93254. Rest of the calculations are as above. It is to be noted that for simplicity we would have obtained the probability for Z=8 instead of Z=7.99 and it would have made only a negligible difference.

CHAPTER 7

Testing of Hypothesis

We are aware that different samples drawn from a population would yield different values for an index, say, mean. In this case, we are confused as to which value of the index is appropriate and to be adopted, and which values to be discarded. Further, it is often not possible to draw different samples to see the variation or consistency of the values of the index. In almost all cases, we draw only one sample, and we derive the index based on that. As such, we come across the question of sampling fluctuations in the estimation of the index for the population based on one-sample. Further, we are also often faced with the problem of deciding whether the index (say mean) derived based on a sample, that is slightly different from an expected value, is to be considered equal to, same as, or acceptable to the expected value, with the assumption that the small difference is attributable to sampling fluctuations. Another, but similar, problem would be: Can the indices for two subgroups, say males and females, of a sample be assumed to be the same even if there is a small difference, assuming that the difference might have occurred due to sampling fluctuations? So, when we are unable to take a decision as to whether two values have come from the same population or not, we apply statistical principles to take a decision. The statistical principles followed in the decision-making process are called *testing of statistical significance* or *testing of hypothesis*.

CERTAIN CONCEPTS AND DEFINITIONS

Before we go in to testing of hypothesis, we need to understand a few terms and concepts related to hypothesis testing.

Sampling Distribution

We have seen in the chapter on 'Measures of Central Tendency and Dispersion' that, for a sample of n observations $x_1, x_2, \ldots, x_n$, the mean is $\bar{x} = (x_1 + x_2 + x_3 + \cdots + x_n)/n$. Let us draw a number of such samples with n observations each and calculate their means. The mean values may differ from sample to sample and, they be denoted as $\bar{x}_1, \bar{x}_2, \bar{x}_3$, etc. Now, let us assume that these mean values are the observations of a sample, then the resulting distribution of the sample means $\bar{x}_1, \bar{x}_2, \bar{x}_3$, etc. is called the sampling distribution of means. Similarly, we can also calculate the standard deviations (SDs) for each sample and call the distribution of the sample SDs as the sampling distribution of SDs. In general, we can calculate an index (like mean and SD) for each sample and the values of the index for a number of samples is called the sampling distribution of the index.

Standard Error

Generally, different samples of the same size drawn from the same population would give different values for the statistic under consideration. We have seen in the previous chapter that in tossing two coins 100 times, we expect zero heads 25 times, one heads 50 times and two heads 25 times, but a practical exercise resulted in zero heads 21 times, one heads 46 times and two heads 33 times, with a mean of 1.1 heads. Let us have another exercise, and in that, the number of times zero heads is 20, one head is 50 and two heads is 30, and the mean is $(20*0 + 65*1 + 15*2)/100 = 0.9$. That is, the values of the mean may differ from exercise to exercise (or, in general, sample to sample) and the differences being due to sampling fluctuations, provided the sampling procedure is the same for each sample. Now, considering the means have been obtained from different samples as observations (i.e., the observations are 1.1, 0.9, ...), we can calculate the mean and the SD for these observations (mean values). The SD so obtained is called the standard error (SE) of the sample mean in estimating the population mean. In general, SE is the SD of the sample statistic (mean, correlation coefficient, etc.) for repeated samples drawn from the same population with the same sampling procedure. In practice, we do not select different samples but obtain the SE based on the single sample, which is used in hypothesis testing (see later in this chapter).

Confidence Interval

When repeated samples are drawn from a population, approximately 95 percent of the sample means likely lie within two times the SE of the population mean if the sample means are normally distributed. That is, there is 95 percent probability that the population mean will lie within the limit of sample mean $\pm 2*SE$. This is called 95 percent confidence interval (CI). For example, if the mean children ever born is 3.0 and the SE is 0.2, then the 95 percent CI of mean children ever born in the population lies in the interval $(3.0 - 2*0.2$ to $3.0 + 2*0.2)$ or $(2.6$ to $3.4)$. That is, when the mean number of children born per woman obtained from the sample is 3 with an SE of 0.2, we can be 95 percent confident that the mean number of children born per woman in the population would be in the range 2.6–3.4, provided the assumption that the sample is drawn at random is true. The estimation of population parameter in the exact value (here 3.0) is called *point estimation*, and the estimation of population parameter in range values (here, 2.6–3.4) is called *interval estimation*. Please note that still there is a 5 percent chance that the mean number of children born per woman in the population may be less than 2.6, or more than 3.4. That is, in statistics, we are never 100 percent confident or sure and always leave or provide a margin for error.

Null Hypothesis and Alternate Hypothesis

A hypothesis is a statement about a *population* (*parameter*) and not about a *sample* (*statistic*). For example, the occurrence of suicide is more among small farmers than among farmers with large holdings. For applying the test of significance, we first have to set up a hypothesis, that is, a statement about the population parameter. In hypothesis testing, we frame two hypothesises: one is opposite of the other, and are called null hypothesis and alternate hypothesis. A null hypothesis is a hypothesis of *no difference* and is usually denoted by the symbol H_0. For example, the statement H_0: Boys and girls do not differ in their nutritional status (or) the nutritional status of boys and girls is the same, is a null hypothesis. The complementary hypothesis to the null hypothesis (opposite of null hypothesis) is often called alternate hypothesis and it is denoted by the symbol H_1. For example, the statement H_1: Boys and girls differ in their nutritional status (or) the nutritional status of boys and girls is not the same (i.e., different), is the alternate hypothesis to the above null hypothesis. Please note that we can also set the null hypothesis as H_0: The nutritional status of girls is not different from that of boys (a hypothesis of no difference) and the alternate hypothesis as H_1: The nutritional status of girls is poorer than that of boys (one-sided difference). In hypothesis testing, the null hypothesis is tested for possible rejection under the assumption that it is true. The alternate hypothesis is accepted if the null hypothesis is rejected.

Type I and Type II Errors

The main purpose of sampling is to draw inferences about the population and predict the population parameters based on the sample statistics. In practice, as discussed above, we decide to accept or reject the null hypothesis after examining the sample(s). Although we make our decisions based on some statistical principles (such as the assumption that the distribution is normal), still sometimes, our decisions might go wrong. The wrong decisions (called errors) that we may commit to are of two types: (a) rejecting the null hypothesis when it is true and (b) accepting the null hypothesis when it is false. These two errors are respectively called type I and type II errors.

Type I Error: Rejecting H_0 when it is true. Also called alpha (α) error.
That is, accepting H_1 when H_0 is true.

Type II Error: Accepting H_0 when it is false. Also called beta (β) error.
That is, accepting H_0 when H_1 is true.

In practice, type I error amounts to rejecting the sample when it is actually a representative sample from the population, and type II error amounts to accepting the sample when it is not adequate to represent the population. Although committing some errors by chance (and not by choice) is unavoidable, in any investigation, we need to ensure that the chance errors are at a minimum level. In testing of hypothesis, we often set the α level at a low value, usually at 0.05 or 5 percent. That is, the probability of rejecting the null hypothesis when it is true is 0.05 or less (α level 5 percent, confidence level 95 percent). Sometimes the α level is set at a value as low as 0.01 or 1 percent (i.e., the chances of the decision being wrong, or rejecting H_0 when it is true, is lesser and, hence, the confidence on the decision is higher at 99 percent). We can also set the α level as high as 0.1 or 10 percent (i.e., the chances of the decision being wrong are higher and, hence, the confidence in the decision is lesser at 90 percent). It is clear that the lower the α level, the higher the confidence in the decision of accepting or rejecting the null hypothesis.

Sometimes, the type I error is also called *producer's risk* and the type II error is called the *consumer's risk*, because in the former case, rejection of a good quality product is a loss for the producer, while in the latter case, accepting a bad quality product is a loss for the consumer. The type I and type II errors need not be the same (equal), and they may be set at different levels. For example, the decision to accept a job in Mumbai city may be governed by the reputation of the institution, promotion opportunities and a very high salary offered, while a decision to reject the job may be due to the dislike of city life, housing problems, family problems and the like. So, they are somewhat like *push* and *pull* factors.

Let us quantify or measure the probability (P) of committing these errors.

$$P\{\text{Rejecting } H_0 \text{ when it is true}\} = \alpha$$

$$P\{\text{Accepting } H_0 \text{ when it is false}\} = \beta$$

In testing of hypothesis, we apply the type I error strategy. That is, we will try to reject the null hypothesis H_0. While taking a decision to reject H_0, we estimate the amount of error (α) we are committing in taking this decision. If the error is smaller than a predetermined (prefixed) small quantity (say 10 percent, 5 percent or 1 percent, often denoted by α_0), then we will confirm our decision and reject H_0; otherwise we will accept H_0. Often, the α value is called the *significance level*. With regard to β, the value $1 - \beta$ is called the *power* or *statistical power* of the test and is not in common use (though used often by statisticians); hence, it is not further described in this book.

Two-tailed and One-tailed Tests

For a one-sample test, let $\bar{x}$ be the mean of a sample of size n and the corresponding population value estimated be a. (That is, $\mu=a$, please note the difference: μ is the *expected* population value and a is the *estimated* population value based on the sample value, here $\bar{x}$. All the three values may be the same or different.) It is to be noted that an estimate of population mean is the sample mean itself (that is, $a = \bar{x}$), but it need not be the case for all indices and that is why 'a' is used here as a general case instead of $\bar{x}$. For a two-sided test, the null hypothesis of no difference is stated as H_0: $\mu=a$. The alternate hypothesis is H_1: $\mu \neq a$. It is to be noted that $\mu \neq a$ means that either $\mu > a$ or $\mu < a$, and not $\mu=a$, and that is the meaning of the two-tailed test. A two-tailed test is also called a two-sided test or a non-directional test and a one-tailed test is called a one-sided test or a directional test.

We have already seen under the 'type I and type II errors' that $P\{$rejecting H_0 when it is true$\}=\alpha$. That is, $P\{Z< -Z_0$ or $Z > +Z_0\}=\alpha$, where Z_0 is the Z value corresponding to the α value under the standard normal variate. In a two-tailed test, the α value is equally divided into two parts: $P\{Z< -Z_0\}=\alpha/2$ and $P\{Z> +Z_0\}=\alpha/2$. It is to be noted that when $\alpha=0.05$, $\alpha/2=0.025$ or 2.5 percent as shown in Figure 7.1. Also, please note that the 2.5 percent area corresponds to the x-axis value (Z value) -1.96 on the left and $+1.96$ on the right (close to -2 and $+2$, respectively) as shown in Figure 7.1. So, in a two-tailed test, for the null hypothesis to be true and accepted, the calculated α value (also called the significance level) needs to be greater than the prefixed value (often 0.05). Alternatively, to reject H_0 the calculated α value needs to be less than the prefixed value. Please note that if a test statistic is significant at a particular level of significance with a two-tailed test, it goes without saying that the test statistic is automatically significant at that level of significance with a one-tailed test.

In common language, it is the matter of a negative decision and the amount of opposition to the decision. The negative decision is 'to reject the null hypothesis' and the amount of opposition is 'the error committed', the α value. It is natural that for any decision there would be some opposition from some sections of the stakeholders, and the defendable (tolerable or ignorable) amount of opposition (in rejecting the null hypothesis) is the α_0 level (type I error or critical region). If the amount of opposition (rejection error, α) is within the defendable amount (the α_0 level), then go on to reject the null hypothesis, and if the amount of opposition is higher than the defendable amount, then drop the decision to reject the null hypothesis, that is, accept the null hypothesis.

Figure 7.1 Two-tailed Test α Regions

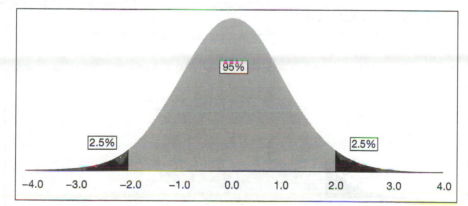

In the same way, in hypothesis testing, for a two-tailed test, if the α value is greater than the prefixed value (say 0.05), the null hypothesis is accepted and the alternate hypothesis is rejected. Alternatively, we may also calculate the Z value and if it is within ± 1.96 (corresponding to $\alpha=0.05$), then the null hypothesis is accepted, else rejected. It is to be noted that for $\alpha=0.1$, $Z=1.65$, the significance level is 10 percent and the confidence level is 90 percent. Similarly, for $\alpha=0.01$, $Z=2.58$, the significance level is 1 percent and the confidence level is 99 percent.

For a one-tailed test, if the research problem is to test if $\bar{x} \le a$, then the null hypothesis is $H_0: \mu \le a$ and the alternate hypothesis is $H_1: \mu > a$. Similarly, if the research problem is to test if $\bar{x} \ge a$, then the null hypothesis is $H_0: \mu \ge a$ and the alternate hypothesis is $H_1: \mu < a$. It is to be noted that the decision as to whether to apply two-tailed test or one-tailed test, and if one-tailed test, whether the null hypothesis is $H_0: \mu \le a$ or $H_0: \mu \ge a$ depends on the research problem and is not taken arbitrarily.

In a one-tailed test, the α value is not divided into two parts, but is kept as a single part, either as $P\{Z<Z_0\}=\alpha$ or $P\{Z>Z_0\}=\alpha$, as appropriate for the null hypothesis. The one-tailed $\alpha=0.05$ (5 percent) area of the standard normal variate corresponds to the x-axis value $Z_0=-1.65$ on the left tail end (as shown in Figure 7.2) or $Z_0=1.65$ on the right tail end. Similarly, for $\alpha=0.01$, the 1 percent area on one side of the standard normal variate corresponds to the x-axis value $Z_0=-2.33$ on the left tail end or $Z_0=2.33$ on the right tail end. So, it is clear that the area on one side of $\alpha=0.1$ for a two-tailed test is equivalent to $\alpha=0.05$ for a one-tailed test. That is, the significance level (α) of a one-tailed test is just half of the significance level of a two-tailed test.

Some software programs output the significant levels for both one-tailed and two-tailed tests, irrespective of whether we have asked for it or not, and we have to choose the one we want. At the same time, some other programs, including SPSS, output the significant level for a two-tailed test only. In the latter case, if the hypothesis is one-tailed, we have to manually divide the output (two-tailed) significance value by 2, and let the new value be α_1 (if the output value of α is 0.08, α_1 is 0.08/2=0.04). Now, if $\alpha_1<0.05$, then reject the null hypothesis at 5 percent level of significance, else accept it.

For a two-sample test, let $\bar{x}_1$ and $\bar{x}_2$ be the means of the two-samples of sizes n_1 and n_2 drawn from two different populations (two subgroups of the same population), and their respective population estimates be μ_1 and μ_2. For a two-tailed test, the null hypothesis is $H_0: \mu_1=\mu_2$ and the alternate hypothesis is $H_1: \mu_1 \ne \mu_2$. For a one-tailed test to examine $\bar{x}_1 \le \bar{x}_2$, the null hypothesis is $H_0: \mu_1 \le \mu_2$ and the alternate hypothesis is $H_1: \mu_1>\mu_2$. Similarly, to examine $\bar{x}_1 \ge \bar{x}_2$, the null hypothesis is $H_0: \mu_1 \ge \mu_2$ and the alternate hypothesis is $H_1: \mu_1<\mu_2$.

Figure 7.2   One-tailed Test α Regions (Left)

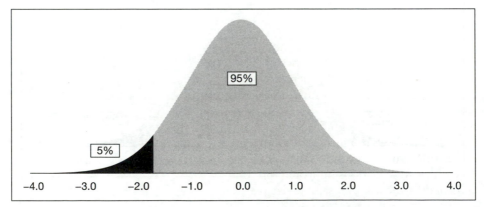

Significance Levels

Let us begin with an example. Let the population proportion be 0.75 (or 75 percent) and let us see what happens if the sample proportion deviates on either side of the population value of 75 percent. Let the estimates of population proportion based on different samples of size 200 each be 66 percent, 68 percent, 70 percent, 72 percent, 78 percent, 80 percent, 82 percent and 84 percent as shown by the following data. The t and α values obtained based on the one-tailed test are also presented (calculation part deferred for the time being).

Estimate p (%)	66.0	68.0	70.0	72.0	78.0	80.0	82.0	84.0
t value	2.680	2.117	1.539	0.943	0.943	1.539	2.117	2.680
α level	0.011	0.042	0.122	0.256	0.256	0.122	0.042	0.011

For the population estimate of 72 percent, the calculated t value of 0.943 is (much) less than the value of 1.65 at the 5 percent level of significance with one-tailed test ($\alpha=0.256>0.05$, the null hypothesis is not rejected). That is, the null hypothesis that the population estimate 72 percent is close to 75 percent is accepted, and the small difference observed ($75-72=3$ percent points) can be attributed to sampling fluctuations. When the population estimate decreases to 70 percent, the t value increases to 1.54 and it is still less than 1.65 ($\alpha=0.122>0.05$). But when the population estimate further decreases to 68 percent, the t value increases to 2.12 and it is greater than 1.65 ($\alpha=0.042<0.05$). That is, if the population estimate is 68 percent or less, then we can confidently say that even if we draw different samples, we are sure (with 95 percent confidence) that the population estimate based on the sample will not be close to 75 percent, even after allowing for sampling fluctuations.

So, we can be 95 percent confident that the population estimate of 68 percent is significantly lower than the expected 75 percent, but still there is a 5 percent chance of the estimate being equal to the 75 percent mark. Suppose the population estimate is 66 percent. Then, the t value will further increase to 2.68. If this is the case, we can be 99 percent confident that repeated samples will not give an estimate of 75 percent.

Now, consider the population estimate being on the other (upper) side of the expected value; that is, when the population estimate is greater than 75 percent. It is clear that as the difference between the expected value and the population estimate increases, the t value also increases and the α value decreases. The values are same as that observed in the opposite direction for the difference between the expected value and the population estimate. So, in a one-tailed test, the direction of the null hypothesis does not matter for hypothesis testing, but the inference we draw and the explanation we give should be made based on the direction of the relationship.

Important Notes

1. A relationship is 'significant' does not mean that the relationship is 'important', in that, significant implies a difference in the statistical relationship of two variables, whereas important implies a person's judgement about a difference as to whether it is important or not for a particular purpose. As such, a significant difference may or may not be important for a particular purpose.
2. A relationship is 'not significant' does not mean that there is no relationship between the variables involved. It only means that the given sample or samples do not support a statistical relationship between the variables.
3. Sometimes, the relationship would turn out to be significant if we increase the sample size and conduct the test. So, sample size plays an important role in determining the statistical

significance of the relationship between variables via their SEs. We have already discussed that as the sample size increases, the SE decreases. So, adequate sample size is important for ensuring a significant or non-significant relationship between variables.

Degrees of Freedom

In statistics, the number of degrees of freedom is the number of values in the final calculation of a statistic that are free to vary. Estimates of statistical parameters are often based on the different amounts of information or data (observations). The degrees of freedom of an estimate is equal to the number of independent values (observations) that go into the estimate minus the number of parameters estimated as intermediate steps in the estimation of the parameter itself. In case of estimation of population variance, sample variance is used, and since the sample mean is the only intermediate step involved, the number of degrees of freedom is one minus the number of observations.

The concept of degrees of freedom is a bit tricky to explain to non-statisticians. However, it is explained in the form of a small example. Let us consider four observations with the mean $\bar{x} = 5$. Now, let the value of the first observation be 4, second be 6, third be 7; automatically, the fourth value is 3, so that $4+6+7+3=20$ and $\bar{x} = 20/4 = 5$. That is, when 3 of the 4 values are chosen, the fourth value is automatically fixed, so that the total and mean values are unchanged. In general, if there are n observations, $n-1$ values can vary and the remaining one (nth) value is fixed, and so the number of degrees of freedom is $n-1$. The degrees of freedom need not be always $n-1$ and will vary depending on the number of variables involved and the number of indices associated with them in the estimation processes.

When to Apply the Test of Significance

In a one-sample case with a reasonably large sample size, if the *sample value* is far different from the *population value* (often assumed), we can confidently say that the sample value cannot be considered as the population value and that there is no need for a test to substantiate it. Similarly, in a two-sample case with reasonably large sample sizes, if the values (say means) of the two samples are far different, then we can confidently say that the populations from which the samples are drawn are different and there is no need for a test to substantiate it. On the other hand, if both the values are equal or almost equal, then also without conducting a test, we can say that the two populations (from which the samples are drawn) are equal. The confusion in taking a decision arises when the values are neither too close nor too different, the sample size is small and/or the SD (coefficient of variation) is large. In such cases, the small difference observed may or may not be real (the difference being attributed to sampling fluctuations). So, we have to rule out the possibility that the differences are due to sampling fluctuations alone, before deciding that the two values are the same or different. In this case, we need appropriate statistical principles to rule out this possibility, and there are different tests for different situations. Some of the common tests are described further in the text.

TEST STATISTIC

Sample Value against a Population Value

Let u be a sample statistic, $E(u)$ be the estimated value of u in the population (or estimated population parameter) and $SE(u)$ be the SE of u. Then for large samples ($n > 30$, often $n > 100$), according to the central limit theorem, $Z = \dfrac{u - E(u)}{SE(u)}$ follows normal distribution with mean 0 and SD

1 [often denoted as $Z \sim N(0,1)$]. Please note that u can be the arithmetic mean, SD, correlation coefficient, regression coefficient and the like, and, hence, a general symbol u is used.

For testing the null hypothesis H_0, we compute the value of Z assuming that Z follows a normal distribution with mean 0 and SD 1 and get the value, say, Z_0. That is, $Z = \dfrac{u - E(u)}{SE(u)} = Z_0$ assuming $Z \sim N(0,1)$.

For the given problem, let the probability of the absolute value (negative value is also considered as positive value) of Z being greater than Z_0 be α. That is, $P(|Z| > Z_0) = \alpha$ (significance level). To reject the null hypothesis H_0 under the assumption that it is true, the α value is to be less than a prefixed value α_0 (usually 0.05). In other words, we reject H_0 if the significance level α is smaller than α_0 ($\alpha < \alpha_0$), and if $\alpha > \alpha_0$, then we accept H_0.

For large samples, the critical values of α for one-sided (one-tailed) and two-sided (two-tailed) test and the corresponding Z (Z_0) values and confidence levels are available (see last two rows of Table E.1 in Appendix E). So, when we have (or can estimate) SD of the population, we can compute the Z score and use the normal distribution. But when sample sizes are small ($n < 30$, often $n < 100$), and SD of the population is not known, we often use the 't statistic' (or the t score) that follows the t *distribution*, specifically the *Student t distribution*. It is to be noted that the 't statistic' is associated with what is called the degrees of freedom that refer to the number of independent observations in the dataset. In general, if a sample size n is small, then Z follows a t distribution with ($n-1$) degrees of freedom.

The critical values for small samples are to be obtained from the t table in Table D.1 in Appendix D. The Z *value* approximates the t *value* for higher degrees of freedom (often $n > 1,000$). The Z or t value for 95 percent CI (5 percent level of significance) is often used.

In this chapter, we discuss a few tests that are commonly applied in social sciences. The tests are categorised into a combination of one sample test and two samples test; large sample test and small sample test; and mean test, proportion test, correlation test and chi-square test, as appropriate. Let us see them one by one with manually worked-out and SPSS examples.

ONE-SAMPLE MEAN TEST

The one-sample mean test deals with testing a single observed sample mean value against a predetermined population mean value. Let $\bar{x}$ be the observed sample mean based on n observations and μ be the expected (predetermined or assumed) population mean value. To test whether $\bar{x}$ differs significantly from μ, the test statistic is:

For large samples $\quad Z = \dfrac{|\bar{x} - \mu|}{\dfrac{\sigma}{\sqrt{n}}}$

For small samples $\quad t = \dfrac{|\bar{x} - \mu|}{\dfrac{\sigma}{\sqrt{n-1}}}$ with ($n-1$) degrees of freedom

Alternatively $\quad t = \dfrac{|\bar{x} - \mu|}{\dfrac{s}{\sqrt{n}}}$ with (n 1) degrees of freedom

where
$\bar{x}$ is the observed sample mean.
s is the observed sample SD.
μ is the expected population mean (often assumed).
σ is the expected population SD (often assumed).
n is the sample size.

Important notes
Please note that σ and s (or σ^2 and s^2) are defined as:

$$\sigma^2 = \frac{1}{n}\sum x_i^2 - \bar{x}^2 \quad s^2 = \frac{1}{n-1}\left(\sum x_i^2 - n\bar{x}^2\right).$$

While conducting the one-sample mean test for large samples, often the population mean μ and the population SD σ are assumed (hypothetical values are set), and the assumed values of μ and σ cannot be taken as population estimates of mean and SD. In this case, in the denominator of the test statistic, the sample SD 's' is used instead of the assumed population SD. That is, in the denominator, the $\frac{\sigma}{\sqrt{n}}$ is changed to $\frac{s}{\sqrt{n}}$ while conducting one-sample mean test for large samples.

Please note that for large samples, the test statistic is Z, and for small samples, the test statistic is t. Please also note that the test statistic t is always associated with a certain number of degrees of freedom.

The critical value of t for large samples is $t=Z=1.96$ at 5 percent level of significance for two-tailed test and for small samples it is to be obtained from the t table corresponding to the applicable degrees of freedom (see Table E.1 in Appendix E).

Assumptions/Conditions: The one-sample mean test assumes that the observations are independent, the sample is sufficiently large (for large sample test) and $n>30$ (for small sample test), the sample is drawn using simple random sampling (SRS) method from a large population (at least 10 times larger than the sample size) and the population is normal.

Example: A family planning programme was designed to bring down the number of children per sterilisation accepters to 2.5 on the average from the current level of 3.5 over a period of 10 years. At the end of 10 years, a sample of 527 women who were sterilised during the one-year period before the survey showed an average number of children of 2.93 with a SD of 0.983. Can we consider that the programme has achieved its objective of 2.5 children per sterilisation acceptor?

The null hypothesis is $\quad$ H_0: $\mu \leq 2.5$

The alternate hypothesis is $\quad$ H_1: $\mu > 2.5$

$$n = 527, \quad \bar{x} = 2.93, \quad \mu = 2.5 \quad \text{and} \quad \sigma \text{ is unknown.}$$

Since the sample is large, we may assume $\sigma=0.983$ (the sample SD)

$$Z = \frac{|2.93 - 2.5|}{\dfrac{0.983}{\sqrt{527}}} = 0.43/(0.983/22.96) = 0.43 / 0.0428 = 10.04$$

The Z value of 10.04 is greater than 1.65 (for one-tailed test at 5 percent level of significance) and also greater than 2.33 (for one-tailed test at 1 percent level of significance). That is, the difference in the target and achievement is highly statistically significant. So, we reject the null hypothesis that the mean number of children per sterilisation acceptor is (or has reached a level of) 2.5. As the sample mean of 2.93 is higher than the target value of 2.5, we conclude that the programme has not achieved its objective of reducing the mean number of children per sterilisation acceptor to a level of 2.5.

Note: If it is a two-tailed test, then the Z value (of 10.04) is compared with 1.96 at 5 percent level of significance or with 2.56 at 1 percent level of significance.

An SPSS Example of One-sample Mean Test

Let us continue with the NFHS-3 Goa data that we have used earlier, and test whether the mean weight of children of age group 24–35 months is far less than 12 kg.

$H_0: \mu \geq 12$ (kg) and $H_1: \mu < 12$ (kg).

In SPSS, first we have to select the children of age group 24–35 months using the menu 'Data => Select cases' and then choosing the option 'If' and setting the age group 24–35. Next, choose the menu 'Analyze => Compare means => One-sample t-test'. In the pop-up window, transfer the variable 'weight' (study variable) to the box labelled 'Test Variable(s)' and enter the assumed population mean 12 (for 12 kg) in the box labelled 'Test value' as shown in Figure 7.3, and click 'OK'. The output is shown in Tables 7.1a and 7.1b.

It is seen from Table 7.1a that the number of children of age group 24–35 months in the sample is 170, and their mean weight is 11.384 kg with a SD of 1.9553 kg. The SE of the estimate is worked out to be 0.1500 $\left(\dfrac{s}{\sqrt{n}} = \dfrac{1.9553}{\sqrt{170}} = 0.149965 = 0.15 \right)$. In the Table 7.1b, it can be seen that the test value is 12 (i.e., 12 kg), the t value is –4.107 ($t = 11.384118 - 12)/0.149965 = -4.10685 = -4.107$, with internal values in the calculation), degrees of freedom (df) is 169, the significance level for two-tailed test is 0.000. It means that the mean weight of 11.384 kg of the children of age group 24–35 months estimated from the sample is significantly different from the expected mean weight of 12 kg.

Since our alternate hypothesis is $H_1: \mu < 12$, we have to undertake one-tailed t-test. As SPSS does not produce one-tailed t-test significance values for one-sample mean test, we have to calculate the

Figure 7.3 SPSS Window for One-sample t-test

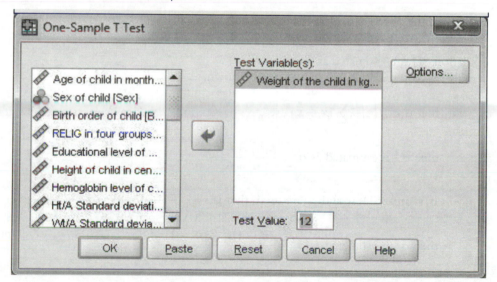

Table 7.1a   SPSS Output of One-sample Mean Test Statistics

	N	Mean	SD	SE Mean
Weight of the child in kg	170	11.384	1.9553	0.1500

Table 7.1b   SPSS Output of One-sample Mean Test

					95% Confidence Interval of the Difference	
	t	df	Sig. (two-tailed)	Mean Difference	Lower	Upper
Weight of the child in kg	−4.107	169	0.000	−0.6159	−0.912	−0.320

Test Value = 12

significant value manually. We have Sig. (two-tailed) value $\alpha=0$ and so the Sig. (one-tailed) value $\alpha/2=0$. That is, the observed weight is significantly lower than the expected weight of 12 kg. Alternatively, we can use the t table, from which we get $t_0=1.66$ at 5 percent level of significance and $t_0=2.364$ at 1 percent level of significance for 169 degrees of freedom. As the calculated value $t=4.107$ is far higher than the table values, even at 1 percent level of significance, we reject the null hypothesis and accept the alternate hypothesis, and say that the sample estimate of the mean weight of 11.38 kg of the children is significantly lower than the expected mean weight of 12 kg.

TWO-SAMPLES MEAN TEST

The two-samples mean test statistic if the two samples are drawn from the same population is:

$$z = \frac{|\bar{x}_1 - \bar{x}_2|}{\sigma\sqrt{\dfrac{1}{n_1} + \dfrac{1}{n_2}}},$$

where
$\bar{x}_1$ and $\bar{x}_2$ are the observed sample means.
n_1 and n_2 are the respective sample sizes.

The population SD σ is estimated as follows:
If the sample-based population SD σ_1 and σ_2 are known,

$$\text{that is,} \sigma = \left(\sqrt{\frac{1}{n}\sum(x_i - \bar{x})^2}\right),$$

then σ^2 is estimated as $\sigma^2 = \dfrac{n_1\sigma_1^2 + n_2\sigma_2^2}{n_1 + n_2}$.

If sample SDs s_1 and s_2 are used, that is, $s = \left(\sqrt{\dfrac{1}{n-1}\sum(x_i - \bar{x})^2}\right),$

then σ^2 is estimated as $\sigma^2 = \dfrac{(n_1 - 1)s_1^2 + (n_2 - 1)s_2^2}{n_1 + n_2 - 2}$.

When the samples are drawn from different populations or the population variances of the two groups are not the same (i.e., when the variances are not assumed to be equal), then:

$$z = \frac{|\bar{x}_1 - \bar{x}_2|}{\sqrt{\dfrac{s_1^2}{n_1} + \dfrac{s_2^2}{n_2}}}.$$

When n_1 and n_2 are small samples, z follows t with $(n_1 + n_2 - 2)$ degrees of freedom.

Assumptions/Conditions: The two-samples mean test assumes that the groups are independent, and within the groups, the observations are also independent; the samples are sufficiently large (for large sample test) and $n_1, n_2 > 30$ (for small sample test). The samples are drawn from (same or different) large normal populations (at least 10 times larger than the sample size) using SRS method.

Example: A family planning survey of 514 women who got sterilised during a particular year showed that illiterate women had an average number of 3.05 children with a sample SD of 1.01 children, and literate women had an average number of 2.79 children with a sample SD of 0.88 children. Of the sample size, 288 women were illiterate and the rest were literate. Can we confidently say that illiterate and literate women differ in their numbers of children at sterilisation acceptance?

$$n_1 = 288 \qquad\qquad \bar{x}_1 = 3.05 \quad s_1 = 1.01$$
$$n_2 = 514 - 288 = 226 \quad \bar{x}_2 = 2.79 \quad s_2 = 0.88$$

The null hypothesis is H_0: Literate and illiterate women have the same number of children at sterilisation acceptance and the alternate hypothesis is H_1: Number of children at acceptance is different for literate and illiterate women. And, equal variance is assumed (default assumption).

$$\sigma^2 = \frac{(n_1 - 1)s_1^2 + (n_2 - 1)s_2^2}{n_1 + n_2 - 2} = (287 * 1.01 * 1.01 + 225 * 0.88 + 0.88) / 512 = 0.96025$$

$$\sigma = \sqrt{0.96025} = 0.9799$$

$$z = \frac{|\bar{x}_1 - \bar{x}_2|}{\sigma\sqrt{\dfrac{1}{n_1} + \dfrac{1}{n_2}}} = \frac{|3.05 - 2.79|}{0.9799\sqrt{\dfrac{1}{288} + \dfrac{1}{226}}} = 2.9858$$

The Z value of 2.9858 is greater than 1.96 and also greater than 2.56, and so the difference in the mean numbers of children between illiterate and literate women is statistically highly significant. So, we reject the null hypothesis that the number of children of sterilisation acceptor is the same for both illiterate and literate women. As the mean number of children for literate women is 2.79 against 3.05 children for illiterate women, we conclude that literate women have lesser number of children than illiterate women at sterilisation acceptance.

An SPSS Example of Two-samples Mean Test

Let us continue with the data used for the one-sample mean test, and test whether the mean weight differs between the male and female children of age group 12–59 months.

The null hypothesis is that the mean weight is the same for male and female children, and the alternate hypothesis is that male and female children differ in their weights.

For this, choose the menu 'Analyze => Compare means => Independent Samples *t*-test'. In the pop-up window, transfer the variable 'weight of child' (study variable) into the box labelled 'Test Variable(s)' and transfer the variable 'Sex of child' into the box labelled 'Grouping Variable'. Then click the 'Define groups' and assign the codes for male and female (see Figure 7.4) and then click 'OK'. The output is shown in Tables 7.2a and 7.2b.

Table 7.2a gives the group statistics and Table 7.2b gives the test results. The *t* value is 3.161 if the variances are assumed to be equal, and is 3.165 otherwise. The significance levels (for two-tailed test) are 0.002 and 0.002 (both < 0.01), respectively, and both reveal that the observed sex difference in the weight is statistically highly significant. That is, the weights of male and female

Figure 7.4 SPSS Window for Independent Samples *t*-test

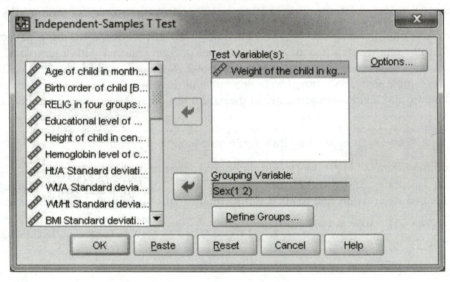

Table 7.2a Independent Sample Group Statistics

	Sex of Child	N	Mean	Std. Deviation	Std. Error Mean
Weight of the child in kg	Male	417	11.595	3.3879	0.1659
	Female	392	10.860	3.2207	0.1627

Table 7.2b Independent Samples Test Statistics

		Levene's Test for Equality of Variances		*t*-test for Equality of Means					95% Confidence Interval of the Difference	
		F	Sig.	t	df	Sig. (two-tailed)	Mean Difference	Std. Error Difference	Lower	Upper
Weight of the child in kg	Equal variances assumed	0.132	0.716	3.161	807	0.002	0.7355	0.2327	0.2787	1.1923
	Equal variances not assumed			3.165	806.9	0.002	0.7355	0.2323	0.2794	1.1916

children are different and further as we see from Table 7.2a (group statistics) the weight of male children is higher than the weight of female children.

Manual Calculation with Equal Variance

$$\sigma^2 = \frac{(n_1 - 1)s_1^2 + (n_{2-1})s_2^2}{n_1 + n_2 - 2}$$

$$= (416 * 3.3879 * 3.3879 + 391 * 3.2207 * 3.2207) / (417 + 392 - 2) = 10.9425027$$

$$\sigma = \sqrt{10.9425027} = 3.30793 \quad \text{and} \quad \sqrt{\frac{1}{417} + \frac{1}{382}} = 0.070349854$$

$$z = (11.595 - 10.860) / (3.30793 * 0.070349854) = 3.1605$$

Manual Calculation with Unequal Variance

$$\sqrt{\frac{s_1^2}{n_1} + \frac{s_2^2}{n_2}} = \sqrt{\frac{3.3879 * 3.3879}{417} + \frac{3.2207 + 3.2207}{392}} = 0.23234965$$

$$Z = (11.595 - 10.860) / (0.23234869) = 3.1655$$

(**Note:** Calculations are made with the internal values of the computer output.)

ONE-SAMPLE PROPORTION TEST

The one-sample proportion test deals with testing a single observed sample proportion value against a predetermined population proportion value. Let p be the observed sample proportion based on n observations and P be the expected (predetermined or assumed) population proportion value. To test whether p differs significantly from P, the test statistic is:

$$\text{For large samples,} \quad Z = \frac{|p - P|}{\sqrt{\dfrac{PQ}{n}}}$$

$$\text{For small samples,} \quad t = \frac{|p - P|}{\sqrt{\dfrac{pq}{n-1}}} \quad \text{with } (n-1) \text{ degrees of freedom,}$$

where $q = 1 - p$ and $Q = 1 - P$.

Important Notes

As in one-sample mean test, for deriving SE (in the denominator), the sample proportion p is used instead of the population proportion P, if assumed. That is, in the denominator of the Z test statistic, PQ needs to be replaced with pq while conducting one-sample proportion test with assumed population proportion.

SPSS has no provision for 'proportion test', but we can use the 'mean test' for it by converting the test variable into a dummy variable (with 0s and 1s). It is to be noted that the proportion test is a special case of mean test, and as such, the mean test will produce the same result as the proportion test.

Assumptions/Conditions: Same as for one-sample mean test.

Example: The government has set a target of 75 percent coverage of children of age group 6–11 months for DPT and Polio immunisation. At the end of the year, a sample survey of 200 children of age group 6–11 months was conducted, and it was found that the immunisation coverage was only 72 percent. Test whether the shortfall in the coverage can be attributed to the fluctuations in the sampling or to the low performance of the workers in the programme.

Here, we are testing a single sample proportion against an expected population proportion. The null hypothesis and alternate hypothesis are as follows.

H_0: Immunisation coverage of children is 75 percent.

H_1: Immunisation coverage is below 75 percent (one-tailed test).

That is, H_0: P percent ≥ 75 percent or H_0: $P \geq 0.75$ and H_1: $P < 0.75$

The sample proportion is $p = 72$ percent $= 72/100 = 0.72$

The population proportion is $P = 75$ percent $= 75/100 = 0.75$

Since the sample size is 200 (large sample), we can apply the large sample test. However, as the population proportion is only assumed, the SE is derived from the sample proportion. As such $pq = 0.72 * (1-0.72) = 0.72 * 0.28 = 0.2016$ and the sample size is $n = 200$. The test statistic is

$$Z = \frac{|p - P|}{\sqrt{\dfrac{pq}{n}}} = \frac{|0.72 - 0.75|}{\sqrt{\dfrac{0.72 * 0.28}{200}}} = \frac{|-0.03|}{\sqrt{0.00108}} = \frac{0.03}{0.031749} = 0.9449.$$

For the one-tailed test, the table value of Z is 1.645 at $\alpha = 0.05$ or 5 percent level of significance and Z is 2.326 at $\alpha = 0.01$ or 1 percent level of significance. The calculated value of $Z = 0.9449$ is (much) less than the table value of $Z = 1.645$ at 5 percent level of significance for the one-tailed test. Alternatively, we can derive α from $Z = 0.9449$ and it is 0.172335 ($\alpha = 0.172 > 0.05$). Please note that in MS Excel NORMSDIST(0.9449) = 0.827645 and $\alpha = 1 - 0.827645 = 0.172355$. We can also obtain the α value from Z table in Table D.2 in Appendix D. The probability value corresponding to $Z = 0.9449$ (0.945) is $(0.82639 + 0.82894)/2 = 0.827665$ and $\alpha = 1 - 0.827665 = 0.172335$, which is almost same as that obtained from the Excel function. So, the null hypothesis that the program reached 75 percent coverage is not rejected but rather accepted. That is, the small shortfall (difference) in the survey estimate may be attributed to the fluctuations in the sampling. Hence, as per the test result, we may conclude that the program has achieved the target.

Let us consider the small sample test for single proportion. The t value is

$$t = \frac{|p - P|}{\sqrt{\dfrac{pq}{n-1}}} = \frac{|0.72 - 0.75|}{\sqrt{\dfrac{0.72 * 0.28}{199}}} = \frac{|-0.03|}{\sqrt{0.0010131}} = \frac{0.03}{0.0318286872} = 0.943.$$

The table value of t is calculated as follows. The table gives the t values for the degrees of freedom (df) 100 and 1,000 and not in-between. Usually, the t value for an intermediate df is obtained by interpolation. From the table, we get that the t value is 1.660 for df 100 and 1.646 for df 1,000 and so the t value for df 199 would be approximately 1.65 (not necessary to do the exact arithmetic calculation). The calculated t value of 0.943 is (much) less than the value of 1.65 at 5 percent level of significance with one-tailed test. So, the null hypothesis that the program reached the 75 percent coverage can be accepted.

An SPSS Example of One-sample Proportion Test

A part of the NFHS-3 data for Goa gives the nutritional status indicators for the children of age group 12–59 months. Using the data, test whether the percent of children underweight (weight-for-age Z score below –2 SDs) in the population is (a) 20 percent and (b) 20 percent or less.

(1) The null hypothesis is H_0: $P = 0.2$ and alternate hypothesis is H_1: $P \neq 0.2$.

(2) The null hypothesis is H_0: $P \leq 0.2$ and alternate hypothesis is H_1: $P > 0.2$.

For the application of SPSS, the data need to be in the SPSS format and the underweight variable is to be coded as 1 if a child is underweight, and 0 otherwise. To run one-sample proportion test in SPSS, choose the menu 'Analyze => Compare means => One-sample t-test'. Soon a window as shown in Figure 8.1 will appear. In the window, transfer the variable 'Underweight of child' (study variable) into the box labelled 'Test Variable(s)', enter the assumed population proportion (percent of children underweight) 0.2 in the box labelled 'Test value' and then click 'OK'.

The SPSS output is shown below in two tables (Tables 7.3a and 7.3b). It is seen from Table 7.3a that the sample proportion is 0.25 (internal value is 0.2536873) and is shown under the column 'mean', and the sample size N is 678. From Table 7.3b, it is seen that the test value is 0.2 (i.e., 20 percent, specified on top of the table), the t value is 3.210, degrees of freedom (df) is 677 and the significance level for two-tailed test is 0.001. It is to be noted that while doing the exercise manually, we calculate only the t value and compare it with the table value. On the other hand, SPSS goes one step further and calculates the probability level at which the difference becomes significant. It is presented under the column 'Sig. (two-tailed)'.

For the given example (1) of two-tailed test, the 'Sig.' value is 0.001 ($\alpha < 0.01$) and the difference is significant at 1.0 percent level. So, we are more than 99 percent confident that the estimate of proportion of children underweight 0.25 (or 25 percent) is significantly *different* from the expected level of 20 percent. For one-sample test, $\alpha = 0.001/2 = 0.0005 < 0.005$ and so we are more than 99.5 percent confident that the estimate of proportion of children underweight 0.25 (or 25 percent) is significantly *higher* than the expected level of 20 percent. Please note the use of the words (a) 'different' meaning that the difference is either on the upper or lower side (two-sided), and (b) 'higher' meaning that the difference is on the upper side (one-sided).

The t value can be obtained manually from the first table (using the internal values for precision of calculation) as follows:

Table 7.3a SPSS Output of One-sample Statistics

	N	Mean	Std. Deviation	Std. Error Mean
Underweight of child	678	0.25	0.435	0.017

Table 7.3b SPSS Output of One-sample Test

	Test Value = 0.2					
					95% Confidence Interval of the Difference	
	T	df	Sig. (two-tailed)	Mean Difference	Lower	Upper
Underweight of child	3.210	677	0.001	0.054	0.02	0.09

$$t = \frac{|p - P|}{\sqrt{\dfrac{pq}{n-1}}} = \frac{|0.2536873 - 0.2|}{\sqrt{\dfrac{0.2536873 * (1 - 0.2536873)}{678 - 1}}} = \frac{|0.05368732|}{0.016723049} = 3.21$$

The table value of t for 677 df is 1.964 (approximately from Table E.1 in Appendix E) or simply 1.96 (as n is large). The calculated value of $t = 3.21$ is greater than the table value of 1.964 (at 5 percent level) and even greater than 2.58 (at 1 percent level). So, the null hypothesis is rejected at 1 percent level of significance, that is, the alternate hypothesis that the proportion underweight is >20 percent is accepted. It means that the prevalence of underweight among children in the population is significantly higher than the expected level of 20 percent.

TWO-SAMPLES PROPORTION TEST

The test of significance for difference of two proportions is often called 'Independent samples t-test' and the test statistic is given below.

When the samples are drawn from the same population or from different populations with same variance (i.e., when the variances are assumed to be equal):

For large samples, $\quad Z = \dfrac{|p_1 - p_2|}{\sqrt{PQ \left\{ \dfrac{1}{n_1} + \dfrac{1}{n_2} \right\}}}$

For small samples, $\quad t = \dfrac{|p_1 - p_2|}{\sqrt{PQ \left\{ \dfrac{1}{n_1 - 1} + \dfrac{1}{n_2 - 1} \right\}}} \quad$ with $(n_1 + n_2 - 2)$ df

If p_1 and p_2 are the sample proportions and n_1 and n_2 are the respective sample sizes, then

$$P = \frac{n_1 p_1 + n_2 p_2}{n_1 + n_2} \quad \text{and} \quad Q = 1 - P.$$

When the samples are drawn from two different populations or the population variances from which the two samples are drawn are not the same (i.e., when the variances are assumed to be not equal):

For large samples, $Z = \dfrac{|p_1 - p_2|}{\dfrac{P_1 Q_1}{n_1} + \dfrac{P_2 Q_2}{n_2}}$

For small samples, $t = \dfrac{|p_1 - p_2|}{\sqrt{\dfrac{P_1 Q_1}{n_1 - 1} + \dfrac{P_2 Q_2}{n_2 - 1}}} \quad$ with $(n_1 + n_2 - 2)$ df where p_1 and p_2 are the sample proportions, n_1 and n_2 are the respective sample sizes, and $P_1 = p_1, Q_1 = 1 - P_1$ and $P_2 = p_2, Q_2 = 1 - P_2$.

Assumptions/Conditions: Same as for two-samples mean test.

Example: A sample survey of 200 children of age group 6–11 months was conducted to assess the coverage of children for DPT/Polio immunisation. Of the 200 children surveyed, 105 were males and the remaining were females. The survey showed that the immunisation coverage was 74.1 percent for the males and 69.6 percent for the females. Test whether there is any sex differential in the coverage of children for immunisation in the study population.

Let n_1 and n_2 be the number of male and female children in the sample and p_1 and p_2 be the respective proportions of children covered for immunisation. Then, $n_1 = 105$ and $p_1 = 0.741$ (male sample) and $n_2 = 95$ and $p_2 = 0.696$ (female sample).

Let P_1 and P_2 be the estimates of proportions of children immunised in the population. As there is no reason to believe that the SD in the coverage of children to be different for male and female children, we can safely assume that the two samples are drawn from the same population with equal SD. Furthermore, as the samples are large, we apply the large sample test.

H_0: $P_1 = P_2$ (immunisation coverage is the same for male and female children)

$$P = \frac{n_1 p_1 + n_2 p_2}{n_1 + n_2} = \frac{105 * 0.741 + 95 * 0.696}{105 + 95} = 0.719625.$$

$$Q = 1.0 - 0.719625 = 0.280375$$

$$Z = \frac{|p_1 - p_2|}{\sqrt{PQ\left\{\frac{1}{n_1} + \frac{1}{n_2}\right\}}} = \frac{|0.741 - 0.696|}{\sqrt{0.7196 * 0.2804\left\{\frac{1}{105} + \frac{1}{95}\right\}}} = \frac{0.045}{\sqrt{0.202 * 0.02005}} = 0.7075$$

The Z value of 0.7075 is (much) less than the table value of 1.96 (at 5 percent level of significance). So, we accept the null hypothesis that the immunisation coverage is the same among both male and female children and the small difference observed in the survey estimates can be attributed to sampling fluctuations. The conclusion is that immunisation coverage does not differ significantly between male and female children. In other words, there appears to be no sex differential in the immunisation coverage of children in the study population.

Extension of the Example: Let us see what happens if we increase the sample size by 10 times ($n_1 = 1,050$ and $n_2 = 950$) for the same level of immunisation coverage of 74.1 percent for the male children and 69.6 percent for the female children.

$$Z = \frac{|p_1 - p_2|}{\sqrt{PQ\left\{\frac{1}{n_1} + \frac{1}{n_2}\right\}}} = \frac{|0.741 - 0.696|}{\sqrt{0.72 * 0.28\left\{\frac{1}{1,050} + \frac{1}{950}\right\}}} = \frac{0.045}{\sqrt{0.202 * 0.002005}} = 2.237.$$

Now, $Z = 2.237$ is greater than 1.96 and the difference in the immunisation coverage (male 74.1 percent and female 69.6 percent) is statistically significant. So, we reject the null hypothesis that the immunisation coverage is the same for both male and female children. The conclusion is that the immunisation coverage is significantly different between male and female children.

Form the statistical point of view, it is clear that the sample estimates being the same, the higher the sample size, the higher the Z value and greater the statistical significance. This is because the estimates based on larger samples are more stable (show less fluctuation due to sampling) than that based on small samples and so, with large samples, we are more confident so that even small differences are really different. From this, what we learn is that 'a statistically not significant' result does not automatically mean that the two variables are not really related, it only means that the *given sample does not support to reject the null hypothesis*.

An SPSS Example of Two-samples Proportion Test

Let us continue with the data used for the one-sample test and test whether the proportion of children underweight differs between male and female children.

Let P_1 and P_2 be the estimates of proportions of children underweight. Then

H_0: $P_1=P_2$ (proportion of children underweight is the same among both male and female children) and H_1 is not explicitly stated.

For the application of SPSS, the variable 'underweight' should have been coded as a dummy variable with a value 1 if the child is underweight, and 0 otherwise. Please note that a child is considered underweight if the weight-for-age Z score is less than –2 SDs (a Z score value less than –2 in the dataset).

To run two samples proportion test in SPSS, choose the menu 'Analyse => Compare means => Independent-Samples t-test'. Soon a window as in Figure 7.2 will open. In the window, transfer the variable 'underweight' to the box labelled 'Test Variable(s)', and the group variable 'Sex of child' to the box labelled 'Grouping Variable'. Then click the 'Define groups' and assign the codes for male and female for the group variable. The SPSS output is shown below in two tables (Tables 7.4a and 7.4b). Table 7.4a gives sex-wise number of children (column labelled 'N') and proportion of children underweight (column 'Mean') and Table 7.4b gives the test results.

Table 7.4a SPSS Output of Group Statistics

	Sex of Child	*N*	*Mean*	*Std. Deviation*	*Std. Error Mean*
Underweight of child	Male	351	0.24	0.429	0.023
	Female	327	0.27	0.443	0.024

Table 7.4b SPSS Output of Independent Samples Test

		Levene's Test for Equality of Variances		*t-test for Equality of Means*					*95% Confidence Interval of the Difference*	
		F	*Sig.*	*t*	*df*	*Sig. (two-tailed)*	*Mean Difference*	*Std. Error Difference*	*Lower*	*Upper*
Underweight of child	Equal variances assumed	2.031	0.155	–0.714	676	0.476	–0.024	0.033	–0.090	0.042
	Equal variances not assumed			–0.713	669.038	0.476	–0.024	0.034	–0.090	0.042

The t value is -0.714 if the variances are assumed to be equal, and is -0.713 otherwise. The significance level (for two-tailed test) is 0.476 for both the assumptions and the value reveals that the observed sex difference in the proportion of children underweight is not statistically significant.

The t value can be obtained manually from the first table (using the internal values for precision of calculation) as follows. By assuming equal variance, we can calculate t as:

$$P = \frac{351 * 0.242165 + 327 * 0.266055}{351 + 327} = 0.253687$$

$$t = \frac{|p_1 - p_2|}{\sqrt{PQ\left\{\dfrac{1}{n_1 - 1} + \dfrac{1}{n_2 - 1}\right\}}} = \frac{|0.242165 - 0.266055|}{\sqrt{0.253687 * 0.746313\left\{\dfrac{1}{350} + \dfrac{1}{326}\right\}}} = 0.7136$$

Without assuming equal variance, we calculate t as:

$$t = \frac{|p_1 - p_2|}{\sqrt{\dfrac{P_1 Q_1}{n_1 - 1} + \dfrac{P_2 Q_2}{n_2 - 1}}} = \frac{|0.242165 - 0.266055|}{\sqrt{\dfrac{0.242165 * 0.757835}{350} + \dfrac{0.266055 * 0.733945}{326}}} = 0.7134$$

PAIRED SAMPLE t-TEST

Paired sample t-test is essentially a one-sample test in which the differences in the values of two related variables are compared for their statistical significance. In a paired sample, there will be two measures (usually 'before' and 'after' or 'pre' and 'post' intervention measures) of the same/similar aspect on a number of subjects or observations, that is, measures are made on the same individuals or subjects (observations) at two times, at two levels, by two measurers, or before and after conducting an experiment. In other words, a pair of measures for the same number of individuals or subjects constitutes a paired sample. For example, blood pressure before and after administering a drug, pre and post training scores, income from primary and secondary occupations and the like are paired samples.

The paired t-test is a modification of the one-sample t-test. For this test, we first calculate the difference (including negative sign) in each pair of scores/values and treat the difference of the values as a single sample (one-sample). Let n be the number of cases with paired values, $\bar{D}$ be the mean of the difference of values and s be the SD of the difference of values. Since the null hypothesis is a hypothesis of no difference, here, for the null hypothesis, we consider that the differences in the paired values are zero, and hence, the population mean of the differences is assumed to be 0, that is, H_0: $\mu = 0$.

We have already seen that the test statistic for one-sample test is

$$t = \frac{|\bar{x} - \mu|}{\dfrac{s}{\sqrt{n}}} \text{ with } (n-1) \text{ degrees of freedom.}$$

Substituting the above values in the equation, we get

$$t = \frac{\bar{D}}{\dfrac{s}{\sqrt{n}}} \text{ with } (n-1) \text{ degrees of freedom.}$$

Assumptions/Conditions: The paired sample t-test assumes that the observations are independent, the data are matched, the sample size $n > 30$, the sample is drawn using the SRS method from a large population (at least 10 times larger than the sample size) and the population (difference, that is, D) is normal.

Example: Table 7.5 gives the blood pressure (BP) reading before and after administering a drug on 12 patients in a hospital (first three columns). Test whether the drug has an effect on reducing the BP level among the patients.

In this exercise, H_0: $\mu = 0$ and H_1: $\mu > 0$, where μ is the difference in the BP level (before –after) and $\bar{D}$ is an estimate of μ.

First obtain the difference D and square of D as in Columns 4 and 5 in the table, and then obtain their totals as in the last row.

$$\text{Calculate } \bar{D} = 66 / 12 = 5.5$$

$$\text{Calculate } s^2 = (1036 - 5.5 * 5.5) / (12 - 1) = 61.18, \text{ and } s = 7.82$$

$$\text{Calculate } t = 5.5 / (7.82 / 3.464) = 2.436.$$

For the one-tailed test with 11 degrees of freedom, $t = 2.436 > 1.80$ (at 5 percent level) but $t < 2.72$ (at 1 percent level), we reject the null hypothesis at 5 percent level of significance that the differences in the BP level before and after administering the drug is zero. As the mean difference is 5.5 (before – after is positive, that is, the BP level decreased), we can conclude that the administration of the drug on high BP level patients brings down their BP level significantly.

To run the test in SPSS, copy the data in the 'Data view' sheet of SPSS and choose the menu 'Analyze => Compare means => Paired Samples t-test'. In the pop-up window, transfer the variable 'BPBefore' to the column 'Variable 1' and the variable 'BPAfter' to the column 'Variable 2' in the box labelled 'Paired Variables' as shown in Figure 7.5, and then click 'OK'.

The output is presented in Table 7.6 (in three subtables). It is seen from the third subtable that $t = 2.436$ (same as that obtained from the manual calculation) and the significance level is $0.033/2 = 0.0165$. The inferences and explanations are the same as above.

Table 7.5   Blood Pressure Before and After Administering a Drug

Patient	Before	After	Difference (D)	D Square
(1)	(2)	(3)	(4)	(5)
1	142	130	12	144
2	134	130	4	16
3	132	136	–4	16
4	145	140	5	25
5	151	152	–1	1
6	140	140	0	0
7	130	125	5	25
8	136	132	4	16
9	142	134	8	64
10	140	130	10	100
11	148	150	–2	4
12	155	130	25	625
Total	NA	NA	66	1,036

Figure 7.5 SPSS Window for Paired Samples *t*-test

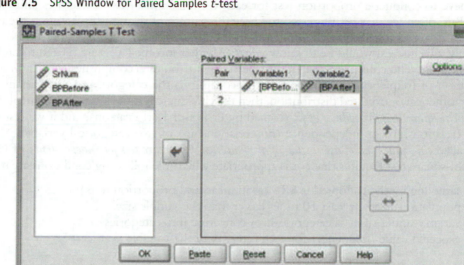

Table 7.6 SPSS Output for Paired Samples *t*-test

Paired Samples Statistics		Mean	N	Std. Deviation	Std. Error Mean
Pair 1	Before	141.25	12	7.629	2.202
	After	135.75	12	8.357	2.412

Paired Samples Correlations		N	Correlation	Sig.
Pair 1	Before and After	12	.524	.080

		Paired Samples Test							
		Paired Differences							
					95% Confidence Interval of the Difference				
		Mean	Std. Deviation	Std. Error Mean	Lower	Upper	t	df	Sig. (2-tailed)
Pair 1	Before – After	5.500	7.822	2.258	.530	10.470	2.436	11	.033

CHI-SQUARE TEST OF SIGNIFICANCE

The mean tests are applicable to the numerical (continuous and discrete) variables only, while the proportion tests are applicable to both numerical and categorical variables but the variables need to be classified into only two categories (e.g., educational level as literate and illiterate, income as high and low). If there are more than two categories (e.g., educational level as illiterate, primary education, high school education and college level education, and income as low, medium and high), we have to conduct a proportion test for each combination of two categories and draw inferences. But, often we may be interested to know the pattern of relationship between the two variables (all categories together) such as income level by educational level.

Specifically, our interest would be to know whether higher income levels are related to higher levels of education. The chi-square test of association of attributes accomplishes this. If we test the distribution of frequencies (or proportions) according to the categories of one variable as against a hypothetical or expected distribution, then the chi-square test of association of attributes is called the *chi-square test of goodness of fit* (coined by Professor Karl Pearson), and if we test the association (relationship) or independence (non-relationship) of two categorical variables, then the test is called *chi-square test of association of attributes* or *chi-square test for independence* of variables. The chi-square test requires that (or is appropriate when) the following conditions are met:

1.   The sampling method adopted is SRS (as in mean and proportion tests).
2.   The population size is at least 10 times larger than the sample size.
3.   The variable under study is categorical (or converted into categories).
4.   The expected value (frequency) for each category of the variable is at least 5.

Chi-square Test for a Single Variable

The chi-square test procedure for a single variable, often called *chi-square test of goodness of fit*, tabulates a variable into categories and tests the hypothesis that the observed frequencies do not differ from their expected values. The goodness-of-fit test compares the observed frequencies with the expected frequencies in each category and computes a chi-square statistic. The null and alternate hypotheses for a chi-square goodness-of-fit test take the following form:

H_0:   The empirical data are consistent with the specified/hypothesised distribution.

H_1:   The data are *not* consistent with the specified distribution.

Example:

H_0:   The religious composition of households in a population is according to the pattern: Hindus 70 percent, Muslims 20 percent and others 10 percent.

H_1:   The religious composition in the population is not as per that in the null hypothesis (at least one proportion is different).

Pearson's chi-square test of goodness of fit for a single variable is given by the formula:

$$\chi_P^2 = \sum \frac{(O_i - E_i)^2}{E_i} \text{ with } (r-1) \text{ degrees of freedom}$$

The *likelihood ratio test* of goodness of fit is given by the formula:

$$\chi_{LR}^2 = -2\sum O_i * \log_e\left(\frac{E_i}{O_i}\right) \text{ with } (r-1) \text{ degrees of freedom}$$

The symbol χ^2 is read as hi-square, ki-square, or chi-square; $i = 1, 2, ..., r$, the number of categories or groups considered; and O_i and E_i are respectively the observed and expected frequencies in the ith category. If the proportions and numbers of observations in different categories are given, then we have to estimate the observed and expected frequencies. Let n be the sample size, and p_i and P_i be the observed and expected proportions for category I, then $O_i = n * p_i$ and $E_i = n * P_i$.

Assumptions/Conditions: The chi-Square test assumes that the data are counts (frequencies), observations are independent, the sample is sufficiently large, the sample is drawn using the SRS method from a large population (at least 10 times larger than the sample size) and the expected cell frequencies are all ≥ 5.

Example: A large hospital schedules discharge support staff assuming that patients leave the hospital at a fairly constant rate throughout the week. However, because of increasing complaints of staff shortage, the hospital administration wants to determine the number of staff to be put on duty depending on the number of discharges made by the day of the week. Columns 1 and 2 of Table 7.7 show the number of discharges made each day of the week during the four weeks period. Test whether the number of discharges varies by the day of a week.

H_0:   The number of discharges is *the same* on the days of a week.

H_1:   The number of discharges is *not the same* on the days of a week.

To test the null hypothesis, we have to estimate the expected discharges assuming that it is the same on all the days of a week, that is, the total number of discharges, that is 589, is to be distributed equally to each day of a week. It is $589/7 = 84.14$ (please retain decimal places) and the same is given in Column 3. Columns 4 and 5 are obtained as per the formula specified.

Pearson's $\chi_P^2 = 29.39$
Likelihood ratio $\chi_{LR}^2 = -2*(-16.38) = 32.76$

The tabulated value of χ^2 for $(r-1)=(7-1)=6$ degrees of freedom (from Table F.1 in Appendix F) is 12.592 at 0.05 probability or 5 percent level of significance; is 16.812 at 0.01 probability or 1 percent level of significance, and is 18.548 at 0.005 probability or 0.05 percent level of significance.

As the calculated value of $\chi^2=29.39$ (Pearson's chi-square test) and 32.76 (likelihood ratio test) are both greater than the tabulated value of $\chi_{0.005}^2=18.55$ at 0.5 percent (<1 percent) level of significance, the null hypothesis that the number of patients discharged is the same on the days of a week is rejected at below 1 percent level of significance (much lower level than the normal 5 percent level). In other words, the number of patients discharged varied widely by the days of the week. So, the number of staff on duty needs to be increased on certain days and may be decreased

Table 7.7 Number of Patients Discharged during the Days of the Week and Chi-square Test

Day of Week	Number of Patients Discharged	Expected Patients Discharged (589/7)	Pearson's Chi-square Statistic	Likelihood Ratio
	(O)	(E)	{(O–E)^2}/E	O*Log(E/O)
(1)	(2)	(3)	(4)	(5)
Sunday	44	84.14	19.15	28.52
Monday	78	84.14	0.45	5.91
Tuesday	90	84.14	0.41	–6.06
Wednesday	94	84.14	1.15	–10.42
Thursday	89	84.14	0.28	–5.00
Friday	110	84.14	7.95	–29.48
Saturday	84	84.14	0.00	0.14
Total	589	589.00	29.39	–16.38

on certain other days of the week. It is seen from the data that discharges are the highest (110 discharges) on Fridays and the lowest on Sundays (44 discharges) and on all other days, it was in the range 78–94 discharges. So, it appears that more number of staff is required to be deployed on Fridays and lesser number of staff is sufficient on Sundays.

Chi-square Test for Association of Attributes

The chi-square test procedure for two variables (cross-classified data) is often called the *chi-square test for independence* or the *chi-square test for association of attributes*. Please note that this test is more appropriate for categorical variables and not nominal variables or at least one variable (the study variable) needs to be a categorical variable. Let two variables be cross-classified into 'r' rows and 'c' columns, excluding the rows and columns containing the captions/labels and marginal totals. The example of educational level by religion is given below (Table 7.8, shaded area) for a better understanding of the situation. The two-way table is also called two-way contingency table. It has four rows and three columns (excluding the rows and columns containing captions and totals). This table is a 3×4 (to be read as 3 by 4, that is, $c=3$ columns by $r=4$ rows) contingency table.

Let r be the number of rows and c be the number of columns. Let O stand for the observed (tabulated) frequencies in each cell. In Table 7.8, the O's are $O_{11}, O_{12}, \ldots, O_{43}$. Let E stand for the expected frequency corresponding to the observed frequency O, which is estimated as

$$E = \frac{\text{Corresponding Row Total * Corresponding Column Total}}{\text{Grand Total}}$$

In general, $E_{ij} = \dfrac{R_i C_j}{G}$ $i=1$ to r and $j=1$ to c,

where R_i is the ith row, C_j is the jth column marginal totals and G is the grand total. Accordingly, in the table,

$$E_{11}=R_1{}^*C_1/G, \quad E_{12}=R_1{}^*C_2/G, \quad E_{21}=R_2{}^*C_1/G, \quad \text{etc.}, \quad E_{43}=R_4{}^*C_3/G$$

Pearson's chi-square test of independence of two variables is given by the formula:

$$\chi_P^2 = \sum \frac{(O_{ij} - E_{ij})^2}{E_{ij}} \text{ with } (r-1)*(c-1) \text{ degrees of freedom}$$

The *Likelihood Ratio test* of independence of two variables is given by the formula:

$$\chi_{LR}^2 = -2\sum O_{ij}{}^*Log_e\left(\frac{E_{ij}}{O_{ij}}\right) \text{ with } (r-1)*(c-1) \text{ df}$$

where the summation is from $i = 1$ to r and from $j = 1$ to c.

Table 7.8 The Format of a Two-way Contingency Table

Educational Level	Religion			Row Total
	Hindu	Muslim	Other	
Illiterate	O_{11}	O_{12}	O_{13}	R_1
Primary	O_{21}	O_{22}	O_{23}	R_2
High school	O_{31}	O_{32}	O_{33}	R_3
College	O_{41}	O_{42}	O_{43}	R_4
Column Total	C_1	C_2	C_3	Grand Total (G)

This chi-square value is compared with the table value (obtained from chi-square table for the above degrees of freedom). If the chi-square value is greater than the table value, then the row and column variables are said to be significantly associated or related with each other, otherwise the two variables are said to be not associated or independent of each other.

Assumptions/Conditions: The chi-square test association of attributes assumes that the data are counts (frequencies), observations are independent, the sample is sufficiently large and is drawn using the SRS method from a large population (at least 10 times larger than the sample size) and the expected cell frequencies are all ≥ 5.

Example: Table 7.9a gives frequency distribution of sterilised women by number of children at sterilisation, classified by literacy status of the women. Apply appropriate statistical test to confirm whether the number of children at sterilisation acceptance is different for illiterate and literate women.

For applying chi-square test of significance, first we need to ensure that the expected cell frequencies are at least 5. From the data, we understand that the first row may not yield expected frequency 5 and so it is desirable to merge the first row with the second row. That is, the 'number of children' groups 0–1 and 2 may be merged as 0–2 children group and it is done as step 1 in Table 7.9b. Next, we need to work out the expected frequency and it is done as step 2, and the final calculated figures are presented in step 3 in the table. It is to be noted that step 2 is not required to be presented but it is shown here as an illustration of how the calculations are made.

From step 1 and step 3 we can derive Pearson's and likelihood ratio chi-square values. The null hypothesis is that literate and illiterate women have equal number of children at sterilisation acceptance and the alternate hypothesis is that the number of children of sterilisation acceptors differs by literacy status of the women.

Pearson's $\chi^2 = 11.57$ with $(3-1)*(2-1) = 2$ df
Likelihood Ratio $\chi^2 = 11.77$ with $(3-1)*(2-1) = 2$ df
χ^2 value for 2df is 5.99 at 5 percent level and 9.21 at 1 percent level of significance.

The calculated value of chi-square test is greater than the tabulated value even at 1 percent level of significance and so, the null hypothesis is rejected. The conclusion is that the number of children of women at sterilisation differs by their literacy status. But the test does not show who has more and who has less number of children.

The percentage distribution of sterilised women by the number of living children classified by literacy status of women is shown in step 4. It is seen that the literate women have lesser number of children than the illiterate women. For example, about 42 percent of the literate women had two or less number of children at sterilisation acceptance, whereas it is only 31 percent among the illiterate women. On the other hand, only 16 percent of the literate women had four or more

Table 7.9a Sterilisation Acceptors by Number of Children

Children	Illiterate Women	Literate Women	Total
0–1	5	2	7
2	83	92	175
3	120	95	215
4+	80	37	117
Total	288	226	514

Table 7.9b   The Process of Calculation of Chi-square Test

Step 1: Merge Rows/Columns for Ensuring a Minimum Frequency of 5 per Cell			
	Observed Frequency		
No. of Children	*Illiterate Women*	*Literate Women*	*Total*
0–2	88	94	182
3	120	95	215
4+	80	37	117
Total	288	226	514

Step 2: Workout Expected Frequency			
	Expected Frequency		
No. of Children	*Illiterate Women*	*Literate Women*	*Total*
0–2	=182*288/514	=182*226/514	182
3	=215*288/514	=215*226/514	215
4+	=117*117/514	=117*226/514	117
Total	288	226	514

Step 3: Expected Frequency			
	Expected Frequency		
No. of Children	*Illiterate Women*	*Literate Women*	*Total*
0–2	102.0	80.0	182
3	120.5	94.5	215
4+	65.6	51.4	117
Total	288	226	514

Step 4: Percentage Distribution of Sterilised Women by Number of Living Children at Sterilisation, Classified by Literacy Status of Women			
	Observed Frequency (%)		
No. of Children	*Illiterate Women*	*Literate Women*	*Total*
0–2	30.6	41.6	35.4
3	41.7	42.0	41.8
4+	27.8	16.4	22.8
Total	100.0	100.0	100.0

children, but it was as high as 28 percent of the illiterate women. That means more literate women accept sterilisation with lesser the number of children than the illiterate women.

An SPSS Example of Chi-square Test

In SPSS, the chi-square test is to be made through the 'Crosstabs' menu and for the cross-classified tables only. In case of three-way tables, the chi-square test is conducted separately for each two-way table (corresponding to each layer category). It is not available for single variable (or frequency table). To run chi-square, choose the menu 'Analyze => Descriptive Statistics => Crosstabs'. Soon a pop-up window with the caption 'Crosstabs' will open (left side part of Figure 7.6), and in that, among the two variables involved in the chi-square test, transfer one variable to the box labelled 'Row(s)'

Figure 7.6   SPSS Window for Chi-square Test

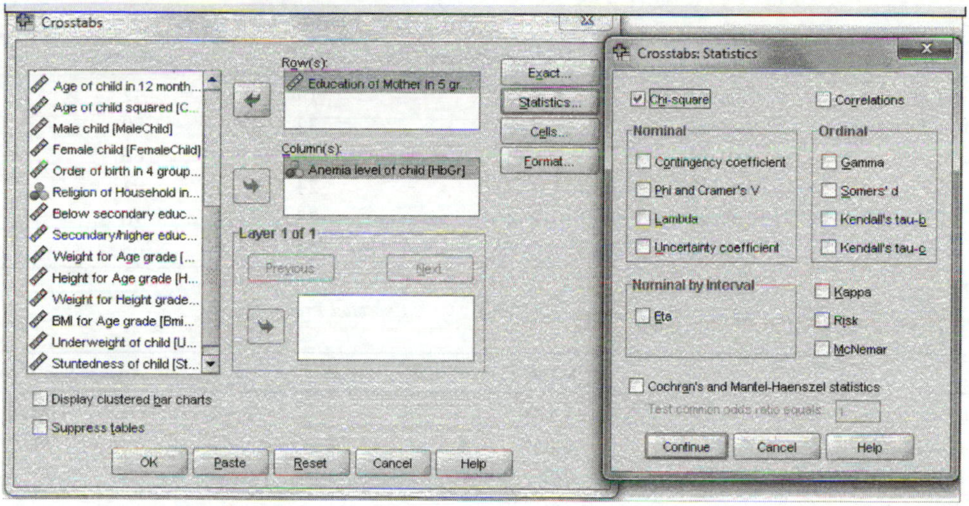

and the other to the box labelled 'Column(s)'. In our example, we have transferred 'Education of mother' and 'Anaemia level' as shown in the figure. Next, click 'Statistics' button and another pop-up window will open (right side part of Figure 7.6), and in that, check 'Chi-square' as shown in the figure. Then click 'Continue' to close this window and then click 'OK'. The output is ready.

The SPSS output consists two tables, one for cross-tabulation (Table 7.10a) and the other for chi-square test results (Table 7.10b). The cross-tabulation is nothing but the usual cross-table and it needs no explanation.

For the chi-square test, the null hypothesis is: the anaemia level of children is independent of educational level of their mothers. The alternate hypothesis is: the anaemia level of children is related to the educational level of their mothers (or anaemia level of children differs by educational level of their mothers).

Table 7.10b consists of three chi-square test results, namely 'Pearson Chi-Square', 'Likelihood Ratio' and 'Linear-by-Linear Association'.

The value of Pearson's chi-square test is 24.415 and that of likelihood ratio is 25.041, and both are significant at 0.002 percent level of significance. Please note the words in the SPSS output table '*Asymp. Sig. (two-sided)*' as against the words *Sig. (two-sided)* that we have seen in the one-sample and two-sample *t*-tests. It is because, in chi-square test, the chi-square distribution is skewed (asymptotic) as seen in 'Figure 5.2: Skewness' under the section 'Skewness' of the chapter on 'Measures of Central Tendency and Dispersion', whereas in one-sample and two-sample *t*-tests the distribution is assumed to be normal (symmetric).

As the significance values are far less than 0.05 (and also less than 0.01), we reject the null hypothesis that the anaemia level of children is independent of educational level of their mothers. That is, the anaemia level of children is strongly associated with the educational level of their mothers, but in which direction, is to be inferred from the data itself. The data in Table 7.10a is presented in Table 7.10c in terms of percentage distribution.

It is seen from the table that as the educational level of mother increases, the proportion of children anaemic decreases. The proportion of children anaemic was 49.4 percent (severe, moderate

Table 7.10a   SPSS Output of Cross-tabulation of Education of Mother and Anaemia Level of Child

		Anaemia Level of Child			
		Moderate/Severe	Mild	Not Anaemic	Total
Education of	Illiterate	22	19	42	83
Mother in 5 groups	1–7 std	28	32	70	130
	8–9 std	17	16	66	99
	10–11 std	18	24	94	136
	12+ std	10	23	96	129
	Total	95	114	368	577

Table 7.10b   SPSS Output of Chi-square Tests

	Value	df	Asymp. Sig. (two-sided)
Pearson Chi-square	24.415[a]	8	.002
Likelihood Ratio	25.041	8	.002
Linear-by-Linear Association	22.503	1	.000
No. of Valid Cases	577		

Note: [a] 0 cells (.0%) have expected count less than 5. The minimum expected count is 13.67.

Table 7.10c   Percentage Distribution of Children by Anaemia Level, Classified by Education of Mother (from Table 7.10a, Row-wise Percentage)

Education of Mother	Anaemia Level of Child			Total (%)	Total (N)
	Moderate/Severe	Mild	Not Anaemic		
Illiterate	26.5	22.9	50.6	100.0	83
1–7 std	21.5	24.6	53.8	100.0	130
8–9 std	17.2	16.2	66.7	100.0	99
10–11 std	13.2	17.6	69.1	100.0	136
12+ std	7.8	17.8	74.4	100.0	129
Total	16.5	19.8	63.8	100.0	577

and mild anaemia combined) if their mothers were illiterate, and it decreased to 25.6 percent if their mothers had completed 12th standard. Furthermore, the proportion of children moderately or severely anaemic was 26.5 percent if their mothers were illiterate and it decreased to 7.8 percent if their mothers had completed 12th standard. So, it is clear that prevalence of anaemia among children decreases as the educational level of their mothers increases.

CHAPTER 8

Measures of Correlation

CORRELATION

Correlation (or co-relation) refers to the relationship between two (random) *numerical* variables. A correlation coefficient measures the strength and the direction of a *linear relationship* between the two variables. Correlation coefficient is very widely used in social sciences as a measure of the strength of linear dependence between two variables.

COVARIANCE

Let x and y be two variables, n be the sample of size, and $\bar{x}$ and $\bar{y}$ be their respective means. Then the covariance (or co-variance) is the relative variance between x and y (i.e., the variation in x values corresponding to the variation in y values, and vice versa) and is given by the formula:

$$\sigma_{xy} = \frac{1}{n}\sum(x_i - \bar{x})(y_i - \bar{y}).$$

The equation can be simplified as:

$$\sigma_{xy} = \frac{1}{n}\sum x_i y_i - \bar{x}\,\bar{y}.$$

Notes: Variance applies to a single variable, whereas covariance applies to two related variables taken together. For example, height and weight are two different single variables and covariance measures as to how much height and weight vary in relation to each other. Please note from $\sum x_i y_i$ (the first part of the second formula) that for the calculation of covariance, we take the sum of the product of the corresponding values of the variables, whereas for the calculation of variance, we take the sum of the square of the values of the individual variables (i.e., $\sum x_i^2$ and $\sum y_i^2$).

As far as the calculation of covariance from tabulated data is concerned, it is slightly difficult and lengthy. For this, the data need to be cross-tabulated and so the calculation of covariance from tabulated data is not considered here. Generally, we do not end with the calculation of covariance, but rather it is used in the derivation of indices such as the correlation coefficient (discussed later). As such, we often need not calculate sample covariance (i.e., covariance with $n-1$ in place of n).

If the two variables x and y have one-to-one correspondence (proportional increase or decrease), then $\sigma_{xy} = \sigma_x * \sigma_y$, and if both the variables are not related (as one variable increases or decreases, the other variable remains constant), then $\sigma_{xy} = 0$. It can be mathematically proved, but it is beyond the scope of this book. Alternatively, the reader can try with some trial data. Often, covariance is used in correlation to measure the relationship between two variables.

PEARSON'S PRODUCT-MOMENT CORRELATION COEFFICIENT

A number of different correlation coefficients are derived and used in different situations. The best known correlation coefficient is *Pearson's product-moment correlation coefficient*, which is obtained by dividing the covariance of two numerical variables by the product of their standard deviations. Pearson's correlation coefficient can be obtained for continuous and discrete (numerical) variables.

Formula: Let x and y be two random numerical variables. For a sample of n observations, let $\bar{x}$ and $\bar{y}$ be their means and σ_x and σ_y be their (population) standard deviations. Then, the Pearson's product-moment correlation coefficient, r, between x and y is given by the formula:

$$r = \frac{1}{n} \sum \left(\frac{x_i - \bar{x}}{\sigma_x} \right) \left(\frac{y_i - \bar{y}}{\sigma_y} \right)$$

The r is called *Pearson's product-moment correlation coefficient* or simply *correlation coefficient*. The 'product-moment' part of the name is because of the fact that the correlation coefficient is calculated by summing up the products of the deviations of the individual values from their respective means. Please note that 'r' (lower case) is used to denote bivariate (two variables) correlation coefficient (as discussed above), whereas 'R' (upper case) is used to denote multiple (many variables) correlation coefficient (to be discussed later).

By rearranging the terms, the correlation coefficient can be expressed in terms of (population) standard deviations and the covariance of x and y as:

$$r = \frac{1}{n} \sum \left(\frac{x_i - \bar{x}}{\sigma_x} \right) \left(\frac{y_i - \bar{y}}{\sigma_y} \right) = \frac{1}{n} \sum \left(\frac{(x_i - \bar{x})(y_i - \bar{y})}{\sigma_x * \sigma_y} \right) = \frac{\sigma_{xy}}{\sigma_x \sigma_y},$$

where

$$\sigma_{xy} = \frac{1}{n} \sum (x_i - \bar{x})(y_i - \bar{y}) \quad \text{or} \quad \sigma_{xy} = \frac{1}{n} \sum x_i y_i - \bar{x}\,\bar{y}$$

$$\sigma_x = \sqrt{\frac{1}{n} \sum (x_i - \bar{x})^2} \quad \text{or} \quad \sigma_x = \sqrt{\frac{1}{n} \sum x_i^2 - \bar{x}^2}$$

$$\sigma_y = \sqrt{\frac{1}{n} \sum (y_i - \bar{y})^2} \quad \text{or} \quad \sigma_y = \sqrt{\frac{1}{n} \sum y_i^2 - \bar{y}^2}$$

If we are manually computing the correlation coefficient, then we can simplify the formula by expanding σ_x and σ_y, and, thereby, cancelling out the $1/n$ from the numerator and the denominator, we get:

$$r = \frac{\sum (x_i - \bar{x})(y_i - \bar{y})}{\sqrt{\sum (x_i - \bar{x})^2 \sum (y_i - \bar{y})^2}} \quad \text{or}$$

$$r = \frac{\sum x_i y_i - n\bar{x}\,\bar{y}}{\sqrt{\left(\sum x_i^2 - n\bar{x}^2\right) * \left(\sum y_i^2 - n\bar{y}^2\right)}}.$$

Please note that all the formulae used here for the calculation of r are the same but are expressed in different formats, and the user may use any one as per convenience. If we are manually computing the correlation coefficient from raw data, then the above (last) formula is the simplest one. In this case, we need to first calculate $\sum x$, $\sum y$, $\sum x^2$, $\sum y^2$ and $\sum xy$, and then the other calculations follow very easily. On the other hand, if we have already calculated the variance or the standard deviations (σ_x and σ_y) and covariance σ_{xy}, then we can easily use the formula:

$$r = \frac{\sigma_{xy}}{\sigma_x \sigma_y}.$$

We can also compute the correlation coefficient using sample standard deviations s_x and s_y and sample covariance s_{xy} as follows:

$$r = \frac{s_{xy}}{s_x s_y},$$

where $s_{xy} = \dfrac{1}{n-1}\sum(x_i - \bar{x})(y_i - \bar{y})$,

$$s_x = \sqrt{\frac{1}{n-1}\sum(x_i - \bar{x})^2} \quad \text{and} \quad s_y = \sqrt{\frac{1}{n-1}\sum(y_i - \bar{y})^2}.$$

Properties of Correlation Coefficient

The correlation coefficient is defined (exists) only if the standard deviations of both the variables are finite and non-zero. The range of correlation coefficient is from -1 to $+1$. The correlation coefficient is an absolute number (free from the unit of measurement of the variables).

The correlation coefficient detects only the linear relationships and not any non-linear relationships between variables (see the table and charts in the next section for an explanation of linear relationship). If two variables are independent, then the correlation coefficient is 0 (zero), but it does not mean that the two variables are not at all related. It only means that there is no linear relationship between the two variables and non-linear relationships may exist.

If $r > 0$, then the two variables are said to be directly (positively) correlated or related, that is, the values of both the variables increase or decrease together. If $r < 0$, then the two variables are said to be inversely (negatively) correlated or related, that is, when the values of one variable increase, the values of the other variable decrease, and vice versa.

If $r > 0.5$, then we can say that the two variables are *positively and highly* correlated. If $r < -0.5$, then we can say that the two variables are *negatively and highly* correlated. If r is >0 but <0.5, then the two variables are said to be positively but weakly correlated. If r is <0 but >-0.5, then the two variables are said to be negatively but weakly correlated. However, a correlation coefficient in the range -0.25 to -0.50 or 0.25 to 0.50 may be said to be moderately correlated. A correlation coefficient in the range 0.75 to 1.0 or -0.75 to -1.0 is said to be very highly correlated, positively and negatively, respectively. In general, we can say that the closer the correlation coefficient to -1 or $+1$, the stronger the relation between the two variables, and the closer the coefficient to 0, the weaker the relation between the two variables.

Important Note: The interpretation of the correlation coefficient should depend on the context, and one need not strictly follow the ranges (mentioned above) for terming weak, moderate, high and very high correlations. For example, a correlation coefficient of 0.8 may indicate a strong relationship between education and income, but it may indicate a weak relationship (or conformity) between two instruments measuring the same items. It is because in the latter case, we expect both the instruments to give the same reading for each item measured so that the correlation of the readings of the two instruments is expectedly or almost equal to +1. In this case, a correlation coefficient of 0.8 may be an indication of serious problem with (or robustness of) the instruments.

A Graphical Representation of Linear Relationship between Variables

The table in Figure 8.1 clearly illustrates the behaviour of correlation coefficient. In the table, the YA values are exactly the double of the corresponding Y values, that is, there is an exact positive relationship between Y and YA, so the correlation coefficient is +1, and the observations form an exact ascending straight line (the line labelled YA in the first chart). On the other hand, the YB values decrease by two points for every five points increase in Y values, that is, there is an exact negative (linear) relationship between Y and YB and so the correlation coefficient is −1, and the observations form an exact descending straight line (the line labelled YB in the first chart).

Figure 8.1 Graphical Representation of Linear Relationships

Y	YA	YB	YC	YD	YE
5	10	120	31	191	154
10	20	118	26	152	125
15	30	116	48	110	118
20	40	114	32	198	82
25	50	112	71	181	71
30	60	110	120	167	51
35	70	108	49	154	18
40	80	106	70	170	7
45	90	104	66	159	31
50	100	102	97	129	46
55	110	100	71	139	77
60	120	98	90	104	104
65	130	96	113	93	75
70	140	94	87	93	102
75	150	92	110	104	129
80	160	90	98	63	180
85	170	88	133	61	167
90	180	86	113	46	92
95	190	84	136	56	59
100	200	82	158	33	41
Cor	1.00	-1.00	0.86	-0.89	0.05

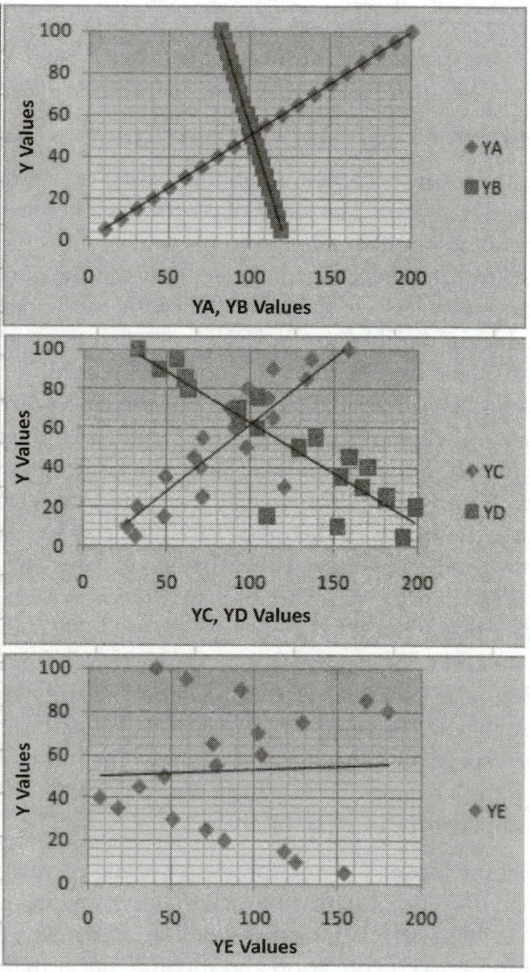

With respect to the relationship between Y and YC, and Y and YD, as the values of Y increase, generally (i.e., by and large), the values of YC also increase and the values of YD decrease, but not in any exact proportions, that is, there is a positive relationship between Y and YC and a negative relationship between Y and YD, and the correlation coefficients are worked out to be $+0.86$ and -0.89, respectively. Correspondingly, although the plotted values (second chart) do not lie on a straight line, most values are located close to it. On the other hand, the plot of the values of Y and YE (third chart) does not show any ascending or descending pattern of relationship. The values are just spread or clustered over the graph area. This is an indication of a very weak correlation or no linear relationship between the variables. The correlation coefficient obtained for this data is just 0.05, almost close to 0 (no correlation).

A few inferences can be drawn from this exercise. For two variables to be perfectly or highly correlated, it is not needed that a change in one variable should bring about substantial or multiple

Table 8.1 Calculation of Correlation Coefficient

Item	Weight (kg)	Height (cm)	NA	NA	NA
(1)	(2)	(3)	(4)	(5)	(6)
i	x	y	x^2	y^2	xy
1	6.3	68.0	39.69	4,624.00	428.40
2	9.1	73.5	82.81	5,402.25	668.85
3	16.1	104.3	259.21	10,878.49	1,679.23
4	15.3	98.4	234.09	9,682.56	1,505.52
5	12.0	93.5	144.00	8,742.25	1,122.00
6	12.3	85.3	151.29	7,276.09	1,049.19
7	11.5	88.5	132.25	7,832.25	1,017.75
8	12.7	95.0	161.29	9,025.00	1,206.50
9	13.7	102.1	187.69	10,424.41	1,398.77
10	8.0	72.0	64.00	5,184.00	576.00
11	15.0	100.0	225.00	10,000.00	1,500.00
12	19.3	97.3	372.49	9,467.29	1,877.89
13	9.4	90.0	88.36	8,100.00	846.00
14	8.7	77.2	75.69	5,959.84	671.64
15	8.5	70.3	72.25	4,942.09	597.55
16	9.4	78.8	88.36	6,209.44	740.72
17	9.5	84.0	90.25	7,056.00	798.00
18	11.0	86.6	121.00	7,499.56	952.60
19	23.7	107.3	561.69	11,513.29	2,543.01
20	8.6	75.4	73.96	5,685.16	648.44
21	9.3	80.5	86.49	6,480.25	748.65
22	9.4	81.8	88.36	6,691.24	768.92
23	11.0	92.0	121.00	8,464.00	1,012.00
24	13.4	96.0	179.56	9,216.00	1,286.40
Sum	283.2	2,097.8	3,700.78	186,355.46	25,644.03
Mean	11.8000	87.4083			
SD/Covariance			3.8677	11.1622	37.0829
Correlation Coefficient					0.859

times of change in the other variable. It is only sufficient that the change is constant or almost constant over the range of the variables, irrespective of whether the magnitude of the change is small or large. For example, the change in YA values is double than the change in Y values, but the change in YB values is only 0.2 times higher than the change in Y values, but still in both the cases, the correlation coefficient is exactly 1 (+ or −). Also, it is clear from the exercise that the correlation coefficient measures only the linear relationship between the variables. A weak or no correlation does not mean that the variables are not at all related; it only means that there is no linear relationship, and there might be other forms of (or non-linear) relationships. For example, though the correlation between Y and YE is 0.05 only, the chart 'YE' looks like a 'Z' type of relationship.

Example: The weights and heights of 24 children of age 1–4 are given in Table 8.1 (Columns 2 and 3). Calculate the correlation coefficient for the weights and heights of the children.

Method 1: Using x^2, y^2 and xy

Let the variable weight be x and height be y. First, calculate the square of the variable weight (x^2) and height (y^2), and the product of the weight and height ($x * y$) as in Columns 4–6 in the table, and obtain the sums for these columns (x, y, x^2, y^2 and xy). Then calculate the correlation coefficient r as follows:

$$r = \frac{\sum x_i y_i - n\bar{x}\,\bar{y}}{\sqrt{\left(\sum x_i^2 - n\bar{x}^2\right) * \left(\sum y_i^2 - n\bar{y}^2\right)}}$$

$$r = \frac{25,644.0324 - 24*(11.8000*87.4083)}{\sqrt{\{3,700.78 - 24*(11.8000*11.8000)\}*\{186,355.46 - 24*(87.4083*87.4083)\}}}$$

$$r = \frac{890.0018}{\sqrt{\{359.02\}*\{2,990.3982\}}} = \frac{890.0018}{\sqrt{1,073,612.76}} = \frac{890.0018}{1,036.153} = 0.8589.$$

Method 2: Using Mean, Standard Deviation and Covariance

$$\sigma_x^2 = \frac{1}{n}\sum x_i^2 - \bar{x}^2 = \frac{3,700.78}{24} - (11.8)*(11.8) = 14.9592 \text{ (and) } \sigma_x = 3.868$$

$$\sigma_y^2 = \frac{1}{n}\sum y_i^2 - \bar{y}^2 = \frac{186,355.46}{24} - (87.4083)*(87.4083) = 124.594 \text{ (and) } \sigma_y = 11.162$$

$$\sigma_{xy} = \frac{1}{n}\sum x_i y_i - \bar{x}\,\bar{y} = \frac{25,644.03}{24} - (11.8)*(87.408) = 37.083$$

$$r = \frac{\sigma_{xy}}{\sigma_x \sigma_y} = \frac{37.083}{3.868*11.162} = 0.8589.$$

Thus, the correlation coefficient between heights and weights of children is 0.86. As the sign of the correlation coefficient is plus (+), we can say that the correlation between heights and weights of children is positive, that is, as the heights of children increase, their weights also increase, and vice versa. Furthermore, as the absolute value of the correlation coefficient (0.86) is very high (>0.75), we can say that the correlation between the heights and weights is very strong, or the two variables are highly correlated.

Notes: In the regression analysis of a predictor (independent) variable (say X) on a criterion (dependent) variable (say Y), the squared term of the correlation coefficient (r^2) is often termed as the 'coefficient of determination'. It indicates the amount of variance in the dependent variable Y, which is explained or accounted for by the variation in the independent variable X. That is, r^2 is a measure of variance explained and it is called the coefficient of determination (see Chapter 11).

Pearson's correlation coefficient is a parametric statistic (theoretical or probability distribution based, or the relationship is assumed to be of specific nature, here, *linear*) and is applicable to discrete and continuous (numerical) variables, except categorical variables. The correlation coefficient is less useful if the distribution of the two variables is not normal (see Chapter 6). If the distributions are not normal, then the non-parametric correlation methods such as Spearman's rank correlation coefficient (ρ), chi-square (χ^2), correlation ratio, Kendall's tau coefficient (τ), and Goodman and Kruskal's lambda (λ) are useful. (Only the Spearman's rank correlation coefficient and Kendall's Tau, which are often used, are discussed in this book.)

SPEARMAN'S RANK CORRELATION COEFFICIENT

Pearson's product-moment correlation coefficient is a parametric measure, and assumes that the relationship between two (random) variables is linear. Often, the linear relationship may not be valid and the pattern of relationship is not known. Charles Spearman devised a method to measure the correlation between two variables, without any assumption of the nature of relationship between the two, that is, Spearman's rank correlation coefficient is a non-parametric (distribution-free, more details in Chapter 10) rank statistic, and it measures the strength of association between two variables without making any assumptions about the frequency distribution of the variables. Unlike Pearson's product-moment correlation coefficient, Spearman's rank correlation coefficient does not assume that the relationship between the variables is linear. Furthermore, Pearson's correlation coefficient requires that the variables are measured on interval scales, but Spearman's rank correlation coefficient can be used for variables measured at the ordinal level as well.

Spearman converted the raw scores or values of the two variables into ranks and used the difference between the ranks of the two variables, for each observation, for the calculation of the correlation coefficient. As this correlation coefficient is based on the ranks of the variables, it is called *Spearman's rank correlation coefficient* or simply *rank correlation coefficient*. It is denoted by the symbol ρ (rho).

Let X and Y be two variables, and X_i and Y_i ($i = 1$ to n) be the pairs of n observations of the variables X and Y. Let us assume that each of the n values of X and Y, $X_1, X_2, \ldots, X_n$ and $Y_1, Y_2, \ldots, Y_n$, respectively, are distinct among themselves (i.e., no two values are the same, and later we will relax this condition). Let $(x_1, x_2, \ldots, x_n)$ be the ranks of $(X_1, X_2, \ldots, X_n)$, and $(y_1, y_2, \ldots, y_n)$ be the ranks of $(Y_1, Y_2, \ldots, Y_n)$, so that the values $(x_1, x_2, \ldots, x_n)$ and $(y_1, y_2, \ldots, y_n)$ lie in the range 1 to n. Also, let $d_i = x_i - y_i$ be the difference between the ranks of corresponding values X_i and Y_i. Then the Spearman's rank correlation coefficient is given by the formula:

$$\rho = 1 - \frac{6 \sum d_i^2}{n(n^2 - 1)}.$$

If any two or more values are the same (called bracketed or tied or equal), Spearman's rank correlation coefficient method breaks down. In this case, the repeated values are assigned consecutive ranks and their average value is taken as the final rank for each of these cases. For such occasion of repetition, a correction factor $\frac{1}{12} m(m^2 - 1)$ is to be added to the term $\sum d_i^2$, where m is the number of values repeated in each occasion.

The correction factor may be applied one by one as above or, incorporating the correction factors for all repetitions of X and Y values, the formula may be written as:

$$\rho = 1 - \frac{6\sum d_i^2 + CF}{n(n^2-1)}, \text{ where } CF = \frac{1}{12}\sum_{j=1}^{r} m_j(m_j^2-1)$$

Here, r is the number of values of X and Y that are repeated, m_j is the number of repetitions of the jth value (among the repeated ones) and $j=1$ to r.

The equation can be rewritten incorporating the correction factor (CF) as:

$$\rho = 1 - \frac{6\sum_{i=1}^{n} d_i^2 + \frac{1}{12}\sum_{j=1}^{r} m_j(m_j^2-1)}{n(n^2-1)}.$$

Notes:

1. The rank correlation coefficient takes a value between −1 and +1 and the strength of relationship is interpreted in the same way as the product moment correlation coefficient.
2. If the number of observations is large, then the number of ties would be many and the manual calculation of rank correlation would be difficult.
3. Since the rank correlation coefficient is a non-parametric index, it is not amenable (useful) for further statistical analysis.

Calculation of Tied Ranks

A simple way to determine the ranks in case of ties (of values) is as follows. In Table 8.2, Column 1 is the serial numbers of the observations and Column 2 is the values of the observations (say, X values). First, look at the values and assign ranks in ascending order of the values in such a way that repeated values will take subsequent ranks (in Excel sheet it is easy: simply sort the values in ascending order [as in Columns 3 and 4] and assign serial numbers as in Column 5). For example, the lowest value 33 (original serial number 20) takes the rank 1 and the value 34 is repeated twice and takes ranks 2 and 3. Similarly the value 41 is repeated thrice taking ranks 6, 7 and 8 and so on. As the ranks are not final we call them as initial ranks. Please note that the 20 observations have 20 ranks from 1 to 20 without repetition even though some values are repeated. In the next step, identify the repeating values and for each repeating value, work out the mean of the corresponding ranks.

For example, the mean of the ranks for the repeating value 34 is $(2+3)/2=2.5$ and the mean of the ranks for the repeating value 41 is $(6+7+8)/3=7.0$. The mean ranks for the tied values are presented in Column 6. The third step is to replace the initial ranks with the mean rank for the tied values and retain the original initial ranks for the non-repeating values, and accordingly Column 7 gives the final ranks. Please note that the final ranks in Column 7 need to be re-sorted according to original serial number in Column 1 before further calculations. In a similar way, determine the final ranks for the variable Y. The calculation of rank correlation coefficient is given below in two examples. In addition, an example using SPSS is also presented.

Simplified Spearman's Rank Correlation Coefficient

An alternate but simplified form of Spearman's rank correlation coefficient is calculated as the product-moment correlation of the ranks instead of the original values. It is often denoted by the symbol r_s.

Table 8.2   Calculation of Ranks for Tied Values

Original Order		Sorted in Ascending Order of X Values				Final Ranks
Serial Number	X Values	Serial Number	X Values	Initial Ranks	Tied Ranks	
(1)	(2)	(3)	(4)	(5)	(6)	(7)
1	40	20	33	1	–	1
2	49	14	34	2	(2+3)/2=2.5	2.5
3	51	19	34	3	(2+3)/2=2.5	2.5
4	43	17	37	4	–	4
5	67	1	40	5	–	5
6	41	6	41	6	(6+7+8)/3=7.0	7
7	41	7	41	7	(6+7+8)/3=7.0	7
8	42	12	41	8	(6+7+8)/3=7.0	7
9	51	8	42	9	–	9
10	43	4	43	10	(10+11+12+13)/4=11.5	11.5
11	46	10	43	11	(10+11+12+13)/4=11.5	11.5
12	41	13	43	12	(10+11+12+13)/4=11.5	11.5
13	43	18	43	13	(10+11+12+13)/4=11.5	11.5
14	34	11	46	14	–	14
15	47	15	47	15	–	15
16	62	2	49	16	–	16
17	37	3	51	17	(17+18)/2=17.5	17.5
18	43	9	51	18	(17+18)/2=17.5	17.5
19	34	16	62	19	–	19
20	33	5	67	20	–	20

Example 1: The weights of 10 couples measured in kg are given below. Obtain the rank correlation coefficient.

Husband	50	40	55	64	80	68	75	75	64	64
Wife	45	48	50	58	60	62	68	68	70	81

Solution: The calculations are presented in Table 8.3.

In this data, husbands' weight 64 has occurred three times, 75 has occurred two times, and wives' weight 68 has occurred two times. So the correction factor is:

$$CF = \frac{3(3^2 - 1) + 2(2^2 - 1) + 2(2^2 - 1)}{12} = \frac{36}{12} = 3$$

$$\rho = 1 - \frac{6\sum d_i^2 + CF}{n(n^2 - 1)} = 1 - \frac{6*72 + 3}{10(10*10-1)} = 1 - \frac{435}{990} = 1 - 0.4394 = 0.5606$$

$r_s = 0.5556$ (usual correlation coefficient is based on the corrected ranks,

i.e., based on Columns 'Rank (RH)' and 'Rank (RW)'.)

The rank correlation coefficient for the given data is 0.56. As the rank correlation coefficient $0.56 > 0.5$, we can say that the weights of husbands and wives are highly positively correlated, that is, the higher the weight of husband, the higher the weight of wife, and vice versa.

Table 8.3   Calculation of Rank Correlation Coefficient

Wt (H)	Wt (W)	Rank (RH)	Rank (RW)	d = RH − RW	d * d
50	45	2	1	1	1
40	48	1	2	−1	1
55	50	3	3	0	0
64	58	5	4	1	1
80	60	10	5	5	25
68	62	7	6	1	1
75	68	8.5	7.5	1	1
75	68	8.5	7.5	1	1
64	70	5	9	−4	16
64	81	5	10	−5	25
Sum					72

Example 2: Table 8.4 gives the weight and height of 24 women of age 15–49 (first three columns). Find out the rank correlation between the weight and height of the women.

The steps involved in the calculation of rank correlation coefficient are already explained. The calculation and results are presented in the following two tables (Tables 8.4 and 8.5).

$$\rho = 1 - \frac{6 \sum d_i^2 + CF}{n(n^2 - 1)} = 1 - \frac{6 * 1331.5 + \dfrac{138}{12}}{20(20 * 20 - 1)} = 1 - \frac{8000.5}{7980} = 1 - 1.0026 = -0.002569$$

$r_s = -0.00986$ (Usual correlation coefficient is based on adjusted ranks).

KENDALL'S TAU

Kendall's τ (tau) is a non-parametric measure of correlation between two ranked variables. It is similar to Spearman's ρ and Pearson's r as it, too, measures the relationship between two variables. Its interpretation is also very similar to ρ and r, that is, for two paired variables, say X and Y, a positive value of τ implies that as X increases, Y also increases and as X decreases, Y also decreases, while a negative value of τ implies that as X increases, Y decreases and as X decreases, Y increases. There are two variants of Kendall's tau: tau-a and tau-b. They differ only in the way they handle rank ties; while tau-a is calculated for data without any ties, tau-b is calculated for data with ties.

The calculation of tau-a (τ_a) is better explained with a small example. The marks scored by five students in Physics and Chemistry are given below.

Student	1	2	3	4	5
Physics	79	72	69	93	92
Chemistry	55	77	97	59	68

The first step in the calculation of tau-a is sorting the data according to the values of one variable, say, Physics, and labelling the order as a, b, c, d, e as shown here under.

Student	3	2	1	5	4
Physics	69	72	79	92	93
Chemistry	97	77	55	68	59
Order	a	b	c	d	e

Table 8.4   Calculation of Spearman's Rank Correlation Coefficient

Item	Weight (kg)	Height (cm)	Ranks for X		Ranks for Y		Difference in Adjusted Ranks	
i	*X*	*Y*	*Consecutive*	*Adjusted*	*Consecutive*	*Adjusted*	*d*	*d * d*
1	40	153	5	5	12	12	−7.0	49.00
2	49	143	16	16	3	2.5	13.5	182.25
3	51	151	17	17.5	8	8	9.5	90.25
4	43	143	10	11.5	2	2.5	9.0	81.00
5	67	160	20	20	20	20	0.0	0.00
6	41	154	6	7	13	13	−6.0	36.00
7	41	158	7	7	18	18	−11.0	121.00
8	42	142	9	9	1	1	8.0	64.00
9	51	152	18	17.5	11	10	7.5	56.25
10	43	150	11	11.5	7	7	4.5	20.25
11	46	152	14	14	9	10	4.0	16.00
12	41	149	8	7	6	6	1.0	1.00
13	43	147	12	11.5	5	5	6.5	42.25
14	34	157	2	2.5	16	16.5	−14.0	196.00
15	47	152	15	15	10	10	5.0	25.00
16	62	159	19	19	19	19	0.0	0.00
17	37	145	4	4	4	4	0.0	0.00
18	43	157	13	11.5	17	16.5	−5.0	25.00
19	34	155	3	2.5	15	14.5	−12.0	144.00
20	33	155	1	1	14	14.5	−13.5	182.25
Sum							0	1,331.50

Note: Repetition: X values: 34*2, 41*3, 43*4, 51*2 times; Y values: 143*2, 152*3, 155*2, 157*2 times.

Table 8.5   Correction Factor Table

Variable	Value	Repetitions (m)	$m(m^2 - 1)$
X	34	2	6
X	41	3	24
X	43	4	60
X	51	2	6
Y	143	2	6
Y	152	3	24
Y	155	2	6
Y	157	2	6
Sum			138

Now, look at the order of the pairs of Chemistry marks $(ab, ac, ad, ae, bc, bd, be, cd, ce, de)$. For example, $a=97$ and $b=77$, that is, b is less than a, and so order ab is negative and it is marked as $ab=-1$. Similarly, $ac=-1$, $ad=-1$, $ae=-1$, $bc=-1$, $bd=-1$, $be=-1$, $cd=+1$, $ce=+1$ and $de=-1$. Now count the number of the concordant pairs (+pairs); they are two in our example (cd and ce). In a similar way, count the number of the discordant pairs (–pairs); they are eight in our example. Please check that the total of concordant pairs ($C=2$) and discordant pairs ($D=8$) should add to $n(n-1)/2=5(5-1)/2=10$.

$$\tau_a = \frac{C-D}{C+D} = \frac{C-D}{\frac{1}{2}n(n-1)} = \frac{2-8}{2+8} = \frac{-6}{10} = -0.6.$$

The formula for the computation of tau-b is given below:

$$\tau_b = \frac{C-D}{\frac{1}{2}\sqrt{n(n-1)-T_x}\sqrt{n(n-1)-T_y}},$$

where C, D and n are as defined above. T_x and T_y are explained below. Let one value of X repeat m times and another value repeat k times, and so on. Then, $T_x=(m^2-m)+(k^2-k)+\ldots$. Similarly, T_y is also calculated. These calculations are very similar to the CF calculation in Spearman's rank calculation. Numerical example for computation of tau-b is not presented.

TEST OF SIGNIFICANCE OF CORRELATION COEFFICIENTS

Test for Pearson's Correlation Coefficient

With respect to the hypothesis testing of Pearson's correlation coefficient, the hypothesis is that there exists no linear relationship between the two variables as seen in the correlation coefficient (r). The null hypothesis (H_0) is that 'there exists no linear relationship between the two variables' and the alternate hypothesis (H_1) is that 'there exists a linear relationship between the two variables'. As in all the hypotheses testing, the goal is to reject the null hypothesis and to accept the alternate hypothesis, that, there exists a linear relationship between the two variables.

Let n be the sample size, r be the correlation coefficient (Pearson's product-moment correlation coefficient) and μ be an estimate of the population correlation coefficient. The null and alternate hypothesises are:

H_0: $\mu=0$ (no correlation between the two variables)

H_1: $\mu \neq 0$ (or $\mu <> 0$, the two variables are correlated)

The test statistic is $t = r\sqrt{\dfrac{n-2}{1-r^2}}$ with $(n-2)$ degrees of freedom

Assumptions/Conditions: The Pearson's correlation coefficient test assumes that the observations are measured in interval or ratio scale, there is no correlation between the observations (i.e., no autocorrelation), outliers, if any, are minimum, there exists a linear relationship between the two variables, the sample is drawn using the SRS method from a large population (at least 10 times larger than the sample size) and the variables are approximately normally distributed, and there exists homoscedasticity (i.e., constant variance) of the errors.

Test of Significance of Spearman's Rank Correlation Coefficient

Spearman's rank correlation test uses the ranks to test for the association (and not the correlation in the real sense). However, association is a broad term covering different types of relationships. For the Spearman's rank correlation test to work, the underlying relationship must be monotonic, that is, either the variables increase in value together or, when one increases, the other decreases. The null hypothesis is written in terms of 'no association between the two variables'. It is not appropriate to state that 'no rank correlation between the variables' as it would be incorrect and confusing.

H_0: There is no association between the variables in the underlying population.

H_1: There is some association between the variables in the underlying population.

The test statistic is $t = r_s \sqrt{\dfrac{n-2}{1-r_s^2}}$ with $(n-2)$ degrees of freedom.

Test of Significance of Kendall's Tau

Kendall's tau correlation test also uses the ranks to test for the association. The null hypothesis is written in terms of 'no association between the two variables'.

The test statistic for tau without ties is $Z = \dfrac{C-D}{\sigma}$,

where $\sigma^2 = \dfrac{1}{18} n(n-1)(2n+5)$.

The test statistic for tau with ties is $Z = \dfrac{C-D+\delta}{\sigma_s}$,

where $\sigma^2 = \dfrac{1}{18}(n(n-1)(2n+5) - T_x'' - T_y'')$,

δ, T_x'' and T_y'' are the adjustment factors for the ties (they consist of a few lengthy mathematical equations and, hence, they are not presented here).

AN SPSS EXAMPLE OF CORRELATION COEFFICIENTS AND SIGNIFICANT TESTS

It is hypothesised that the children of higher orders grow slower in terms of height and weight due to lesser care by their parents. To test this hypothesis, we will analyse height, weight and birth order of the children of age 1–4 years (12–59 months) of Goa, obtained from NFHS-3 using Pearson's, Kendall's and Spearman's correlation coefficients.

To run the correlation in SPSS, choose the menu 'Analyze => Correlate => Bivariate' and a window will open as in Figure 8.2. In the resulting window, transfer the variables of interest (here weight of child, height of child and birth order of child) to the box labelled 'Variables', and choose under options 'Correlation Coefficients', the correlations desired (here all the three correlations, namely, Pearson, Kendall and Spearman) and 'Two-tailed' under 'Test of Significance'. The SPSS output is given in Tables 8.6a and 8.6b.

Table 8.6a gives Pearson's correlation coefficients, significant level of the correlation coefficients with the two-tailed test and the number of cases in each of the combination of variables. Similarly, Table 8.6b gives Kendall's and Spearman's correlation coefficients, significant level of the correlation coefficients with the two-tailed test and the number of cases in each of the combination of variables. Please note that the matrix of figures in the tables is symmetric from the diagonal and so we need to give our attention to the figures above (or below) the diagonal only.

Figure 8.2 SPSS Window for Bivariate Correlations

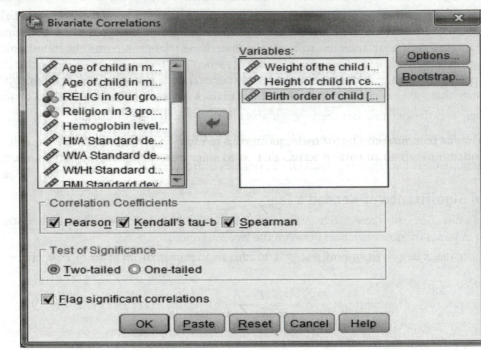

Table 8.6a SPSS Output of Pearson's Correlations and Their Significant Levels

		Weight of the Child in kg	Height of Child in cm	Birth Order of Child
Weight of the child in kg	Pearson Correlation	1	.849**	−.066
	Sig. (two-tailed)		.000	.061
	N	809	803	809
Height of child in cm	Pearson Correlation	.849**	1	−.022
	Sig. (two-tailed)	.000		.525
	N	803	806	806
Birth order of child	Pearson Correlation	−.066	−.022	1
	Sig. (two-tailed)	.061	.525	
	N	809	806	962

Note: **Correlation is significant at the 0.01 level (two-tailed).

From Table 8.6a, it is seen that Person's correlation between the weight and height of children is 0.849 and the relationship is positive and highly significant ($p = 0.00 < 0.01$) at 1 percent level of significance. On the other hand, the correlation between weight and birth order is −0.066 and the relationship is negative (as $r < 0$) but not significant ($p = 0.061 > 0.05$) even at 5 percent level of significance. Similarly, the correlation between height and birth order is −0.022 and the relationship is negative ($r < 0$) but not significant ($p = 0.525 > 0.05$) at 5 percent level of significance. It is to be noted that SPSS does not print out the t-values for correlation tests.

Table 8.6b   SPSS Output of Kendall's Tau and Spearman's Rho and Their Significant Levels

			Weight of the Child in kg	*Height of Child in cm*	*Birth Order of Child*
Kendall's tau-b	Weight of the child in kg	Correlation Coefficient	1.000	.716**	−.041
		Sig. (two-tailed)		.000	.136
		N	809	803	809
	Height of child in cm	Correlation Coefficient	.716**	1.000	−.011
		Sig. (two-tailed)	.000		.678
		N	803	806	806
	Birth order of child	Correlation Coefficient	−.041	−.011	1.000
		Sig. (two-tailed)	.136	.678	
		N	809	806	962
Spearman's; rho	Weight of the child in kg	Correlation Coefficient	1.000	.875**	−.052
		Sig. (two-tailed)		.000	.139
		N	809	803	809
	Height of child in cm	Correlation Coefficient	.875**	1.000	−.014
		Sig. (two-tailed)	.000		.682
		N	803	806	806
	Birth order of child	Correlation Coefficient	−.052	−.014	1.000
		Sig. (two-tailed)	.139	.682	
		N	809	806	962

Note: **Correlation is significant at the 0.01 level (two-tailed).

In a similar way, it is seen from Table 8.6b that Kendall's tau correlation between weight and height of children is 0.716 and the relationship is positive and highly significant ($p=0.00<0.01$) at 1 percent level of significance. On the other hand, the correlation between weight and birth order is −0.041 and the relationship is negative (as $r<0$) but weak ($p=0.136>0.05$) at 5 percent level of significance. Similarly, the correlation between height and birth order is −0.011 and the relationship is negative ($r<0$) but weak ($p=0.678>0.05$) at 5 percent level of significance.

Spearman's rank correlation coefficient (rho) between weight and height is 0.875, that is, they are highly and positively associated. On the other hand, the relationships between weight and birth order, and between height and birth order are negative, but weak.

In this exercise, all the three methods consistently reveal that the height and weight of children are highly positively related but they are not influenced by the birth order of the children, that is, the height and weight of children are not influenced by the birth order of the children and so, we cannot say that the children of higher orders receive lesser child care than the children of lower orders, as far as Goa is concerned.

Note: SPSS uses the r_s algorithm for the calculation of Spearman's rank correlation coefficient, and so the coefficient value may slightly differ from the ρ method.

PARTIAL CORRELATION

Let the two variables x and y be correlated, and let z be another variable (say, control variable) that affects the relationship between x and y. A measure of the correlation between x and y controlling or adjusting for the effect of z is called partial correlation and is denoted by the symbol $r_{xy.z}$.

The partial correlation coefficient is a measure of the linear relationship between two variables, while controlling or adjusting for the effect of one or more additional variables. Examples: (a) correlation between the number of children ever born and age of woman controlling for duration of marriage, and (b) correlation between household income and expenditure controlling for household size (the number of members in the household).

Let there be three numerical variables x, y and z. Let the correlation between x and y be r_{xy}, between y and z be r_{yz} and between x and z be r_{xz}. The partial correlation between x and y controlling for the effect of z is given by the formula:

$$r_{xy.z} = \frac{r_{xy} - r_{xz}r_{yz}}{\sqrt{(1 - r_{xz}^2)(1 - r_{yz}^2)}}.$$

The partial correlation coefficient varies between –1 and +1.

A correlation coefficient between two variables is often called 'zero order' correlation coefficient as no factor is controlled or kept constant. A partial correlation between two variables by keeping one variable (the third variable) constant is called 'first-order' correlation coefficient (as per the number of variables kept constant). Similarly, a partial correlation between two variables by keeping two variables (the third and the fourth variable) constant is called 'second-order' correlation coefficient, and so on. Partial correlation analysis assumes the significance where the phenomena under investigation have multiple factors influencing them or where various interrelated phenomena are to be investigated.

An SPSS Example of Partial Correlation Coefficient

Let us use the same NFHS-3 Goa data and obtain partial correlation between the height and weight of children controlling for age. To obtain partial correlation, choose the menu 'Analyze => Correlate => Partial'. In the pop-up window (Figure 8.3), transfer the height and weight variables to the box labelled 'Variables' and the age variable to the box labelled 'Controlling for' as shown in the figure. If zero-order correlation is also desired, click 'Options' and select 'Zero-order correlations' (selected in this example) and press 'continue'. Then press 'OK'.

The SPSS output is presented in Table 8.7. In the table, the upper panel (control variables 'None') contains the zero-order correlations and the lower panel (control variables 'age of child in months') contains the partial correlations.

It is seen from the table that the zero-order correlation between weight and height is 0.785, between weight and age is 0.663, between height and age is 0.830, and the partial correlation between weight and height controlling age is 0.562. The partial correlation between the weight (w), height (h) and controlling age (a) can be calculated manually also (using the zero-order correlations) as:

$$r_{hw.a} = \frac{r_{hw} - r_{ha}r_{wa}}{\sqrt{(1 - r_{ha}^2)(1 - r_{wa}^2)}} = \frac{0.785207 - 0.663463*0.830244}{\sqrt{(1 - 0.663463*0.663463)(1 - 0.830244*0.830244)}}$$
$$= 0.56197.$$

Note: Higher order correlation coefficients are not discussed due to the fact that the formulae are more complex and the calculations are difficult. However, SPSS provides higher order correlation coefficients. For that, we only need to add the desired variables into the box 'Controlling for' in the SPSS window.

Figure 8.3   SPSS Window for Partial Correlation Coefficient

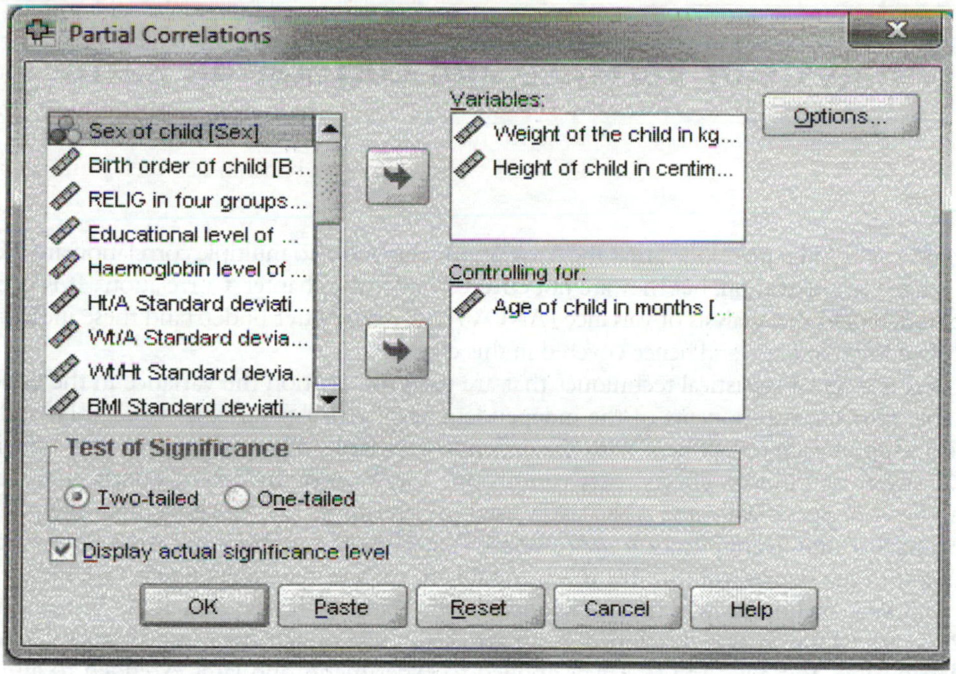

Table 8.7   SPSS Output of Partial Correlation Coefficients and Significance Levels

Control Variables			Weight of the Child in kg	Height of Child in cm	Age of Child in Months
-none-[a]	Weight of the Child in kg	Correlation	1.000	.785	.663
		Sig. (two-tailed)		.000	.000
		df		673	673
	Height of child in centimetres	Correlation	.785	1.000	.830
		Sig. (two-tailed)	.000		.000
		df	673		673
	Age of child in months	Correlation	.663	.830	1.000
		Sig. (two-tailed)	.000	.000	
		df	673	673	
Age of child in months	Weight of the child in kg	Correlation	1.000	.562	
		Significance (two-tailed)		.000	
		df		672	
	Height of child in cm	Correlation	.562	1.000	
		Sig. (two-tailed)	.000		
		df	672		

Note: [a]Cells contain zero-order (Pearson) correlations.

CHAPTER 9

Analysis of Variance and Correlation Ratio

At the outset, it is to be mentioned that the correlation ratio and also multiple correlation are indices that are related to correlation, but they are not covered under the chapter 'Correlation'. It is because once we understand the analysis of variance (ANOVA), we can better understand these indices and also calculate these indices, and hence covered in this chapter.

ANOVA is a set of statistical techniques that are used to partition the variance in the dependent variable into the components of the independent (explanatory) variables or factors, and test the relationship of each component with the dependent variable. The components may be within group variation or random effects, between groups variation or treatment effects, interaction effects and so on. Specifically, the ANOVA is used to determine: (a) which factors (independent variables) have a significant effect on the response (dependent) variable and/or (b) how much of the variation in the dependent variable is attributable to each of the independent variables.

The ANOVA technique was first developed by the famous Statistician R.A. Fisher during the 1920s and 1930s. It was developed as a part of the test of statistical significance based on the F-distribution. Initially, ANOVA was applied to experiments and later extended to all types of data including cross-sectional data. There are several types of ANOVA procedures available depending on the number of treatments and the way they are applied to the subjects. The simplest of the ANOVA procedures is the one-way or one-factor ANOVA.

Generally, in ANOVA, the dependent variable is a numerical (continuous or discrete) variable and the independent/explanatory variables are categorical (nominal or ordinal) variables. In addition, if numerical variables are converted into categorical variables, then they also can form a part of the independent variables list. Numerical variables with actual values (without making categories) can also form a part of the independent variables list and they are termed as 'covariates' in SPSS.

It is to be noted that ANOVA is a complex statistical procedure but found in most statistical analyses, especially in multivariate statistical analyses. However, in order for the readers to have some understanding of the technique, simplest of the ANOVA procedure, that is, one-way ANOVA is discussed in this chapter.

ONE-WAY ANALYSIS OF VARIANCE

If there is only one explanatory variable, then the ANOVA procedure is called one-way or one-factor ANOVA. In one-way ANOVA, the explanatory variable is a categorical variable with two or more categories (groups). If there are only two categories (groups) in the explanatory variable (factor), then the one-way ANOVA is equivalent to the two-sample t-test. As such, the one-way ANOVA generalises the t-test to k categories, where k is equal to or greater than 2. The ANOVA is used to test the hypothesis that the group means are all equal.

The technical aspect of the one-way ANOVA is given in Appendix B as it is a bit complex. For a social scientist, it would be sufficient to understand the following. The total variance (called the total sum of squares, TSS) of a dependent numerical variable can be partitioned into two parts. One part is due to its variation within the categories of the independent variable (called within sum of squares, WSS) and the other part is due to the variation between the categories of the independent variable (called between sum of squares, BSS), so that TSS = WSS + BSS. For the categories (or groups) to be significantly different, the BSS needs to be larger and the WSS smaller, so that the ratio BSS/WSS is larger.

Let n be the number of observations and k be the number of groups in the independent variable; then, the quantity BSS is associated with $(k-1)$ degrees of freedom and the quantity WSS is associated with $(n-k)$ degrees of freedom.

Then, the ratio $\dfrac{\text{BSS}/(k-1)}{\text{WSS}/(n-k)}$ follows the F-distribution with $(k-1, n-k)$ degrees of freedom.

The F-test is a simultaneous test of the hypothesis that all the group means are the same, that is, the null hypothesis is

$H_0 : \bar{Y}_1 = \bar{Y}_2 = \ldots = \bar{Y}_k.$

H_1 : Not all means are the same (statistical statement bit tricky).

If one is interested in terms of the statistical statement, it would be a series of statement as: H_1: $\bar{Y}_1 \neq \bar{Y}_2 = \cdots = \bar{Y}_k$ or $\bar{Y}_1 = \bar{Y}_2 \neq \cdots = \bar{Y}_k$ or $\bar{Y}_1 = \bar{Y}_2 = \cdots \neq \bar{Y}_k$, and so on, that is, there should be at least one $\neq$ sign in it and, not all.

Table 9.1 is the ANOVA table.

A Numerical Example

The following table gives the number of children ever born (CEB) to 35 women classified by the education of woman (EduW). The EduW variable is classified into three groups, namely 0=illiterate, 1=1–7 std and 2=8+ std. Test whether the number of CEB differs by the educational level of women.

Case	1	2	3	4	5	6	7	8	9	10	11	12	13	14	15	16	17	18	19	20	21	22	23	24	25	26	27	28	29	30	31	32	33	34	35
EduW	0	1	0	0	1	0	1	0	2	0	1	0	0	1	0	0	1	0	1	0	0	0	0	1	1	2	2	0	1	2	1	2	2	2	0
CEB	4	2	3	2	2	2	3	3	2	5	2	7	5	3	2	2	5	2	3	2	3	4	6	3	3	2	1	5	3	3	2	2	2	2	2

The calculations for the ANOVA are given in Table 9.2.

Number of cases $n=35$ and number of EduW groups $k=3$.

TSS = 62.9714

Table 9.1   Analysis of Variance (ANOVA) Table

Source of Variation	Variation or Sum of Squares	Degrees of Freedom	Mean Sum of Squares or Variance	F-ratio
Between groups	BSS $= \Sigma_{i=1}^{k} \Sigma_{j=1}^{n_i} (\bar{Y}_i - \bar{Y})^2$	$k-1$	MBSS $= \dfrac{\text{ESS}}{k-1}$	$F = \dfrac{\text{MBSS}}{\text{MWSS}}$
Within group	WSS $= \Sigma_{i=1}^{k} \Sigma_{j=1}^{n_i} (\bar{Y}_i - \bar{Y})^2$	$n-k$	MWSS $= \dfrac{\text{USS}}{n-k}$	
Total	TSS $= \Sigma_{i=1}^{k} \Sigma_{j=1}^{n_i} (\bar{Y}_i - \bar{Y})^2$	$n-1$	NA	$(k-1, n-k)$df

Table 9.2 ANOVA Table (Sum of Squares) for the Numerical Data

Edu Group	No. of Cases	Children Ever Born (CEB)	Mean CEB	$\sum(CEB^2)$	Sum of Squares[$]
Illiterate	17	4,3,2,2,3,5,7,5,2,2,2,2,3,4,6,5	3.4706	247	42.2353
1–7 std	11	2,2,3,2,3,5,3,3,3,3,2	2.8182	95	7.6364
8+ std	7	2,2,1,3,2,2,2	2.0000	30	2.0000
Combined	35	All the above values	2.9714	372	62.9714

Notes: [$] Deviation from mean $=\sum(CEB^2) - \#$ cases $*$ (Mean $CEB)^2$; Combined may not tally with Edu Groups.

$$WSS = 42.2353 + 7.6364 + 2.0000 = 51.8717$$
$$BSS = TSS - WSS = 62.9714 - 51.8717 = 11.0998$$
$$MWSS = WSS/(n-k) = 51.8717/32 = 1.6210$$
$$MBSS = BSS/(k-1) = 11.0998/2 = 5.5500$$
$$F = MBSS/MWSS = 5.5500/1.6210 = 3.4237.$$

The F-table value for (2, 32) degrees of freedom is 3.29 at the 5 percent level and 5.31 at the 1 percent level (obtained through interpolation). The F-table is not presented in this book as it is lengthy but can be download from the web. Also, the F-table value can be obtained using the Excel function F.INV.RT, that is, F.INV.RT(0.05, 2, 32) = 3.294537. (In this function, 0.05 is the 5 percent significance level, and 2 and 32 are the degrees of freedom.) Alternatively, the probability value α can be obtained for $F = 3.4237$ using the Excel function F.DIST.RT(3.4237, 2, 32) = 0.0449. (In this function, 3.4237 is the calculated F value, and 2 and 32 are the degree of freedoms.) The calculated F value of 3.4237 is higher than the table value of 3.29 at the 5 percent level of significance, or $\alpha = 0.0449 < 0.05$. So we reject the null hypothesis that the group means are all equal, that is, the numbers of children ever born to women of different education groups differ significantly. In other words, we can conclude that women of different education groups have the different numbers of children ever born to them. However, at this stage, we cannot say which pairs of groups differ and which pairs do not differ and that has to be obtained using post hoc tests (described below).

An SPSS Example of One-way ANOVA

Let us use SPSS to conduct the one-way ANOVA for the same data. First, open an Excel sheet, copy the given data, transpose the data and paste it in another area in the Excel sheet (to make it as a column data). Then, open SPSS, turn on 'Data View' sheet and copy the dataset (excluding the labels) onto the SPSS data sheet. Next, turn to 'Variables View' and rename the variables as Case, EduW and CEB. Now, go to the menu 'Analyze => Compare means => One-Way ANOVA' and click. The One-Way ANOVA program window is open as shown in Figure 9.1. Now, transfer the variable 'CEB' to the box labelled 'Dependent List' and the variable 'EduW' to the box labelled 'Factor' as shown in the figure.

If descriptive statistics is desired for the dependent variable (here CEB), go to 'Options' and choose 'Descriptive'. If you want a plot of means for the groups of the independent variable (here EduW), choose 'Means Plot' (not chosen). Then click 'Continue' and then click 'OK'. The output is presented in Tables 9.3a and 9.3b.

Figure 9.1 SPSS Window for One-way ANOVA

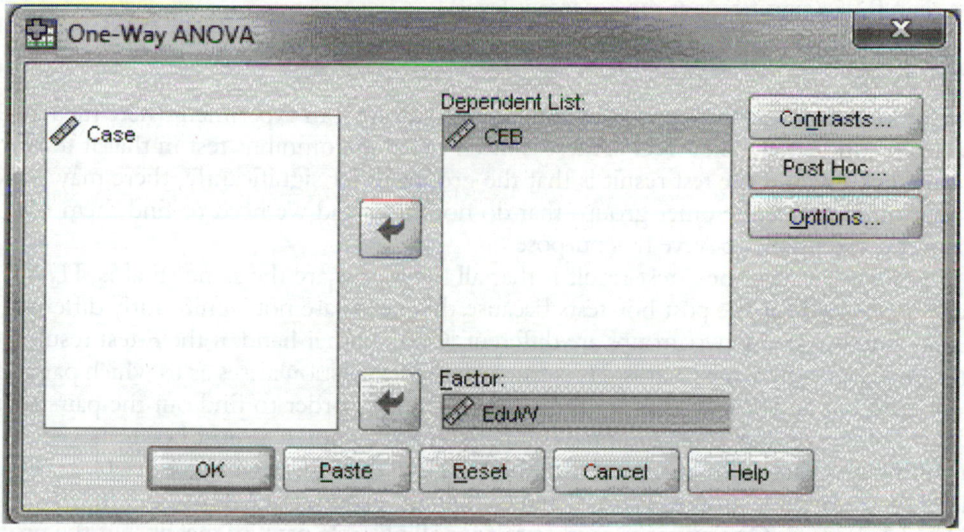

Table 9.3a SPSS Output of Descriptive for One-way ANOVA

Descriptives

CEB

| | | | | | 95% Confidence Interval for Mean | | | |
	N	*Mean*	*Std. Deviation*	*Std. Error*	*Lower Bound*	*Upper Bound*	*Minimum*	*Maximum*
Illiterate	17	3.47	1.625	.394	2.64	4.31	2	7
1–7 std	11	2.82	.874	.263	2.23	3.41	2	5
8+ std	7	2.00	.577	.218	1.47	2.53	1	3
Total	35	2.97	1.361	.230	2.50	3.44	1	7

Table 9.3b SPSS Output of ANOVA Table for One-way ANOVA

ANOVA

CEB

	Sum of Squares	*df*	*Mean Square*	*F*	*Sig.*
Between Groups	11.100	2	5.550	3.424	.045
Within Groups	51.872	32	1.621		
Total	62.971	34			

It can be seen from the table that the values are the same as that obtained from our manual calculation presented earlier. The ANOVA result shows that the *F* value 3.424 is statistically significant as the Sig. value 0.045 is less than the cut-off value of 0.05 for the 5 percent level of significance. Please note that SPSS gives the level at which the *F*-ratio is significant under the column 'Sig.' and we need to check if the value is less than 0.01 (significant at the 1 percent level) or is less than 0.05 (significant at the 5 percent level).

Post Hoc Tests

Post hoc (or 'after this') analysis means looking at the data after an experiment (here the ANOVA test) has been conducted. The ANOVA test is often called the omnibus test in that it tests many groups together. Even if the test result is that the groups differ significantly, there may be some groups that differ and some other groups that do not differ and we need to find them out. The post hoc test is essentially to serve this purpose.

In the ANOVA test, if the F-test result is that all the means are the same (that is, H_0 is true), then there is no need for the post hoc tests because the means are not significantly different, but still we may find out if any two groups are different. On the other hand, if the F-test result is that all the means are not the same (that is, H_1 is true), then the question arises as to which pairs of the means are different and which pairs are the same (if any). In order to find out the pairs that are different, we often conduct some multiple comparison tests, known as post hoc tests.

If the number of factors or groups in the ANOVA is k, then there will be k $(k-1)/2$ pairs. For example, if there are three groups, say A, B and C, then the groups are AB, AC and BC, that is, 3 * $(3-1)/2 = (3 * 2)/2 = 3$. One way is to apply t-test for all possible pairs of means, but the problem is that even when all means are equal, some of the pairs may turn out to be significant. Multiple comparison tests protect against this by setting stringent criteria for declaring differences significant. There are a number of post hoc tests available and a few tests available in SPSS are Fisher LSD, Tukey, Dunnett, Bonferroni, Scheffe. A brief description of a these tests is given below, and a detailed derivation and presentation of the tests are beyond the scope of this book.

The Fisher least significant difference (LSD) test is basically a set of individual t-tests and in each t-test, a pooled standard deviation is computed from only the two groups being compared. The LSD test has been criticised for not sufficiently controlling for Type I error.

The Bonferroni test simply calculates a new pairwise alpha to keep the family-wise alpha value at 0.05. The Bonferroni is probably the most commonly used post hoc test, because it is highly flexible, very simple to compute and can be used with any type of statistical test including ANOVA.

Scheffé's method applies to the set of estimates of all possible contrasts among the factor-level means, not just the pairwise differences. Having an advantage of flexibility, it can be used to test any number of post hoc simple and/or complex comparisons that appear interesting. However, the drawback of this flexibility is low on Type I error and has a low power.

Tukey's test calculates a new critical value that can be used to evaluate whether differences between any two pairs of means are significant. This test is usually recommended because it has greater power than the other tests under most circumstances.

The Dunnet test is similar to the Tukey test but is used only if a set of comparisons are being made to one particular group.

For post hoc tests in SPSS, we need to click the 'Post Hoc' button and in the emerging popup window we have to choose the desired tests as shown in Figure 9.2, and the results for Bonferroni tests are presented in Table 9.4.

It can be seen from the table that the difference in the mean children ever born between illiterate women and women with education 8+ std is significant (Sig. = 0.045) and that between illiterate women and women with education 1–7+ std and also that women with education 1–7+ std and women with 8+ std are not statistically significant. So, as per the data, it appears that attempts

Figure 9.2   SPSS Window for the Post Hoc Test in ANOVA

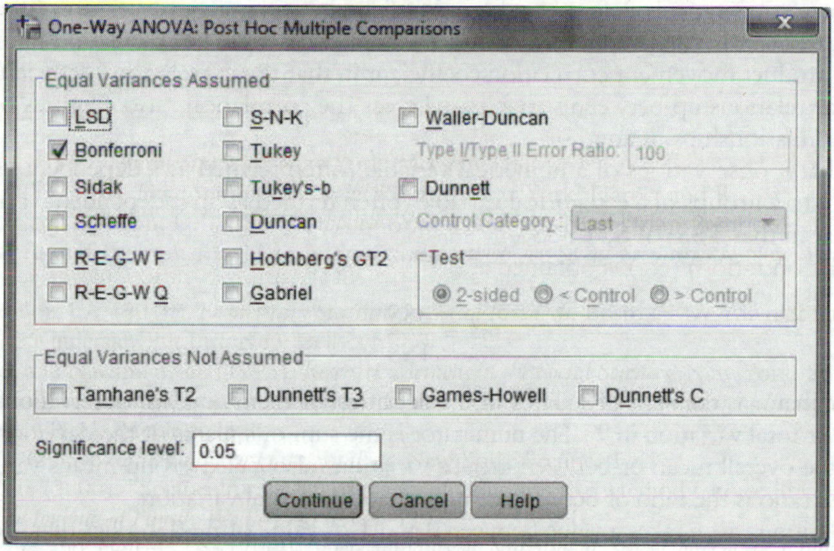

Table 9.4   SPSS Output of Post Hoc Tests

Multiple Comparisons

Dependent Variable: CEB

Bonferroni

(I) EduW	(J) EduW	Mean Difference (I-J)	Std. Error	Sig.	95% Confidence Interval Lower Bound	95% Confidence Interval Upper Bound
Illiterate	1–7 std	.652	.493	.584	−.59	1.90
	8+ std	1.471*	.572	.045	.03	2.92
1–7 std	Illiterate	−.652	.493	.584	−1.90	.59
	8+ std	.818	.616	.580	−.74	2.37
8 std	Illiterate	−1.471*	.572	.045	−2.92	−.03
	1–7 std	−.818	.616	.580	−2.37	.74

Note: *The mean difference is significant at the 0.05 level.

to provide primary education to illiterate women may not be sufficient to bring down children ever born to them, but progressive attempts to take them to secondary-level education will tend to decrease children ever born substantially.

Important Note: Two-way ANOVA is presented with an example later in Chapter 13.

CORRELATION RATIO

Pearson's product moment correlation coefficient can be calculated only if the two variables are numerical variables. If one variable is a numerical variable (example weight) and the other variable is a categorical variable (example religion), an alternative index called the correlation ratio is obtained. Correlation ratio is defined as the ratio of the between-group variation (due to a categorical variable) to the total variance (of the numerical variable). The correlation ratio is different from the product movement correlation coefficient in that the correlation coefficient captures only the linear relationship between variables, whereas the correlation ratio captures both linear and nonlinear relationships, if any.

Suppose that n observations of a numerical variable (often termed as a dependent variable) Υ are classified into k groups of a categorical variable (often termed as an independent variable). We have already seen that TSS=WSS+BSS.

The correlation ratio η (eta) is obtained as

$$\eta^2 = \frac{\text{BSS}}{\text{TSS}}.$$

The denominator is the sum of squares of the deviation of the individual observations from the overall mean or total variation in Υ. The numerator is the sum of squares of the deviation of group means from the overall mean or between groups variation (also called group means variation). So the correlation ratio is the ratio of between-group variation to total variation.

The correlation ratio η takes a value between 0 and 1. A value of $\eta=0$ implies that the numerator value is zero, that is, $\bar{y}_1 = \bar{y}_2 = \cdots = \bar{y}_k = \bar{y}$, so that the differences are all zero. It means that there is no variation between groups or categories, and all groups have the same mean. It implies that there is no correlation (difference) between groups with respect to the dependent variable. On the other hand, a value of $\eta=1$ implies that the numerator value is equal to the denominator value, that is, the between-group variation is equal to the total variation and so no within-group variation. It means that all observations in each category are the same (no within-group variation) and the total variation is completely accounted for by the variation between the categories. In other words, with respect to the dependent variable, all the members of each group are the same and the members of different groups are different. If $\eta>0$ and $\eta<1$, the interpretation of η is almost the same as that of a positive correlation coefficient. However, in practice, the η value tends to be smaller than what we would otherwise expect in terms of the correlation coefficient and so the η value needs to be interpreted accordingly.

Please note that η is undefined if all observations across all categories are the same because both numerator and denominator values are zero and $\eta^2=0/0$ is indeterminate.

Example: In Table 9.5, the mean children ever born (dependent variable) and the sample standard deviation by the educational level of their mothers (same example used for ANOVA) are given. Now, obtain the correlation ratio.

Table 9.5 Mean and Standard Deviation of CEB by Education of Women

EduW	N	Mean CEB	Std. Dev.
Illiterate	17	2.94118	1.95162
1–7 std	11	2.27273	1.34830
8+ std	7	2.00000	0.57735
Total	35	2.54286	1.59674

$$\eta^2 = \frac{\text{BSS}}{\text{TSS}} = \frac{\sum_i n_i (\bar{y}_i - \bar{y})^2}{\sum_j (y_j - \bar{y})^2}.$$

Please note that $\sum_j (y_j - \bar{y})^2 = n\sigma^2 = (n-1)s^2$

$$\eta^2 = \frac{17 * (2.94118 - 2.54286)^2 + 11 * (2.27273 - 2.54286)^2 + 7 * (2.0 - 2.54286)^2}{(35-1) * 1.59674 * 1.59674}$$

$$= \frac{5.56272}{86.68571} = 0.06417$$

$$\eta = \sqrt{0.06417} = 0.253.$$

That is, $\eta = 0.253$. A correlation ratio of 0.253 indicates that the correlation between children ever born and education of mothers is only moderate.

From Table 9.5, we see that as the educational level of mothers increased, the mean CEB decreased and so we may say that the higher the educational level of mothers, the lower the number of children ever born to them, but as $\eta = 0.253$, we may say that the relationship is only moderate.

An SPSS Example of One-way ANOVA and Eta

To obtain eta including ANOVA for the same example as used above, choose Analyze=>Means. In the pop-up window transfer, choose the variable 'CEB' to 'Dependent list' and 'EduW' to 'Independent list'. Then click the options and choose 'ANOVA table and Eta' as shown in Figure 9.3. The output is presented in Table 9.6. The value of η obtained from the SPSS output is 0.253, which is the same as that obtained from the manual calculation.

Figure 9.3 SPSS Window for Correlation Ratio

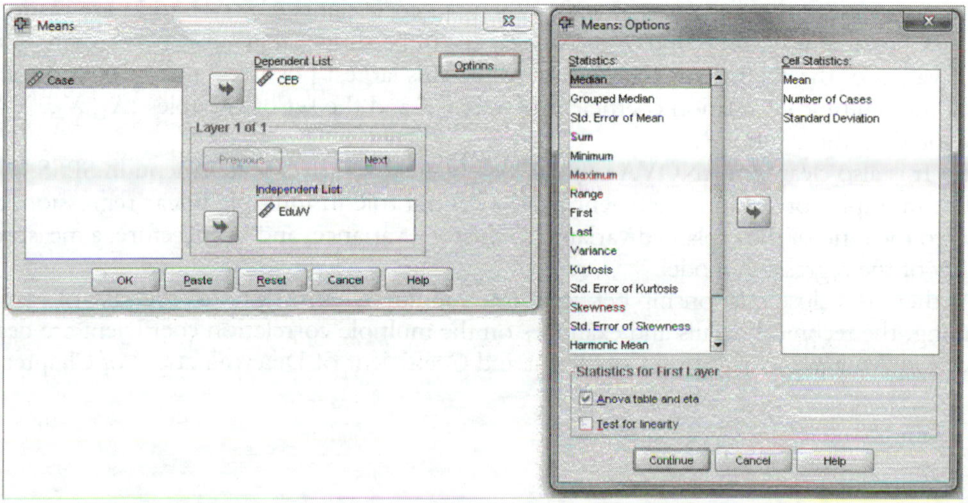

Table 9.6   SPSS Output of the Correlation Ratio

ANOVA Table

			Sum of Squares	df	Mean Square	F
Children ever born*	Between	(Combined)	5.563	2	2.781	1.097
Education of mother	Groups	Within Groups				
			81.123	32	2.535	
		Total	86.686	34		

Measures of Association

	Eta	Eta Squared
Children ever born* Education of mother	.253	.064

MULTIPLE CORRELATION COEFFICIENT

A multiple correlation is the linear relationship between a set of (more than one) independent variables on the dependent variable and is denoted by the symbol R (upper case letter). If the number of independent variables is only 1, it is the usual bivariate correlation coefficient r. As there are more than one independent variables involved and some of their effects on the dependent variable may be positive or negative, usually the square of multiple correlation coefficient R^2 is calculated, and then R is obtained if required. As such, a multiple correlation coefficient is always positive and it varies from 0 to $+1$. A value of $R = 0$ implies no linear relationship and a value of $R = 1$ implies a full linear relationship between the independent variables and the dependent variable. The formulae and the manual calculation of R are a bit complex. Furthermore, R^2 is used more often than the R, for many reasons.

Let Y be a dependent variable, and $(X_1, X_2,..., X_k)$ be a set of independent variables. Let Y be a linear combination of the X_i variables so that

$$Y = b_0 + b_1 X_1 + b_2 X_2 + b_3 X_3 + \cdots + b_k X_k.$$

Let us consider the function $\rho(Y, X)$. When the coefficients b_i's ($i=1$ to k) are made to vary in every possible way, the value of ρ changes. It can be shown that, in general, there is a single set of values of the coefficients that maximises ρ. This largest possible value of $\rho(X, Y)$ is usually called the multiple correlation coefficient between Y and the set of variables $(X_1, X_2,..., X_k)$ and is denoted by the symbol R.

Note: It is also clear that ANOVA can also be obtained via the 'Means' menu in SPSS.

The multiple correlation coefficient plays a central role in multiple linear regression, as R^2 is equal to the ratio of the explained variance to the total variance, and is, therefore, a measure of the quality of the regression model.

As there is a close relationship between R and multiple regression, for the sake of easy understanding, the technical details and examples on the multiple correlation coefficient are dealt with in section 'Multiple Correlation Coefficient and Coefficient of Determination' of Chapter 11.

CHAPTER 10

Non-parametric Tests

WHAT IS A NON-PARAMETRIC TEST?

Testing of hypotheses about *parameters* or indices of population is called a parametric test, which implies that the nature of distribution of the population from which samples are drawn to estimate the parameter is known, that is, the population distribution is pre-specified. For example, the sample tests such as the *t*-test and *z*-test of significance are based on the assumption that the frequency distribution of the units in the population from which the samples are drawn is normal, that is, the distribution is symmetric from the middle (see the middle normal distribution curve in Figure 10.1).

In a non-parametric test (NP test), the frequency distribution of the parent population is not known or not assumed. For this reason, NP tests are often used in place of parametric tests if and when the assumptions of the parametric tests have been grossly violated, that is, the distribution is not normal or not of the specified nature. For example, if the population distribution is severely skewed to the right or to the left (see the skewed-left and skewed-right curves in Figure 10.1), the normality assumption is violated and in such cases, the *t*-test or *z*-test is not appropriate and if applied, the results may lead to draw wrong conclusions. It can be noted from the figure that the skewness is only moderate but in many occasions, it would be highly skewed. Although some NP tests do require certain assumptions, they do not assume any specific or rigorous assumptions about the population from which the samples are drawn. In other words, NP tests are generally valid, whatever may be the population distribution. So, NP tests are often referred to as *distribution-free tests*. Distribution-free statistical procedures do not require the normality or any particular mathematical form of the underlying population.

The advantages of NP methods are that they require no theoretical assumption about the population. They are simple and easy to apply. Further, parametric tests cannot be applied to non-numerical variables (categorical variables) but NP tests can be applied to such data. The main disadvantage of NP tests is that they are usually less powerful than parametric tests. Further, NP tests are meant for hypothesis testing only and are not useful for parameter estimation such as mean and standard deviation of the population. Though certain indices are derived for NP tests they are not amenable for any further statistical treatment or application apart from using them in the hypothesis testing. Non-parametric tests are often not appropriate for large samples (of sizes say 100 and above) as there would be many ties (repetition) of values, that is, many observations may have the same value.

In short, NP tests are preferred to the standard parametric tests when there are evidences of serious violations of the assumptions about the underlying population that would invalidate the outcome of the parametric tests and when the sample sizes are small. Another situation is when the variables of interest are not suitable to the numerical measurement but can be categorised or ranked. It is to be noted that most NP tests just require the observations to be arranged in an ascending or a descending order of values, ranking of values, differencing of values, taking

Figure 10.1   Normal and Skewed Frequency Distributions

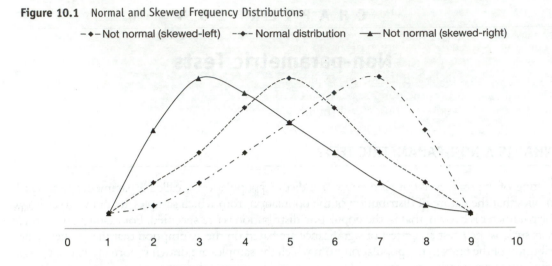

the positive or negative sign of the difference of values, a pattern of sequence of values and the like, and not obtaining mean, median, standard deviation, correlation and the like. Some of the common NP tests vis-à-vis their parametric counter parts are presented below.

Type of Data/Test	*Parametric Methods*	*Non-parametric Methods*
One-sample test for randomness of observations		Wald–Wolfowitz Runs test
One-sample test for goodness of fit or normality of quantitative data		One-sample Kolmogorov–Smirnov test
Compare two paired groups or two related samples	Paired *t*-test	Sign test, Wilcoxon signed-rank test
Compare two unpaired groups or two independent samples	Two-sample *t*-test (or unpaired *t*-test)	Mann–Whitney *U* test (or) Wilcoxon rank sum test
Compare three or more unmatched groups or several independent samples	One-way ANOVA	Kruskal–Wallis test
Quantify association between two variables	Pearson correlation	Spearman rank correlation

ONE-SAMPLE WALD–WOLFOWITZ RUNS TEST

The one-sample Wald–Wolfowitz Runs test (or simply, Runs test) is meant for checking the randomness of observations. Most parametric statistical tests assume that the observations are drawn from the population at random. One way of checking the randomness of the observations is to ensure that the order in which observations were made was random and not selective. If the order does matter (or selective), then the sample is said to be not drawn at random, and we cannot draw conclusions about the population from which the sample is drawn.

The Runs test procedure tests whether the order of occurrence of observations of a variable is random. A run is a sequence of similar observations. A sample with too many or too few runs would suggest that the sample is not random. The procedure first classifies each value of the variable as falling above or below a cut-point and then tests if there is no specific order to the resulting sequence. The cut-point is either a measure of central tendency (mean, median or mode) or a custom (fixed or assumed) value.

Let $X_1, X_2, \ldots, X_N$ be a set of N observations arranged in the order in which they are measured or occurred. Choose a cut-point, say, X within the range of the values of the N observations. Often the cut-point is the mean or median of the observations. Then, against each observation write 'A' if the observation is equal to or above the cut-point and write 'B' if it is below the cut-point and obtain the sequence of As and Bs. Let the sequence of 10 observations be ABBABBAABB. Let N_A be the number of As, N_B the number of Bs and R the number of sequences of As and Bs. In the above example of 10 observations, $N_A = 4$ (number of As) and $N_B = 6$ (number of Bs) and $R = 6$ (A BB A BB AA BB, the number of underlines).

Test Procedure

The null hypothesis is H_0: *The sequence of observations is random.*

The sampling distribution of the number of runs (R) is approximately normal with

$$\text{Mean } \mu_R = \frac{2 N_A N_B}{N} + 1 \quad \text{and} \quad \text{SD } \sigma_R = \sqrt{\frac{2 N_A N_B (2 N_A N_B - N_A - N_B)}{(N_A + N_B)^2 (N_A + N_B - 1)}}$$

Then the two-sided significance level is based on the normal variate $Z = \dfrac{R - \mu_R}{\sigma_R} \sim N(0,1)$ asymptotically. When $N \geq 50$, Z can be considered as a normal variate with mean 0 and SD 1. When $N < 50$, the following approximation is made:

$$Z = \frac{(R - \mu_R) + 0.5}{\sigma_R} \quad \text{if } |R - \mu_R| \leq 0.5$$

$$Z = \frac{(R - \mu_R) - 0.5}{\sigma_R} \quad \text{if } |R - \mu_R| > 0.5$$

A Numerical Example

Given below is a set of 32 observations arranged row-wise. Test whether the sequence of observations is made at random. Use median as the cut-point.

8	7	8	6	10	8	6	7
8	9	7	10	7	8	12	10
12	9	11	12	10	13	13	12
11	14	9	14	11	12	11	13

The null hypothesis is H_0: *The set of observations is random.*

The median of the observations is 10 and so we put A if the value is ≥ 10 and B if it is <10. The number of runs is 10. Details are given in Table 10.1.

$$\text{Mean } \mu_R = \frac{2 N_A N_B}{N} + 1 = \frac{2 * 18 * 14}{32} + 1 = \frac{504}{32} + 1 = 16.75$$

$$\sigma_R = \sqrt{\frac{2 N_A N_B (2 N_A N_B - N_A - N_B)}{(N_A + N_B)^2 (N_A + N_B - 1)}} = \sqrt{\frac{2 * 18 * 14 * (2 * 18 * 14 - 18 - 14)}{(18 + 14) * (18 + 14) * (18 + 14 - 1)}}$$

$$\sigma_R = \sqrt{\frac{237,888}{31,744}} = \sqrt{7.49395} = 2.737508$$

Table 10.1   One-sample Wald–Wolfowitz Runs Test Exercise

Sl No.	Obs	A/B	Runs	Sl No.	Obs	A/B	Runs
1	8	B	1	19	11	A	8
2	7	B		20	12	A	
3	8	B		21	10	A	
4	6	B		22	13	A	
5	10	A	2	23	13	A	
6	8	B	3	24	12	A	
7	6	B		25	11	A	
8	7	B		26	14	A	
9	8	B		27	9	B	9
10	9	B		28	14	A	10
11	7	B		29	11	A	
12	10	A	4	30	12	A	
13	7	B	5	31	11	A	
14	8	B		32	13	A	
15	12	A	6	Median	10.0		
16	10	A		$N=$		32	
17	12	A		$N_A=$		18	
18	9	B	7	$N_B=$		14	
(Continue)=>				$R=$		10	

Table 10.2   SPSS Output for One-sample Wald–Wolfowitz Runs Test

Runs Test

Items	Values
Test value (median)	10
Cases < test value	14
Cases ≥ test value	18
Total cases	32
Number of runs	10
Z	−2.283
Asymp. Sig. (two-tailed)	0.022

Since $R - \mu_R = |10.0 - 16.75| > 0.5$, we use the formula for Z as

$$Z = \frac{(R - \mu_R) + 0.5}{\sigma_R} = \frac{10 - 16.75 - 0.5}{2.737508} = \frac{-6.25}{2.737508} = -2.2831$$

Since $|Z| > 1.96$, we reject the null hypothesis that the set of observations is random.

SPSS Output

Enter the data in SPSS and use the menu 'Analyze=>Nonparametric Tests=>Runs'. In the resulting window, select the variable and choose the default cut-point median. The SPSS output is shown in Table 10.2.

The number of runs (10) is statistically significant at 5 percent level of significance (as Asymp. Sig. value 0.022 is less than 0.05). So, we reject the null hypothesis that the set of observations is drawn at random.

ONE-SAMPLE KOLMOGOROV–SMIRNOV TEST

The one-sample Kolmogorov–Smirnov test is meant for testing goodness of fit or normality of a quantitative data. The test procedure compares the observed cumulative distribution function of a variable with a specified theoretical distribution, which may be normal, uniform, Poisson or exponential. The Kolmogorov–Smirnov Z is computed from the largest difference (in absolute value) between the observed (computed directly from the data) and theoretical cumulative distribution function. In SPSS, four theoretical distribution functions are available, namely normal, uniform or equal distribution, Poisson and exponential. The goodness-of-fit test tests whether the observations could reasonably have come from the specified distribution. The one-sample Kolmogorov–Smirnov test is often used to test whether a variable (i.e., income) is normally distributed.

A Numerical Example Using SPSS

The annual household income of 1,000 families is obtained. Test whether the income distribution is normal.

Null hypothesis H_0: *The household income is normally distributed*.

Enter the data in SPSS and use the menu 'Analyze=>Nonparametric Tests=>1 Sample Kolmogorov–Smirnov Test'. The SPSS output is given in Table 10.3.

Inference: The Kolmogorov–Smirnov Z statistic is asymptotically significant at 1 percent level of significant. So, we reject the null hypothesis that household income is normally distributed, that is, the household income is not normally distributed.

TWO-PAIRED SAMPLES TESTS

Two-paired samples or two-related samples means 'a single group with two measures of the same variable', that is, two measures of the same aspect are made at two times, at two levels, with two equipment, by two measurers and before and after conducting an experiment. The measurements should be at least at the ordinal level, preferably in interval or ratio scale. A two-paired-samples test compares the equality of the distributions of the two measures of related variables for the

Table 10.3   SPSS Output for One-sample Kolmogorov–Smirnov Test

		Household Income (in thousands)
N		1,000
Normal Parameters[a]	Mean	77.535
	SD	107.04416
Most extreme differences	Absolute	0.261
	positive	0.231
	negative	−0.261
Kolmogorov–Smirnov Z		8.254
Asymp. Sig. (two-tailed)		000

Note: [a]Test distribution is normal.

same group or for the same sample of observations. There are many procedures available for hypothesis testing of these types of data (nominal, ordinal or interval data type) and the appropriateness of a test depends on the types of data, and few tests are described below.

The Sign Test

The Sign test is used when the data are numerical in nature (measured in interval or ratio scale). The sign test computes the difference between two paired variables for each case in the sample or group and classifies the differences as positive, negative or tied (equal). If the two variables are similarly distributed, the number of positive and negative differences will not differ significantly.

Consider a situation in which we have to compare two variables (say, pre and post training scores), for which the measurements are made under similar conditions (i.e., using the same set of questions) but in different environments (before and after the training). The different environments under which measurements are made imply that the normality condition of the observations (drawn at random) is violated and the parametric paired t-test is invalid. In such situations, we use the Sign test.

Procedure

Let (x_i, y_i), $i=1, 2,..., n$ be n paired sample of observations. Let $x_1, x_2,..., x_n$ are drawn from a population with probability density function (f_x) and $y_1, y_2,..., y_n$ are drawn from the same or another population with probability density function (f_y). We want to test the null hypothesis $H_0: f_x = f_y$, that is, the two sets of observations have come from the same population or the two measures are the same. When H_0 is true, each set of x_i and y_i observations constitute a random sample of size 2 from the same population. With the assumption that $x_i \neq y_i$, the probability that $x_i > y_i$ is $\frac{1}{2}$ and $x_i < y_i$ is $\frac{1}{2}$, so that the sum of these two probabilities add to 1.

The null hypothesis is that there is no difference between the two measures (or variables). If it is so, then the number of $+$ signs (or $-$ signs) should have a *binomial distribution* with $p=$Prob $(x_i > y_i) = 0.5$. To carry out the Sign test, our statistic is the number of $+$ signs. Let n be the sample size, s_1 be the number of $+$ signs (number of successes) and s_2 be the number of $-$ signs (number of failures). Let s be the minimum of s_1 and s_2. The null hypothesis would be H_0: the two variables are similarly distributed, that is, the numbers of $+$ and $-$ signs are equal. The alternative hypothesis would be that the number of $+$ and $-$ signs is different, that is, there is an extreme number of $+$ signs (or $-$ signs), be it small or large. So, we would find the probability of the number of $+/-$ signs being $\leq s$ and $\geq (n-s)$ or two times the probability of the number of $+/-$ sign being $\leq s$.

Let x be a random variable of number of successes. Then, in an experiment of n trials with a probability of success p, the probability of at least s successes P $(x \leq s)$ can be obtained from binomial probability table. Alternatively, the probability value can be obtained from the MS Excel worksheet function BINOMDIST(). The format is $=$BINOMDIST(s, n, p, TRUE) where s, n and p are as defined above and the option 'TRUE' is to obtain the cumulative probability $x \leq s$ (if the option 'FALSE' is used, then we will obtain the probability $x = s$ only). For example, for $n = 14$ trials, $s = 3$ successes, $p = 0.5$ probability of success, the value of BINOMDIST(3,14,0.5,TRUE) is 0.028687 and double the values is 0.057373. This is the probability of significance.

The Sign Test for Large Samples

Let (x_i, y_i), $i = 1, 2,..., n$ be n paired sample of observations. Let us define that U_i is 1 if $x_i > y_i$ and 0 if $x_i < y_i$. Then, U_i is a Bernoulli variate with probability $p = P (x_i > y_i) = \frac{1}{2}$. Since U_is are independent, $U = \sum_{i=1}^{n} U_i$, the total number of positive deviations is a binomial variate with parameters n and p (here $p=1/2$). For large samples, we may regard U to be asymptotically normal with expected values of U being $\mu_U=E(U)=np=n*(1/2)=n/2$ and variance of U is $\sigma_U^2=V$ $(U)=npq=n*(1/2)*(1/2)=n/4$. Therefore, $Z = \dfrac{U - E(U)}{\sqrt{V(U)}} = \left(U - \dfrac{n}{2}\right) / \sqrt{n/4}$ is asymptotically N $(0, 1)$ and we may use the normal test.

A Numerical Example

In a class, 15 students scored less than 40 marks in statistics examination and these students were given a special lecture on the subject and a supplementary examination was conducted for them in the same line of the regular examination. The marks scored by these students in the main examination and in the supplementary examination are given in Table 10.4 (Columns 1–3) under the captions 'pre' and 'post'. Test whether the students have shown improvement in the statistics subject after the special lecture.

The Sign test is applied to test the null hypothesis that the marks scored by the students in the main and supplementary examinations are the same. For this, the marks scored in the main and supplementary examinations are compared and a '+' sign is given if the score in the supplementary examination is greater than the marks scored in the main examination and a '−' sign is given if the marks scored in the supplementary examination are less than the marks scored in the main examination.

If the marks scored in the two examinations are the same, then it is called a tie and assigned the sign '=' or '0'. The details are presented in the last column of the table. With the probability of success $p=0.5$, among the 15 students, 9 students have scored higher marks (+ sign) and 5 students have scored less marks (− sign) and one student scored equal marks. In our example $n=14$ (the total of the + and − signs, excluding the ties), $s=5$ (minimum of + and − signs) and $p=0.5$. So, $2*P$ $(x \le 5)=2*0.211975=0.42395$ (the Excel function BINOMDIST(5,14,0.5,TRUE) gives the value

Table 10.4   The Sign Test Procedure

Student	Test-marks		Sign
	Pre	Post	
1	20	40	+
2	28	25	−
3	24	38	+
4	14	27	+
5	35	31	−
6	20	20	=
7	15	32	+
8	29	38	+
9	15	25	+
10	19	18	−
11	25	32	+
12	31	28	−
13	35	33	−
14	12	29	+
15	25	29	+

Table 10.5   SPSS Output for Sign Test

Sign Test	Frequencies	
		N
SuppExam − MainExam	Negative Differences[a]	5
	Positive Differences[b]	9
	Ties[c]	1
	Total	15

Test Statistics[e]	
	SuppExam − MainExam
Exact Sig. (two-tailed)	0.423950[d]

Notes: [a] SuppExam < MainExam.
[b] SuppExam > MainExam.
[c] SuppExam = MainExam.
[d] Binomial distribution used.
[e] Sign test.

0.211975). As the probability of significance 0.42395 > 0.05, we accept the null hypothesis that the marks scored by the students in the main and supplementary examinations are the same, that is, there is no significant improvement in the performance of the students due to the special lecture.

SPSS Output

To do this exercise with SPSS, enter the data in Columns 2 and 3 into SPSS editor and name the variables as 'MainExam' and 'SuppExam'. Now, go to the SPSS menu 'Analyze => Non parametric Tests => 2 Related Samples' and click. We have got the output in Table 10.5.

The upper panel in the table with the caption 'Frequencies' displays the number of negative differences (SuppExam–MainExam) as 5 and number of positive differences as 9 and the panel captioned 'Test Statistics' gives the significance level for a two-tailed test as 0.423950. For one-tailed test, it would be $0.423950/2 = 0.211975$. As the Sig. value is greater than 0.05, we accept the null hypothesis that the two groups are drawn from the same population, that is, the two groups are not significantly different from each other and the inference is as mentioned above.

Wilcoxon Signed-rank Test

The Wilcoxon signed-rank test is an extension of the sign test and considers not only the sign but also the magnitude of the differences. Because the Wilcoxon signed-rank test incorporates more information about the data, it is more powerful than the Sign test. Let (x_i, y_i), $i = 1, 2, \ldots, n$ be n paired sample of observations. Since (x_i, y_i) are two different measures with different magnitudes, the ranks of the deviation of the observations are considered. Let $d_i = x_i - y_i$ be the difference (including the sign) and r_j be the rank order of $|d_i|$ (i.e., the positive value of d_i, ignoring the negative sign, if any) where $i, j = 1, 2, \ldots, n$. Let T_1 be the sum of the ranks for the positive differences $(T_1 = \sum r_j$ for $d_i > 0)$, T_2 be the sum of the ranks $(r_j s)$ for the negative differences $(T_2 = \sum r_j$ for $d_i < 0)$ and T be the smaller of the two sums T_1 and T_2.

For the null hypothesis H_0 to be true, the sum of the positive ranks and the sum of the negative ranks are expected to be nearly equal. If H_0 is false then we expect one of the sums to be substantially smaller than the other, and therefore T is expected to be quite small. The most extreme

Table 10.6 Wilcoxon *T* Table: Wilcoxon Signed-ranks Test Critical Values (CI=95%)

Number (n)	Two-sided	One-sided	Number (n)	Two-sided	One-sided
6	0	2	16	29	35
7	2	3	17	34	41
8	3	5	18	40	47
9	5	8	19	46	53
10	8	10	20	52	60
11	10	13	21	58	67
12	13	17	22	65	75
13	17	21	23	73	83
14	21	25	24	81	91
15	25	30	25	89	100

Note: Two distributions are significantly different if the calculated *T* value is less than the value presented in this table.
Source: Wilcoxon and Wilcox (1964).

outcome for the rejection of H_0 is $T=0$. The sampling distribution of T can be found in Wilcoxon *T* table (Table 10.6).

Distribution of d_i for Large Samples

For large samples, under the null hypothesis H_0, the distribution of d_i is symmetric about 0 and follows a normal distribution. Now, we can calculate mean and variance of T as follows:

$$\mu_T = E(T) = \frac{n(n+1)}{4} \quad \text{and} \quad \sigma_T^2 = V(T) = \frac{n(n+1)(2n+1)}{24}.$$

The test statistic is $Z = \dfrac{T - \mu_T}{\sigma_T} = \dfrac{T - \dfrac{n(n+1)}{4}}{\sqrt{\dfrac{n(n+1)(2n+1)}{24}}}.$

Since Z follows a normal distribution with mean 0 and SD 1 for large samples, we can apply the '*t*-test' significance levels.

A Numerical Example

Continuing with the example used for the Sign test, the marks scored by 15 students in the main examination and in the supplementary examination are given in the Table 10.7 under the captions 'Pre' and 'Post'. We have to test whether the students have shown improvement in the statistics subject after the special lecture. For this, we add three columns, namely 'actual difference' in the marks (i.e., with sign), 'absolute difference' in the marks (i.e., without sign) and the rank order of the absolute difference. It is to be noted that cases with absolute difference of zero are not included for the ranks. If the absolute difference is the same for more than one observation (i.e., in case of ties), the average of the ranks is considered for each of the observations with the same absolute difference. In the next step, the ranks for the positive differences and for the negative differences in two separate columns are copied and the sum of the rank values is obtained. Details are presented in Table 10.7.

Table 10.7   Wilcoxon Signed-rank Test Exercise

Student	Test-marks		Differences		Ranks (Absolute)	Positive Ranks	Negative Ranks
	Pre	Post	Actual	Absolute			
1	20	40	20	20	14	14	
2	28	25	−3	3	3.5		3.5
3	24	38	14	14	11	11	
4	14	27	13	13	10	10	
5	35	31	−4	4	5.5		5.5
6	20	20	0	0	0		
7	15	32	17	17	12.5	12.5	
8	29	38	9	9	8	8	
9	15	25	10	10	9	9	
10	19	18	−1	1	1		1
11	25	32	7	7	7	7	
12	31	28	−3	3	3.5		3.5
13	35	33	−2	2	2		2
14	12	29	17	17	12.5	12.5	
15	25	29	4	4	5.5	5.5	
Total						89.5	15.5

Sum of positive ranks $T_1 = 89.5$
Sum of negative ranks $T_2 = 15.5$
The minimum of T_1 and T_2 is $T = 15.5$

Critical T value for 14 observations (zero-difference observations excluded) at 5 percent level of significance from the T table (given above) is 21. That is, $T_c = 21$.

As per the rule, we accept the null hypothesis H_0 if the calculated value T is greater than the critical table value T_c and reject H_0 if T is equal to or less than Tc. In our example, $T < T_c$ (15.5 < 21), and therefore we reject the null hypothesis that the marks scored by the students in the supplementary examination are the same as the marks scored in the main examination.

We can also test the hypothesis using the Z statistic:

$$Z = \frac{T - \mu_T}{\sigma_T} = \frac{T - \dfrac{n(n+1)}{4}}{\sqrt{\dfrac{n(n+1)(2n+1)}{24}}} = \frac{15.5 - (14*15)/4}{\sqrt{14*15*29/24}} = \frac{-37.0}{15.92953} = -2.32273.$$

As $n = 14$, it is a small sample and so we can obtain the Z value for $n − 1 = 13$ df from the t table for two-tailed test at the 5 percent level of significance. It is $Z_0 = 2.160$. As the calculated value of $Z = 2.32273$ is greater than the table value of $Z_0 = 2.160$, we reject the null hypothesis that the marks scored by the students in the main and supplementary examinations are the same.

We can also go one step forward and calculate the probability level at which differences are significant. For two-tailed test, the probability that $Z \leq −2.323$ is obtained as $2 * P(Z \leq −2.323) = 2 * 0.01009 = 0.02018$ (NORM.S.DIST($−2.323$,TRUE) = 0.01009) or (=NORMSDIST($−2.323$) = 0.01009). As the probability value of 0.0202 is less than 0.05 (at 5 percent level), we reject the null hypothesis that the scores in the two examinations are the same.

That is, we would conclude that there is significance difference in the marks scored by the students in the supplementary examination as compared to the main examination. At the same time, from the test result, we cannot say whether the difference is positive or negative, that is, improvement or deterioration in the performance of the students and is be inferred from the number of positive and negative differences or from the sum of ranks for the positive and negative differences. There are more positive differences (9) than negative differences (5) and further the sum of positive ranks (89.5) is far greater than the sum of negative ranks (15.5). A positive difference (supplementary exam marks minus main exam marks) means an improvement in the marks, and so we can conclude that there is an improvement in the performance of the students in the supplementary examination and it was due the special lecture.

SPSS Output

For the same above exercise, the SPSS output is given here. To run Wilcoxon signed-rank test, go to the SPSS menu 'Analyze=>Non-parametric Tests=>2 Related Samples'. In the resulting window, choose the variables of interest and then the test type 'Wilcoxon'. The output is given in Table 10.8.

From the table, we see that the results from the SPSS output are almost the same as that obtained from the manual calculation (except for rounding of figures) and the interpretation of the results are already made.

TWO INDEPENDENT SAMPLES TESTS

Two independent samples means 'two groups with one variable', that is, two samples or groups (of same or different sizes) with respect to a single variable. A two independent samples test compares the equality of a measure/variable between two samples or groups.

Table 10.8   SPSS Output for Wilcoxon Signed-ranks Test

Wilcoxon Signed-ranks Test

Ranks		N	Mean Rank	Sum of Ranks
SuppExam − MainExam	Negative ranks	5[a]	3.10	15.50
	Positive ranks	9[b]	9.94	89.50
	Ties	1[c]		
	Total	15		

Test Statistics[e]	*SuppExam − MainExam*
Z	−2.324[d]
Asymp. Sig. (two-tailed)	.020

Notes: [a]SuppExam < MainExam.
[b]SuppExam > MainExam.
[c]SuppExam = MainExam.
[d]Based on negative ranks.
[e]Wilcoxon signed-ranks test.

Mann–Whitney U test

The Mann–Whitney U test is an NP counterpart of the two independent samples t-test for equality of means. The Mann–Whitney U test is also sometimes referred to as Wilcoxon rank sum test or simply Wilcoxon test. It can be noted that the 'Wilcoxon rank sum test for two independent samples' is different from the 'Wilcoxon signed-rank test for paired/related observations'. The Mann–Whitney test tests that two populations from which the two samples are drawn are equivalent in location or order, that is, the population units are randomly mixed and not necessarily to have similar or same frequency distribution. This test can be used to analyse two sets of observations drawn independently from the same population and the measurement is at least ordinal. It analyses the *degree of separation* (or the amount of overlap) between the two groups. It is the most popular method of the two independent samples NP tests. It is equivalent to the Wilcoxon rank sum test and the Kruskal–Wallis test for two groups.

The Mann–Whitney U test tests the *null hypothesis* that two groups or two sets of observations (values/scores for the two groups) are samples from the same population drawn at random or the sets of values/scores of the two groups *do not differ systematically* from each other. The *alternative hypothesis* is that the two groups differ systematically.

The procedure for the Mann–Whitney test is as follows. Let us consider two groups, say A and B, with n_1 and n_2 observations and $n_1+n_2=n$. The observations from the two groups are combined and ranked from 1 to n. It is to be noted that rank 1 is assigned to the lowest value and rank n to the highest value. Further, in case of ties (more than one observation having the same value), the average rank is assigned to each one of them. The number of ties should be small relative to the total number of observations. If the populations are identical in location (order), the ranks should be randomly mixed between the two samples. The test calculates the number of times a score from group A precedes a score from group B (call it as m_1) and the number of times a score from group B precedes a score from group A (call it as m_2). The Mann–Whitney U statistic is the smaller of these two numbers.

Consider the following example (Table 10.9). The base data is given in the first three columns. There are 15 observations (Column 1) and, of them, 7 observations belong to Group 1 and the remaining 8 observations belong to Group 2 (Column 2) and the values are given in Column 3.

The observations sorted by value (lowest to highest) are given in Column 5 and their group representation is given in Column 4. The ranks are given in Column 6. It is to be noted that value 40 occurred twice (tied) with ranks 3 and 4 and so the mean $(3+4)/2=7/2=3.5$ is taken as the common rank for the two observations. Similarly, value 47 has occurred thrice with ranks 9, 10 and 11 and so they take the common rank $(9+10+11)/3=10$. The ranks corresponding to the respective groups are presented in Columns 7 and 8, and the sum of the group ranks is given in the corresponding bottom row.

Calculation of U

Let n_1 be the number of observations in Group 1; $n_1=7$
Let n_2 be the number of observations in Group 2; $n_2=8$
Let R_1 be the sum of ranks for Group 1; $R_1=46.5$
Let R_2 be the sum of ranks for Group 2; $R_2=73.5$

$$U_1 = n_1 n_2 + \frac{n_1(n_1+1)}{2} - R_1 = 7*8 + \frac{7*(7+1)}{2} - 46.5 = 37.5$$

$$U_2 = n_1 n_2 + \frac{n_2(n_2+1)}{2} - R_2 = 7*8 + \frac{8*(8+1)}{2} - 73.5 = 18.5$$

Table 10.9   Mann–Whitney U Test Procedure

	Given Data			*Sorted Data*			*Rank*	
Item	*Group*	*Value*	*Group*	*Value*	*All*	*Group 1*		*Group 2*
(1)	(2)	(3)	(4)	(5)	(6)	(7)		(8)
1	1	40	2	33	1			1
2	2	49	1	34	2	2		
3	2	51	1	40	3.5	3.5		
4	1	43	2	40	3.5			3.5
5	2	67	2	41	5			5
6	2	41	1	42	6	6		
7	1	42	1	43	7	7		
8	1	47	1	45	8	8		
9	1	34	1	47	10	10		
10	2	47	2	47	10			10
11	2	62	1	47	10	10		
12	2	40	2	49	12			12
13	2	33	2	51	13			13
14	1	45	2	62	14			14
15	1	47	2	67	15			15
Sum						46.5		73.5

Note: The repeated values are given in grey.

The next step is to consider U and U' as follows:

$$U \text{ is the smaller of } U_1 \text{ and } U_2: \quad U=18.5$$
$$U' \text{ is the larger of } U_1 \text{ and } U_2: \quad U'=37.5.$$

Now, look at the U table available in most statistical textbooks, or can be downloaded from the web, that will give the *critical values* of U (or U') for different values of n_1 and n_2 and for various significance levels. To reject H_0, the observed (calculated) value of U has to be greater than the critical (given in Table G.1 in Appendix G) value of U. Please note that the maximum separation of the two groups is indicated by $U=0$.

In our example, $n_1=7$ and $n_2=8$ and for a two-tailed test with $\alpha=0.05$, the critical value of U is 10 (obtained from Table G.1 in Appendix G). The observed (calculated) value of $U=18.5$ is far greater than the critical (table) value of $U=10$. As the observations (values) of two groups become more mixed, the value of U becomes larger. Therefore, *large* values of U lead to the acceptance of the null hypothesis H_0 (that the two groups are from the same population) and for *small* values of U lead to the rejection of null hypothesis H_0. As the calculated value of U is greater than the table value (18.5 > 10), we accept the null hypothesis that there is no significant difference in the values between the two groups.

SPSS Output

To do this exercise with SPSS, enter the data in Columns 2 and 3 into SPSS editor and name the variables as 'Group' and 'Value'. Now, go to the SPSS menu 'Analyze => Non- parametric Tests => 2 Independent Samples' and click. We have got the output in Table 10.10.

Table 10.10   SPSS Output for Mann–Whitney Test

Ranks

	Group	N	Mean Rank	Sum of Ranks
Value	1	7	6.64	46.50
	2	8	9.19	73.50
	Total	15		

Test Statistics[a]

	Value
Mann–Whitney U	18.500
Wilcoxon W	46.500
Z	−1.104
Asymp. Sig. (two-tailed)	0.269
Exact Sig.[2*one-tailed Sig.)]	0.281[b]

Notes: [a]Grouping Variable: Group.
[b]Not corrected for ties.

The subtable captioned 'Ranks' displays the sum of Ranks as 46.5 for Group 1 and 73.5 for Group 2. The subtable captioned 'Test Statistics' displays the Mann–Whitney U as 18.5 and it is asymptotically significant (two-tailed) at 0.269. As the Sig. value is greater than 0.05, we accept the null hypothesis that the two groups are drawn from the same population, that is, the two groups are not significantly different from each other.

Mann–Whitney U Test for Large Samples

When the sample size becomes large ($n_1 > 20$, $n_2 > 20$, or $n > 40$), the sampling distribution of U statistic approaches the normal distribution with:

Mean $\mu_U = \dfrac{n_1 n_2}{2}$ and SD $\sigma_U = \sqrt{\dfrac{n_1 n_2 (n_1 + n_2 + 1)}{12}}$ and U follows a normal distribution with mean 0 and SD 1, that is, $U \sim N(0,1)$ asymptotically.

Kruskal–Wallis *H*-test

The Kruskal–Wallis *H*-test is also called *Kruskal–Wallis one-way analysis of variance (ANOVA) by ranks*. It is a test for many independent groups or samples. As the name suggests, it is a NP counterpart of the one-way ANOVA. It is used to compare the differences in the measures of a variable between several (more than two) independent groups or samples. Let the number of groups or samples be k. When $k = 2$, the Mann–Whitney U test can be used and when $k > 2$, the Kruskal–Wallis H-test is appropriate. It can be noted that as the groups or samples are considered independent, they can be of different sizes.

The null hypothesis is that the k samples come from the same population or from populations with equal or identical medians. The alternative hypothesis is that not all the samples are from the same population or from populations with equal medians. It is assumed that the underlying distributions are continuous but it can be even an ordinal measurement.

The statistic H (sometimes also called KW) can be calculated as:

$$H = \frac{12}{n(n+1)} \sum_{i=1}^{k} \frac{R_i^2}{n_i} - 3(n+1)$$

where

k = the number of samples (or groups)
n = the total number of cases (all samples combined)
n_i = the number of cases in the ith sample
R_i = the sum of the ranks in the ith sample

When H_0 is true, if $k > 3$, and all samples have 5 or more scores, then the sampling distribution of H is closely approximated by the chi-squared distribution with df = $k - 1$. If $k = 3$ and the number of scores in each sample is 5 or less, then the chi-squared distribution should not be used. In this case, one should use a table of critical values of H.

A Numerical Example

Table 10.11a displays the scores obtained in a test by four groups of students. Test whether the groups differ in the scores obtained by the students.

The null hypothesis is that the scores obtained by the students are the same in all the four groups. As we have four independent groups and the sample sizes are small, we apply Kruskal–Wallis H-test.

To apply the Kruskal–Wallis H-test, first we have to compute the overall ranks and then obtain group-wise the sum of the ranks as follows. In Table 10.11b, the given data are presented in Columns (1) and (2) and the same data are sorted and presented in Columns (3) and (4) and assigned ranks in Column (5). The Columns (3) and (5) are again sorted group-wise and presented in Columns (6) and (7) and Column (8) gives group-wise total of the overall ranks.

Kruskal–Wallis H-test is: $H = \dfrac{12}{n(n+1)} \sum_{i=1}^{k} \dfrac{R_i^2}{n_i} - 3(n+1),$

that is, $H = \dfrac{12}{26 * 27} * \dfrac{71.5 * 71.5}{5} * \dfrac{82.5 * 82.5}{6} * \dfrac{111 * 111}{8} * \dfrac{86 * 86}{7} - 3 * 27 = 0.256777 \chi^2$ for $k - 1 = 3$ df is 7.815 (obtained from Table F.1 in Appendix F)

That is, the calculated value of 0.256777 is much lower than the table value of 7.815 and so we accept the null hypothesis that the scores obtained by the students are the same in all the four

Table 10.11a   Scores Obtained in a Test by Four Groups of Students

Group	1	2	3	4	5	6	7	8	No. of Obs
A	18	27	8	16	10	*	*	*	5
B	8	19	17	10	12	20	*	*	6
C	12	19	11	22	10	13	15	12	8
D	11	14	13	14	11	12	14	*	7

Table 10.11b   Kruskal–Wallis *H*-test Procedure

Group	Score	Group	Score	Rank	Group	Rank	Sum of Ranks
(1)	*(2)*	*(3)*	*(4)*	*(5)*	*(6)*	*(7)*	*(8)*
A	18	A	8	1.5	A	1.5	
A	27	B	8	1.5	A	4	
A	8	A	10	4	A	19	
A	16	B	10	4	A	21	
A	10	C	10	4	A	26	71.5
B	8	C	11	7	B	1.5	
B	19	D	11	7	B	4	
B	17	D	11	7	B	10.5	
B	10	B	12	10.5	B	20	
B	12	C	12	10.5	B	22.5	
B	20	C	12	10.5	B	24	82.5
C	12	D	12	10.5	C	4	
C	19	C	13	13.5	C	7	
C	11	D	13	13.5	C	10.5	
C	22	D	14	16	C	10.5	
C	10	D	14	16	C	13.5	
C	13	D	14	16	C	18	
C	15	C	15	18	C	22.5	
C	12	A	16	19	C	25	111.0
D	11	B	17	20	D	7	
D	14	A	18	21	D	7	
D	13	B	19	22.5	D	10.5	
D	14	C	19	22.5	D	13.5	
D	11	B	20	24	D	16	
D	12	C	22	25	D	16	
D	14	A	27	26	D	16	86.0

(Header groupings: *Given Data* spans columns (1)–(2); *Sorted Data* spans columns (3)–(5); *Sorted Rank* spans columns (6)–(7).)

groups. In other words, the scores obtained by the students of different groups do not differ significantly between the groups or the scores are the same for all the four groups.

SPSS Output

First recode Group A as 1, B as 2, C as 3 and D as 4, and rearrange the data in two columns (Column 1 the groups and Column 2 the scores). Then, copy the data into SPSS Editor and name the columns as 'Group' and 'Scores'. Now, go to the SPSS menu 'Analyze=>Non-parametric Tests=>*k* Independent Samples' and click. In the resulting window, choose the variables of interest; choose the test type 'Kruskal–Wallis H' and click OK. The output is given in Table 10.11c.

From the subtable 'Test Statistics', it is seen that chi-square value is 0.259 and the asymptotic significance value is 0.968. As the significance value is greater than 0.05, we accept the null hypothesis that the scores obtained by the students are the same in all the four groups.

Table 10.11c   SPSS Output for Kruskal–Wallis Test

Kruskal–Wallis Test

Ranks

	Group	*N*	*Mean Rank*
Score	1	5	14.30
	2	6	13.75
	3	8	13.88
	4	7	12.29
	Total	26	

Test Statistics[a,b]

	Score
Chi-square	0.259
df	3
Asymp. Sig.	0.968

Notes: [a]Kruskal–Wallis test.
[b]Grouping variable: Group.

CHAPTER 11

Regression Analysis

INTRODUCTION

Every statistical model is built upon certain underlying principles and assumptions and so anybody who uses the models should ensure that the principles and assumptions are met by the data before applying the technique. Some principles and assumptions are basic and common to most of the multivariate statistical techniques and others are specific to an individual model or technique. In this chapter on Regression, some of these principles and assumptions are highlighted and how to asses and take into account in the analysis are suggested with examples. It is to be noted that *regression technique is the basis for most of the multivariate techniques*. So this chapter is written with a view to making the reader conversant with not only regression analysis *per se* but also multivariate techniques in general. Hence, this chapter runs lengthy and if one reads and understands this chapter, one will, hopefully, easily understand other multivariate techniques and applications.

MEANING AND IMPORTANCE OF REGRESSION

Meaning

The term 'regression' literally means 'looking back' or 'return to an earlier state'. Accordingly, *in regression analysis, we determine the likely behaviour of a population based on the behaviour of a sample of individuals drawn from the same population who have actually experienced it*. The goal of linear regression is to find a model (an equation of relationship of variables) that best fits the given observations (data) and this model or equation is then considered the expected relationship between the variables and is used to estimate the levels of one (the dependent) variable for a given set of levels of other (independent) variables. In other words, regression techniques help us to assess the strength of relationship between variables and to predict the level of one variable (dependent variable) based on the behaviour of some other related variables (independent variables).

Measuring the Relationship between Variables

Let us assume that in a population the number of children a woman will have depends on, among other things, the educational level of the woman. Generally the relationship is 'the higher the educational level of a woman, the lesser the number of children she will have'. Using regression technique we can estimate the number of children that women of different educational levels will have and the amount of reduction in the number of children that can be achieved for a given increase in the level of education of women. From policy perspectives, it will help planners to decide on the nature and amount of investment in education required for improving the status of women in general and for reducing fertility in particular. If the impact is predictably very less, then the planners have to think twice about investing in education and explore other measures to achieve the goal of reducing fertility.

Identifying Important Factors

Generally, many factors contribute to the behaviour of people or things and our interest is to identify predominant factors that will have greater contribution to the behaviour of people and are easy
to manipulate through action. Regression analysis helps us to identify such factors that are crucial in
bringing about changes in the community behaviour and, thus, makes it easy for the planners and
program implementers to *concentrate on those factors* that will have greater impact in the community.

The Question of Sample Size

Regression analysis or multivariate analysis in general can be applied to data based on reasonably
small samples. We often conduct surveys with very small sample sizes, mainly due to time constraints and high cost of data collection. With small samples it is very difficult to find the relative
importance of variables through the conventional tabular analysis. For example, the number of
children a woman will have is determined basically on her age and duration of marriage. So if we
want to assess the effect of education on children ever born, first we have to control for her age
and/or duration of marriage and then relate education to children ever born. In tabular analysis it is
a three-way tabulation (children ever born by educational level by age or duration of marriage) and
while doing so the cell frequencies tend to become smaller and the percentage distribution of fewer
cases is unstable and drawing inference is difficult, that is, with small sample sizes it is very difficult
to draw inferences through cross-tabulation analysis because of the expected small cell frequencies.
Regression analysis or in general multivariate analysis overcomes this problem to a great extent.

The Assumption of Fixed Amount of Change

Let X refer to age of child measured in months and Y refer to weight in kg. Our interest is to find
how much of weight a child will gain as it grows (in months). First, let us assume that the relationship is linear and later we will consider other relationships as well. Under linear relationship,
the weight of a child increases by a fixed amount every month. For example, if we assume that the
birth weight of a child is 3 kg and it grows by 500 grams (or 0.5 kg) per month then its weight at
the end of 6 months is $3+0.5 * 6=3+3=6$ kg. In regression analysis, our interest is to find how
much is the 'fixed amount' of weight gain.

The Concept of Model Building

The simplest form of relationship is $Y=bX$, where Y is weight of child, X is age in months and b is a
constant value (fixed amount) to be estimated using the given data. In this relationship, as age of child
increases by one month its weight increases by b kg. Though b is to be estimated from the data, for the
time being let us assume a hypothetical value and see what happens to the weight of the child at different ages. If $b=1/4$ (or 0.25), at age 24 months a child's weight is $Y=bX=(1/4) * 24=6$ kg, at age 36
months the child's weight is $(1/4) * 36=9$ kg, and so on. In general, as per this model a child's weight
increases by 1 kg for every 4 months ($9-6=3$ kg in $36-24=12$ months and so 1 kg in 4 months).

But what about its weight at birth? As per the above equation, it is $(1/4) * 0=0$ (zero), which
is not acceptable. To avoid this, let us add an initial weight 'a' to the model and the equation
becomes $Y=a+bX$. Though a is also to be estimated from the data, for the time being let us
assume $a=3$ kg. Now the child's weight is $Y=a+bX=3+(1/4) * 0=3$ kg at birth, 4.5 kg at age 6
months, 6 kg at age 12 months, 9 kg at age 24 months, and so on. This model appears to be more
reasonable than the previous model. The regression line is presented in Figure 11.1.

Figure 11.1   Regression: Weight=3+0.25 * Age

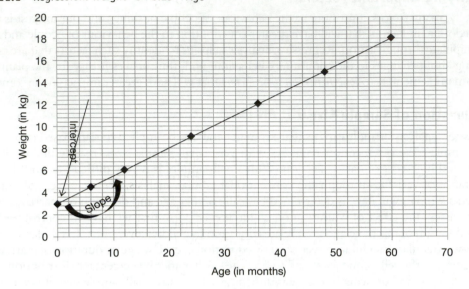

SIMPLE LINEAR OR BIVARIATE REGRESSION

The simplest form of regression analysis is the *simple linear regression* or *bivariate linear regression* of finding the *linear relationship between two variables* of the form $Y=a+bX$. The variable Y is called the *response variable* and the variable X is called the *predictor variable* or *explanatory variable*. That is, the value of X predicts the value of Y and the value of Y is in response to the value of X. Please note that the reverse process (Y predicts X, or X is in response to Y) is not valid. The term b is called the *coefficient of regression* of X (or *slope* of the regression line corresponding to X) and the term a is called the *constant term* or *intercept* of the equation. The other names for the X and Y variables are, respectively, *exogenous* and *endogenous variables*, *independent* and *dependent variables*, *regressor* and *regressand*, and so on. However, the most commonly used names for the X and Y variables are respectively *independent* and *dependent* variables, or *explanatory* and *response* variables.

To be very specific, the *intercept* is the value of Y when $X=0$ and in Figure 11.1 it is the place where the regression line meets, crosses or intercepts the Y-axis. The slope is the gradient or steepness of the regression line from the X-axis (see Figure 11.1). It is to be noted that some textbooks state the bivariate regression equation as:

$$Y=a+bX+e \qquad Y_i=a+bX_i+e_i \qquad Y_i=b_0+b_1X_i+e_i \qquad \text{and so on}$$

In our exercise we have used the regression equation as $Y=a+bX$ just for simplicity. In the above equations, the term e is an *error* or *residual term* to account for the unexplained variation in Y. In the equation $Y=a+bX$ the error term is set aside (or made hidden) for the benefit of non-statisticians to understand the lesson in a simpler way. The meaning and importance of e will be brought out later. In the format $Y_i=a+bX_i+e_i$ the equation is stated for each observation ($i=1$ to n) while the format $Y=a+bX$ it is stated in general without the subscript, again for the understanding of non-statisticians. Also, in the format $Y_i=b_0+b_1X_i+e_i$, the coefficients are b_0 and b_1 instead of a and b, that is all. Otherwise there are no differences in the scope and meaning of these equations.

The regression analysis can handle predictor variables of any type (nominal, ordinal or interval scale variables) but the dependent variable should be a numerical variable without extreme skewness (the condition for normal distribution) or a dummy variable without extreme distribution of cases (very high or very low proportion of cases in one group). It is to be noted that for regression analysis nominal and ordinal variables need to be converted into a set of dummy variables (already discussed in Chapters 1 and 5).

BIVARIATE LINEAR REGRESSION: AN EXERCISE

Running a Bivariate Regression

As of now we only assumed some values for 'a' and 'b' but in practice they are to be estimated from a sample of observations drawn from the population (here, children). The statistical procedures involved in the derivation of a and b are beyond the scope of our discussion and are not required for us. What is important is how to get these values for the population in question. For this, let us draw a sample of children from a population of children, measure their age and height and fit a regression equation using any statistical software. If we have the data in SPSS format, fitting a regression equation is nothing but going to the menu 'regression', placing the variable 'weight' under 'dependent variable' section and placing the variable 'age' under 'independent variables' section and running the program by clicking the 'OK' button (Figure 11.2). The output is ready. Given in Table 11.1 is the regression output from SPSS for 811 children of age 0–59 months from Goa who participated in the National Family Health Survey 2005–06 (NFHS-3). We have fitted a regression model $Y = a + bX$ where Y is weight in kg and X is age in completed months.

Figure 11.2   SPSS Window for Linear Regression

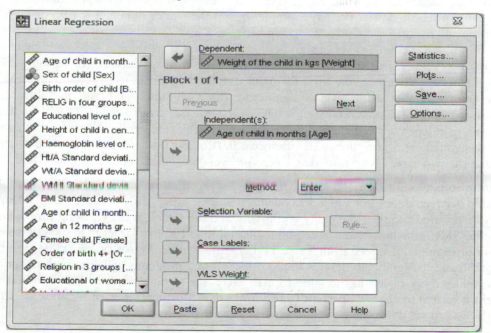

Table 11.1   SPSS Regression Output[a] for the Model Weight=$a+b$ * Age

Model		Unstandardised Coefficients		Standardised Coefficients		
		B	Std. Error	Beta	t	Sig.
1	(Constant)	6.494	.153		42.358	.000
	Age of child in months	.156	.004	.779	35.256	.000

Note: [a]Dependent variable: Weight of child in kilograms (1 decimal).

Fitting the Regression Equation

In this exercise $a=6.494$ and $b=0.156$ (listed under Column 'B'). The regression equation then becomes $Y=a+bX=6.494+0.156 * X$. Or, Weight=$6.494+0.156 *$ Age. That is, for every increase of one month in age, the child's weight increases by 0.156 kg. In other words, for every half a year of age (6 months), the child's weight increases by $0.156 * 6=936$ grams, or the child gains nearly 1 kg of weight every 6 months. Similarly, for every increase of one year (or 12 months) in age, the child's weight increases by 1.872 kg, or nearly 2 kg.

Testing the Significance of the Regression Coefficient

The next question is, 'Is a child's weight significantly related to its age?' Let β be the population value for b, then for the t-test, the null hypothesis is H_0: $\beta=0$ (that is, age is not related to weight) and the alternate hypothesis is H_1: $\beta \neq 0$ (i.e., age is related to weight, whether positively or negatively will be seen later). Please note that H_0: $\beta=0$ implies $b=0$ and hence $bX=0 * X=0$ for all values of X, and so Y is not related to (or not depended on) X.

We have already learned what standard error is, what t-test is, and what significant level is, so these are not repeated here. For large sample sizes, if the t-value obtained is 1.96 or higher, we reject the null hypothesis (of no relationship between X and Y) and say that the two variables are related at 5 percent (0.05) level of significance. Further, if the t-value is 2.58 or higher, we say that the two variables are related at 1 percent (0.01) level of significance (or strongly related). Most statistical software use the t-test for small samples that applies to large samples as well and prints out the t-value and its level of significance (the Columns 't' and 'Sig.' in Table 11.1). If the printed value of significance (Sig.) is 0.05 or less, we can say that the two variables (the corresponding independent variable and the dependent variable) are significantly related at 5 percent level of significance. If the value of significance is 0.01 or less (including the value 0.000), we can say that the two variables are related at 1 percent level of significance, or strongly related.

Assumptions/Conditions: The testing of regression coefficients assumes that the form of relationship between dependent and independent variables is linear, the errors are independent, normally distributed and their variability is constant, and the sample is drawn using simple random sampling (SRS) method from a large population (at least 10 times larger than the sample size). In our example, it is seen from Table 11.1 that the standard error of b is 0.004, the t-value is 35.256 and its significance level is 0.000. All computer programs will automatically print out these values more or less in the same format. Here, the significance level 0.000 indicates that weight is related to age at <1 percent (much lower than 1 percent) level of significance. In other words, we can say that a child's weight is strongly related to its age.

Testing the Significance of the Constant Term

Regarding the constant term a, let α be the corresponding population parameter and in this case the null hypothesis is H_0: $\alpha=0$ and the alternate hypothesis is H_1: $\alpha \neq 0$. For the first model of regression equation $Y=a+bX$ (Table 11.1), $a=6.494$ and the corresponding $t=42.358$ and the t value is significant at 1 percent level of significance (Sig.=0.000). That means $\alpha=0$ is rejected. It implies that when $X=0$, $Y=a+b*0=a$ (that is $Y=a=0$) is rejected. So the alternate hypothesis $\alpha \neq 0$ or $Y \neq 0$ is accepted. In reality, at birth (that is when $X=0$) the weight of a child is always greater than zero ($Y>0$) and there is no need to test whether it is greater than zero. Generally, at birth, the weight of a child may be in the range 2–4 kg (let us say $Y=3$ in general). In this case the test should have been H_0: $\alpha=3$ (or some other value in the range 2–4) but most computer programs assume that the default null hypothesis is H_0: $\alpha=0$ which is not appropriate in most situations. So, very often researchers do not use the test result for the constant term as produced by the computer program. If necessary one may set up his/her own hypothesis and conduct the test manually using the test statistic $t = \dfrac{(a - a_0)}{S_a}$ with $(n-2)$ degrees of freedom, where n is the number of observations, a is the constant/intercept term (obtained from the regression output) and S_a is the standard error of a (obtained from the regression output under the column 'Std. Error') and a_0 is an appropriate value being fixed by the researcher/user.

In our example, $n=811$ (is shown in some other table of the regression output and is not presented here), $a=6.494$, $S_a=0.153$ (from Table 11.1) and $a_0=3.0$ (assumed). And $t=(6.494-3.0)/0.153=22.837$ and is >2.58 (at 1 percent level of significance). That is, as per this model, the weight of a child at birth is significantly different from 3 kg. Please note that while doing manual calculations the significance value for $n<100$ can be obtained from t table and for $n>100$ we may use the large sample values of 1.96 at 5 percent level or 2.58 at 1 percent level of significance.

Checking If the Relationship Is Positive or Negative

The next question is, 'Is the relationship positive or negative'? A positive relationship means that, as the value of the independent variable increases the value of the dependent variable also increases, or as the value of the independent variable decreases the value of the dependent variable also decreases, that is, a positive relationship means that both independent and dependent variables increase or decrease together. On the other hand, a negative relationship means that, as the value of the independent variable increases the value of the dependent variable decreases, or as the value of the independent variable decreases the value of the dependent variable increases. How do we know this from the regression output? It is very simple. If the b value is positive ($b>0$) then the relationship between the corresponding independent variable and the dependent variable is positive and if the b value is negative ($b<0$) then the relationship between the two variables is negative. In our example, the coefficient for age of child is 0.156 and is positive and so the relationship is also positive. As the child's age increases, its weight also increases.

In general, *the sign of the 'b' coefficient tells the direction of the relationship* and *significance value indicates how strong the (linear) relationship is.* Please note that if the relationship is weak, it only means that the *linear relationship is weak,* but the variables may have some form of curvilinear relationship. There are ways of capturing such relationships and some of them are discussed later in this chapter.

The Beta Coefficients

The beta coefficients are standardised regression coefficients. What is a standardised coefficient? Let us start with the same exercise. We have measured weight (Y) in kilograms and age in months. Let us measure weight in grams; a weight of 6.8 kg will take the value 6,800 grams. In this case, the regression equation $Y=a+bX$ will remain the same but the values of the coefficients will change as seen in Table 11.2. Please note that in Table 11.2 the regression coefficients (B values) and their standard errors are 1,000 times higher than that in Table 11.1, only to account for the difference in the unit of measurement of weight. Otherwise the beta coefficient, t-value and its significant level remain the same. A similar exercise can be made by measuring age in years. The 'B' coefficients so obtained are often called *metric coefficients* or *un-standardised coefficients*.

From this we learn that the absolute value of regression coefficients can differ, depending on the unit of measurement but not on the beta coefficients, test results and inference. Another lesson we learn is that we cannot and should not judge the importance of a variable from the numerical value of its regression coefficient (B value in the table) because the numerical value of the coefficient varies with the unit of measurement of the variable. But there is a way to get the coefficients free of unit of measurement by transforming the variables in question into a standardised form as described below.

The 'Beta' coefficient is a standardised coefficient of b with no constant term 'a'. This coefficient is obtained by converting Y into $Y' = \dfrac{Y - \bar{Y}}{S_Y}$ and X into $X' = \dfrac{X - \bar{X}}{S_X}$, exactly the same way standard normal variate is created in Chapter 6. The X' and Y' are standardised variables with mean 0 and SD 1 and are called *standard normal variates*. It is to be noted that a variable with mean 0 and SD 1 is called a standard normal variate (variable). In practice, there is no need to convert the raw data into standardised variables (as stated above) to obtain the β coefficient. The *beta coefficient* or *standardised regression coefficient* is obtained from the metric regression coefficient and the SD of the independent and dependent variables using the formula $\beta = b\dfrac{S_X}{S_Y}$. Please note that after standardisation the constant term vanishes (that is, $a=0$ always, or not applicable). Please note that in the table the cell corresponding to the constant term is left blank, meaning that the term is not applicable.

The SD usually helps to answer the question, 'Which of the independent variables have greater effect on the dependent variable'?, especially when the variables are measured in different units of measurements (for example, weight measured in kilograms and age measured in months). In our example, $\beta=0.779$. As we have only one variable in the regression equation, the importance of the beta coefficient is not felt, but when we have many variables in the equation, its importance will be known.

Table 11.2 SPSS Regression Output[a] for Weight (in grams)=$a+b$ * Age (in Months)

Model		Unstandardised Coefficients		Standardised Coefficients		
		B	Std. Error	Beta	t	Sig.
1	(Constant)	6493.995	153.312		42.358	.000
	Age of child in months	156.282	4.433	.779	35.256	.000

Note: [a]Dependent Variable: Weight of child in grams.

MULTIPLE LINEAR REGRESSION OR MULTIPLE REGRESSION

Multiple linear regression is simply an extension of the bivariate (linear) regression. In multiple regression, there is not just one but many (two or more, or a set of) independent variables (X variables) and only one dependent (response) variable (Y variable), that is, the variable X is not just one variable but a linear combination of many variables, and the dependent variable Y is always only one variable. A multiple regression equation is of the form:

$$Y = a + b_1 X_1 + b_2 X_2 + b_3 X_3 + \cdots + b_k X_k$$

where k is the number of independent variables in the equation; $X_1, X_2, X_3, \ldots, X_k$ are the k independent variables, $b_1, b_2, \ldots, b_k$ are the corresponding regression coefficients and a is the constant term.

Please note that in multiple regression also there is an error term e that is kept hidden here. In regression analysis, often the term n is used to refer to the number of sample observations and k is used to refer to the number of independent variables in the equation. Please also note that multiple regression and multivariate regression are different. In multiple regression, there is only one dependent variable. Multivariate regression, or multivariate multiple regression, is an extension of multiple regression in that there would be *multiple* (two or more) *dependent variables* and *multiple* (two or more) *independent variables*.

In multiple regression, though there can be many independent variables, there is an important condition involved. The condition is that the independent variables should *not be related* among themselves, that is, the independent variables are independent or unrelated among themselves. For example, let us consider weight and height. Generally, both weight and height are closely related, in that, at any age, the higher the height of a child, the higher is its weight, and vice versa. Statistically, when two independent variables are *highly* correlated among themselves either the estimation process breaks down (calculation of coefficients not possible) or the coefficients (parameters) are not stable (that is, small differences in the independent variables would yield large differences in the estimated parameters). In practice, it is often unavoidable to have some amount of correlation between the independent variables and is accepted.

Multiple Linear Regression: An Exercise

Let us assume that weight of a child (Weight) is related not only to age of the child (Age) but also to the order of birth (BirthOrder) and Haemoglobin level (HbLevel) of the child. Later, we may consider a variety of variables as well. We assume that age, order of birth and Hb level are not highly related (independent of each other, which is largely true). The regression equation is:

$$\text{Weight} = a + b_1 * \text{Age} + b_2 * \text{HbLevel} + b_3 * \text{BirthOrder}$$

where a is the intercept (constant) term and b_1, b_2 and b_3 are the regression coefficients corresponding to the independent variables Age, Haemoglobin level and Order of birth, respectively. The output from SPSS for the Goa data is given in Table 11.3.

In this exercise $a = 4.770$, $b_1 = 0.140$, $b_2 = 0.245$ and $b_3 = -0.233$ (listed under Column 'B'). The regression equation then becomes

$$\text{Weight} = 4.77 + 0.140 * \text{Age} + 0.245 * \text{HbLevel} - 0.233 * \text{BirthOrder}.$$

The child's weight increases by 0.14 kg every month and is highly significant (Sig. = 0.000). Similarly, the child's weight is higher by 0.245 kg for an increase of 1 g/dl of Hb level and the increase is highly significant (Sig. = 0.000). On the other hand, the child's weight reduces by 0.233 kg as the birth order of the child increases by one and it is also highly significant (Sig. = 0.007). In other words, other things being same, as the Hb level of a child increases the weight of the child

Table 11.3   Regression Output[a] for Weight=$a+b_1$ * Age+B_2 * HbLevel+b_3 * BirthOrder

Model		Unstandardised Coefficients		Standardised Coefficients		
		B	Std. Error	Beta	t	Sig.
1	(Constant)	4.770	.660		7.229	.000
	Age of child in months	.140	.006	.695	24.928	.000
	Haemoglobin level of child	.245	.059	.117	4.157	.000
	Birth order of child	−.233	.086	−.071	−2.701	.007

Note: [a]Dependent variable: Weight of the child in kg.

also increases at the rate of 0.25 kg per 1 g/dl, irrespective of the child's age and birth order. At the same time, as the birth order of a child increases by one, its weight decreases by 0.23 kg, irrespective of the child's age and Hb level, that is, children of higher order births tend to have lesser weight than children of lower order births at every age and irrespective of Hb level.

The Error or Residual in Linear Regression

Let us continue from the above example. In the above example the fitted regression equation is:

$$\text{Weight}=4.77+0.140 * \text{Age}+0.245 * \text{HbLevel}-0.233 * \text{BirthOrder}.$$

The first case in the sample (child) was 42 months old, had a Hb level of 11.6 g/dl, was born as second order child and had a weight of 13.7 kg (obtained from the raw data). By substituting these values, except the weight of the child, in the above equation we get:

$$\text{Weight}=4.77+0.140 * 42+0.245 * 11.6+0.233 * 2=13.96 \text{ kg}.$$

Now we have two measures of weight for this child, the one we have originally measured (13.7 kg) and the one we have estimated from the regression equation (13.96 kg).

Let us assume that the sample size is n and for each of the n cases we have two Y values: one we have measured (observed) and the other we have calculated from the equation (estimated). Usually, the observed value is termed as Y and the estimated value is termed as $\widehat{Y}$ (read as Y-cap). So, for the ith case the observed and estimated values are Y_i and $\widehat{Y}_i$. In the above example (first case in the sample) $Y_1=13.7$ and $\widehat{Y}_1=13.96$ and the difference is $Y_1-\widehat{Y}_1=13.70-13.96=-0.26$.

If the data make a perfect fit of the regression equation, then we expect that the two values namely Y and $\widehat{Y}$ are the same (equal) and the difference is zero for all cases. In that case, all the Y values fall on the fitted line. But normally it is not the case and there may exist some differences between Y and $\widehat{Y}$ for most cases, and the difference between Y and $\widehat{Y}$ for each case (that is, $Y_i-\widehat{Y}$) is called the unexplained or error component, often referred to as the *residual* and denoted by the symbol e. The same is the e that is mentioned in different formats of the bivariate linear regression equation mentioned above in section 'Simple Linear or Bivariate Regression'.

The residual of Y_i is e_i and is equal to $Y_i-\widehat{Y}_i$, where Y_i is the observed value and $\widehat{Y}_i$ is the predicted value (obtained from the fitted regression equation) and $i=1, 2, \ldots, n$.

Multiple Correlation Coefficient and Coefficient of Determination

The deviation of each case Y_i from the overall mean $\overline{Y}$ (Y-bar and not Y-cap) can be expressed by adding and subtracting $\widehat{Y}_i$ as:

$$Y_i-\overline{Y}=(Y_i-\widehat{Y}_i)+(\widehat{Y}_i-\overline{Y})$$

Rearranging the terms on the right hand side, squaring the terms on both the sides and taking summation over all observations we get:

$$\sum(Y_i - \bar{Y})^2 = \sum(Y_i - \hat{Y}_i)^2 + \sum(\hat{Y}_i - \bar{Y})^2$$

Please note that the term $\sum[2 * (Y_i - \hat{Y}_i) * (\hat{Y}_i - \bar{Y})]$ gets reduced to zero (not shown). Recalling our usual procedure for obtaining variance or SD, the terms in the above equation, as we have seen in ANOVA, are:

$\sum(Y_i - \bar{Y})^2$ is the total sum of squares or *total variation* (TSS).

$\sum(\hat{Y}_i - \bar{Y})^2$ is the regression sum of squares or *explained variation* (ESS).

$\sum(Y_i - \hat{Y}_i)^2$ is the residual sum of squares or *unexplained variation* (USS).

In other words, the total variation (TSS) equals the explained variation (ESS) plus the unexplained variation (USS). Please note that in ANOVA we have used the terms 'Total Sum of Squares' (TSS) for TSS, 'Between-group Sum of Squares' (BSS) for ESS and 'Within-group Sum of Squares' (WSS) for USS and TSS = BSS + WSS. The quantity $\dfrac{\text{ESS}}{\text{TSS}}$ measures the proportion of total variance that is explained by the regression and this quantity is usually termed as *coefficient of determination* and denoted by the symbol R^2.

$$R^2 = \frac{\text{ESS}}{\text{TSS}} = \frac{\sum(\hat{Y}_i - \bar{Y})^2}{\sum(\hat{Y}_i - \bar{Y})^2}$$

It is clear from the above formula that the *coefficient of determination*, R^2, measures the proportion of total variation (sum of squares) that is explained or accounted for by the regression fit (or model or equation). In a bivariate regression (regression of Y on X, two variables only) R^2 is nothing but the square of the Pearson's *product moment correlation coefficient* (r) and in multiple regression (regression of Y on X_1, X_2, ..., three or more variables involved), R^2 is the square of the *multiple correlation coefficient*, R. Please note that the correlation of one variable on another variable is denoted by the lower case letter r and the correlation of a set of variables on another variable is denoted by the upper case letter R.

If all the observations fall on the regression line, then USS = 0 and TSS = ESS and hence $R^2 = 1$. On the other hand if no variation is explained by the regression, then ESS = 0 and $R^2 = 0$. That is, R^2 varies from 0 to 1 and so R also varies from 0 to 1. The multiple correlation coefficient, R, is always positive because when three or more variables are involved, some of the relations may be positive and others may be negative and so the direction of relationship of R cannot be established. Please note that the product moment correlation coefficient (r) lies between -1 and $+1$, whereas the multiple correlation coefficient (R) and also the coefficient of determination (R^2) lie between 0 and $+1$ only (i.e., R and R^2 are always positive).

A problem with the R^2 is that the addition of an irrelevant predictor variable to the regression equation will tend to increase the value of R^2, even if the predictor variable is in no way related to the other variables in the equation. So, a correction to R^2 is required to adjust for the irrelevant or insignificant independent variables in the equation. A corrected or adjusted multiple correlation coefficient $\acute{R}^2$ is given by the formula:

$$\acute{R}^2 = \left(R^2 - \frac{k}{k-1} \right)\left(\frac{n-1}{n-k-1} \right)$$

where n is the sample size and k is the number of predictor or independent variables in the regression equation.

The SPSS and most statistical software produce the corresponding regression output in a table. In SPSS it is printed with the heading 'Model Summary' and the same for the above model is produced in Table 11.4. It is seen from the table that the multiple correlation coefficient is $R=0.747$, the coefficient of determination is $R^2=0.559$ (or variance explained is 55.9 percent), adjusted R Square is $\acute{R}^2=0.557$ and the standard error of the estimate is 2.0855.

That means, in the regression model: Weight$=a+b_1$ * Age$+b_2$ * HbLevel$+b_3$ * BirthOrder; age, Hb level and birth order have jointly explained 0.559 or 55.9 percent of the variation in the weight of children in Goa and the unexplained variation is as high as 44.1 percent. It implies that the regression model is not a robust model or it does not fit well, as the included independent variables in the model, namely, age, Hb level and order of child, do not account for all or at least much of the variation in the weight of the child. This indicates that there are other variables that are related to the weight of children independent of these three variables.

Analysis of Variance or *F*-test

The TSS, ESS and USS can be used to test the combined effect of all the predictor variables (age, Hb level and order of child) on the response variable (weight of child) using analysis of variance (ANOVA) or the *F*-test. First let us put the TSS, ESS and USS in an ANOVA table (see Table 11.5). As per usual convention, the TSS is associated with $(n-1)$ degrees of freedom and the ESS is associated with k degrees of freedom. Please note that n is the number of observations and k is

Table 11.4   Regression Output: Model Summary
(R Square for Weight$=a+b_1$ * Age$+B_2$ * HbLevel$+b_3$ * BirthOrder)

Model	R	R Square	Adjusted R Square	Std. Error of the Estimate
1	.747[a]	.559	.557	2.0855

Note: [a]Predictors: (Constant), Haemoglobin level of child, Birth order of child, Age of child in months.

Table 11.5   Analysis of Variance (ANOVA) Table for Multiple Regression Analysis

Source of Variation	Variation or Sum of Squares	Degrees of Freedom	Mean Sum of Squares or Variance	F-Ratio
Explained by Regression	$ESS = \sum(\widehat{Y}_i - \bar{Y})^2$	k	$MESS = \dfrac{ESS}{k}$	$F = \dfrac{MESS}{MUSS}$ $(k, n-k-1)$ df
Unexplained (or) residual	$USS = \sum(Y_i - \widehat{Y}_i)^2$	$n-k-1$	$MUSS = \dfrac{USS}{n-k-1}$	
Total	$TSS = \sum(Y_i - \bar{Y})^2$	$n-1$	NA	

Table 11.6 Regression Output: ANOVA[a] for Weight $= a + b_1 *$ Age $+ B_2 *$ HbLevel $+ b_3 *$ BirthOrder

Model		Sum of Squares	df	Mean Square	F	Sig.
1	Regression	3,519.243	3	1,173.081	269.726	.000[b]
	Residual	2,779.110	639	4.349		
	Total	6,298.352	642			

Notes: [a]Predictors: (Constant), Birth order of child, Age of child in months, Haemoglobin level of child.
[b]Dependent variable: Weight of the child in kg.

the number of independent variables in the equation. Also note that the number of parameters estimated in the regression is actually $k+1$ (that is, k numbers of b coefficients and the constant term a) and so the degrees of freedom is $(k+1)-1=k$. As such the USS is associated with $(n-1)-(k)=(n-k-1)$ degrees of freedom.

Given the total variance (TSS) constant, it is clear from Table 11.5 that the larger the value of the explained variance (MESS), the smaller the value of the unexplained variance (MUSS) and larger the value of the F-ratio (MESS/MUSS). Please note that the F-ratio is always positive and it ranges from 0 to ∞ (infinity). The omnibus F-test is a simultaneous test of hypothesis that all the β coefficients are zero. That is, the null hypothesis is:

$$H_0: \beta_1 = \beta_2 = \cdots = \beta_k = 0$$

If one is interested in an alternate hypothesis, it would be:

$$H_1: \beta_1 \neq 0 \text{ or } \beta_2 \neq 0 \text{ or } \ldots \text{ or } \beta_k \neq 0 \text{ (that is, not all } \beta\text{'s are zero)}$$

Continuing with the above example, the fitted regression equation is:

$$\text{Weight} = 4.77 + 0.140 * \text{Age} + 0.245 * \text{HbLevel} - 0.233 * \text{BirthOrder}$$

The null hypothesis is $H_0: \beta_1 = \beta_2 = \beta_3 = 0$ and the ANOVA table produced by SPSS is given in Table 11.6.

It is seen from the table that $F = 269.726$ and the degrees of freedom is $(3, 639)$ and the F value is statistically significant at 0.000 level of significance (Sig. $= 0.000$). So we reject the null hypothesis H_0: $\beta_1 = \beta_2 = \beta_3 = 0$ at all levels (including 0.1 percent level) of significance. In other words, the predictor or independent variables in the equation as a whole, namely age, Hb level and birth order, is significantly related to the response or dependent variable, namely, weight of child. It is to be noted that we have seen in Table 11.3 that individually also age, Hb level and birth order are significantly related to weight of child. Please note that it is also possible that while the F value is highly significant, some of the independent variables are not significant. At the same time, as we see from Table 11.4, the model is not a robust model as the percentage variance explained is not very large (55.9 percent only). That means, the three variables, age, Hb level and birth order, are strongly related to weight of child but still there are other factors which need to be identified and considered in the model to make it as a robust model.

UNDERLYING ASSUMPTIONS IN LINEAR REGRESSION

The linear regression analysis rests upon four principal assumptions as follows:

1. *Independence* of the errors (no serial correlation)
2. *Normality* of the error distribution
3. *Linearity* assumption. That is, the dependent and independent variables are linearly related
4. *Homoscedasticity* (that is, constant variance) of the errors

Independence: The observations of the dependent variable Y (that is, the Y_i values) and its error term (e_i) are statistically independent of each other or follow a random process. The observations are not independent if they are based on repeated or related measurements from the same population or experimental units.

Linearity: The mean values $\mu_{Y/X}$ (the mean values of Y for different values of X) all lie on a straight line, which is the population regression line, that is, for a unit increase in the value of X, there is a proportional change (increase or decrease) in the mean value of Y. For example, if the mean weight of children of age 12 months is 6.5 kg and that of children of age 13 months is 6.6 kg (an increase of 100 g in one month) then the same increase of 100 g per month applies to children of all ages. That is, the dependent variable Y increases or decreases linearly with the independent variable X.

Normality: For any fixed value of the independent variable X, the distribution of the dependent variable Y is normal (that is, the Y values corresponding to each of X values are normally distributed) with mean $\mu_{Y/X}$ (the mean of the Y values corresponding to a given value of X). For example, the weights of children of *each* of the age groups 12–17, 18–23,..., 54–59 months are normally distributed. So also, the error term e_i is normally distributed.

Equal variance: For a fixed value of the independent variable X, the values of the dependent variable Y are distributed with mean $\mu_{Y/X}$ and a constant variance σ^2. For example, if the variance of weight of children of age group 12–17 is 4 kg, then the variance weights of children of the age groups 18–23, 24–29,..., 54–59 are all 4 kg. In statistics the equal variance assumption is often called homoscedasticity and violation of this assumption (unequal variance) is called heteroscedasticity.

Overall, in linear regression, it is assumed that the observations (values) are all independent of each other (with respect to the dependent variable), the dependent and each of the independent variables are linearly related and the residuals or the errors of the dependent variable are normally distributed at each level of the independent variables and with a constant variance.

If the population from which the sample was drawn and the applied linear regression model violates one or more of the linear regression assumptions then the results of the analysis may be incorrect and misleading. This is because, if any of these assumptions is violated (that is, if there is nonlinearity, serial correlation, heteroscedasticity and/or non-normality) then the regression coefficients, hypothesis testing, forecasts, confidence intervals and other measures derived from the regression model would be inefficient or seriously biased and the inferences misleading. Some small violations are unavoidable in practical situations and often they will have very little practical effect on the analysis, while other violations may render the linear regression results incorrect and the inferences misleading, and sometimes even the results itself un-interpretable.

Examining Independence of the Residuals (No Serial Correlation)

Serial correlation or autocorrelation is the term used to describe the relationship between the observations of the same variable over periods of time, or order of observations (corresponding values prior and later cases). If the serial correlation of the observations is zero, then the observations are said to be in independent or random order. If the observations are serially correlated, it means that the observations do not evolve in a random process, but they are related to their prior or later cases.

One of the assumptions of regression analysis is that the observations are not related to one another and it is measured in terms of the independency of the residual (error term), that is, the error term of different cases are mutually independent (uncorrelated or random). Although

Table 11.7   SPSS Output of Model Summary[a] with Durbin–Watson Coefficient

Model	R	R Square	Adjusted R Square	Std. Error of the Estimate	Durbin–Watson
1	.779[b]	.606	.606	2.0883	1.731

Notes: [a]Predictors: (Constant), Age of child in months.
[b]Dependent variable: Weight of the child in kg.

there are many ways this assumption might be violated, the most common occurrence is with time series data in the form of *serial correlation*. However, serial correlation is not restricted to time series data alone, but may also occur with cross- sectional data. For example, it is likely that children of the same mother are all heavy in weight (or thin) irrespective of their background characteristics. If many observations in a sample are children of same mothers, then the weights of younger children are related to (not independent of) the weights of their elder siblings, amounting to serial correlation.

The Durbin–Watson test is a well-known method for testing if serial correlation is a serious problem in the data undermining the model's suitability in assessing the predicted values of a dependent variable. The statistic of the Durbin–Watson procedure is d and is calculated as follows:

$$d = \frac{\sum_{i=2}^{n} (e_i - e_{i-1})^2}{\sum_{i=1}^{n} e_i^2}, \text{ where } e_i \text{ is the residual for the } i\text{th case of the } n \text{ cases.}$$

It can be shown that the value of d will be between zero and four (range 0–4) with a 'zero' corresponding to perfect positive correlation, a 'four' to perfect negative correlation and a 'two' to no correlation. In other words, if d is close to 2 ($d \approx 2$) then we can say that the residuals are uncorrelated or independent, and more the deviation of d from 2, the higher the degree of serial correlation.

In SPSS we can get the value of d by choosing 'statistics' in the 'regression menu' and then choosing 'Durbin–Watson'. In the SPSS output the d value is included and printed in the 'model summary' table as shown above (Table 11.7). It is seen from the table that the d value is 1.73 and it is less than 2 but close to 2, meaning that there exists marginal serial correlation. As some amount of serial correlation is unavoidable, we can say that the residuals are largely unrelated.

Examining the Linearity Assumption

Not all the independent variables can be *linearly* related to the dependent variable, and the relationship of some variables may be *curvilinear*. If the relationship is not linear, we can use appropriate transformation and convert the relationship into a liner form in the regression equation. Examining what kind of (linear or curvilinear) relationship the independent variables have with the dependent variable is the responsibility of the researcher and we have many tools to accomplish this. Two such conversion techniques are presented. In the bivariate situation, a scatterplot is a good means for judging how well a straight line fits the data. Figure 11.3 gives SPSS output of scatter plot of weight by age of child and the fitted regression line. It is seen from the chart, though the scatter plots centre around the fitted line, at the beginning and ending portions, relatively more points are located below the fitted line than above it. So it appears that a linear assumption is less appropriate.

Another way to look at the linearity assumption is to obtain the mean of the dependent variable Y (here, weight) for different categories of the independent variable X (here, age) and plot a line graph as shown in Figure 11.4.

Figure 11.3   SPSS Output of Scatter Plot of Weight by Age of Child and Fitted Line

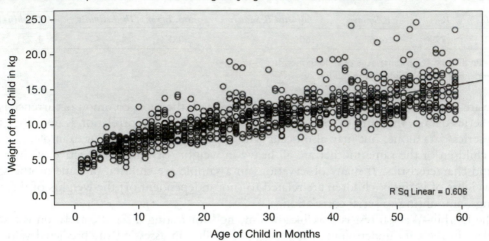

Figure 11.4   Mean Weight by Age Group

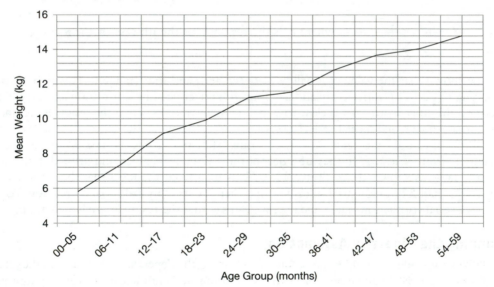

In both the figures (Figures 11.3 and 11.4), though the plots look largely linear, a careful observation indicates that the slop of the points/curve decreases as age increases. The pattern looks like a growth chart of weight for age. A general format of a growth chart of weight for age looks like the one presented in Figure 11.5 (the line named as 'Growth chart'). But at the same time, the regression line of weight for age of child is a straight line as in Figure 11.5 (the line named as Regression fit'). Further, the constant value $a = 6.494$ (weight at age 0 months) appears to be on a higher side. So we need to modify the regression equation to capture the curvilinear pattern of weight for age relationship.

Figure 11.5   Weight for Age Curve

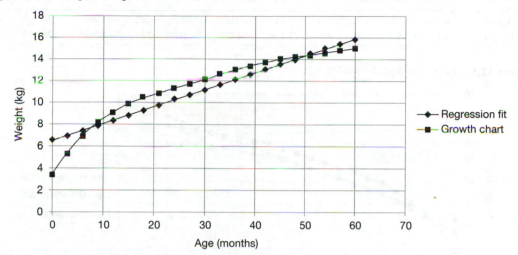

Table 11.8   Regression Output[a] for the Equation $Y = a + bX + cX^2$

Model		Unstandardised Coefficients		Standardised Coefficients		
		B	Std. Error	Beta	t	Sig.
1	(Constant)	5.444	.250		21.739	.000
	Age of child in months	.253	.019	1.259	13.398	.000
	Age of child in months squared	−.002	.000	−.494	−5.253	.000

Note: [a]Dependent Variable: Weight of the child in kilograms(1 decimal).

Capturing Curvilinear Pattern of Relationship

A non-linear or curvilinear pattern of relationship of the dependent variable with an independent variable can be captured in a variety of ways, according to the nature of relationship between the variables. Any change in the scale of measurement or transformation of independent variable does not affect the distribution of the dependent variable. But, at the same time, a transformation can lead to a possible linear relationship with the dependent variable. So we can transform the independent variable according to the nature of its relationship with the dependent variable if it is known or if it can be assumed appropriately, such as logarithmic transformation and exponential transformation. If the underlying model or relationship is not known, a simple way to capture, *to a large extent*, a curvilinear pattern of relationship (such as the above) of an independent variable with the dependent variable is to add a square term of the independent variable in the regression equation. The resultant regression equation will be of the form $Y = a + bX + cX^2$ (a 'parabola' that gives a curvilinear relationship). Table 11.8 is the regression output for the children of Goa as per NFHS-3.

In this exercise, $a = 5.444$, $b = 0.253$ and $c = -0.002$ (listed under Column 'B'). The equation then becomes $Y = 5.444 + 0.253 X - 0.002X^2$. For select values of age (X), the values of weight (Y) are given in Table 11.9. For example, for $X = 6$, $Y = 5.444 + 0.253 * 6 - 0.002 * 6 * 6 = 6.89$.

It is clear from Table 11.9 that as age increases the weight also increases, but not in a constant proportion. For example, for the increase in age from 0 to 12 months the increase in weight is $8.19 - 5.44 = 2.75$ kg. But for the same increase in age from 12 to 24 months, the increase in

Table 11.9　Values of Y for Select Values of X for the Regression Equation $Y = a + bX + cX^2$

X (Age)	0	6	12	18	24	30	36	42	48	54	60
Y (Weight)	5.44	6.89	8.19	9.35	10.36	11.23	11.96	12.54	12.98	13.27	13.42

Figure 11.6　Weight for Age and Age² Curves

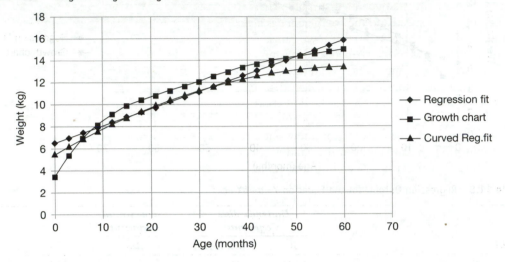

weight is $10.36 - 8.19 = 2.17$ kg. Similarly, for the increase in age from 24 to 36 months, the increase in weight is $11.96 - 10.36 = 1.60$ kg and for the increase in age from 48 to 60 months, the increase in weight is $13.42 - 12.98 = 0.44$ kg only.

If we plot the weight obtained for different ages 0–60 months, we get a curved line as shown in Figure 11.6 (the line named as 'Curved Regfit'). Please note that the shape of the curve 'Curved Regfit' is very similar to the curve 'Growth chart' presented in Figure 11.5, except for the lower end. Please do not compare the height of the two curves (weight values) as the 'Growth chart' values in Figure 11.5 are only hypothetical and not real. Further, the constant term a is reduced from 6.494 to 5.444, but still it appears to be on a higher side. This value corresponds to the weight of child at birth.

What we learn from this is that, if the relationship of an independent variable with the dependent variable is of a curved or nonlinear form, we can capture such relationship to a large extent by adding a square term to it in the regression model. However, in this case, the analysis of the output is slightly difficult as we have to analyse the two coefficients (in this example b and c) jointly.

The next step is to analyse, 'Is the squared term for age is significant?' which is equivalent to saying, 'Is the curvilinear relationship significant'? or 'Is the square term for age is really needed in the model'? In our example, the inclusion of square term for age has reduced the t-value for age from 35.3 (Table 11.1) to 13.4 (Table 11.8), but still b is significant at 0.000 level. Further the t-value for the squared term of age is $t = -5.3$ and is also significant at 0.000 level, indicating that the relationship between age and weight of children is not linear, but more of curvilinear. In other words a curvilinear relationship, and not a linear relationship, of age that explains better the weight of children and hence a squared term for age in the model is preferred and appropriate.

The next question is, 'Is the curvilinear relationship positive or negative?' A positive relationship means 'as X increases, Y changes (increases or decreases) slowly until a certain level of X

and then changes faster as X further increases' (a U-shaped pattern), and a negative relationship means 'as X increases, Y changes (increases or decreases) faster until certain level of X and then changes slowly as X further increases' (an inverted U-shaped pattern). In other words, the sign of the coefficient b implies a positive or negative relationship while the sign of the coefficient c (for the squared term) indicates the U-shape or inverted U-shape pattern of curvilinear relationship of the variable with the dependent variable. It is very similar to speed and acceleration, in that the coefficient b is speed and the coefficient c is acceleration. In our example, as the coefficient for the square term is negative (-0.002), we can say that the relationship between age and weight of children is of an inverted U-shaped relationship. That means, as age increases the weight of child also increases but the rate of increase reduces.

It is not required to present all independent variables in curvilinear form by adding a square term to each one of them. It should be done only if a clear pattern of curvilinear relationship was found. A scatter plot of height on x-axis and weight on y-axis is shown in Figure 11.7. It is very clear from the figure that, except for a few outliers, as height increases the weight also increases almost uniformly. So, if height of the child is also an independent variable in the model, there is no need for a square term for height in the equation. Further, there is no need to consider curvilinear relationship (and hence a square term) for dummy variables as they take only two values (0 and 1) and so Y values fall on two vertical columns only.

It is to be noted that there are many other non-linearity assumptions and related transformations. Some of them are presented below, but a detailed description is beyond the scope of this book.

Figure 11.7   SPSS Output of Scatter Plot of Weight by Height

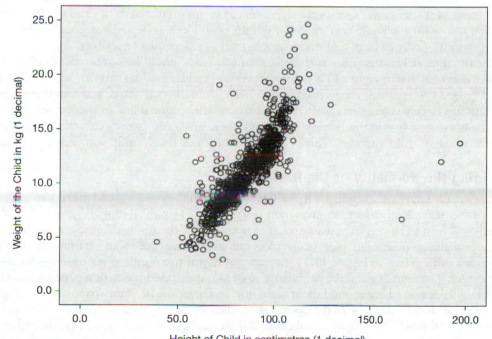

(1) If the distribution of an independent variable is skewed to the right like income distribution then a log transformation is appropriate: $Y = a + b \log(X)$. On the other hand, if the dependent variable is skewed then the transformation would be: $Log\,(Y) = a + bX$. In this case the dependent variable is $Log\,(Y)$ and not Y, and the output should be interpreted and inference drawn accordingly. Please see section 'MCA for logistic regression' under Chapter 13 in this book.

(2) If the distribution of dependent variable by an independent variable tend to show an exponential pattern (like population growth) then an exponential transformation is appropriate: $Y = a + b\,(e^X)$.

(3) Another one is, reciprocal transformation $Y = a + \dfrac{b}{X}$ (or) $Y = a - \dfrac{b}{X}$

When the distribution of the residuals is positively skewed (that is, skewed to the right), a log transformation of the dependent variable ($Log\,Y$) is a better option. On the other hand, when the distribution is negatively skewed (that is skewed to the left), a square transformation (Y^2) is preferred. The transformations apply to the independent variables as well depend on the pattern of distribution of observations of these variables. However, as demonstrated above ($Y = a + bX + cX^2$), as far as possible, transformation of independent variables is preferred than transformation of the dependent variable, mainly from the point of view of easy interpretation of the results and drawing inference.

OVERALL LINEARITY ASSUMPTION TEST

To check if the model as a whole follows a linear pattern, the convenient method is to plot the residuals against the predicted values. Nonlinearity is usually evident in a plot of the *observed* versus *predicted* values or a plot of *residuals* versus *predicted* values, which are a part of standard regression output in most statistical software programs including SPSS. Figures 11.8 and 11.9 are SPSS output of scatter plots of, respectively, observed versus predicted values and residuals versus predicted values for the regression model of weight of children as dependent variable and age of child in months, order of birth and haemoglobin level as independent variables.

If the fitted model is largely linear then the plotted points should be symmetrically distributed around a diagonal line in Figure 11.8 (observed versus predicted values) and around a horizontal line in Figure 11.9 (residuals versus predicted values). From the two charts, it is seen that the plotted points are largely symmetrically distributed around the diagonal line in the former chart and around a horizontal line in the latter plot, though there are some exceptions and the exceptions increases as age of child increases. This implies that the linear relationship is somewhat violated.

Examining the Normality of the Residual

We have already seen that, a residual is the difference between the observed and the model-predicted values of the dependent variable. A histogram (Figure 11.10) or a P-P plot (Figure 11.11) of the residuals will help us to check the assumption of normality of the residuals. Please note that a P-P plot is a probability–probability plot, which plots two cumulative probability distribution functions against each other. Here, in Figure 11.11, the *expected* cumulative standardised residuals are shown by the diagonal straight line and the cumulative *observed* standardised residuals are the plot of values as seen by a thick curved line around the straight line. In Figure 11.10, if the shape of the histogram reflects approximately the shape of the normal curve then we can say that the residuals or error term approximately follows the normal distribution and we can take it for granted that the regression model satisfies the normality condition. On the other hand, if the histogram deviates much from

Figure 11.8   SPSS Output of Scatter Plot of Observed and Predicted Weight of Child

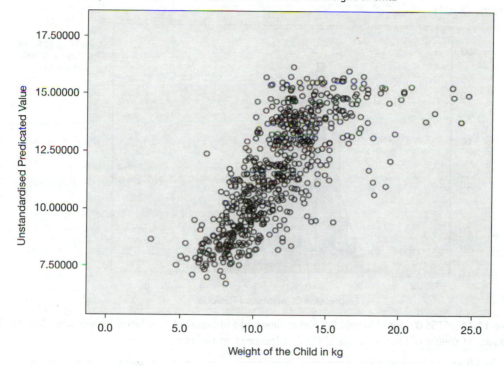

Figure 11.9   SPSS Output of Scatter Plot of Weight by Age of Child and Fitted Line

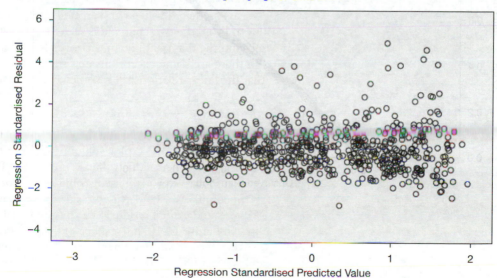

Figure 11.10 SPSS Output of Histogram of Regression Standardised Residuals with Weight of Child as Dependent Variable

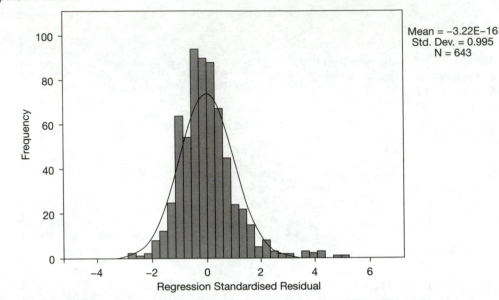

Figure 11.11 SPSS Output of Normal P-P Plot of Observed and Expected Cumulative Probabilities (Standardised Residuals) of Weight of Child with Age of Child as Independent Variable

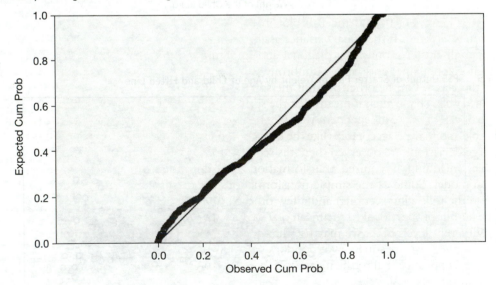

the normal curve or skewed to the right or left to a substantial extent then it means that the model does not satisfies the normality assumption.

The shape of the histogram in Figure 11.10 follows the shape of a normal curve fairly well, but there are a few large positive residuals (standardised residuals with values >3) as seen on the right side of the normal curve (above the label '4'). If there are a few large (positive or negative) residuals in the data then it is an indication that the corresponding observations are most likely outliers. Otherwise, the data by and large reflects a normal distribution with respect to the dependent variable (here weight of child).

The P-P plot of the residuals (Figure 11.11) also helps us to check the assumption of normality of the residuals. If the two distributions are identical, that is, both fall on the straight line, then it means that the residuals follow the normal distribution, that is, the plot of the cumulative observed residuals lie exactly on the cumulative expected residuals (which always form a straight line). By observing how the observed residuals are scatter about the expected straight line we can compare the two distributions. If the cumulative observed residuals lie exactly on the straight line or very close to it, we can assume that the residuals are distributed normally or almost normally, as the case may be. In our example the two curves are not identical but are very close to each other, though the cumulative predicted residuals deviate more on the upper side than on the lower side of the chart. In general, it appears that the distribution is largely normal, of course with some deviations.

Examining the Equality of Variance

The equal variance assumption is that for different values of an independent variable, the variance of the dependent variable or its residuals are the same. The plot of observed and predicted values of the dependent variable (Figure 11.9), the plot of the dependent variable by the independent variable(s) (Figure 11.10) and the P-P plot in Figure 11.11 can indicate if the equal variance assumption is violated. If the equal variance assumption is satisfied, then in Figure 11.9 the plotted points will cluster around the diagonal and in Figure 11.10 the plotted points will cluster around a horizontal line more or less uniformly and at equidistance on both sides throughout the range of the x-axis. On the other hand, if the spread of the points looks like a 'cone' or 'inverted cone' or 'irregular shape' then it means that the spread is not uniform and the variance differs over the range of values of the independent variable. In practice, however, some amount of deviation is unavoidable and may be acceptable (like the deviations seen in the above-mentioned 3 charts), but where large deviations are observed then it is required to incorporate appropriate transformation of variables, including, if required, transformation of the dependent variable, before finalising the regression model. Some of the simple transformations are discussed in this book (in the earlier and also in the following sections) and a few other options are: (a) if the variance of residuals is not constant but proportional to the mean of Y (that is, the coefficient of variation is almost constant) at different levels of X, we may use the square root of Y (that is, $\sqrt{Y}$) provided all values of Y are positive (because square root not does not apply to negative values); and (b) if the SD of the residuals is proportional to the mean of Y, we may try logarithmic transformation.

MORE ABOUT EXAMINING THE DATA

Examining for Outliers

An *outlier* is an observation that is *numerically distinct* from most of the other observations in the dataset. In other words, outliers are observations that are not within the expected range. As discussed under Chapter 5, statistical measures (indices and estimates) derived based on the dataset that included outliers may produce much higher or lower than the real values and inferences drawn based on such indices would be misleading. For example, the mean of 2, 3, 4, 5, 6 is 4 and the mean of 2, 3, 4, 5, 16 is 6. That is, just because one observation is numerically distinct (16), the mean is increased from 4 to 6. In regression analysis, the presence of outliers may increase or decrease the b coefficient even to the extent of altering the significance level from highly significant to not significant, and vice versa. Sometimes the coefficient may even change its sign, from a positive coefficient to a negative coefficient, and vice versa. Further, a few outliers can contribute substantially to the violation of the underlying assumptions even if the data are otherwise fully within the underlying assumptions. So, it is most important first to examine the data for outliers.

Figure 11.12 is a scatter plot of weight by age of child obtained from SPSS using the menu 'Graphs => Legacy Dialogs => Scatter/Dot ... => Simple Scatter'. A scatter plot is nothing but presenting the values of dependent variable plotted against an independent variable on a graph by taking the independent variable (X) on the x-axis and dependent variable (Y) on the y-axis. It is seen from the figure that quite a few cases are outliers.

A sorting of the raw data by age and weight showed that a child of age 2 months had a weight of 36 kg, a child of age 7 months had a weight of 25.5 kg and a child of age 12 months had a weight of 17.1 kg. On the opposite side, a child of age 15 months had a weight of just 3 kg and a child of age 38 months had a weight of 6.7 kg. There are a few other outliers as well. It may be that either the weight is wrong, or age is wrong or both are wrong, or the cases may be exceptional (either too overweight or too thin, as the case may be). But often these would be wrong

Figure 11.12 Checking for Outliers Using Scatter Plot of Weight by Age

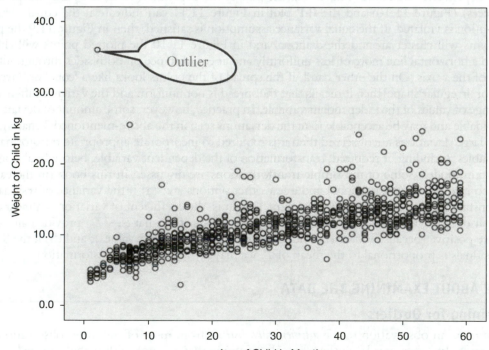

entries. The outliers may occur due to wrong measurement, careless recording of values in the questionnaire or wrong computer entry (say, recording of age 20 months as 02 months).

One way to deal with outliers is to go back to the dataset and see if there was any data entry or coding error and, if so, correct the errors in consultation with the questionnaire. If it is not possible or the questionnaires are not accessible, the other way is to exclude them, or live with them, and there is no standard rule. We cannot arbitrarily correct them because we do not know whether the problem is with the variable X, or with Y, or both, and if we make correction in one variable it may not be consistent with other variables in the dataset concerning the individual observation.

If the outliers are many then exclusion of them from the analysis will rapidly reduce the sample size and systematically change the distribution of cases, and thereby it will severely affect the analysis and the results, that is, inclusion of outliers affect the analysis in one way and exclusion of them affect the analysis in some other way. So the best way is to ensure that the quality of the data is satisfactory. However, if outliers still exist in the data, an appropriate way to deal with it is to exclude only those cases with very extreme values. In our exercise we have excluded only those cases with a weight greater than 15 kg for children of age 12 months or less. Accordingly, the first listed three values (36 kg, 25.5 kg and 17.1 kg with age of child 2–12 months) are excluded from the analysis by treating them as missing.

Robust Regression

Another way to deal with outliers is to use robust regression techniques. Robust regression tries to protect against the estimates of parameters, standard errors, coefficient of determination or variance explained, test statistics and also other statistics being highly biased, by giving lesser weightage to extreme values (outliers) and not excluding them from the analysis. Robust estimation methods can help when the tails in the distribution of the residuals are heavy (an indication is seen in Figure 11.10), that is when there are many outliers compared to the normal distribution.

There is a family of robust regression analysis techniques that replaces the sum of squared errors with one less influenced by outliers. SPSS does not have a procedure for robust regression but statistical packages such as SAS and STATA have some procedures. If the estimated errors (residuals) obtained from Ordinary Least Square (OLS) estimation method (OLS method is the usual method of estimation in linear regression that minimises the sum of the squared vertical distances from the line to the observed data points; this method is not discussed as it is highly technical and not required here) are much different from that obtained using robust estimation method, it means that outliers have influence on the OLS results, making the estimates unreliable. In such cases, the predicted values based on robust estimation will better portray the data. Further, robust residuals will help better to discover which cases are unusual and outliers. However, description and discussion on the methods of robust regression are highly technical and beyond the scope of this book.

Multicollinearity

One of the basic assumptions in multiple regression is that the independent (predictor) variables are unrelated (independent) among themselves but are individually related to the response (dependent) variable, so that the assumption of linear combination of the predictor variables on the response variable is valid. However, in reality, a complete non-relation or independence of the predictor variables is not possible. For example, education of husband and education of wife may not be completely independent. Multicollinearity relates to the issue of the relationship among the predictor (independent) variables themselves.

In general, two predictor variables are said to be collinear if they are highly correlated and, in practice, a correlation coefficient of 0.8 or higher is considered as the two variables being collinear. The existence of very high correlation among different predictor variables is called multicollinearity. Please note that multicollinearity is different from interaction and in that interaction refers to a change in the relationship between a predictor variable and a response variable in the presence of another predictor variable, but multicollinearity refers to the relationship between two predictor variables themselves. However, in interaction, some amount of relationship (correlation) may exist between the predictor variables in question, but not to the extent that they are collinear. As a practical example, let us consider the two predictor variables, namely, number of children ever born and number of children surviving on the age woman at family planning method acceptance. We know that as the number of children ever born increases, the number of children surviving also increases, and in populations where child loss experience is very low the two variables tend to be almost the same, that is, the two variables are closely related or highly correlated and so they are not independent of each other.

Mathematically, two or more variables are said to be collinear if one of the variables can be expressed as a linear combination of the other variables. Let us consider the regression equation $Y=a+bX_1+cX_2+dX_3$ and if $X_3=X_1+2X_2$ then the variables X_1, X_2 and X_3 are multicollinear. As a practical example, we know that current age of woman (CA), age at marriage (AM) and duration of marriage (DM) are all related to number of children ever born (CEB) to a woman. But we know that duration of marriage is equal to current age minus age at marriage. That is, $DM=CA-AM$ and in this case we cannot consider a regression model $CEB=a*CA+b*AM+c*DM$ as the three predictor variables are linearly related. Alternatively we can consider any two of the three variables and the effect of the third variable can be estimated from the regression output using the relationship $DM=CA-AM$.

The problem with multicollinearity is that if two or more predictor variables are *linearly related*, the regression coefficients $a, b, c, \ldots$ are not uniquely solvable and the computer program sends a message to this effect (the technical part is not discussed here). On the other hand if two variables are not exactly linearly related but very closely related (say, correlation coefficient is 0.9), then the regression coefficients $a, b, c, \ldots$ are solvable but the estimates are imprecise or not stable because the standard errors for these variables will be very large. In all, the problem of multicollinearity is one of statistical instability of the regression coefficients due to inappropriate selection of predictor variables and/or inadequate spread of values of the predictor variables.

How to Detect Correlation between Independent Variables?

Most computer programs automatically check for multicollinearity among the predictor variables as a routine exercise, for the sake of the computer processing of the program being not breakdown (in computer terminology 'hanging') while solving the regression equation. If two or more independent variables are exactly multicollinear as in the case Duration-of-Marriage = Current-Age – Age-at-Marriage, the statistical software program itself will detect and inform us. The SPSS will go one step forward by dropping one variable from the model and proceeding with the analysis. At the same time, the statistical software programs will not automatically detect and inform if two independent variables are highly correlated, but not exactly collinear. Thus, we need to detect (by instructing the program to do tests) and treat the variables appropriately in the model.

Now the issue is, how to detect the very high correlation between two numerical and/or categorical variables. If both the variables are numerical variables we can obtain Pearson's product moment correlation coefficient, and if the absolute value of the correlation coefficient is 0.8 or higher we can consider the two variables as highly correlated. If one variable is a numerical variable and the other is a categorical variable, we can obtain correlation ratio, and if the correlation ratio is 0.5 or higher, we can consider that the two variables are highly correlated. We can also go one step further and conduct the *F*-test, and if the relationship is significant at 1 percent level (for small samples) or 0.1 percent level (for large samples) we can treat the two variables as highly correlated. On the other hand, if both the variables are categorical variables, we can perform chi-square test for the association of attributes and if the relationship is significant at 1 percent level (for small samples) or 0.1 percent level (for large samples), we can treat the two variables as highly correlated. The tests can be performed for the different combinations of the independent variables that are perceived to be highly correlated. Though these procedures are suggestive measures to look for highly correlated variables, there is no hard and fast rule to do the exercise. But if we do such exercises, we are more confident about the appropriateness of the model for the data on hand and the results and finding from the exercise.

There are two ways to deal with the situation. If two variables are closely related, discard the less relevant variable from the regression model. Alternatively combine the two variables into one as a linear combination the two variables (example, Duration-of-Marriage=Current-Age−Age-at-Marriage), or as a single categorical variable, or a set of dummy variables (example, education of wife and of husband as 'both literate', 'any one literate' and 'both illiterate'). Please note that dropping one variable is not a good idea if both the variables are important for the research problem on hand.

MORE ABOUT TREATMENT OF VARIABLES

Categorical Variables and Dummy Variables

For regression analysis, the dependent and independent variables should be discrete or continuous variables. But in social science research, often, we have to deal with categorical variables (ordinal and nominal variables). However, in regression analysis there is a way to deal with these variables. The categorical variables are first converted into a set of dummy (dichotomous or binary) variables and then used in the regression equation. The dummy variables concept has already been dealt with in Chapters 1 and 5.

Let us start with an example of a categorical variable having two categories. The variable sex has two categories, namely, male and female, and it can be converted into a dichotomous variable by assigning a numerical code 1 for male and 0 for female. Accordingly, let us call the recoded variable as 'Male' that takes the value 1 if the individual is a male and the value 0 otherwise. Alternatively, we may consider the variable as 'Female' by coding 1 if female and 0 if male. Though the coefficients may differ depending on the coding pattern, the ultimate inference will remain the same and so the coding pattern is immaterial and it can be left to the convenience of the user. The category that takes the value '0' is called the *reference category*. So, in our example, the category 'female' is the reference category. Let us consider how to incorporate the variable 'Male' instead of 'sex' in the regression equation and how to interpret the result. For this, let us consider the regression of weight (Y) on age (X) and Male (Z). The corresponding regression equation is $Y=a+bX+cZ$ (or, Weight=$a+b$ * Age+c * Male). Now create a new variable 'Male' by recoding the original variable 'Sex' and run a regression of weight on Age and Male. The output is given in Table 11.10.

The fitted regression equation is $Y=6.167+0.156$ * Age+0.652 * Male. We see from Table 11.10 that the variable 'Male' is significantly related to weight of child, meaning that, for children of a specified age, the weight is significantly different for male and female children. Let us see how much the difference is.

At any age X, the weight of a male child (Male=1) is:

$$Y=6.167+0.156 * X+0.652 * 1=6.167+0.156 * X+0.652.$$

Table 11.10   Regression Output[a]: Weight=$a+b$ * Age+c * Male

Model		Unstandardised Coefficients		Standardised Coefficients		
		B	Std. Error	Beta	t	Sig.
1	(Constant)	6.167	.168		36.697	.000
	Age of child in months	.156	.004	.777	35.595	.000
	Child male (1M, 0F)	.652	.145	.098	4.491	.000

Note: [a]Dependent Variable: Weight of the child in kg.

Table 11.11   Regression Output[a]: Weight=$a+b$ * Age+c * Female

Model		Unstandardised Coefficients		Standardised Coefficients		
		B	Std. Error	Beta	t	Sig.
1	(Constant)	6.820	.168		40.598	.000
	Age of child in months	.156	.004	.777	35.595	.000
	Child male (1F, 0M)	−.652	.145	−.098	−4.491	.000

Note: [a]Dependent Variable: Weight of the child in kg.

At any age X, the weight of a female child (Male=0) is:

$$Y=6.167+0.156 * X+0.652 * 0=6.167+0.156 * X+0.$$

From the above two equations, it is clear that the difference in weight between male and female children is 0.652 kg. That means a male child tends to weight 0.652 kg higher than a female child of the same age. What difference it will make if we consider the variable 'Female' by coding 1 if female and 0 if male. Now create a new variable 'Female' by recoding the original variable 'Sex' and run a regression of Weight on Age and Female (Table 11.11). As seen from the table, we have got exactly the same regression result but the 'B' coefficient, 'Beta' coefficient and t-value have taken the opposite sign. At any age X, the weight of a female child (Female=1) is:

$$Y=6.820+0.156 * X-0.652 * 1=6.820+0.156 * X-0.652.$$

At any age X, the weight of a male child (Female=0) is:

$$Y=6.820+0.156 * X-0.652 * 0=6.620+0.156 * X-0$$

It is clear from the table that a female child tends to weight 0.652 kg less than a male child of the same age, which is same as saying a male child weighs 0.652 kg higher than a female child of the same age. This implies that the change of reference category may change the output value, but the inference will remain the same. It is to be noted that we can also have other coding pattern as well, say, male=1 and female=2, but the interpretation of the result is rather complex. So the coding system 0 and 1 is ideal and very convenient for analytical and explanatory purposes.

Categorical variables with more than two categories are also treated in a similar way but it will be considered in more than one dummy variable. The number of dummy variables will be one less than the number of categories in the variable. Let us consider the variable 'Religion' with four categories, namely, Hindu, Christian, Muslim and 'other religions'. In our sample it was found that only two cases belonged to 'other religion' category and so the variable OTHER is omitted from the analysis, that is, in our exercise we have only three religions, namely, Hindu, Muslim and Christian, and so we need to construct only two dummy variables. The two dummy variables

Table 11.12 Regression Output[a]: Weight=$a+b$ * Age+c * Christian+d * Muslim

Model		Unstandardised Coefficients		Standardised Coefficients		
		B	Std. Error	Beta	t	Sig.
1	(Constant)	6.332	.165		38.424	.000
	Age of child in months	.157	.004	.780	35.502	.000
	Christian dummy variable	−.128	.233	−.012	−.550	.583
	Muslim dummy variable	.721	.175	.092	4.109	.000

Note: [a] Dependent Variable: Weight of the child in kilograms (1 decimal).

considered are Muslim and Christian, with Hindu as the reference category. So, the regression equation of weight (Y) on age (X) and religion with dummy variables CHRISTIAN (Z_1) and MUSLIM (Z_2) becomes $Y=a+bX+cZ_1+dZ_2$. Now create the two dummy variables and run the regression in SPSS. The output is shown in Table 11.12.

The fitted regression equation is:

$$Y=6.332+0.157 * \text{Age}-0.128 * \text{Christian}+0.721 * \text{Muslim}.$$

We also see from the table that the weight of Christian children is not significantly different from the weight of Hindu children ($t=-0.550$ and Sig.$=0.583>0.05$). But at the same time, the weight of Muslim children is significantly different from Hindu children ($t=4.109$ and Sig.$=0.000<0.05$). Please note that the output allows direct comparison with 'Hindu' (reference category) only but the comparison can be made between any two groups with required arithmetic calculations as follows: At any age X, the estimated weight of a Hindu child is:

$$Y=6.332+0.157 * X-0.128 * 0+0.721 * 0=6.332+0.157 * X$$

At any age X, the estimated weight of a Christian child is:

$$Y=6.332+0.157 * X-0.128 * 1+0.721 * 0=6.332+0.157 * X-0.128$$

At any age X, the estimated weight of a Muslim child is:

$$Y=6.332+0.157 * X-0.128 * 0+0.721 * 1=6.332+0.157 * X+0.721$$

That means a Christian child tends to weigh 0.128 kg less than a Hindu child of the same age, but a Muslim child tends to weigh 0.721 kg more than a Hindu child of the same age. By comparing the two results, we can easily make out that a Muslim child tends to weigh $0.721-(-0.128)=0.849$ kg more than a Christian child of the same age. As we have already seen that the weight of Muslim children is significantly different from that of Hindu children, we may say that the weight of Muslim children is also significantly different from that of Christian children.

Interaction Effect or Confounding Variable

Due to a variety of developmental, environmental and other factors, individuals differ in their behaviour. This means that when we try to see whether variable X_1 causes a difference in variable Y, we should always ask ourselves, 'Is there some other variable X_2 that changes or influences the relationship between X_1 and Y?' Consider the two situations: (a) X_1 and X_2 are related to Y, and the presence of X_2 does not change the extent of relationship between X_1 and Y and also the presence of X_1 does not change the relationship between X_2 and Y, that is, X_1 and X_2 influence Y independent of each other and in this case there is no interaction effect. (b) X_1 and X_2 are related to Y, and when

X_2 is not present the relationship between X_1 and Y is, say, a_1 and when X_2 is present the relationship between X_1 and Y is, say, a_2. If $a_1=a_2$ then we can say that there is no interaction between X_1 and X_2 and if $a_1<a_2$ or $a_1>a_2$ then we say that there is interaction between X_1 and X_2. Further, if $a_2>a_1$ then the interaction of X_1 with X_2 is positive and if $a_2<a_1$ then the interaction is negative.

The positive and negative interaction effects can be explained with two simple examples. Let us assume two salesmen A and B selling the same brand of detergent. For some time, both A and B were visiting households together and they could sell the product for ₹3,000 in a day. Later they divided the area and visited the households individually and as a result their combined sale increased to ₹2,200+₹1,800=₹4,000 in a day. The effect of visiting together contributed the sale less by ₹1,000 in a day and hence the interaction effect (working together) is negative.

In arithmetic terms: Total Sale=Sale by A+Sale by B+Interaction Sale by A&B

In numerical terms, it is: ₹3,000=₹2,200+₹1,800−₹1,000

Now let us consider two labourers C and D. Their job is to transfer bricks from one place to another and they will get ₹20 per 100 bricks. Individually, one could carry 10 bricks at a time, as lifting by oneself more than 10 bricks is difficult. At this rate, worker C could transfer 1,250 bricks and worker D could transfer only 1,000 bricks in a day with a wage of ₹250 and ₹200 respectively (total ₹450). The next day they made an understanding that they will help each other in lifting the bricks to the head or shoulder. As such they could lift and carry 15 bricks at a time and each could transfer 3,000 bricks in a day with a combined wage of ₹600. That is, here the interaction effect (helping each other) is positive.

Total Wage=Wage of A+Wage of B+Interaction Wage of A&B

In numerical terms, it is: ₹600=₹250+₹200+₹150

In general, we say that there is interaction between two independent variables (say, X_1 and X_2) if the effect of one variable (say X_1) on the dependent variable (say Y) depends on the level of the other variable (here X_2). The difference in the effect of X_1 on Y, with and without the presence of X_2 is called the *interaction effect* (of X_2 on the relation between X_1 and Y) and the variable X_2 is called the *interaction or confounding variable*. There can also be interaction effect (of X_1 on the relation between X_2 and Y). But it is not mandatory to have interaction effect on both the ways. However, regression does not make a difference as to whether X_1 interacts with X_2, or X_2 interacts with X_1, or both interact with each other, and it is up to the researcher to make out that, based on theoretical or practical considerations. In regression analysis, we introduce a third variable, say, X_3 based on X_1 and X_2 (as in the examples above, namely, Interaction Sale by A&B and Interaction wage of A&B) to capture interaction effect.

How to Detect If There Is Interaction between Variables?

First and foremost, look at the theoretical relationship between the variables. If there is any reason to believe that the relation between an independent variable and the dependent variable is influenced by another independent variable, an interaction term for the two independent variables is needed. For example, while relating education of woman with children ever born we need an interaction term age, because as age of woman increases the number of children ever born to her also increases and also it is more likely that illiteracy is more among older women than among younger women due to recent improvements in education facilities. If there is no theoretical evidence, one way is to examine the distribution of the dependent variable (or mean) by the two independent variables cross-classified. In SPSS it is equivalent to running Analyse=>Compare

Means=>Means, and taking the dependent variable in the dependent variables list and one independent variable as layer 1 and the other independent variable as layer 2.

Table 11.13 gives the mean weight by age of child and anaemia level. Please note that the age group 0–5 is omitted as Hb level was not measured for them and 'severe' anaemia group is excluded due to a very small number of cases (just 10 cases) in that group. It is seen from the table that the overall the mean weight of children increases from 9.6 kg for the moderately anaemic children to 12.4 kg for the normal children. This implies that the anaemia level of a child is related to the weight. Similarly, the mean weight increases from 7.5 kg for children of the age 6–11 months to 14.5 kg for the children in the age 48–59 months. This implies that the age of the child is related to the weight.

If there is no interaction between anaemic level and age of the child in influencing the weight of children, then, as age increases, the weight of children also increases uniformly in all anaemia groups. But it is not the case. For example, the mean weight of moderately anaemic children in the age group 6–11 months is 7.4 kg and that of normal children is 7.7 kg (the difference is 7.7–7.4=0.3 kg). The corresponding figures for the children in the age group 12–23 months are 9.0 kg and 10.0 kg respectively (the difference is 10.0–9.0=1.0 kg). Further, for the same difference of age, moderately anaemic children have grown by 9.0–7.4=1.6 kg while normal children have grown by 10.0–7.7=2.3 kg. Similar differences can be observed in many other age groups as well, that is, in general, not only normal children have higher weight than anaemic children, but, also, as age increases, their weight also increases faster than that of the anaemic children. Thus, age has an interaction effect on the relationship between anaemic level and weight of children. Though the interaction is not very clear-cut in all the age groups let us assume that there is interaction and see what the regression model reveals.

We have already fitted a regression equation of Weight (Y) on Age (X) with and without curvilinear relationship (X^2). Now we want to add haemoglobin level (Hb) and the equation becomes $Y=a+bX+cX^2+dHb$, where d is the regression coefficient for haemoglobin level (Hb). The regression output is as given in Table 11.14.

It is seen from Table 11.14 that Hb level is significantly related to weight ($t=4.429$ and Sig.=0.000). Please note that the regression coefficient for age of child squared is actually –0.000767 (but shown in the table as .000, corrected to three decimal places). But as per our assumption, the two variables, namely, age and anaemic level, interact with weight, their effects are mixed up. So, our interest would be to find the individual effect of the two variables, here age and Hb level and their joint effects on weight. This can be achieved by adding an interaction term in the equation in addition to the variables age and Hb level. The interaction variable is the product of the two independent variables. In our case, let X be age, H be Hb level and $I=A*H$

Table 11.13   Mean Weight by Age and Anaemic Level of Children

| Age in Months | Anaemia Level | | | | | | | |
| | Moderate | | Mild | | Normal | | Total | |
	Cases	Mean Weight	Cases	Mean Weight	Cases	Mean Weight	Cases	Mean Weight
06–11	27	7.4	13	7.3	26	7.7	68	7.5
12–23	43	9.0	37	9.3	67	10.0	153	9.6
24–35	21	10.6	32	11.0	92	11.6	146	11.3
36–47	14	12.4	25	12.9	96	13.4	135	13.2
48–59	9	12.4	20	13.6	111	14.8	141	14.5
All	114	9.6	127	10.9	392	12.4	643	11.6

Table 11.14 Regression Output[a]: Weight $= a + b$Age $+ c$Age$^2 + d$HbLevel

Model		Unstandardised Coefficients		Standardised Coefficients		
		B	Std. Error	Beta	t	Sig.
1	(Constant)	3.567	.691		5.160	.000
	Age of child in months	.189	.026	.941	7.319	.000
	Age of child in months squared	.000	.000	−.253	−1.978	.048
	Haemoglobin level of child adjusted by altitude (g/dl – 1 decimal)	.260	.059	.124	4.429	.000

Note: [a]Dependent Variable: Weight of child in kilograms (1 decimal).

Table 11.15 Regression Output[a]: Weight $= a + b$Age $+ c$Age$^2 + d$HbLevel $+ e$Age * HbLevel

Model		Unstandardised Coefficients		Standardised Coefficients		
		B	Std. Error	Beta	t	Sig.
1	(Constant)	4.367	1.306		3.342	.001
	Age of child in months	.164	.044	.816	3.770	.000
	Age of child in months squared	.000	.000	−.276	−2.093	.037
	Haemoglobin level of child adjusted by altitude (g/dl - 1 decimal)	.182	.124	.087	1.473	.141
	Age x Hb level (for interaction effect)	.003	.004	.165	.721	.471

Note: [a]Dependent Variable: Weight of child in kilograms (1 decimal).

(the * stands for multiplication) is the interaction variable. Now the regression equation becomes $Y = a + bX + cX^2 + dH + eI$ and the output is shown in Table 11.15.

It is seen from the table that, for the interaction variable I (that is, the term Age * Hb level in the table), the t-value is 0.721 and its significance level is 0.471. It means that the interaction between age and Hb level on the weight of child is not statistically significant and so the interaction term for the two variables may be dropped in the final model.

Interaction Terms for Dummy Variables

Usually the interaction variable for two numerical variables is the product of the two variables. But how to construct interaction terms if one or both the variables are categorical variables. Interaction effect of a dummy variable with another dummy variable or a numerical variable is being done in the same way. The first step is to construct dummy variables for the categorical variables. If one variable is categorical variable and the other is numerical variable, then each of the dummy variables of the categorical variable is multiplied by the numerical variable to form the interaction variables. Here, the interaction variable is not one, but is equal to the number of dummy variables.

For example, we want to establish if any interaction between education and income. Let education be considered in three dummy variables, namely, 'primary education', 'middle/high school education' and 'higher education,' with 'no education/illiterate' as the reference category. In this case the interaction variables are 'income * primary education', 'income * middle/high-school education' and 'income * higher education' (that is, 3 interaction variables). However, it is not necessary to have interaction term for all the dummy variables of the categorical variable, that is, in the above case, if one feels that income interacts with higher education and not with lower education or no education, then we need to have only one interaction term namely 'income * higher education' and the other dummy variables need not have interaction terms. Another example is in finding the effect of educational level of husband and of wife on family income and in that one may be interested in the interaction effect if both are illiterate and not in the other combinations of their educational levels.

If both the variables are categorical variables, then interaction variables can to be constructed for each dummy variable of the first categorical variable with each dummy variable of the second categorical variable. For example if one categorical variable is formed into 3 dummy variables and the other categorical variable is formed into 2 dummy variables then the number of interaction variables is $3*2=6$, and the total number of variables in the regression equation in respect of these two categorical variables is $3+2+6=11$ (the 3 dummy variables of the first categorical variable, the 2 dummy variables of the second categorical variable and the $3*2=6$ interaction variables). However, it is not mandatory to have all possible interaction terms in the equation and some of them may be dropped if they are of less important and their expected interaction effect is negligible.

An alternate way of avoiding interaction terms in case of two categorical variables is to construct dummy variables for each combination of the categories of both the variables. For example, consider religion in 3 categories: Hindu, Muslim and Christian (including others) and order of birth in 4 categories: Ord1, Ord2, Ord3 and Ord4+ and the dummy variables are HinduOrd1, HinduOrd2, ..., MuslimOrd1, MuslimOrd2, ... (in total $3*4=12$ variables). Now keep one group (dummy variable) as the reference category and consider all the remaining 11 dummy variables as independent variables. Here there are no interaction variables as the two categorical variables are now only one categorical variable with 12 categories of mutually exclusive groups. Both the methods yield the same result. However, in the former method we get the interaction effect directly but for obtaining the individual effect we have to add the main effect with the interaction effect. In the latter method, we get the individual effect of each group directly but for obtaining interaction effect we have to do some arithmetic exercise.

MORE ABOUT REGRESSION

Stepwise Regression

Stepwise regression method is sometimes applied when there are a large number of predictor variables and the researcher is unable to decide which of them are important to be in the model. In stepwise regression, the computer is set to consider the variables one by one (one variable or a block of variables at a time), based on certain entry and exit criteria. At the end, only the predictor variables that are more powerful, measured in terms of their significant contribution to the increase in the value of R^2, are retained in the equation.

Stepwise regression has two methods, namely, *forward selection method* and *backward elimination method*. In forward selection method, variables are sequentially added to the model one by one, or group by group. The first variable considered for entry into the equation is the one that has the largest and significant (positive or negative) relationship with the dependent variable. Once the first variable is entered, the next variable to be considered for inclusion is the variable that has the largest partial correlation with the dependent variable. The procedure stops when there are no more variables that meet the entry criterion.

In backward elimination method, first all the variables are entered into the equation and then, sequentially, variables are removed one by one, or group by group. The variable with the smallest partial correlation with the dependent variable is considered first for removal and is removed if it meets the exit criterion. The next variable to be considered for removal is the variable that has the smallest partial correlation with the dependent variable. The procedure stops when there are no more variables in the equation that satisfy the removal criteria.

Please note that the forward selection and backward elimination methods may not yield the same result. This is because, in stepwise regression the relative importance of variables changes step after step whether it is forward selection method or backward elimination method, that is, in stepwise regression, it is the computer that decides the model rather than the user. The user decides the model based on theory whereas the computer decides the model based on significance of the variables irrespective of whether the variables are logically/theoretically related to the dependent variable or not. In this process, one may end up with theoretically important variables remaining out of the model and less important variables remaining in the model. Further, stepwise regression violates the logic of hypothesis testing because at every step the stepwise regression considers a hypothesis of its own and not a model based on theory.

Considering all these issues, it is preferable that model specification be made by the user based on theatrical considerations rather than allowing the computer to decide on the variables based on entry and exit criteria. So, it is preferable to avoid performing stepwise regression as far as possible.

Optimal Number of Independent Variables

Generally the number and the choice of variables are dictated by theory or the nature of investigation on hand. From statistical point of view, there are some considerations. Let n be the number of observations (valid cases for the analysis) and k be the number of independent variables in the model. Please note that each of the dummy and interaction variables is also an independent variable in the model and hence k is the sum of all individual, dummy and interaction variables, and not merely the original numerical and categorical variables. At the lower end, there should be at least one independent variable in the model and so the minimum value for k is 1. The theoretical maximum value for k is $(n-1)$ because there are $(k+1)$ coefficients (the constant a and the k number of b coefficients) and to determine their values we need $(k+1)$ simultaneous equations in the $(k+1)$ coefficients. So the range of k is $0 < k < n$.

If $k = n - 1$ then we can estimate the regression coefficients provided no two observations have equal value for any of the independent variables (the question of multicollinearity), but we cannot estimate standard error because the degrees freedom for the residual term is zero. If k is less than $n - 1$ but very closed to n, then the degrees of freedom for the residual sum of squares $(n - k - 1)$ is very small, resulting in very high standard error of the estimate. So it is desirable that the number of independent variables should be *much less* than the number of observations (sample size) so that estimate of standard error is not severely affected.

Another consideration is the amount of variance explained, measured in terms of adjusted R^2. Adding more and more independent variables generally increases the R^2 (even if it did not increase, it will never decrease). However, the adjusted R^2 may decrease, as it is adjusted for the number of degrees of freedom due to regression (or number of variables in the equation). So, adjusted R^2 does not necessarily increase if more variables are added to the model. All these suggest that *keeping a large number of independent variables* in a regression model is not a good idea unless the nature of investigation warrants it. Keeping irrelevant or less relevant variables will only increase the standard errors, without adding more to the variance explained. Further, a model with many variables is often difficult to interpret and to draw valid conclusions. At the same time, having a very few variables without ensuring a very high R^2 (variance explained) will amount to 'lack of goodness of fit' of the model.

Thus, overall, there is no hard and fast rule for the optimum number of independent variables in the regression equation. But, it should be kept in mind that each dummy variable and interaction term in the model is a variable as far as the regression equation is concerned. Taking together the number of independent variables in the equation should be far less than the number of observations. If two variables are closely related, it is preferable to keep only one of them or they may be combined into a set of mutually exclusive dummy variables to avoid multicollinearity. Further, it is better to avoid (irrelevant or less relevant) variables as per theory and not as per the significant level revealed by the regression output.

A Note of Caution

The above few sections clearly demonstrate that application of multivariate techniques in general, and regression models in particular, involves understanding of a number of assumptions and also verification of the applicability of the models to the particular situation and to the data on hand. Also, the choice of appropriate model and variables is also very important. On the other hand, social scientists often apply any statistical technique to any type of data as they like, just because software packages are readily available. Further, it is not only the application of the statistical technique but also the appropriate interpretation of the output and drawing valid conclusion that are very important. In this direction, this book would be a good reference material for social scientists and students to enhance their knowledge and skill in the application of common statistical techniques. My advice to social scientists and students is not to consider the materials presented in this book as too lengthy or inappropriate, but to understand the various issues involved in the application of the statistical techniques.

AN ILLUSTRATIVE EXAMPLE OF REGRESSION MODEL

A survey was conducted in Goa on a sample of about 3,000 households (NFHS-3). In this survey, first, an enumeration of all members of the selected households was made and then, in respect of all children age below 5 years (<60 months), weight, height and Hb level were obtained. In addition the mothers of these children were asked of their age, educational level, occupation, and so on, and of their children's date of birth, order of birth, and so on. Also some information about their husbands (fathers of children) was also obtained. The data were coded and a file in SPSS format was created. For more details, please refer to the last section of Chapter 2.

Model Building

The objective is to determine the effect of education of mother on the weight of children in Goa using multiple regression analysis.

Generally many (independent) variables influence a (dependent) variable. In our case though, our aim is to assess the effect of education of mother on the weight of children, we should not restrict our analysis to these two variables alone and we need to identify and control for the relevant variables that may have influence on weight of children. We know that as age of a child increases, its weight also increases and so we need to add the variable 'age of child' in the model to control for age. We also know from theory/practice (weight for age growth chart) that the relationship between age and weight is not linear but curvilinear. In order to capture the curvilinear pattern of the relationship between age and weight of child, we propose to add a square term for age to account for the curvilinear pattern of the relation of age with weight of child.

Studies have shown that male and female children have different patterns of weight for age. So, in addition to age, we also consider sex of the child as a basic factor (or intervening variable) of weight of children. In addition, we expect that women of poor families will have more children, and as the order of birth increases, the weight of the child decreases. So we would like to control for the order of birth of the child as well, while seeking the effect of education of mothers on the weight of children. We have not included any interaction term as we do not have sufficient evidence of any of the independent variables having interaction effect with weight. Please note that though our interest is on the relationship between education of mother and weight of child, we have considered a few other variables also in the model as control variables so that we will be able determine the net effect of education of mother on weight of children.

Regarding the effect of education of mother on weight of children, the hypothesis is that the higher the education of a mother, the higher the weight of her children. In other words, the higher the education of mother, the better the child care, including health and nutritional care, and hence the higher the growth of her children. In India and in different states, as illiteracy is common and higher education is rare among women, in this exercise, we have considered education of mother in three categories, namely, 'illiterate' (no education), 'education below secondary level' and 'secondary or higher level education'. Further the three categories are converted into two dummy variables namely 'education below secondary level' and 'secondary or higher level education' with 'no education' (or illiteracy) as the reference category.

The details of the variables and the SPSS output are given below.

Variable	Variable Description
Weight	Weight of child in kg (dependent variable)
Age	Age of child in months (numerical variable)
Age2	Age squared (to capture curvilinear relationship)
SexM	Sex of the child as dummy variable (Male=1 and female=0)
Order	Order of birth (numerical variable)
BelowSec	Secondary education dummy (1–9 standard=1, else=0)
SecEdu	Secondary/higher education (10+ standard=1, else=0)
Illiterate	Reference category (not in the regression equation)

The regression model is:

$$\text{Weight} = b_0 + b_1\text{Age} + b_2\text{Age2} + b_3\text{SexM} + b_4\text{Order} + b_5\text{BelowSec} + b_6\text{SecEdu}$$

Now create appropriate new variables including dummy variables in the data file and run regression for the above model. The R-square table, the ANOVA table and the regression coefficients table are presented in Tables 11.16a to 11.16c. Please note that in the tables with the caption 'Model Summary' and 'ANOVA', the variables list is given at the bottom.

Table 11.16a 'Model Summary' shows that the independent variables namely age of child, age of child squared, sex of child, order of birth and educational of mother (in three groups) combined explained 65.6 percent of the variation in the weight of children. Though the variance explained by the model is large, still a substantial proportion (more than one third) of the variance is unexplained indicates that there are other variables that explain a significant proportion of the variation in the weight of children. Table 11.16b 'ANOVA' indicates that the variables in the regression model (age, sex and order of birth of children and education of mother) are jointly significantly related (below 0.01 level) to weight of children.

It is seen from Table 11.16c 'Regression Coefficients' that the weight of a child in Goa is significantly related to age and sex of the child at 0.001 (or 99.9 percent) level. It is also seen that 'age of child squared' is also significantly related to weight of child confirming that the relationship between age and weight of child is not linear but curvilinear. Further, the negative coefficient of this variable indicates that in the initial ages of the child the increase in weight is faster and as

Table 11.16a   SPSS Regression Output: Model Summary

Model	R	R Square	Adjusted R Square	Std. Error of the Estimate
1	.810[a]	.656	.654	1.9575

Note: [a]Predictors (Constant), Secondary/higher education (10+ standard), Male child (1M, 0F) Age of child squared, Birth order of child, Below secondary education (1–9 standard), Age of child in months.

Table 11.16b   SPSS Regression Output: ANOVA[a]

Model		Sum of Squares	df	Mean Square	F	Sig.
1	Regression	5,866.590	6	977.765	255.160	.000[b]
	Residual	3,073.236	802	3.832		
	Total	8,939.826	808			

Notes: [a]Dependent variable: Weight of the child in kg.
[b]Predictors (Constant), Secondary/higher education (10+ standard), Male child (1M, 0F) Age of child squared, Birth order of child, Below secondary education (1–9 standard), Age of child in months.

Table 11.16c   SPSS Regression Output: Regression Coefficients[a]

Model		Unstandardised Coefficients		Standardised Coefficients	t	Sig.
		B	Std. Error	Beta		
1	(Constant)	4.439	.353		12.591	.000
	Age of child in months	.256	.018	1.276	14.253	.000
	Age of child squared	−.002	.000	−.509	−5.689	.000
	Male child (1M, OF)	.644	.138	.097	4.670	.000
	Birth order of child	−.045	.075	−.013	−.595	.552
	Below secondary education (1–9 standard)	.277	.220	.040	1.260	.208
	Secondary/higher education (10+ standard)	1.251	.220	.188	5.678	.000

Note: [a]Dependent variable: Weight of the child in kg.

age increases further, the increase in weight decreases, which is expected. At the same time, the weight of a child is not related to birth order of the child when other factors are controlled.

Regarding the education of the mother, the weight of children of women with schooling below secondary education is not significantly higher than the weight of children of illiterate mothers as the corresponding regression coefficient 0.277 is not statistically significant (Sig.=0.208, greater than 0.05). However, the weight of children of women who completed secondary education is significantly higher than the weight of children of illiterate mothers. The regression analysis shows that, other things being equal, on average, the weight of children of mothers with education below secondary level is only 277 grams higher than that of children of illiterate mothers, but the weight of children of mothers who completed secondary education is as much as 1,251 grams higher than that of children of illiterate mothers. The difference in the weight of children of mothers who have completed secondary education as against children of mothers who are literate but not completed secondary education was 1,251−277=974 grams. The analysis indicates that for any substantial improvements in the weight and health of new born children, mothers need to have education at least up to secondary level. This implies that education of girls at least up to secondary level is required so that after marriage and child birth, they can take better care of their children.

CHAPTER 12

Logistic Regression Analysis

The regression analysis can handle predictor (independent) variables of any type (nominal, ordinal or interval/scale variables), but the dependent variable should be a numerical variable without extreme skewness (the condition for normal distribution). Furthermore, dummy variables can also be considered as dependent variables, but they should not have the extreme distribution of cases (a very high or very low proportion of cases in one group). Now, the question is: What to do if the dependent variable is a dummy variable with extreme skewness or a very high or very low proportion of cases in one group? The logistic regression is an answer to this question. It is a special case of multiple regression, which can handle non-normal-dependent variables.

The multiple regression fits a straight line that has many limitations as follows:

- The estimated dependent variable can take impossible values. Let us consider the example of regression of weight for age. Although negative age is impossible, still we can get a weight for a negative age in linear regression.
- Violate the linearity assumption. Often the relationship between an independent variable and a dependent variable is not linear, but we impose the assumption that it is linear.
- Homoscedasticity assumption of equal variance at all levels of the independent variable, which is often not true. For example, the standard deviation of the weight of children at age 12 months may not be the same as that at age 60 months.
- Inappropriate hypothesis testing. When the linearity and homoscedasticity assumptions are not appropriate, our usual procedure of hypothesis testing (the assumption of normal distribution) is not valid.
- Low variance explained (R^2). Because of the linearity and homoscedasticity assumptions, often the variance explained in the dependent variable by the independent variables in linear regression may turn out to be very low, though the independent variables are strongly but nonlinearly related to the dependent variable.

The logistic regression overcomes these problems at least partly. In the logistic regression, we fit a curved line of 'S' shape (more specifically elongated or slanted integral ∫ symbol) or 'inverted S' shape and not a straight line. When the dependent variable assumes only two values, yes and no, coded as 1 and 0, respectively, the dependent variable is interpreted as a probability (p) instead of a value (Y). In the linear regression, the regression of an independent variable, say Z, on a dependent variable, say p, is modelled as $p = a + bZ$, whereas in the logistic equation, the model is

$$p = \frac{1}{1 + e^{-Z}},$$

where Z is the predictor (independent) variable and e is the base of the natural logarithm ($e = 2.71828$). When the dependent variable is dichotomous (yes/no type), the logistic regression model has many advantages over the linear regression model. A few properties of the logistic function are explained in the following.

First, let us find the value of p for different values of Z. Table 12.1 gives the values of p for $Z=-\infty$, $Z=0$ and $Z=+\infty$ (the symbol ∞ is to be read as infinity, very large). It is clear from the table that when Z varies from $-\infty$ to $+\infty$ (that is, whatever be the values of Z), the p varies from 0 to 1 only.

The shape of the logistic curve is illustrated in Figures 12.1a and 12.1b. For this, we consider two equations: one with the independent variable Z and the other with the independent variable $-Z$ (i.e., $-Z$ is replaced with $+Z$) as follows:

$$p = \frac{1}{1+e^{-Z}}$$

$$p = \frac{1}{1+e^{+Z}}.$$

Table 12.2 gives the values of p for different values of Z (ranging from -10 to $+10$) and the data are plotted in Figures 12.1a and 12.1b. It is clear from the figures that the logistic curve is of the shape 'S' for the first equation $p=1/[1+\text{Exp}(-Z)]$ and is of the shape 'inverted S' for the second equation $p=1/[(1+\text{Exp}(+Z)]$. Please note that, as in the case of the normal curve, the logistic curve is also symmetric from $Z=0$ (or $p=0.5$). Also, please note that, although the logistic curves look like touching the x-axis at $p=0$ and the top horizontal line at $p=1$ for higher (positive and negative) values of Z, it never touches 0 or 1 but goes on indefinitely (see the values of p in the table).

Now, as in the case of multiple regression, the Z can be thought of as a single variable or as a linear combination of a number of variables, that is, Z can be thought of as a linear combination of a set of k variables:

$$Z \text{ as } a + b_1X_1 + b_2X_2 + b_3X_3 + \cdots + b_kX_k.$$

Table 12.1   The Range of Values of a Logistic Function

Z	e^{-Z}	$p=1/(1+e^{-Z})$
$-\infty$	$e^{-(-\infty)}=e^{\infty}=>\infty$	$1/(1+\infty)=1/\infty=>0$
0	$e^{-0}=1/e^{0}=1/1=1$	$1/(1+1)=1/2=0.5$
$+\infty$	$e^{-\infty}=1/e^{\infty}=1/\infty=>0$	$1/(1+0)=1/1=>1$

Figure 12.1a   The Shape of Logistic Curve of Type 1

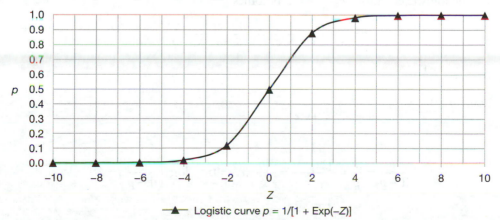

Logistic curve $p = 1/[1 + \text{Exp}(-Z)]$

Table 12.2   Some Sample Values of Logistic Functions

Z	$p = 1/[(1 + Exp(-Z)]$	$p = 1/[(1 + Exp(+Z)]$
-10	0.00005	0.99995
-8	0.00034	0.99966
-6	0.00247	0.99753
-4	0.01799	0.98201
-2	0.11920	0.88080
0	0.50000	0.50000
2	0.88080	0.11920
4	0.98201	0.01799
6	0.99753	0.00247
8	0.99966	0.00034
10	0.99995	0.00005

Figure 12.1b   The Shape of Logistic Curve of Type 2

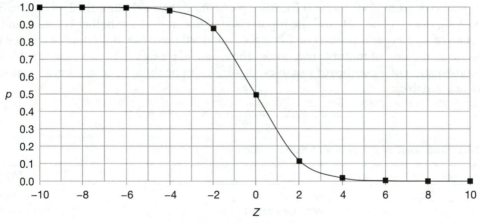

—■— Logistic curve $p = 1/[1 + Exp(+Z)]$

Now, the logistic equation $p = \dfrac{1}{1+e^{-Z}}$ becomes

$$p = \frac{1}{1 + e^{-(a + b_1\,X_1 + b_2\,X_2 + b_3\,X_3 + \cdots + b_k\,X_k)}}.$$

Since $p = \dfrac{1}{1+e^{-Z}}$,

We obtain $q = 1 - p = 1 - \dfrac{1}{1+e^{-Z}} = \dfrac{e^{-Z}}{1+e^{-Z}}$,

where $q = 1 - p$ and

$$\frac{p}{1-p} = \frac{p}{q} = \frac{\dfrac{1}{1+e^{-Z}}}{\dfrac{e^{-Z}}{1+e^{-Z}}} = \frac{1}{e^{-Z}} = e^{Z} \quad \text{or} \quad \log_e\left(\frac{p}{1-p}\right) = Z.$$

The term $\dfrac{p}{1-p}$ or $\dfrac{p}{q}$ is called *odd* and is often denoted by the symbol omega Ω.

The quantity $\log_e\left(\dfrac{p}{1-p}\right)$ is called *log odd* or the *logit of p* (log Ω). This implies that

$$\log\ \Omega = \log_e\left(\frac{p}{1-p}\right) = a + b_1 X_1 + b_2 X_2 + b_3 X_3 + \cdots + b_k X_k.$$

Here, the dependent variable p is a dichotomous variable taking values 0 and 1 and $X_1, X_2, X_3,$ ..., X_k are independent variables of any type, namely nominal, ordinal and/or interval variables. It is the logistic regression model.

Now, the model can be fitted to the observed data using the logistic regression estimation procedure which is slightly different from that of the multiple regression estimation procedure. While the multiple regression model is estimated using the ordinary least-squares (OLS) estimation method, the logistic regression model is estimated using the maximum likelihood (ML) estimation method. The estimation procedures are technical in nature and, hence, not discussed here and also not necessary for us. But what is required to know is that, just like multiple regression, we can estimate the values of a, b_1, b_2 and so on, and fit a logistic regression model as above. As the model is slightly different from multiple regression, the interpretation of the coefficients is also slightly different and discussed in the following.

INTERPRETATION OF COEFFICIENTS

Let us assume that we have only one numerical variable X in the model and the equation becomes $\log\ \Omega = a + bX$ or $\Omega = e^{a+bX}$. Now, for a one unit increase in X (i.e., setting or replacing X by $X+1$), the equation becomes $\Omega^* = e^{a+b(X+1)}$. Taking the ratio of the two equations, we obtain

$$\frac{\Omega^*}{\Omega} = \frac{e^{a+b(X+1)}}{e^{a+bX}} = e^{[a+b(X+1)]-[a-bX]} = e^b.$$

This means that, with other things being equal, a one unit increase in X multiplies the ratio of the odds by the factor e^b. In general, we can say that a one unit increase in an independent variable, say X, multiplies the ratio of the odds by the factor e^b, where b is the logistic regression coefficient of X. The quantity e^b is called the *odds ratio*. Similarly, we can show that the odds ratio of a dummy variable to its reference category is e^b, where b is the logistic regression coefficient of the dummy variable. Please note that, to measure the effect of one unit change in a variable in the linear regression, we take the difference in the values, whereas in the logistic regression, we take the ratio of the values, as it is convenient for interpretation.

An odds ratio of 1 ($e^b = 1$) means that the odds are equal irrespective of whether the independent variable increases or decreases. This means that a change in the independent variable does not make a corresponding change in the dependent variable. An odds ratio greater than 1 implies that an increase in the independent variable (by one unit) increases the odds ratio by the factor (e^b) or the dependent variable (event) is more likely to occur by the factor e^b. In other words, as the value of the independent variable increases, the likelihood of the occurrence of the dependent variable (event occurring) is e^b times, or [100 * e^b – 100] or [100 * (e^b – 1)] percent. On the other hand, an odds ratio lesser than 1 implies that an increase in the independent variable (by one unit) decreases the odds ratio by the factor (e^b), or the dependent variable (event) is less likely to occur by $[100 - 100 * e^b]$ or $[100 * (1-e^b)]$ percent. In general, if $e^b=1$ or close to 1, then we can say that a change in the independent variable does not affect a change in (or does not alter) the dependent variable. If $e^b > 1$, we can say that the independent variable and the dependent variable are positively related. If $e^b < 1$, then the independent variable and the dependent variable are negatively related.

Please note that 'close to 1' is relative to the magnitude of the corresponding variable, say X. If X takes large values, then b tends to be small and e^b tends to be very close to 1, that is, only large differences in the values of X will make substantial differences in e^b from 1, and one unit change may not make much difference in e^b from 1. In such cases, we should evaluate the change in 10 units, 100 units, 1,000 units and see the change in e^b from 1. For example, if X is the family size, then we can evaluate the effect of one unit change in the family size (increase or decrease of one member) on the difference in e^b from 1. But if X is the annual income, then we may have to evaluate the effect of 1,000 units change in the annual income (increase or decrease of ₹1,000) on the difference in e^b from 1. This is because given the same effect of the family size and the annual income on the dependent variable, the value of b will much smaller for the annual income than that for the family size, primarily due to the sheer large numerical value of the annual income (usually a 5–6 digit figure) as compared to the family size (usually, a 1–2 digit figure). However, if we measure the annual income in '1,000' rupees (i.e., if we measure ₹25,000 as 25), then we will get the new b as 1,000 times the old b and the new e^b may make a difference from 1.

With regard to dummy independent variables, let us assume that we are interested in education in three categories namely illiterate (reference category), below secondary education ($X_1=1$ or 0) and secondary or higher education ($X_2=1$ or 0). Please see under regression as to how to create dummy variables. Now, the logistic regression equation is

$$\log \Omega = a + b_1 X_1 + b_2 X_2.$$

For 'illiterate' the equation is $\log \Omega = a$ because $X_1=0$ and $X_2=0$.
For 'below secondary education', $\log \Omega^* = a + b_1$ $X_1=1$ and $X_2=0$.
For 'secondary or higher education', $\log \Omega^{**} = a + b_2$ $X_1=0$ and $X_2=1$.
The odds ratio for 'below secondary education' as against 'illiterate' is

$$\frac{\Omega^*}{\Omega} = \frac{e^{a+b_1}}{e^a} = e^{a+(b_1)-(a)} = e^{b_1}.$$

Similarly, the odds ratio for 'secondary or higher education' as against 'illiterate' is

$$\frac{\Omega^{**}}{\Omega} = \frac{e^{a+b_2}}{e^a} = e^{a+b_2-(a)} = e^{b_2}.$$

And the odds ratio for 'secondary or higher education' as against 'below secondary education' is

$$\frac{\Omega^{**}}{\Omega^*} = \frac{e^{a+b_2}}{e^{a+b_1}} = e^{a+b_2-(a+b_1)} = e^{b_2-b_1}.$$

In the following, we will see as to how to derive e^b coefficients and how to interpret them. Please do not bother if you are not conversant with the mathematical derivations, but only keep in mind the concepts *odds*, *odds ratio* and the e^b coefficients.

AN EXAMPLE USING SPSS

The Data

In a study in Goa with a sample of about 3,000 households, the anthropometric measurements of children aged below 60 months were made to study the extent of under-nutrition among them, that is, all children below age 60 months were weighed, their height measured and their Hb level (for the children of age 6+ months only) obtained. In addition, the mothers of these children were asked about their ages at birth of their children, order of birth, educational level, occupation and so on. The data obtained in the survey were coded and a file in the SPSS format was created. The data were used to determine the effect of the education of mother on underweight among children (measured in terms of weight-for-age Z-score less than –2SD) in Goa using the logistic regression analysis. It is to be noted here that weight-for-age Z-scores are derived by the survey authorities and given in the dataset. What we need to do is to recode the Z-score as 1 (under-weight) if it is less than –2 and 0 (normal) otherwise.

Model Building

We know that as the age of a child increases, his/her weight also increases. Similarly, studies have shown that male and female children have different patterns of weight-for-age index. In addition, we expect that women of poor families will have more children than those of rich families and as such, if the order of birth increases, the weight-for-age Z-score also decreases and, hence, under-weight increases. So we need to control the age, sex and order of birth of the child while seeking the effect of the education of mother on underweight among children. We have not included any interaction terms as we do not have evidence of any of the independent variables having interaction effect with weight. Please note that, although our interest is to investigate only the effect of education on underweight, we have to control the effect of other factors that have a bearing on underweight (dependent variable) and that is why we have included age, sex and order of birth of children into the model or equation.

Regarding the effect of the education of mother on underweight among children, the hypothesis is that, the higher the education of mother, the lower the chances of her children being underweight. It may be that higher education means better child care including health and nutrition care and, hence, the higher growth of children (weight for age). In this exercise, our interest is to see the effect of 'secondary or higher education' as against 'below secondary education' and 'no education' of mothers on underweight among their children. So the education of mother is considered in two dummy variables, namely 'below secondary education' and 'secondary or higher education' with 'no education' (or illiteracy) as the reference category.

The details of the variables are given in Table 12.3.

The logistic regression model is

$$\log_e\left(\frac{p}{1-p}\right) = b_0 + b_1 \text{ Age} + b_2 \text{ SexM} + b_3 \text{ Order} + b_4 \text{ Below Sec Edu}$$

$$+ b_5 \text{ Above Sec Edu.}$$

Now, load SPSS, open the data file, create appropriate new variables including dummy variables in the data file and run the logistic regression for the above model. To run the logistic regression in SPSS, from the main menu, choose 'Analyze => Regression => Binary Logistic' and click.

Table 12.3 Description of the Variables in the Logistic Regression Model

Variable	Variable Description
WtAgeBM2 (say p)	A child with weight-for-age Z-score less than −2 (underweight) is coded as 1, else 0 (dependent variable)
Age	Age of the child in months (numerical variable)
SexM	Sex of the child as a dummy variable (male=1 and female=0)
Order	Order of birth (numerical variable)
BelowSec	Below secondary education dummy (1–9 standard=1, else=0)
SecEdu	Secondary/higher education (10+ standard=1, else=0)
Illiterate	Reference category (not in the regression equation)

Figure 12.2 SPSS Window for Logistic Regression

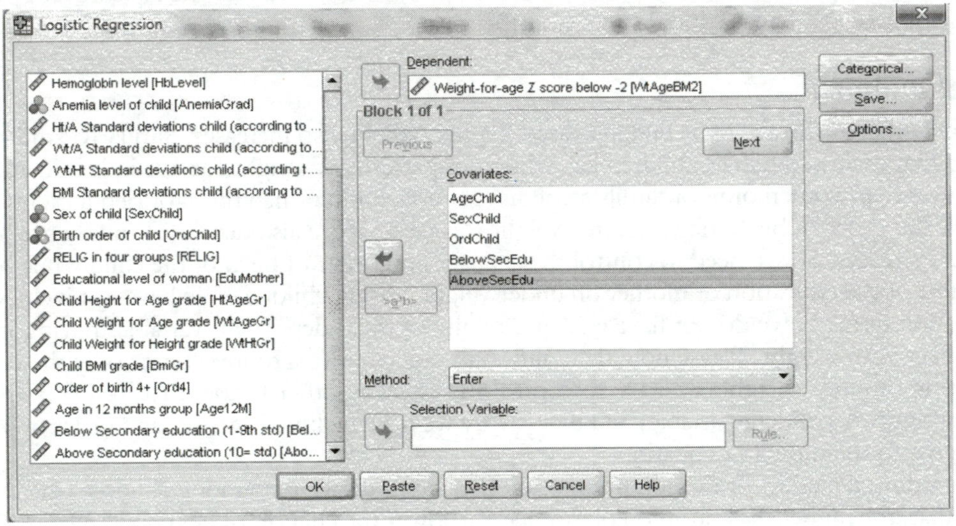

Soon the logistic regression window opens with the variables in the data file listed on the left of the window as shown in Figure 12.2.

Now, click the dependent variable (WtAgeBM2: weight-for-age Z-score below −2) and move it into the dependent variable box and transfer the independent variables, namely AgeChild, SexM, BelowSecEdu and SecEduEdu into the 'Covariates' box. Keeping all options at their default levels (as shown in the figure), click 'OK' to process the data. Soon the outputs are produced in a series of tables and are given in Tables 12.4–12.7, and discussed one by one.

The binary logistic regression output in SPSS will consist of 'Case Processing Summary' table (not presented here) that will give details of valid cases for the analysis. It is to be noted that in SPSS, for the linear regression, categorical variables are to be converted into dummy variables by the user, whereas for the logistic regression, it is done by SPSS and the user only needs to declare it as a categorical variable (why this facility is not available for the linear regression is not known). The table 'Dependent Variable Encoding' (not presented here) gives the internal coding structure of the categorical variables.

Table 12.4 is the 'Omnibus Test of Model Coefficients'. After running the model, first we need to determine whether the model reasonably describes the data. For this purpose, the binary logistic

Table 12.4   SPSS Logistic Regression Output of Omnibus Tests of Model Coefficients

		Chi-square	df	Sig.
Step 1	Step	66.687	5	0.000
	Block	66.687	5	0.000
	Model	66.687	5	0.000

Table 12.5   SPSS Logistic Regression Output of Model Summary

	–2 Log Likelihood	Cox and Snell's R^2	Nagelkerke's R^2
Step 1	812.372[a]	0.083	0.122

Note: [a] Estimation terminated at iteration number 4 because parameter estimates changed by less than 0.001.

Table 12.6   SPSS Logistic Regression Output[a] of the Classification Table

			Predicted		
			Underweight of Child		
	Observed		Not Underweight	Underweight	Percentage Correct
Step 1	Underweight of child	Not underweight	564	10	98.3
		Underweight	182	16	8.1
		Overall percentage			75.1

Note: [a] The cut value is 0.500.

Table 12.7   SPSS Logistic Regression Output of 'Variables in the Equation'

		B	SE	Wald	df	Sig.	Exp(B)
Step 1	Age	0.018	0.005	12.112	1	0.001	1.019
	BirOrd	0.106	0.087	1.476	1	0.224	1.112
	Female	0.190	0.173	1.214	1	0.270	1.209
	BelowSecEdu	−0.451	0.240	3.527	1	0.060	0.637
	SecEdu	−1.488	0.262	32.247	1	0.000	0.226
	Constant	−1.145	0.343	11.173	1	0.001	0.318

regression procedure in SPSS by default applies the Hosmer–Lemeshow goodness of fit. The Hosmer–Lemeshow statistic will be an indicator of a good fit of the model if the corresponding significance value is less than 0.05. In our exercise, the Sig. value for the 'Model' is 0.000 which is not only less than 0.05 but also less than 0.01. So we can say that the model adequately fits the data.

In the linear regression model, the coefficient of determination, R^2, summarises the proportion of variance in the dependent variable that is explained by the predictor (independent) variables. In the logistic regression model, it is not possible to compute a single R^2 statistic that has all of the characteristics of R^2. However, in SPSS, the following methods are used to estimate the coefficient of determination. The Cox and Snell's R^2 is based on the log likelihood for the model compared to the log likelihood for a baseline model. However, with categorical outcomes, even for a 'perfect' model, the theoretical maximum value will be less than 1. Nagelkerke's R^2 is an adjusted version of the Cox and Snell R^2 that adjusts the scale of the statistic to cover the full range from 0 to 1. Table 12.5 gives the results.

Unlike the linear regression, in the logistic regression, we cannot expect a very high value for R^2 and what constitutes a 'good' R^2 value varies between different areas of application. While these statistics can be suggestive of their own, they are useful for comparing competing models for the same data. The model with the largest R^2 statistic is 'best' according to this measure. In our exercise, the Cox and Snell's R^2 is 0.083 or 8.3 percent and Nagelkerke's R^2 is 0.122 or 12.2 percent. Both the statistics suggest that the variance explained in the dependent variable by the independent variables is very less, or not substantial. The –2 Log likelihood value of 812.372, as it is, is not much informative.

Table 12.6 gives the cross-classification of the dependent variable according to the 'observed' status by the 'predicted' status. It is to be noted that the observed values of p are 0 and 1 (in our example normal=0 and underweight=1, two values only), whereas the predicted values are obtained for each observation by substituting the values of the independent variables into the fitted equation. As such the predicted values are probabilities (decimal values) in the range from 0 to 1 and for classification purposes a value less than 0.5 is taken as 0 (normal) and a value 0.5 or above is taken as 1 (underweight). In our model, as per the survey data, the total number of cases is $564+182+10+16=772$, and, of them, $182+16=192$ cases are underweight and $564+10=574$ cases are normal, and the proportion underweight is 24.87 percent. Based on the logistic regression model, $10+16=26$ cases are underweight and $564+182=746$ cases are normal (the proportion underweight is 3.37 percent).

At the same time, the table shows that 564 cases are correctly classified as normal (not underweight) and 16 cases are correctly classified as underweight by both the methods (observed and predicted), and the total number of cases correctly classified is $564+16=580$ or $580/772=75.13$ percent of total cases (as shown in the table), that is, the model has correctly predicted 75 percent of the cases which is reasonably high.

Table 12.7 may repeat many times and we have to consider the last/final one (presented here) as the earlier ones are those obtained in the initial or intermediate steps. This is because the logistic regression model is estimated using the ML method that involves an iterative process. The interpretation of Table 12.7 is very similar to that of the corresponding table in multiple regression with two exceptions, namely Columns 6 (Wald) and 8 (Exp(B)). The Wald statistic is an alternative to the t-statistic and the Exp(B) is nothing but the (e^b), the exponent of the logistic regression coefficient, that is, the odds-ratios. In our exercise, the variables sex and order of child are not statistically significant (Sig. values are 0.270 and 0.224, respectively), whereas age is significantly related to underweight (Sig. value is 0.001). Correspondingly, the Exp(B) value of 1.019 for the age indicates that, other things being equal, as age increases by 1 month, the likelihood of a child becoming underweight increases by $100 * (1.019-1.000)=1.9$ percent, or nearly 2 percent. Please note that the increase in likelihood is in the 'underweight' of the child as we have coded 1 for underweight (0 for normal) for a dependent variable 'WtAgeBM2'. In general, the increase or decrease in likelihood is with reference to the category that is coded as 1 (here underweight).

Similarly, we can see from the table that as compared to the children of illiterate mothers, the children of mothers with education 'below secondary education' are better nourished because the likelihood of the children underweight is about $(100-100 * 0.637)=36.3$ or 36 percent less, that is, the children of mothers with 'below secondary education' are 35 percent less likely to be underweight as those of the children of 'illiterate' mothers, but the difference is not statistically significant. However, the significance level (Sig.=0.060) is very close to the verse of significance at the 5 percent level. It is to be noted that, although the likelihood is 35 percent less, the relationship is not statistically significant and it is because of the relatively high standard error (SE) of this variable (0.24) as compared to the coefficient (B) value –0.451. At the same time, the value of Exp(B)=0.226 indicates that children of mothers with education 'secondary or higher' levels are [100 * (1.0 – 0.226)] = 77.4 percent less likely to be underweight as that of children of illiterate mothers. However, if our interest is the odds ratio for children of mothers with secondary or higher education as against children of mothers with below secondary education, we need to do a small manual calculation. The odds ratio, as seen earlier, is $e^{b_2 - b_1} = e^{-1.335 - (-0.451)} = e^{-0.884} = 0.4131$ or 41 percent, that is, children of mothers with secondary or higher education are 41 percent less likely to be underweight as that of children of mothers with below secondary education.

Important Note: It is to be noted that even if the e^b value is substantially higher or lower from 1, we should not attach much importance to it if the corresponding variable is not statistically significant. A logistic regression coefficient (b) that is much different from 0 (zero) or $e^b <> 1$ and the coefficient not significant implies that the difference is not stable or confidence level very low due to high SE. So we are not confident that the difference is real and the same difference will be maintained if different samples are drawn. So, it is not meaningful to discuss the odds ratios (e^b) of variables that are not statistically significant, even if the values are substantially different from 1, and it is because of statistical instability as inferred from their high SE.

MULTINOMIAL LOGISTIC REGRESSION

Binary logistic regression deals with the analysis of binary (two categories) variables as dependent variable and multinomial logistic regression is an extension of binary logistic regression in which the dependent variable can have more than two categories. For example, given a variety of (often a few but more than 2) brands of a consumer product, which brand is preferred more often by which category of people is analysed using the multinomial logistic regression method. Based on the background characteristics of the people (such as urban/rural residence, age, education, occupation and monthly income), who buys which brand, the preferred brand can be determined using the multinomial logistic regression method. Another example may be choosing a family-planning method by couples. There are family-planning methods like female sterilisation, male sterilisation, intrauterine device (Copper T), condom and oral pills, and each method has its own advantages and disadvantages. Furthermore, people may be aware of some methods better than the other; in some places, some methods are available more than other methods, government supplies some methods and with less or no cost, some methods have more side effects than other and so on. Couples have to decide which method to adopt or remain without adopting any method. So, what factors that determine the choice of a family-planning method can be analysed using the multinomial logistic regression method.

As making a choice is a complex phenomenon, the multinomial logistic regression analysis is also relatively more complex and so it is not discussed in this book, but this method is available in SPSS under the menu 'Analyze => Regression => Multinomial Logistic'.

Interested readers may refer to my article in which binary logistic regression was applied (Rajaretnam and Hallad 2000). Similarly, one may refer to my article in which multinomial logistic regression was used (Rajaretnam 2000).

Multiple Classification Analysis

Multiple classification analysis (MCA) is a method used primarily to estimate the levels of the dependent variable for different levels of an independent variable, while controlling the effect of other independent variables (in the equation). For example, we can estimate the level (or extent) of under-nutrition (underweight) among the children of mothers who have completed secondary education after controlling the effect of the sex of child, order of birth and religion of the household. The estimated levels for two or more groups are then compared to obtain what is called the *adjusted* or *net* effect of the change in the independent variable on the dependent variable. The estimation of the net effect is important because the difference we get directly through cross-tabulation (called *unadjusted* or *gross* effect) is often misleading due to the fact that it is mixed up with the effect of other independent and confounding factors.

MCA is primarily an additive model and is an extension of the multiple regression and ANOVA. In ANOVA, the response variable is quantitative (numerical variable) and the predictor variables are all categorical variables. As such, an MCA with one categorical variable is equivalent to one-way ANOVA, and an MCA with two categorical predictor variables is equivalent to two-way ANOVA. In addition to categorical variables, numerical variables (without categories) can also be included as control variables (called covariates) in the list of predictor variables of the MCA model. Although primarily MCA is applied to multiple regression, it can also be applied to many other multivariate techniques, such as logistic regression, multinomial logistic regression and survival/hazards models. Here, MCA is applied to multiple regression with an SPSS example.

RUNNING MCA IN SPSS: AN EXAMPLE

The latest versions of SPSS do not have a menu for running MCA, but it can be obtained through the ANOVA command via the syntax editor. Let us consider an example of running ANOVA using the NFHS-3 survey data for Goa. In the survey, children below age 5 (<60 months) were weighed, their height was measured and Hb levels were obtained. In addition, the mothers of these children were asked for their age at the birth of their children, order of birth, educational levels, occupation, religions and so on. The data obtained in the survey were coded and a file in the SPSS format was created for selected variables.

A model relating the weight of children to education and the religion of mothers and sex of the children, controlling the ages of the children and age-squared, is considered. The model-building procedure is the same as that for multiple regression.

Let age (AGE) and age-squared (AGE^2) be the control variables (numerical variables). Let MEDU4 be the education of mother considered in four categories as 0=illiterate, 1=1–7 std, 2=8–12 std and 3=12+ std, RELIG3 be the religion considered in three categories as 1=Hindu, 2=Muslim and 3=Christian (a few cases of other religions are included under Christians), and SEX be the sex of child in two categories as 1=Male and 2=Female. Please note that for running

ANOVA with SPSS, there is no need to create dummy variables for the predictor/categorical variables, but the codes for different categories should be contiguous integers without a gap, and it may start at 0 or 1 or any other number. For example 1 = Hindu, 2 = Muslim and 3 = Christian are permitted because Codes 1–3 are contiguous integers, but 1 = Hindu, 2 = Muslim and 4 = Christian are not permitted because Code 3 is undefined (not allocated to any category).

Now, load the data file in SPSS and then choose the menu 'File => New => Syntax'. Soon a window named 'SPSS Syntax Editor' will open. In the syntax editor, place the command **ANOVA** followed by two subcommands **METHOD** and **STATISTICS** in the following format:

ANOVA VARIABLES = <DepVar> **BY** <CatVar1 (LoCode, HiCode)>
<CatVar2 (LoCode, HiCode)> etc. **WITH** <Covariate1> <Covariate2>, etc./
METHOD = EXPERIMENTAL/**STATISTICS** = MCA.

Please note that the part <DepVar> needs to be replaced with the name of the dependent variable of interest. In the <CatVar1 (LoCode, HiCode)>, 'CatVar1' is the name of the first categorical variable, 'LoCode' is the code for the first category and 'Hicode' is the code for the last category of the first categorical variable. The part <CatVar2 (LoCode, HiCode)> etc. is optional (need to be present if more than one categorical variable is considered). If there are any numerical (discrete/continuous) variables (called covariates), enter them as <Covariate1>, <Covariate2>, etc. The 'WITH <Covariate1> <Covariate2>, etc.' part is not required if no covariates are considered in the model. The **METHOD** and **STATISTICS** subcommands are to be placed in the model exactly in the same way. The method subcommand /**METHOD** = HIERARCHICAL instead of /**METHOD** = EXPERIMENTAL can also be used. For our model, the **ANOVA** command is as follows:

ANOVA VARIABLES = WEIGHT **BY** RELIG3(1,3) SEX(1,2) MEDU4(0,3)
WITH AGE AGE^2/**METHOD** = **EXPERIMENTAL**/**STATISTICS = MCA.**

The SPSS output obtained for the above ANOVA command is presented in Tables 13.1–13.5.

Table 13.1 gives the statistics of the total number of cases in the SPSS file, the number of valid cases 'included' in the analysis and the number of cases 'excluded' from the analysis due to missing or not applicable information.

Table 13.2 provides the results of ANOVA. The table has five blocks of information, namely covariates, main effects, two-way interactions, three-way interactions and model summary. A covariate is a numerical variable without grouping (categories). In this exercise, 'age of child in months' and 'square of age of child in months' are covariates and both the variables are individually and together significant at the 1 percent level of significance. The next block is 'main effects' of the categorical variables in the model namely 'sex of child', 'religion' and 'education of mother', and all the variables are individually and together significant at the 1 percent level of significance except religion that is significant at the 5 percent level of significance. The next two blocks 'two-way interactions' and 'three-way interactions' are, as defined under regression analysis, a multiplicative

Table 13.1   ANOVA Procedure: Case Processing Summary[a]

			Cases				
Included			*Excluded*			*Total*	
N	*%*		*N*	*%*		*N*	*%*
807	83.9		155	16.1		962	100.0

Note: [a] Weight of the child in kg by religion in three groups, sex of child, education of women in four groups with the age of child in months, age of child in months squared.

Table 13.2   ANOVA Procedure: ANOVA Output[a,b]

			Experimental Method				
			Sum of Squares	df	Mean Square	F	Sig.
Weight of the child in kilograms	Covariates	(Combined)	5,530.440	2	2,765.220	732.034	.000
		Age of child in months	759.122	1	759.122	200.962	.000
		Age of child in months squared	117.034	1	117.034	30.982	.000
	Main effects	(Combined)	392.485	6	65.414	17.317	.000
		RELIG in three groups	42.625	2	21.312	5.642	.004
		Sex of child	84.283	1	84.283	22.312	.000
		Education of woman in four groups	211.713	3	70.571	18.682	.000
	Two-way interactions	(Combined)	39.856	11	3.623	0.959	.483
		RELIG in three groups * Sex of child	11.931	2	5.965	1.579	.207
		RELIG in three groups * Education of woman in four groups	28.112	6	4.685	1.240	.283
		Sex of child * Educational of woman in four groups	0.739	3	0.246	0.065	.978
	Three-way interactions	RELIG in three groups * Sex of child * Educational of woman in four groups	18.053	6	3.009	0.797	.573
	Model		5,980.833	25	239.233	63.332	.000
	Residual		2,950.186	781	3.777		
	Total		8,931.019	806	11.081		

Notes: [a]Weight of the child in kg by RELIG in three groups, sex of child, education of woman in four groups with age of child in months, age of child in months squared.
[b]Covariates entered first.

Table 13.3   ANOVA Procedure: MCA Output[a]

				Predicted Mean		Deviation	
			N	Unadjusted	Adjusted for Factors and Covariates	Unadjusted	Adjusted for Factors and Covariates
Weight of the child in kilograms	Religion in three groups	Hindu/Other	522	11.203	11.099	−.0388	−.1425
		Muslim	94	10.551	11.186	−.6904	−.0551
		Christian	191	11.687	11.658	.4459	.4166
	Sex of child	Male	415	11.602	11.557	.3604	.3156
		Female	392	10.860	10.907	−.3816	−.3341
	Education of woman in four groups	Illiterate	110	10.408	10.559	−.8333	−.6824
		1–7 std	173	10.881	10.648	−.3606	−.5940
		8–11 std	321	11.430	11.330	.1884	.0888
		12+ std	203	11.702	11.977	.4610	.7356
	Total	**NA**	**807**	**11.241**	**11.241**	**NA**	**NA**

Note: [a]Weight of the child in kilograms by religion in three groups, sex of child, educational of woman in four groups with the age of child in months, and age of child in months squared.

Table 13.4   ANOVA Procedure: Factor Summary[a]

		η	Beta Adjusted for Factors and Covariates
Weight of the child in kilograms	RELIG in three groups	0.097	0.070
	Sex of child	0.111	0.098
	Education of women in four groups	0.131	0.159

Note: [a]Weight of the child in kg by religion in three groups, sex of child, education of women in four groups with the age of child in months, and the age of child in months squared.

Table 13.5   ANOVA Procedure: Model Goodness of Fit

	Factors and Covariates	
	R	R-squared
Weight of the child in kilograms by RELIG in three groups, sex of child, education of women in four groups with age of child in months, age of child in months squared	0.814362169	0.663185742

combination of the dummy variables taken two and three at a time, respectively. The SPSS output shows that both the interaction effects are not statistically significant. The 'model' block shows that the model as a whole is statistically significant at the 1 percent level of significance.

Now let us come to the 'MCA', that is, Table 13.3. The table gives, for all categories of the categorical variables, the unadjusted and adjusted mean weight and also their deviation from the overall mean value. The overall mean, presented in row 'Total' and is not part of the SPSS output, can be obtained from any category using the identity: Overall mean=Category mean−Deviation. Accordingly, the overall mean is the mean value for the Muslim category (10.551) minus the corresponding deviation value (−0.6904), that is, $10.551 - (-0.6904) = 11.2414$. Please note that in linear regression, the overall unadjusted mean is the same as the overall adjusted mean. For the purpose of analysis, we may consider either the adjusted mean or the adjusted deviation from the mean. For example, the adjusted deviation figures indicate that, with respect to religion, the mean weight of Christian children is the highest with 416.6 g higher than the overall mean, whereas the mean weight of Muslim children is 55 g lesser than the overall mean. Furthermore, the mean weight of Muslim children is $417+55=472$ g lesser than those of Christian children and $143 - 55 = 87$ g higher than those of Hindu children. The description of the effect of the other categorical variables is very similar and not repeated here.

It is important to note that the unadjusted values are the same values we get from the usual crosstab or mean analysis, and the adjusted values are the values we obtain from the fitted regression equation by substituting the mean values of all variables except for the category for which we seek the adjusted mean value. For an example, please see section 'Multiple Linear Regression: An Exercise' and sub-section 'Categorical Variables or Dummy Variables' in Chapter 11.

Table 13.4 presents the unadjusted correlation ratio *eta* (η) and the adjusted correlation coefficient *beta* (β) coefficients. The η coefficient is equivalent to the multiple correlation coefficient with a single predictor variable and so it may also be mentioned as R. The β coefficient is otherwise the partial correlation coefficient. It can be seen from the table that the correlation ratio between the independent categorical variables and the weight of child is only moderate, or below moderate, as the η values are all below 0.2. Furthermore, after controlling for other factors and covariates, the correlation ratio between the religion and weight of child reduced from 0.097 to 0.07 and between the sex and weight of child from 0.111 to 0.098, whereas the correlation ratio between the education of mother and weight of child increased from 0.131 to 0.159. It is to be noted that in this model the 'covariates' are the age of child and age-squared, and the 'factors' are religion, sex of child and education of woman.

Table 13.5 shows that the variables in the model together explain 66 percent of the variation in the weight of children and it is the same as that obtained in the regression analysis.

MCA FOR LOGISTIC REGRESSION

The MCA table for linear regression is direct and straightforward, and it is directly obtained through ANOVA of the SPSS procedure with a request for MCA statistics. But for logistic regression, there is no provision in SPSS (probably in most other statistical software programs) for direct MCA table but one can easily construct one. In this section, we explain how to construct MCA for logistic regression, and the same procedure can be applied to other models as well including the linear regression.

Let us consider the logistic regression model: underweight as a function of age, age-squared, sex of child, order of birth, education of mother and religion of head of household, for the NFHS-3 Goa data. In this model, age and age-squared are considered as numerical variables and the other variables as categorical variables. The coding categories and their mean values (mean and proportions as applicable) are given in Table 13.6. The means and proportions are obtained as usual using the frequencies and means procedures in SPSS. Please note that, by default, SPSS rejects all cases with missing (system missing or user missing) codes in any of the variables, from the logistic regression model. So, the unadjusted means and proportions should be obtained only for the valid cases included in the logistic regression.

With these variables, let us run binary logistic regression. The SPSS output is not shown, but part of it (specifically the regression coefficients) is shown in Table 13.7. For the MCA table, the logistic regression coefficients and the corresponding mean values are sufficient as input and the rest are only calculations. For this, from the SPSS output, first copy the logistic regression variables and categories along with their B coefficients in a new worksheet in Excel and then copy and paste the corresponding mean and proportion values (except for the reference categories, which are anyway not listed) in the next column as shown in Columns 1–3 corresponding to the rows 'Age' to 'Constant' in the table. In Column 4, the product of 'B coefficient' and 'Mean' is obtained so that we can get the overall adjusted level of the dependent variable. Next, Columns 5–19 are the list of the categories (including reference categories) of the independent variables for which adjusted values are desired.

For numerical variables, 'Categories' do not apply but we can get the adjusted values for different levels of the numerical variables (in this example, we obtain the adjusted underweight for the children of age 12 months and 24 months). Now, copy the mean values in Column 3 to all Columns 5–19; it means that we are setting the level of the independent variables (categories) at their respective mean values.

Now, for each numerical and categorical variable in Column 1, replace the mean values of the corresponding categories in Rows 5–19 with their respective values (numerical values for numerical variables, 1's and 0's for categorical variables as per the coding procedure adopted for that variable), while retaining the mean values for the rest of the categories. For example, the variable 'AGE' takes the value 12 corresponding to the category 'Age of child 12 months' and the value 24 corresponding to the category 'Age of child 24 months'. Also, the variable 'AGE^2' (age-squared)

Table 13.6   Description of Variables for Logistic Regression-based MCA Table

Variable Description	SPSS Name	Type	Categories	SPSS Category	Mean/ Proportion (%)
Underweight	Underweight	Dependent	NA	NA	25.58
Age of child	Age	Numerical	NA	NA	30.87
Age-squared	Age²	Numerical	NA	NA	1,224.43
Sex of child	Female	Categorical	Female	Female	27.49
			Male	RefCat	23.81
Order of birth	Ord4	Categorical	One	RefCat	21.32
			Two	Ord4(1)	27.45
			Three	Ord4(2)	30.59
			Four+	Ord4(3)	40.00
Mother's education	MEDU4	Categorical	Illiterate	RefCat	44.12
			Std 1–7	MEDU4(1)	38.69
			Std 8–11	MEDU4(2)	21.36
			Std 12+	MEDU4(3)	10.99
Religion	RELIG3	Categorical	Hindu	RefCat	28.51
			Muslim	RELIG3(1)	29.41
			Christian	RELIG3(2)	15.56

Note: RefCat: reference category; mean applies to age and age-squared only.

takes the value $12 * 12 = 144$ corresponding to the category 'Age of child 12 months' and the value $24 * 24 = 576$ corresponding to the category 'Age of child 24 months'. Similarly, the categorical variable 'RELIG(1)' (Muslim) takes the value 0 for the category 'Hindu', 1 for the category 'Muslim' and 0 for the category 'Christian'. The procedure is similar for all the variables in the equation. At the same time, the value of the 'Constant' is 1 for all categories, that is, for all Columns 5–19. The values that changed are shaded in the table.

With p representing underweight, the logistic regression equation becomes

$$\log_e\left(\frac{p}{1-p}\right) = b_0 + b_1 \text{AGE} + b_2 \text{AGE}^2 + b_3 \text{RELIG}(1) + b_4 \text{RELIG}(2) + b_5 \text{FEMALE}$$
$$+ b_6 \text{ORD}(1) + b_7 \text{ORD}(2) + b_8 \text{ORD}(3) + b_9 \text{MEDU}(1) + b_{10} \text{MEDU}(2)$$
$$+ b_{11} \text{MEDU}(3).$$

It is clear that Column 4, that is, multiplying the B coefficients (Column 2) by the corresponding mean values (Column 3) and then summing the products (row Sum-Product), give the RHS value of the above equation. This can be easily obtained by using the Excel function SUMPRODUCT. For example, let the B coefficients be in the Column range B6–B17 and the mean values be in the Column range C6–C17; then, '=SUMPRODUCT(B6:B17,C6:C17)' will yield the value -1.210 shown in Column 4 corresponding to the row item 'Sum-Product'.

Now, anchor B6–B17 (B$6:B$17) (the $ sign keeps the B column unchanged while copying the cell to other cells in the worksheet) and copy the formula '=SUMPRODUCT(B$6:B$17,C6:C17)' through Columns 5–19 (the same row) and we have obtained the RHS values for

Table 13.7 Multiple Classification Analysis (MCA) for Logistic Regression

Factors	Overall			Age of Child		Religion			Sex of Child		Order of Birth				Education of Mother			
Categories: Original →	NA		B*	12m	24m	Hindu	Muslim	Christian	Male	Female	One	Two	Three	Four+	Illiterate	Std 1-7	Std 8-11	Std 12+
Categories: Equation →	B Coef	Means	Means	NA	NA	RefCat	RELIG(1)	RELIG(2)	RefCat	Female	RefCat	ORD(1)	ORD(2)	ORD(3)	RefCat	MEDU(1)	MEDU(2)	MEDU(3)
(1)	(2)	(3)	(4)	(5)	(6)	(7)	(8)	(9)	(10)	(11)	(12)	(13)	(14)	(15)	(16)	(17)	(18)	(19)
AGE	.0050	30.87	.154	12.0	24.0	30.9	30.9	30.9	30.9	30.9	30.9	30.9	30.9	30.9	30.9	30.9	30.9	30.9
AGE²	.0002	1224.4	.221	144.0	576.0	1224.4	1224.4	1224.4	1224.4	1224.4	1224.4	1224.4	1224.4	1224.4	1224.4	1224.4	1224.4	1224.4
RELIG(1)	−.0945	.110	−.010	.110	.110	0	1	0	.110	.110	.110	.110	.110	.110	.110	.110	.110	.110
RELIG(2)	−.5498	.234	−.129	.234	.234	0	0	1	.234	.234	.234	.234	.234	.234	.234	.234	.234	.234
FEMALE	.1734	.482	.084	.482	.482	.482	.482	.482	0	1	.482	.482	.482	.482	.482	.482	.482	.482
ORD(1)	.2365	.331	.078	.331	.331	.331	.331	.331	.331	.331	0	1	0	0	.331	.331	.331	.331
ORD(2)	.1247	.110	.014	.110	.110	.110	.110	.110	.110	.110	0	0	1	0	.110	.110	.110	.110
ORD(3)	.2680	.065	.017	.065	.065	.065	.065	.065	.065	.065	0	0	0	1	.065	.065	.065	.065
MEDU(1)	−.2627	.218	−.057	.218	.218	.218	.218	.218	.218	.218	.218	.218	.218	.218	0	1	0	0
MEDU(2)	−1.0273	.401	−.412	.401	.401	.401	.401	.401	.401	.401	.401	.401	.401	.401	0	0	1	0
MEDU(3)	−1.7355	.248	−.430	.248	.248	.248	.248	.248	.248	.248	.248	.248	.248	.248	0	0	0	1
Constant	−.7385	1	−.739	1.000	1.000	1.000	1.000	1.000	1.000	1.000	1.000	1.000	1.000	1.000	1.000	1.000	1.000	1.000
Sum-product $Z=\text{Log}(p/(1-p))$	−1.210		−1.210	−1.499	−1.361	−1.071	−1.165	−1.620	−1.293	−1.120	−1.319	−1.082	−1.194	−1.051	−.309	−.572	−1.337	−2.045
Exponent $p/(1-p)=\text{EXP}(Z)=y$	0.298		0.298	0.223	0.256	0.343	0.312	0.198	0.274	0.326	0.267	0.339	0.303	0.350	0.734	0.564	0.263	0.129
Adjusted underweight $p=y/(1+y)$	0.230		0.230	0.183	0.204	0.255	0.238	0.165	0.215	0.246	0.211	0.253	0.232	0.259	0.423	0.361	0.208	0.115
% Adjusted underweight $100*p$	23.0		23.0	18.3	20.4	25.5	23.8	16.5	21.5	24.6	21.1	25.3	23.2	25.9	42.3	36.1	20.8	11.5
% Unadjusted underweight From means procedure	25.6		25.6	NA	NA	28.5	29.4	15.6	23.8	27.5	21.3	27.5	30.6	40.0	44.1	38.7	21.4	11.0

Note: Calculations are made in Excel and are based on values with many decimal places but only a few decimal places are presented here. Required explanation on the method of construction of the table is given in the text.

Table 13.8   MCA for Binary Logistic Regression on Percent of Children (0–59 Months) Underweight by Factors in the Model

Factors and Categories	Unadjusted Underweight		Adjusted Underweight	
	%	Deviation[@]	%	Deviation[@]
Overall	25.58	NA	22.98	NA
Age of child				
12 months	NA	NA	18.26	4.71
24 months	NA	NA	20.41	2.57
Sex of child				
Male[$]	23.81	1.77	21.53	1.45
Female	27.49	−1.91	24.61	−1.63
Order of birth				
One[$]	21.32	4.27	21.10	1.88
Two	27.45	−1.87	25.30	−2.32
Three	30.59	−5.00	23.25	−0.27
Four+	40.00	−14.42	25.90	−2.92
Religion				
Hindu[$]	28.51	−2.93	25.53	−2.55
Muslim	29.41	−3.83	23.77	−0.80
Christian	15.56	10.03	16.52*	6.46
***Education of mother**				
Illiterate[$]	44.12	−18.53	42.33	−19.35
Std 1–7	38.69	−13.11	36.07	−13.10
Std 8–11	21.36	4.23	20.80*	2.17
Std 12+	10.99	14.59	11.46*	11.52

Notes: [$]Reference category.
*Corresponding logistic regression coefficient is significant.
[@]Deviation from overall proportion (percent).

all categories of the variables. Let us assume the value be Z, that is, $\log_e\left(\dfrac{p}{1-p}\right) = Z$. Now, the question is to obtain the value p.

We know that if $\log_e(x) = y$, then $x = e^y$, that is, $\dfrac{p}{1-p} = e^Z = y$ (say) and $p = \dfrac{y}{1+y}$ (by simple arithmetic operation). These calculations are presented in rows corresponding to 'Exponent' and 'Adjusted underweight'. The next row is '% Adjusted underweight' which is just $100 *$ Adjusted underweight (in percentage). The last row is '% Unadjusted underweight' which is the unadjusted underweight as obtained from the 'Means' procedure in SPSS. In general, unadjusted underweight is the *gross* effect and the adjusted underweight is the *net* effect (independent or free of the effect of other variables/factors in the model).

The final figures of the adjusted percent of children underweight along with the corresponding unadjusted figures, and also their deviation from the overall proportion (%) are presented in Table 13.8. The table also gives the statistical significance of the corresponding logistic regression coefficients (marked based on the values of 'Sig.' in the logistic regression output). The

Figure 13.1 Unadjusted and Adjusted Percent of Children Underweight

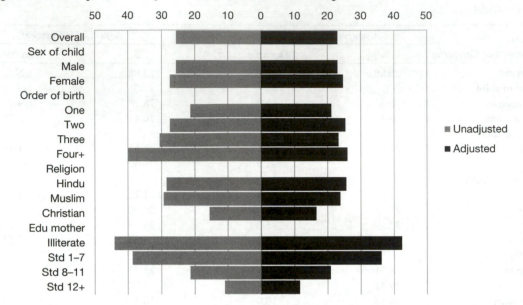

unadjusted and adjusted percentages of children underweight by the factors in the model are also depicted in Figure 13.1. It is to be noted that the interpretation of logistic regression coefficients, significance of regression coefficients, odd ratios, goodness of fit, omnibus tests of model coefficients and so on are already dealt with in Chapter 12.

In linear regression, the overall unadjusted and adjusted values will be equal (because of linearity assumption, see Table 13.3), but in logistic regression, it may be slightly different (due to the nonlinear model specification and also rounding of figures). From the table, we get that the unadjusted proportion of children underweight is 25.6 percent and the adjusted proportion of children underweight is 23.0 percent. It is to be noted that the small difference in the level of the unadjusted and adjusted estimates does not matter for comparison between groups.

Among the various factors, the effect of order of birth on underweight is very clear from the unadjusted and adjusted figures. The unadjusted figures show that underweight increased from 27.5 percent among the children of the first order births to 40 percent among the children of fourth and higher order births, whereas the adjusted figures indicated no such differences (the figures are 25.3 percent and 25.9 percent, respectively, or only 3 percentage points difference from the overall value). This clearly shows that the order of birth has no independent effect on underweight among children. Generally, we expect that higher order births are associated with the illiteracy of mothers, and once the effect of education of mother is removed, order of birth does not show any independent effect on underweight among children. Please note that the corresponding regression coefficients are not statistically significant.

But at the same time, the effect of education of mother on underweight among children remained the same even after controlling for the effect of other factors in the model. The adjusted proportion of children underweight was 42 percent if their mothers were illiterate but below 12 percent if their mothers completed higher secondary education, clearly indicating a strong effect of education of mothers on reducing underweight among children. However, it is seen from the significance level of the regression coefficients that the children of illiterate mothers and those of mothers with education below the high school level (primary level education or just literate) do not differ in their level of underweight, but the children of mothers with education at the high school or higher level show a remarkable reduction in underweight.

The sex differences in underweight remained almost the same even after controlling the effect of other factors, but the differences are only marginal and also not statistically significant.

With respect to religion, underweight among Christian children remained the lowest (16.5 percent) but between Hindu and Muslim children, underweight was lower among Muslim children (23.8 percent) than that among Hindu children (25.5 percent) while the pattern was the reverse with the unadjusted figures, though the difference was marginal. The differences between Hindu and Christian children are statistically significant, but the differences between Hindu and Muslim children are not statistically significant.

As far as the age of child is concerned, we have obtained the adjusted figures for only two ages namely 12 months and 24 months, but it is clear enough to show that underweight increases with the age of child. The proportion of children underweight was 18 percent at the age of 12 months and 20 percent at the age of 24 months, but the differences are not statistically significant.

In a very similar way, multiple classification analysis can be applied to many other statistical models, such as multinomial logistic regression and survival or hazard models.

CHAPTER 14

Factor Analysis

WHAT IS FACTOR ANALYSIS?

Statistically speaking, factor analysis is a method for investigating whether a larger number of highly correlated variables of interest, say $y_1, y_2, \ldots, y_k$, are linearly related to a smaller number of uncorrelated and unobservable factors, say $F_1, F_2, \ldots, F_r$, where $r < k$. The word 'uncorrelated' means that the factors are not correlated among themselves, whereas the y variables are correlated, often highly correlated, among themselves. The word 'unobservable' means that the factors are not directly measurable from the sample of observations but are derived from the correlation matrix of the variables, whereas the y variables are directly measurable. With factor analysis, one can produce a small number of mutually exclusive (or unrelated or uncorrelated) 'factors' from a large number of highly correlated 'variables', which are capable of explaining the observed variance in the larger number of variables. The small number of factors can then be used in further (multivariate) analysis instead of a large number of variables which often violate independence among them due to their high correlation.

The starting point of factor analysis is a correlation matrix, in which the inter-correlations between the y variables of interest are presented. The dimensionality (rows and columns) of this matrix can be reduced by looking for a set of a lesser number of new variables that are uncorrelated among themselves but each of which is highly correlated with one set of the original variables and weakly correlated with the remaining set of the original variables, and each one of the new variables is called a *factor*.

It is to be noted that a 'factor' is different from a 'variable' and that a factor is largely (need not be fully) an amalgamation of a set of variables. Furthermore, a 'factor' is different from a 'group' in that in groups, a variable can find a place in only one group, whereas in factors, a variable can have a representation in more than one factor, but its strength or degree of representation may differ from one factor to another. In factor analysis, the belonging of a variable to a factor is largely determined by the strength of representation of the variable to that factor.

The original variables on a factor lead to two results, namely *factor scores* and *factor loadings*. Factor scores are the scores of the subjects (observations or cases, and not variables) on a factor and factor loadings are the correlation of the original variables with the factors. The factor loadings are also sometimes called *latent* (unmeasured) variables. The factors can then be used as new variables (instead of the original variables that are highly correlated) with factor scores as their values in multivariate analysis. The factor loading is essentially a correlation value and its squared value determines the amount of variance accounted for by the particular variable, and is especially useful in determining the substantive importance of the variable to the corresponding factor. Because a factor loading for a variable is a measure of how much the variable contributes to the factor, a high factor loading score indicates that the dimensions of the factors are better accounted for by the variables.

Applications

Factor analysis is basically used to condense a larger set of correlated variables into a smaller number of unrelated factors to describe the phenomenon of interest. It can also be used to construct indices by identifying weight for each variable in the index, thereby precisely grading individual observations for classification. The factor scores can be used in the further analysis of data. As the factors are a few and unrelated, the use of factor scores in multivariate analysis can improve the explanatory power of the factors instead of the original variables in terms of higher degrees of freedom and larger variance explained but at the cost of understanding the contribution of the individual variables.

In general, factor analysis allows researchers to investigate aspects that are not easily and directly measurable. By asking a variety of questions or recording behaviours, we can reduce a large number of variables (answers/behaviours) into a few interpretable underlying factors. As such, factor analysis is a useful tool for investigating relationships among variables of complex concepts and constructing indices such as socio-economic status, dietary patterns and psychosocial behaviours.

The relationship between original variables and factors is explained with an example. Let us assume that there are nine variables, and let us describe them in terms of three factors, say loosely, background (in which the subjects live), social factors and economic factors. Let as assume that each variable is related (in varying degrees) to all the three factors plus a set of unknown factors. Often, the known factors are called *common factors* and the unknown factors (i.e., the variance not explained by the known factors) are together termed as a single *unique factor* and also called *uniqueness* of the variable.

Let $y_1, y_2, ..., y_9$ be the nine variables, F_1, F_2 and F_3 be the three factors and e be the unique factor. Now, we can write

$$y_1 = \alpha_1 F_1 + \beta_1 F_2 + \gamma_1 F_3 + e_1$$
$$y_2 = \alpha_2 F_1 + \beta_2 F_2 + \gamma_2 F_3 + e_2$$

$$...$$

$$y_9 = \alpha_9 F_1 + \beta_9 F_2 + \gamma_9 F_1 + e_9,$$

where α (alpha), β (beta) and γ (gamma) values are the coefficients of the factors, namely F_1, F_2 and F_3, respectively. Note that α, β and γ have each nine values and the subscripts are omitted just for convenience. In factor analysis, the set of values for α, β and γ are called *factor loadings* or simply *loadings*. For example, β_1 is called the *loading* of variable y_1 on factor F_2. The loadings can range from −1 to +1. A factor loading close to +1 or −1 is an indication that the factor is strongly related to the corresponding variable positively or negatively (as the case may be), and a factor loading close to 0 (zero) is an indication that the factor is weakly related to the corresponding variable, that is, the factor loadings give us an idea about how much the variable has contributed to the factor; the larger the factor loading, the stronger the correlation between the variable and the factor and, hence, the larger the variable has contributed to that factor.

The mathematical model for factor analysis (presented above) appears somewhat similar to a multiple regression equation. In a regression equation, the dependent variable is represented as a linear combination of the independent variables, whereas in factor analysis, each of the variables (of interest) is represented as a linear combination of a small number of unobservable factors. However, there are differences between the equations of regression analysis and factor analysis. An important difference is that in regression analysis, there are two categories of variables (a dependent variable and a set of independent variables), whereas in factor analysis, there is no such categorisation of variables, and we only condense a large number of variables into a small number of factors. In regression analysis, the independent variables are individual variables, whereas in factor analysis, the factors are only labels for the groups of variables. Furthermore, in regression analysis, there is only one equation, whereas in factor analysis, there are as many equations as the number of variables. Similar to regression analysis, in factor analysis also it would appear that the loadings can be estimated and tested by regressing each *y* variable against the factors, but such an approach is not feasible because the factors are not observed (measured). So, a new strategy is required for the estimation.

Requirements for Factor Analysis

The requirements for factor analysis are listed below:

1. The data used for factor analysis need to be free from outliers, or at least free from severe outliers. This is a common requirement for many multivariate analyses.
2. The variables should be normally distributed, that is, there has to be univariate and multivariate normality within the data. This is also a common requirement for many multivariate analyses.
3. It is assumed that there exists a linear relationship between the factors and each of the variables.
4. The error term (unique factor) is assumed to be normally distributed with mean 0 and variance 1.
5. A factor should have at least three variables, else labelling and interpretation of the factors would be difficult and should be done with caution.
6. The correlation coefficient between the variables must be 0.3 or higher since a lower value implies a weak relationship between the variables.
7. Factor analysis requires a large sample size, preferably more than 300 observations.

Important Note: For the factors to be considered stable, it is desirable that the number of observations is at least 10 times the number of variables in the analysis and at least 30 times the number of factors considered. For example, for a factor analysis with 40 variables and seven factors, the minimum sample size desired is the maximum of 40 * 10=400 and 7 * 30=210, which is 400. However, a smaller sample size may be sufficient if many factor loading scores are very high, say >0.8.

Limitations

One of the limitations of factor analysis is the problem of appropriately naming the factors. We can see easily from the factor equations that some, often many, variables may load into more than one factor, which is known as *split loading*. If a variable loads into more than one factor, the factors themselves cannot be said to be uniquely referring to a single dimension but a mix of dimensions, and in this case, naming or labelling them is problematic, that is, the label may refer to one dimension, but the factor variables are from different dimensions. In the above example, if income loads into both economic and social factors, then the labelling of the factors—economic and social—is not very appropriate. As such, the factor names may not accurately reflect the variables within the factor.

Difference between Principal Component Analysis and Factor Analysis

Principal component analysis and factor analysis are similar because both the procedures are used to simplify the structure of a set of variables. However, the analyses differ in several ways.

In principal component analysis, the components are calculated as the linear combinations of the original variables, that is, all the original variables are constituents of each of the components.

Figure 14.1 Difference between Factor Model and Principal Component Model

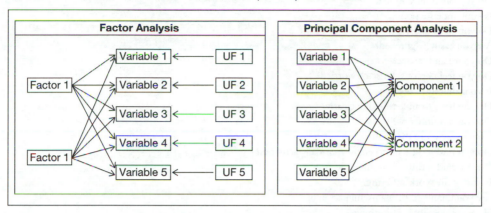

Note: UF stands for the unique factor (see the equations under the subsection 'A Simple Example').

In factor analysis, the original variables are defined as the linear combinations of the factors, that is, all the factors are constituents of each of the original variables. However, the strength of the relationship may vary from variable to variable in the former case and factor to factor in the latter case. Figure 14.1 illustrates the relationships.

In principal component analysis, the goal is to explain as much of the total variance in the variables as possible with a few components of the original variables. The goal of factor analysis is to explain the covariances or correlations between the variables.

So, we may use principal component analysis to reduce the variables into a smaller number of components and use them in factor analysis to understand what constructs underlie the data, that is, principal component analysis can be an intermediate step in the factor analysis.

STEPS IN FACTOR ANALYSIS

In factor analysis, firstly, a correlation matrix is generated for all the variables. Secondly, the dimensionality (rows and columns) of the matrix is reduced by looking for a set of lesser number of new variables (factors), each of which is highly correlated with one set of the original variables and weakly correlated with the remaining set of the original variables. Thirdly, the factors are rotated in order to maximise the relationship between the variables and the factors.

The steps in factor analysis are illustrated with data drawn from a household survey conducted in the Vidarbha region of Maharashtra state. The study was conducted in 2009 to understand the livelihood aspects of the people who are often prone to crop failure and distress. Often we hear news that farmers of the Vidarbha region have committed suicide due to crop failure and related psychiatric distress. World Health Organization (WHO) developed a self-reporting questionnaire (SRQ) as an instrument designed to screen psychiatric disturbance, especially, in the developing countries. The SRQ consisted of 20 questions that have to be answered yes or no. It may be used as a self-administered or as an interview administered questionnaire. In the household questionnaire, a section was devoted to understand the distress among the farmers by asking a series of 20 questions suggested in the SRQ manual (WHO, 1994). The questions are listed here.

V01 Do you often have headache?

V02 Is your appetite poor?

V03 Do you sleep badly?

V04 Are you easily frightened?

V05 Do your hands shake?

V06 Do you feel nervous, tense or worried?

V07 Is your digestion poor?

V08 Do you have trouble thinking clearly?

V09 Do you feel unhappy?

V10 Do you cry more than usual?

V11 Do you find it difficult to enjoy your daily activities?

V12 Do you find it difficult to make decisions?

V13 Is your daily work suffering?

V14 Are you unable to play a useful part in life?

V15 Have you lost interest in things?

V16 Do you feel that you are a worthless person?

V17 Has the thought of ending your life been on your mind?

V18 Do you feel tired all the time?

V19 Do you have uncomfortable feelings in your stomach?

V20 Are you easily tired?

The data pertain to 4,908 farmers (males) in the age group of 20–69. The survey was conducted during September–November (kharif crops growing/harvesting stage) of 2009. In this example, the intention is to determine the underlying construct of farmers' susceptibility to the risk of distress, and the research question may be put as: What are the underlying mechanisms or factors that can produce correlation amongst the farmers at the risk of distress?

Examining the Data

In the first step, we need to examine the data for outliers and missing cases. The problems of outliers and how to deal with them are already discussed in Chapter 11 and are not repeated here. If there are missing values, then we need to decide on the SPSS options, namely exclude cases list-wise (cases with missing values for any one variable will be excluded from the analysis), exclude cases pair-wise (cases with missing values for a variable will be excluded from computation of indices involving that variable only), or replace with mean (missing values will be replaced with mean of the non-missing values of the variable).

Examining Correlation Matrix

After the preliminary look at the data, the first step in factor analysis is to obtain the correlation matrix and related statistics to check the relationship between the variables, and to identify the variables that do not appear to be related to other variables. The analysis of the correlation matrix will indicate the appropriateness of the application of factor model to the data. SPSS provides the correlation matrix and two summary indices to evaluate the data. The indices are Bartlett's test of sphericity (BTS) and Kaiser–Meyer–Olkin measure of sampling adequacy (KMO).

In the latest version of SPSS, the menu 'Analyze=>Dimension Reduction=>Factor' displays the factor analysis window. In the open window, choose the command 'Descriptives' and select the options 'Correlation coefficients', 'Determinant', 'KMO and Bartlett's test of sphericity' and other statistics as desired (Figure 14.2).

Figure 14.2   Factor Analysis: Descriptives

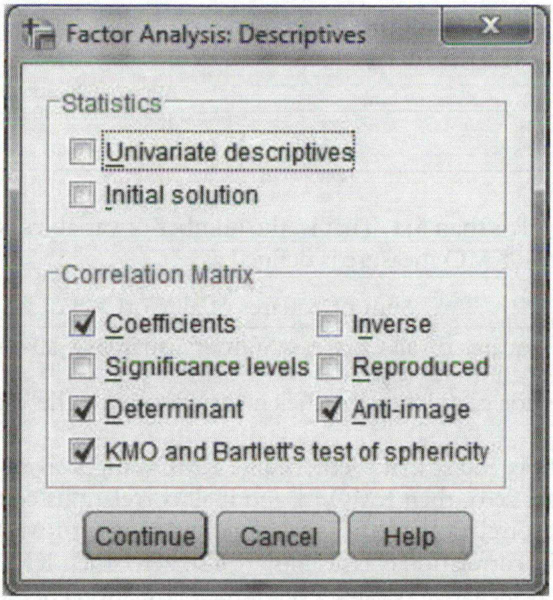

Bartlett's Test

Bartlett's test is used to test the hypothesis that a correlation matrix is an identity matrix. An identity matrix is a square matrix with all the diagonal values 1 and all other values 0. If a correlation matrix is an identity matrix, then it means that all the variables in the matrix are unrelated to each other. So, in Bartlett's test, the null hypothesis is that the variables are all unrelated to each other with correlation coefficient zero (the correlation matrix is an identity matrix) and the alternative hypothesis is that not all correlation coefficients are zero. That is:

H_0: All the correlation coefficients are zero (except for the variables themselves)

H_1: Not all the correlation coefficients are zero.

Bartlett's test assumes that the sample data are drawn from a multivariate normal population. The test is based on a chi-square transformation of the determinant of the correlation matrix. The derivation of the test statistic is beyond the scope of this book. A higher value of the test statistic is associated with a higher level of significance (or a lower significance value). A significance level of $p < 0.05$ is a confirmation of significant relationship between the variables.

Table 14.1 is the SPSS output of KMO index and Bartlett's test results. Bartlett's test result produced a very high chi-square value and it is highly significant ($p < 0.001$). It means that the null hypothesis that the correlation coefficients are zero is rejected and the alternate hypothesis that they are all not zero is accepted. So, the correlation matrix is not an identity matrix and the variables are correlated.

Kaiser–Meyer–Olkin Measure of Sampling Adequacy

Kaiser–Meyer–Olkin measure of sampling adequacy (KMO measure) is an index for comparing the magnitudes of the observed correlation coefficients to the magnitudes of the partial correlation coefficients. The KMO measure is particularly recommended when the number of cases to

Table 14.1 KMO and Bartlett's Test SPSS Output

KMO and Bartlett's Test		
Kaiser–Meyer–Olkin Measure of Sampling Adequacy		.877
Bartlett's Test of Sphericity	Approx. Chi-Square	26,294.523
	df	190
	Sig.	.000

the number of variables is less than 5:1. That is, the number of variables is higher than 20 percent of the observations (cases). KMO measure is defined as:

$$KMO = \frac{\text{Sum of squares of all CorCoefs}}{\text{Sum of squares of all CorCef} + \text{Sum of squares of all partial CorCoefs}},$$

where 'CorCoefs' stands for correlation coefficients, exclusive of the diagonal ones (which are always 1).

It is clear from the above index that theoretically, KMO ranges from 0 to 1. If all the partial correlation coefficients are zero, then KMO = 1 and if all correlations coefficients are zero and at least some of the partial correlation coefficients are non-zero, then KMO = 0. Please note that in the latter case, if all partial correlation coefficients are also zero, then KMO is indeterminate. Also note that KMO will not be negative because even if the correlation coefficients are negative, their square values will be positive.

If many variables share a common factor, then it means that they are correlated among themselves. At the same time, a low partial correlation coefficient means that not only the two variables are correlated among themselves but also with other variables, and a high partial correlation coefficient means that the two variables are highly correlated but weakly correlated with other variables. Accordingly, when the partial correlations are high, the KMO value will be less and it implies a weak correlation among the variables. As such, if the KMO value is low, factor analysis is not appropriate. On the other hand, factor analysis is appropriate if the KMO value is large. According to Kaiser–Meyer–Olkin, a KMO value of 0.90+ is marvellous, 0.80+ is meritorious, 0.70+ is middling, 0.60+ is mediocre, 0.50 is miserable and below 0.50 is unacceptable for factor analysis, that is, a KMO measure of 0.70 or above is a reasonably high value to go ahead with factor analysis, though 0.50 or higher is also acceptable.

The KMO measure for the present data is 0.877, which is meritorious for factor analysis. It means both BTS and KMO measure of sampling adequacy are favourable to the data for the application of factor analysis.

Selection of Variables for Inclusion in Factor Analysis

In the above exercise, both the tests support the factor analysis. What if the tests fail? One way is to abandon factor analysis and another way is to remove the variables that are not correlated with other variables. One procedure to accomplish this is explained below.

Table 14.2 gives the correlation matrix obtained from the SPSS output (reformatted and presented), except the last row. The suitability of the variables for factor analysis can be assessed using this correlation matrix. For this, look for correlation values that are close to zero. Variables that have large number of correlation coefficients, usually in the range $-0.25 \leq r \leq 0.25$, with other variables may be excluded. Please note that some books suggest the range $-0.3 \leq r \leq 0.3$.

A practical way is to assign the value 0 if the correlation coefficient is $-0.25 \leq r \leq 0.25$, else 1, and then count the number of 1's row-wise or column-wise. From this number we will less 1, as

Table 14.2 Correlation Matrix for All Variables from SPSS Output for Factor Analysis (Reformatted)

Correlation Matrix (V01, V02,..., V20 are the Variables Listed Above); NVC – No. of Variables Correlated

	V01	V02	V03	V04	V05	V06	V07	V08	V09	V10	V11	V12	V13	V14	V15	V16	V17	V18	V19	V20
V01	1.00	0.06	0.18	0.35	0.37	0.28	0.11	0.03	0.32	0.23	0.16	0.33	0.26	0.22	0.21	0.25	0.25	0.30	0.30	0.23
V02	0.06	1.00	0.19	0.08	0.04	0.03	0.10	0.56	0.04	0.06	0.12	0.09	0.04	0.09	0.10	0.03	0.01	0.02	0.06	0.01
V03	0.18	0.19	1.00	0.20	0.15	0.17	0.41	0.13	0.15	0.10	0.44	0.26	0.14	0.20	0.39	0.13	0.10	0.13	0.21	0.08
V04	0.35	0.08	0.20	1.00	0.51	0.27	0.14	0.09	0.30	0.33	0.18	0.31	0.21	0.26	0.22	0.29	0.29	0.31	0.35	0.30
V05	0.37	0.04	0.15	0.51	1.00	0.29	0.12	0.03	0.31	0.28	0.18	0.28	0.25	0.24	0.21	0.30	0.28	0.35	0.37	0.31
V06	0.28	0.03	0.17	0.27	0.29	1.00	0.08	0.02	0.45	0.18	0.16	0.32	0.25	0.19	0.21	0.21	0.19	0.30	0.29	0.30
V07	0.11	0.10	0.41	0.14	0.12	0.08	1.00	0.11	0.13	0.15	0.45	0.22	0.11	0.17	0.36	0.10	0.06	0.13	0.22	0.14
V08	0.03	0.56	0.13	0.09	0.03	0.02	0.11	1.00	0.02	0.05	0.13	0.07	-0.01	0.08	0.07	0.01	-0.02	0.01	0.05	0.02
V09	0.32	0.04	0.15	0.30	0.31	0.45	0.13	0.02	1.00	0.33	0.15	0.41	0.29	0.21	0.20	0.32	0.28	0.29	0.30	0.28
V10	0.23	0.06	0.10	0.33	0.28	0.18	0.15	0.05	0.33	1.00	0.16	0.26	0.21	0.27	0.14	0.12	0.14	0.20	0.24	0.23
V11	0.16	0.12	0.44	0.18	0.18	0.16	0.45	0.13	0.15	0.16	1.00	0.29	0.16	0.30	0.53	0.12	0.14	0.20	0.26	0.12
V12	0.33	0.09	0.26	0.31	0.28	0.32	0.22	0.07	0.41	0.26	0.29	1.00	0.34	0.32	0.33	0.27	0.26	0.29	0.36	0.24
V13	0.26	0.04	0.14	0.21	0.25	0.25	0.11	-0.01	0.29	0.21	0.16	0.34	1.00	0.30	0.25	0.33	0.24	0.31	0.29	0.28
V14	0.22	0.09	0.20	0.26	0.24	0.19	0.17	0.08	0.21	0.27	0.30	0.32	0.30	1.00	0.37	0.32	0.21	0.26	0.32	0.17
V15	0.21	0.10	0.39	0.22	0.21	0.21	0.36	0.07	0.20	0.14	0.53	0.33	0.25	0.37	1.00	0.20	0.19	0.26	0.30	0.19
V16	0.25	0.03	0.13	0.29	0.30	0.21	0.10	0.01	0.32	0.12	0.12	0.27	0.33	0.32	0.20	1.00	0.45	0.30	0.30	0.29
V17	0.25	0.01	0.10	0.29	0.28	0.19	0.06	-0.02	0.28	0.14	0.20	0.26	0.24	0.21	0.19	0.45	1.00	0.25	0.28	0.20
V18	0.30	0.02	0.13	0.31	0.35	0.30	0.13	0.01	0.29	0.20	0.26	0.29	0.31	0.26	0.26	0.30	0.25	1.00	0.52	0.57
V19	0.30	0.06	0.21	0.35	0.37	0.29	0.22	0.05	0.30	0.24	0.26	0.36	0.29	0.32	0.30	0.30	0.28	0.52	1.00	0.48
V20	0.23	0.01	0.08	0.30	0.31	0.30	0.14	0.02	0.28	0.23	0.12	0.24	0.28	0.17	0.19	0.29	0.20	0.57	0.48	1.00
NVC	5	1	3	7	6	3	3	1	7	3	3	8	4	5	5	5	1	5	8	5

the diagonal values are always 1 that refer to the correlation of a variable with itself and is given in the last row with the label 'NVC' (number of variables correlated). Now, if this number is less than one-fifth (20 percent) of the number of variables in the list (rows or columns), then it is clear that the corresponding variable lacks a patterned relationship with other variables and it may be removed. As a rigid condition, one may even set the number to one-fourth (25 percent). In this example, cut-off number is $(20/5) - 1 = 3$, and only three variables namely V02, V08 and V17 (with NVC < 3) fall in this category. If desired, we may exclude them from factor analysis.

Anti-image Correlation

Please note that we have learned partial correlation in Chapter 8. In KMO, the partial correlation is the correlation between two variables after eliminating the effect of all the other variables (not just one variable) in the model. The negative of the partial correlation coefficient is called *anti-image correlation*. In SPSS, we can also obtain the matrix of anti-image correlations by choosing the option 'Anti-image' in the 'Factor Analysis: Descriptives' window (as shown above, output not presented here). From the anti-image correlations matrix, we can identify correlations that are large as described above. However, what value is 'large' is not well defined, but we may consider absolute values greater than 0.3 as large. If many anti-image correlations are very high, it is not advisable to apply factor analysis to that data.

FACTOR EXTRACTION

The next step is factor extraction. There are a number of methods to accomplish this and a few are explained in brief.

Principal Component Method

Principal component method is a standard extraction method in factor analysis. It extracts uncorrelated linear combinations of the variables. The first extracted factor explains the maximum variance and the second and all the following factors explain the smaller portions of the variance and are all the factors are uncorrelated with each other. That is, we can extract as many factors as there are uncorrelated linear combinations of the observed variables.

Principal Axis Factoring Method

The second most common analysis is *principal axis* factoring, also called *common factor analysis*, or *principal factor analysis*. It is very similar to principal component method. The principal axis method identifies the latent constructs behind the observations, whereas principal component method identifies similar groups of variables.

Maximum Likelihood Method

Maximum likelihood method assumes that the data are drawn from a population having multivariate normal distribution (other methods make no such an assumption), and hence, the residuals of correlation coefficients must be normally distributed at around 0. The loadings are iteratively estimated by maximum likelihood approach. So, computationally, it is a resource intensive method for estimating loadings that maximises the likelihood of sampling the observed correlation matrix from a population.

Unweighted Least Squares Method

Ordinary or unweighted least squares method is aimed at minimising the residuals between the input correlation matrix and the one reproduced by the factors, while diagonal elements as the sums of communality and uniqueness are aimed to restore 1s. In short, this method minimises off-diagonal residuals between the reproduced and the original correlation matrix.

Generalised (Weighted) Least Squares Method

Generalised or weighted least squares method is a modification of the ordinary or unweighted least squares method. The modification is that, when minimising the residuals, it weights correlation coefficients differentially such that correlations between variables with high uniqueness (at the current iteration) are given less weight. We may use this method if we want the factors to fit highly *unique* variables (i.e., those weakly driven by the factors) worse than highly *common* variables (i.e., strongly driven by the factors). In general, this method minimises off-diagonal residuals, and the variables with larger communalities are given more weight.

Choice of Extraction Method

For factor extraction in factor analysis, principal component method and maximum likelihood method are the two methods commonly used, and principal axis factoring method is also used often. As a general principle, the maximum likelihood method is used to obtain maximum likelihood estimates of the factor loadings if the factors and the errors in the factor model are assumed to follow a normal distribution. On the other hand, principal component method is used if the factors and errors in the factor model are not assumed to follow a normal distribution. Between principal component and principal axis factoring methods, principal component method is preferred when using factor analysis in causal modelling and principal axis factoring method is used when the factor analysis is to reduce data.

Eigenvalues and Eigenvectors

Eigenvalues (also called characteristic values or latent roots) are the variances of the principal components. Eigenvalues are used to determine the number of factors to be extracted in principal component analysis. Usually, factors are extracted as long as the eigenvalue is 1 or higher.

Eigenvalues and eigenvectors are related to matrix algebra and are highly mathematical in nature. So, only the definition or outline is given here. Let A be a matrix of size n by n (n rows and n columns) and x be a non-zero ($x \neq 0$) vector of size n by 1. A scalar λ is said to be an eigenvalue of A, if $Ax = \lambda x$. The vector x is called an eigenvector corresponding to λ. More about eigenvalues or its derivation is beyond the scope of this book.

Communalities

As explained earlier, the known factors are called common factors and the unexplained variance is attributed to the unique factor. The proportion of variance explained by the common factors is called *communality* of the variable. Communalities can range from 0 to 1, with 0 indicating that the common factors explain none of the variance and 1 indicating that all the variance is explained by the common factors.

Factor Extraction Output

Now, with an example, we will obtain estimates of initial (not final) factors from principal component analysis and communalities. As mentioned earlier in principal component method, factors are extracted as a linear combination of the observed variables. For this, in the SPSS windows, click 'Extraction' and in the popup window, choose the option 'Principal Component' from the pulled down menu. Also choose the analyse options 'Correlation matrix', extract option 'Based on Eigenvalue' and set eigenvalue greater than 1, and display options 'un-rotated factor solution' and 'Scree plot' (Figure 14.3).

Table 14.3 gives component matrix and communalities vector obtained from SPSS by principal component method of factor extraction (only a part of the table is presented). It is to be noted that the table of 'variance explained' by the components is presented in Table 14.5 in the next section, along with the variance explained by the components after rotation.

It is seen from Table 14.3 that the principal component method extracted five components (factors) that have an eigenvalue 1 or higher. Furthermore, as it will be seen from Table 14.4 that the five components together accounted for 55 percent of the total variance in the data.

FACTOR ROTATION

Although the extracted factor matrix indicates the relationship between the factors and the individual variables, often the variables and factors may not be correlated in an interpretable pattern. In order for the factors to be substantially meaningful and interpretable, factor analysis attempts to transform the initial matrix into one that is easier to interpret and this attempt is called *factor rotation*. In other words, in factor analysis, rotation is a procedure to obtain a new set of factor loadings (weights) from the initial one. It is to be noted that factor rotation is not applicable if only one factor is extracted.

Figure 14.3 Factor Analysis: Extraction

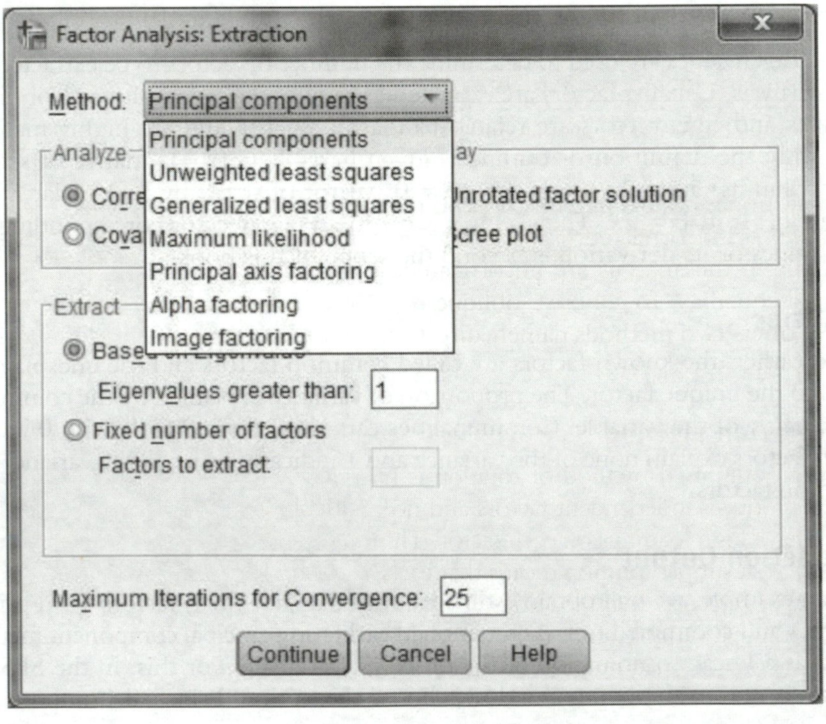

Table 14.3   Component Matrix and Communalities Vector Obtained from SPSS by Principal Component Method of Factor Extraction

Variables	1	2	3	4	5	Communalities
			Component			
V01 Do you often have headache?	0.548	−0.128	0.081	0.066	−0.297	0.415
V02 Is your appetite poor?	0.149	0.495	0.702	−0.042	0.051	0.765
V03 Do you sleep badly?	0.425	0.551	−0.189	0.027	−0.162	0.547
V04 Are you easily frightened?	0.603	−0.125	0.173	0.057	−0.124	0.428
V05 Do your hands shake?	0.603	−0.195	0.116	−0.013	−0.130	0.432
Etc. (variables V06 to V19)	x	x	x	x	x	x
V20 Are you easily tired?	0.563	−0.262	0.032	−0.541	0.187	0.714

Notes: Extraction Method: Principal Component Analysis. Five components are extracted. The coefficients are sorted by size.
In SPSS output the 'Communalities' column is given in a separate table and it is presented with this table for convenience.

Table 14.4   Total Variance Explained as Obtained from SPSS Output

Component	Extraction Sums of Squared Loadings			Rotation Sums of Squared Loadings		
	Total	*% of Variance*	*Cumulative %*	*Total*	*% of Variance*	*Cumulative %*
1	5.471	27.353	27.353	2.541	12.704	12.704
2	1.974	9.872	37.226	2.499	12.497	25.201
3	1.417	7.083	44.308	2.296	11.482	36.683
4	1.159	5.793	50.101	2.128	10.640	47.323
5	1.022	5.110	55.211	1.578	7.888	55.211

Note: Extraction Method: Principal Component Analysis. Rotation Method: Varimax with Kaiser Normalisation.

Factor extraction is done differently depending upon whether the factors are believed to be correlated (*oblique*) or uncorrelated (*orthogonal*). Simply put, orthogonal rotation methods assume that the factors in the analysis are uncorrelated. SPSS offers three methods, namely, varimax, quartimax and equamax. In contrast, oblique rotation methods assume that the factors are correlated. SPSS offers two methods namely direct oblimin and promax. A brief description of these rotation methods is given here.

Varimax Rotation Method

The most commonly used method of rotation is *varimax*. This method is an orthogonal rotation method (that produces independent factors and no multicollinearity) that minimises the number of variables that have high loadings on each factor. This method simplifies the interpretation of the factors. For varimax, a simple solution means that each factor has a small number of large loadings and a large number of zero (or small) loadings. This simplifies the interpretation because after a varimax rotation, each original variable tends to be associated with one or a small number of factors, and each factor represents only a small number of variables. In addition, the factors can often be interpreted from the opposition of few variables with positive loadings to few variables with negative loadings.

Quartimax Rotation Method

The second frequently used method is *quartimax*. This method rotates the factors in order to minimise the number of factors needed to explain each variable. This method simplifies the interpretation of the observed variables.

Equamax Rotation Method

Another method is *equamax*. This method is a combination of the *varimax* method that simplifies the factors, and the *quartimax* method that simplifies the variables. The number of variables that load highly on a factor and the number of factors needed to explain a variable are minimised.

Oblimin Rotation Method

In oblimin method, a parameter called δ (delta) controls the extent of obliqueness. When δ is zero, the factors are most oblique. For negative values of δ, the factors become less oblique as δ becomes more negative. So, δ can be either zero or negative.

Promax Rotation Method

For oblique rotations, the promax rotation has the advantage of being fast and conceptually simple. It tries to fit a target matrix which has a simple structure. It necessitates two steps. The first step defines the target matrix, almost always obtained as the result of a varimax rotation whose entries are raised to some power (typically between 2 and 4) in order to 'force' the structure of the loadings to become bipolar. The second step is obtained by computing a least square fit from the varimax solution to the target matrix.

Choice of Rotation Method

Perhaps the best way to decide between orthogonal and oblique rotation is to request oblique rotation (direct oblimin or promax) with the desired number of factors, and look at the correlations among the factors. If the factor correlations are not driven by the data, the solution remains nearly orthogonal. For this, look at the factor correlation matrix for correlations 0.3 and above, and if so, there is at least 10 percent overlap in variance among the factors and it is enough to warrant oblique rotation, unless there are compelling reasons for orthogonal rotation.

FACTOR ROTATION OUTPUT

In the SPSS factor analysis window, click 'Rotation' and a window with the caption 'Factor Analysis: Rotation' will pop-up, and in that choose the method option 'Verimax' and display option 'Rotated Solution' as shown in Figure 14.4. The SPSS output is briefly explained in Table 14.4.

Percentage of Variance Explained

The retained components cumulatively explain a certain percentage of variation. The acceptable level of explained variance depends on how we use the principal components or common factors. For descriptive purposes, we may need 80 percent of the variance explained. In our example, the five components together accounted for only 55 percent of the variation. However, the variance explained is more evenly distributed after rotation than before rotation. The large changes in the individual totals (the 'Total' column) suggest that the rotated component matrix will be easier to interpret than the unrotated matrix.

Figure 14.4 Factor Analysis: Rotation

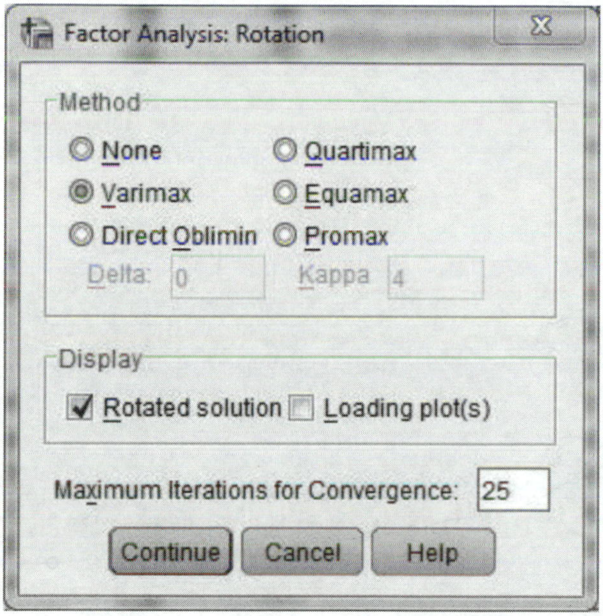

Scree Test

The ideal pattern in a scree plot is a steep curve, followed by a bend and then a flat or horizontal line. The curve looks like a rubble or landslip or avalanche and hence the name *scree*. In factor analysis, it indicates the number of factors that can be retained. We retain those components or factors in the steep curve before the first point that starts the flat line trend.

Figure 14.5 depicts the scree plot. It is seen that the first five points (factors) are on the slide portion, and thereafter, the points are almost flattened. So, it appears that a five-factor model would be sufficient for the communality of the variables or common factors.

Rotated Component Matrix

Table 14.5 gives the rotated component matrix obtained from the SPSS output in sorted form. The 20 variables (questions) are sorted according to the components that they largely represent. Accordingly, the first component is largely a factor of the first six variables (listed in the table), the second component is largely a factor of the next four variables, the third component is largely a factor of next five variables, the fourth component is largely a factor of next three variables and the fifth and last component is largely a factor of the remaining two variables. This is very clear from the values of the components that are demarcated by shading.

The rotated component matrix helps us to determine which variables or categories of the variables the components represent. We may name the components based on their coefficients representing the category of the variables. The problem can be easily solved if the variables of the components are of the same nature or all belong to a common category, else it would be a problem. The variables in the present exercise may be grouped as under:

Figure 14.5 Scree Plot of SPSS Output

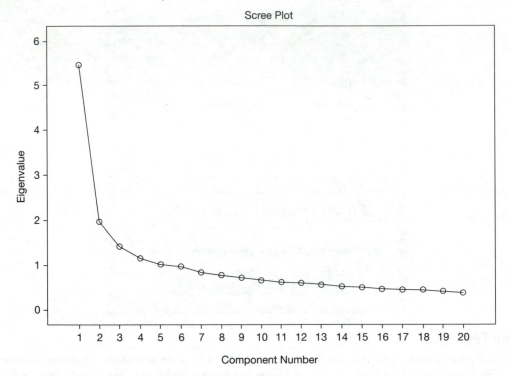

Component 1: **Feelings of nervous:** Feeling nervous, tense or worried, or unhappy.
Component 2: **Mental difficulties:** Finding it difficult to enjoy daily activities, losing interest in things.
Component 3: **Feeling of worthless:** Feeling of worthless or ending life.
Component 4: **Physical feeling:** Easily tired, feeling tired all the time, uncomfortable feelings in stomach.
Component 5: **Mental feeling:** Trouble in thinking clearly and poor appetite.

Note: It is clear from the above description that the labelling of factors is only tentative and is highly influenced by the user.

Component or Factor Score

Often the main aim of factor analysis is to reduce a large number of variables into a small number of factors, and so it is desirable to estimate factor scores for each case and add them to the original dataset. For each case and each component, a factor or component score is computed by multiplying the case's standardised variable values by the component's score coefficients. The resulting component score variables are representative of, and can be used in place of, the original variables, that is, the factor scores can be used in subsequent analysis to represent the values of the factors (in lieu of the original variables). Please note that for each case, there will be as many factor scores as there are components.

In any subsequent analysis, the few component score variables, instead of the many original variables, will explain the total variance explained by the components only, that is, the loss of

Table 14.5   Rotated Component Matrix Obtained from SPSS Output (Sorted)

Variables/Questions	Component 1	2	3	4	5
V06 Do you feel nervous, tense or worried?	.713	.098	−.029	.203	−.030
V09 Do you feel unhappy?	.710	.071	.223	.082	−.024
V01 Do you often have headache?	.588	.103	.202	.131	.025
V12 Do you find it difficult to make decisions?	.515	.336	.258	.111	.021
V05 Do your hands shake?	.508	.057	.288	.293	.045
V04 Are you easily frightened?	.500	.084	.324	.224	.123
V11 Do you find it difficult to enjoy your daily activities?	.075	.789	.114	.083	.049
V15 Have you lost interest in things?	.098	.713	.212	.170	−.014
V07 Is your digestion poor?	.054	.709	.001	.086	.052
V03 Do you sleep badly?	.209	.697	.005	−.020	.131
V16 Do you feel that you are a worthless person?	.144	.033	.734	.187	−.005
V17 Has the thought of ending life been on your mind?	.188	.014	.694	.078	−.050
V10 Do you cry more than usual?	.298	.046	.556	.026	.075
V14 Are you unable to play a useful part in life?	.048	.353	.546	.162	.067
V13 Is your daily work suffering?	.232	.152	.413	.271	−.047
V20 Are you easily tired?	.208	.023	.110	.811	.003
V18 Do you feel tired all the time?	.206	.111	.170	.794	−.008
V19 Do you have uncomfortable feelings in stomach?	.242	.228	.226	.664	.029
V08 Do you have trouble thinking clearly?	.012	.078	−.005	.020	.876
V02 Is your appetite poor?	.034	.105	.029	−.008	.867

Notes: Extraction Method: Principal Component Analysis. Rotation Method: Varimax with Kaiser Normalisation. Rotation converged in five iterations.

information would be 100 minus the variance explained. If the variance explained by the components is 80 percent, then the replacement of the components in place of the original variables will result in 20 percent loss in the variance explained by the original variables. But at the same time, there is an advantage of a gain in the degrees of freedom as the number of variables in the subsequent analysis is reduced.

In SPSS, we can add the factor scores to the dataset by clicking the command 'Scores' and in the resulting popup window choosing the option 'Save as Variables'. There are several methods of estimating the factor scores. SPSS provides three methods namely regression, Bartlett and Anderson–Rubin, and all result in scores with a mean 0. The Anderson–Rubin method always produces uncorrelated scores with standard deviation 1, even when the original factors are estimated to be correlated. The regression factor scores have a variance equal to the squared multiple correlations between the estimated factor scores and the true factor values. If principal component extraction method is used, all three methods result in the same factor scores, which are no longer estimated but are exact.

CONFIRMATORY FACTOR ANALYSIS

There are basically two types of factor analysis: exploratory factor analysis (EFA) and confirmatory factor analysis (CFA). While EFA attempts to discover the nature of the constructs influencing a set of responses (variables or measures), CFA tests whether a specified set of constructs is influencing the responses in a predicted way. The primary objective of EFA is to determine the number of common factors influencing a set of measures (variables) and the strength of the relationship between each factor and each observed measure. On the other hand, the primary objective of CFA is to determine the ability of a predetermined factor model to fit an observed dataset.

Some of the common uses of CFA are: to validate a model, to compare the ability of different models to account for the same set of data and to select the best model, to test the relationship between two or more models (factor loadings), to test if a set of factors are correlated or not, and the like.

Both types of factor analyses are based on the same common factor model (as discussed under 'A Simple Example') but the difference is that in EFA, the number of factors, nature of loading between loadings and the measures (variables) are not predefined or prefixed, while in the CFA they are. The illustration given in this book is basically EFA and similar demonstration of CFA is beyond the scope of this book.

Inequality Measures

$\mathbf{I}$nequality means the possession of resources differently by different people. In other words, inequality is the variation (dispersion) in the resources possessed by (or made available to) the people of a community. The most often quoted example of inequality is the income inequality. If each individual or family in a community earns or receives the same amount of income, then we say that the distribution (of income) is 'equal' and if some families earn more whereas others earn less, then we say that the distribution of income is 'unequal'. Measures of inequality deal with the measurement or quantification of the inequality (in resources) so that the measures can be compared between communities and over period. In this chapter, we discuss a few commonly used inequality measures namely the Lorenz curve, Gini coefficient, dissimilarity index and human development index (HDI).

LORENZ CURVE

The Lorenz curve and Gini coefficient are widely used as measures of the degree of inequality of wealth (or resource, not restricted to income alone) in a society. Suppose that a wealth of quantity X is distributed among n individuals. We say that the distribution of wealth is equal if every individual receives the exact quantity X/n, and all other distributions are unequal. The measurement of the extent of unequal distribution of wealth is often called the *measurement of inequality*, or *measure of concentration and diffusion* of wealth. The Lorenz curve is a graphical presentation of the inequality of wealth, and Gini coefficient is an index of the measurement of the inequality of wealth based on the Lorenz curve. In other words, the Lorenz curve illustrates the degree of inequality in the distribution of wealth in terms of graphical presentation, and the Gini coefficient quantifies the inequality in the distribution of wealth (into a single index) in terms of the area represented by the Lorenz curve.

The Lorenz curve was developed by Max O. Lorenz in 1905 for representing income distribution. With the individuals arranged in ascending order of the quantity of wealth possessed by them, the Lorenz curve is simply a graph showing the distribution of cumulative percentage of wealth as against the cumulative percentage of individuals possessing it. This curve is compared with a curve drawn with a hypothetical equal distribution of wealth possessed by the individuals. It looks like Figure 15.1. The horizontal axis (x-axis) measures the cumulative percentage of individuals and the vertical axis (y-axis) measures the corresponding cumulative percentage of wealth. The curve visually reveals how much of wealth is in possession of the bottom a percent of individuals and how much of wealth is in possession of the top b percent of individuals. A perfectly equal wealth distribution would be one in which every person has the same wealth. In this case, the bottom a percent of households would have a percent of the wealth and the top b percent of households would have b percent of the wealth. By contrast, a perfectly unequal distribution would be one in which one person has all the wealth and everyone else has none. The Lorenz curve is better explained using a graph based on a numerical example.

Figure 15.1 Lorenz Curve for Landholding Distribution of Households (Grouped Data)

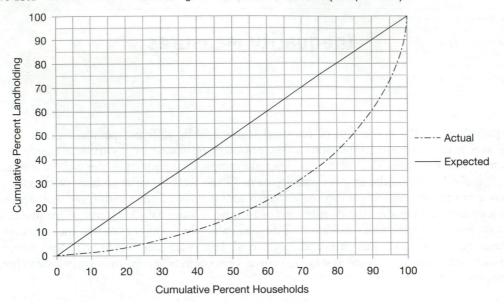

A Numerical Example

Table 15.1 gives the landholding of 1,417 households (if desired, landless households can also be included) and related calculations for drawing the Lorenz curve.

How to Get This Table Using SPSS?

Suppose, we have coded the actual landholding (say, in acres) of households in SPSS, or for that matter in any software. To get the total landholding by landholding groups, first run and obtain a frequency distribution of landholding of households and decide on the landholding class intervals (CIs) (the lesser the width of the intervals or the higher the number of CIs, the better the results), then recode the landholding variable into another variable with the desired CIs and run 'mean' statistics with the original landholding variable as dependent variable and the recoded landholding variable as independent variable. The total landholding in each group can be obtained either by choosing the option 'sum' in the program menu or by multiplying the mean by the corresponding frequency in the output.

Steps to Draw the Lorenz Curve

The following steps are required to draw the Lorenz curve:

1. Make appropriate number of landholding groups with lower and upper limits (Columns 1 and 2).
2. Distribute the households by landholding groups (Column 3) and obtain mean landholding (Column 4), and using Columns 3 and 4, obtain the sum of total landholding by landholding group (Column 5).
3. Obtain cumulative distribution of households and also cumulative distribution of landholding by landholding group (Columns 6 and 7).

Table 15.1   Landholding Pattern of Rural Households in Maharashtra, NFHS-3

Landholding (in acres)		Number of Households	Mean Land-holding	Total Land-holding	Cumulative		% Cumulative	
Lower Limit	Upper Limit				House-holds	Land-holding	House-holds	Land-holding
(1)	(2)	(3)	(4)	(5)	(6)	(7)	(8)	(9)
0							0	0
0.1	1	272	0.82	223.5	272	223.5	19.2	3.1
1.1	2	297	1.88	559.7	569	783.2	40.2	10.8
2.1	3	193	2.87	553.0	762	1,336.2	53.8	18.4
3.1	4	140	3.90	545.7	902	1,881.9	63.7	26.0
4.1	5	153	4.95	757.7	1,055	2,639.6	74.5	36.4
5.1	6	58	5.99	347.5	1,113	2,987.1	78.5	41.2
6.1	8	85	7.50	637.7	1,198	3,624.8	84.5	50.0
8.1	10	88	9.76	858.5	1,286	4,483.3	90.8	61.9
10.1	15	62	13.11	812.8	1,348	5,296.1	95.1	73.1
15.1	20	35	18.23	638.0	1,383	5,934.1	97.6	81.9
20.1	25	14	23.86	334.0	1,397	6,268.1	98.6	86.5
25.1	30	7	29.29	205.0	1,404	6,473.1	99.1	89.3
30.1	40	4	36.75	147.0	1,408	6,620.1	99.4	91.4
40.1	50	2	47.50	95.0	1,410	6,715.1	99.5	92.7
50.1	60	4	57.50	230.0	1,414	6,945.1	99.8	95.9
60.1	80	2	75.00	150.0	1,416	7,095.1	99.9	97.9
80.1	999	1	150.00	150.0	1,417	7,245.1	100.0	100.0
Total		1,417	5.11	7,245.1	1,417	7,245.1	100.0	100.0

4. Add two more columns (Columns 8 and 9) and also add a row on top of the data-range of each column and fill the cells of Columns 1, 8 and 9 with the value zero (for origin).

5. In Columns 8 and 9, cumulate the 'percentage of households' and 'percentage of landholding' based on Columns 6 and 7.

6. Insert a graph type 'scatter with smooth lines' in MS Excel (Menu: Insert=> Charts=> Scatter=> Smooth lines).

7. Right click on the graph, choose 'Select data' and add two 'Data series' as follows:

    a. Series 1: Cumulative percentage of households (Column 8) on the x-axis and cumulative percentage of landholding (Column 9) on the y-axis. This will give the actual landholding distribution curve.

    b. Series 2: Cumulative percentage of households on the x-axis and again cumulative percentage of households on the y-axis (the same Column 8 on both the axes). This will give the equal distribution (straight line) curve.

8. Format the graph as shown, or as desired. This is the Lorenz curve (Figure 15.1).

Some Observations from the Graph

The area between the diagonal straight line and the curved line (see Figure 15.1) represents the amount of inequality in the landholding of households. The inequality is nil (zero) if the curved line falls on the diagonal straight line. The inequality is 100 percent if the curved line falls on the horizontal x-axis. In general, the larger the area between the diagonal straight line and the curved line, the larger the inequality (here landholding of households). From the curve, we could see that 40 percent of the households (40 on the x-axis) possess approximately 10 percent of the land (10 on the y-axis), that is, the bottom 40 percent of the households own just 10 percent of the total land area. On the other hand, from the right end, we could see that the upper 10 percent of the households (90 on the x-axis) correspond to approximately $100 - 60 = 40$ percent of the landholding (60 on the y-axis), that is, the top 10 percent of the households own as much as 40 percent of the total land area. Please note that here, a household means a landholding household (excluding landless households).

GINI COEFFICIENT

The Gini coefficient, or Gini index or Gini ratio or Gini concentration ratio, is a *measure of statistical dispersion* often used to measure social and economic inequality in societies or populations. The Gini coefficient is defined as the ratio of the two parts of the diagonal area on the Lorenz curve. If the area between the line of perfect equality and Lorenz curve is A, and the area below the Lorenz curve is B (see Figure 15.2), then the Gini coefficient is $\dfrac{A}{(A+B)}$.

If the cumulative distribution of the individuals and their wealth are expressed in terms of units (and not in terms of percentages), the total area of the x-axis and y-axis of the Lorenz curve (rectangular chart area as a whole) is one and the area below the diagonal is 0.5, that is, $A+B=0.5$. Then the Gini coefficient is $G=A/(A+B)=A/(0.5)$. Multiplying both numerator and denominator by 2, we get $G=2*A/(2*0.5)=2A/1=2A$. It is clear from the graph that $G=2A=1-2B$. It is the whole rectangular area (1) minus two times the B area.

Let there be r ranges (groups or CIs) of wealth placed in ascending order with $k=1$ to r. In the example, the landholding groups ranges are 0.1–1.0, 1.1–2.0 and so on, and the number

Figure 15.2 Calculation of Gini Coefficient Using the Lorenz Curve

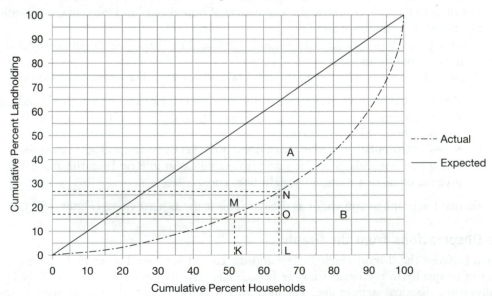

of ranges is $r=17$. Now, let us partition the B area into 17 slices and each slice will look like the figure represented by the points K, L, N and M in the figure. Although the line MN is not a straight line, we can assume it as a straight line for practical purposes as it is very short, that is, the figure KLNM can be assumed as a trapezium (a quadrilateral with two sides parallel). Now, the area of the trapezium KLNM is the area of the rectangle KLMO plus the area of the right angled triangle MNO. Alternatively, the area of the trapezium KLNM is KL * (LO+NO/2). The same principle is applied in calculating the area under B for obtaining the Gini coefficient.

Let X_k and Y_k be the cumulative percentage of individuals and wealth, respectively, corresponding to the class k. The quantity $X_k - X_{k-1}$ is the percentage of individuals in the $k-1$ to k wealth range (say P_k) and $(Y_k + Y_{k-1})/2$ is the average amount of wealth (say $Q_k/2$) corresponding to the $X_k - X_{k-1}$ individuals (see Table 15.2). So, the area B is the sum of product of all P_k and Q_k values. If the data are in percentages, we have to divide the sum by 100 * 100 = 10,000 so that the total number of individuals and total wealth are set to one each.

That is, $$B = \frac{1}{10,000} \sum (P_k * Q_k)/2$$

and, $$G = 1 - 2B = 1 - \frac{2}{10,000} \sum (P_k * Q_k)/2 = 1 - \frac{1}{10,000} \sum (P_k * Q_k)$$

that is, $$G = 1 - \frac{1}{10,000} \sum (P_k * Q_k)$$

(or) $$G = 1 - \frac{1}{10,000} \sum_{k=1}^{r} (X_k - X_{k-1}) * (Y_k + Y_{k-1}),$$

where $X_0 = 0$ and $Y_0 = 0$.

The area $2B$ ranges from 0 to 10,000 in percentage terms, or 0 to 1 in unit (one) terms, and, hence, the Gini coefficient G ranges from 0 to 1. The coefficient $G=0$ corresponds to perfect equality (i.e., every individual having exactly the same wealth) and $G=1$ corresponds to perfect inequality (i.e., one individual possessing the entire wealth and all others having nothing). Hence, a low value of the Gini coefficient is an indication of low inequality, or more equal distribution of wealth, while a high value is an indication of a high unequal distribution of wealth.

As far as the income/wealth distribution is concerned, the Gini coefficient requires that no individual to have a negative net income or wealth, and if so, it should be taken as zero. A world-wide analysis of the income distribution showed that the Gini coefficient ranged from approximately 0.232 for Denmark to 0.707 for Namibia. Most free market nations have a Gini coefficient between 0.25 and 0.50.

The Gini coefficient is often expressed in the percentage terms. So a Gini coefficient 0.232 can be expressed as 23.2 percent, or 23.2%, or 23.2 by omitting the symbol '%' or the word 'percent'.

A Numerical Example

Following the previous example, Table 15.2 gives the landholding of 1,417 households (if desired, landless households can also be included) and related calculations for obtaining the Gini coefficient.

Steps of the Calculation

1. Add a row on top of the data range in the table with all values zero (0), that is, as the top shaded row in Table 15.2.

Table 15.2   Calculation of Gini Coefficient

Group (k)	Households	Total Land	%Cum HHs (X)	%Cum Land (Y)	$P_k=(X_k-X_{k-1})$	$Q_k=(Y_k+Y_{k-1})$	P_k*Q_k
0			0.0	0.0	0.0	0.0	
1	272	223.5	19.2	3.1	19.2	3.1	59.2
2	297	559.7	40.2	10.8	21.0	13.9	291.2
3	193	553.0	53.8	18.4	13.6	29.3	398.4
4	140	545.7	63.7	26.0	9.9	44.4	438.8
5	153	757.7	74.5	36.4	10.8	62.4	673.8
6	58	347.5	78.5	41.2	4.1	77.7	317.9
7	85	637.7	84.5	50.0	6.0	91.3	547.4
8	88	858.5	90.8	61.9	6.2	111.9	695.0
9	62	812.8	95.1	73.1	4.4	135.0	590.6
10	35	638.0	97.6	81.9	2.5	155.0	382.9
11	14	334.0	98.6	86.5	1.0	168.4	166.4
12	7	205.0	99.1	89.3	0.5	175.9	86.9
13	4	147.0	99.4	91.4	0.3	180.7	51.0
14	2	95.0	99.5	92.7	0.1	184.1	26.0
15	4	230.0	99.8	95.9	0.3	188.5	53.2
16	2	150.0	99.9	97.9	0.1	193.8	27.4
17	1	150.0	100.0	100.0	0.1	197.9	14.0
	1,417	7,245.1	100.0	100.0			4,802.2

Note: $G = 1 - 4,820.2/10,000 = 0.518$ (or) 51.8 percent.

2. Obtain the cumulative number of cases and cumulative landholding (optional, not shown in this example).
3. Obtain the percentage of cumulative households and the percentage of cumulative landholding (the X and Y Columns).
4. Calculate P, the difference of X values of consecutive two rows (of Column X).
5. Calculate Q, the sum of Y values of two consecutive rows (of Column Y).
6. Calculate $P*Q$, the product of P and Q values of each row and obtain their sum.
7. Calculate $G = 1 - \text{sum}/10,000$. Since the X and Y values are in percentage terms, we have to divide the sum by $100*100 = 10,000$ to make it for unity.
8. To express G in percentage terms, multiply the value by 100.

DISSIMILARITY INDEX

The index of dissimilarity or dissimilarity index (DI) is a measure of the summary difference between two related percentage distributions. In the Lorenz curve, the dissimilarity index is the sum of the vertical deviation (difference) between the Lorenz curve and the line of perfect equality, and so the index of dissimilarity is also known as the *summation of Lorenz differences*.

Let there be n units in a region (say n districts in a state). Let X_i be the number of households in unit i and Y_i be the total wealth of these households. Let the x_i and y_i ($i = 1$ to n) be the corresponding percentage values (percentage of households and percentage of wealth). Then $x - y$ is the difference in the corresponding percentage values and $|x - y|$ is the absolute (negative sign ignored) difference. Table 15.3 shows the details. (Please note that the greyed rows are for later use only.)

Table 15.3   Distribution of Households (*X*) and Wealth (*Y*)

Unit	Households	Wealth	Percent Households	Percent Wealth	Difference
i	*X*	*Y*	*x*	*y*	$\lvert x-y \rvert$
1					
2					
...					
j	X_j	Y_j	$x_j = 100$	$y_j = 0$	$\lvert x_j - y_j \rvert = 100$
...					
k	X_k	Y_k	$x_k = 0$	$y_k = 100$	$\lvert x_k - y_k \rvert = 100$
...					
n					
Total			100.0	100.0	

The index of dissimilarity is half of the sum of the differences in the two percentage values, that is,

$$\text{DI} = \frac{1}{2} \sum_{i=1}^{n} \lvert x_i - y_i \rvert.$$

The sum of $\lvert x_i - y_i \rvert$ ranges from 0 to 200. When the distribution of x_i and y_i is the same (i.e., X_i and Y_i are proportionate to their respective totals), then $x_i = y_i$ and $\lvert x_i - y_i \rvert = 0$ for every *i*, and the sum (of the differences) is 0. On the other extreme, let us assume that when $i = j$, $x_j = 100$ and $y_j = 0$, and when $i = k$, $x_k = 0$ and $y_k = 100$ (where *k* is different from *j*). In this case, $x_i = 0$ and $y_i = 0$ for all cases other than *j* and *k*, so that the sum of all x_i ($i = 1$ to *n*, including *j* and *k*) is 100 and sum of all y_i ($i = 1$ to *n*, including *j* and *k*) is 100. Now, $\lvert x_j - y_j \rvert = 100 - 0 = 100$, $\lvert x_k - y_k \rvert = \lvert 0 - 100 \rvert = 100$ and $\lvert x_i - y_i \rvert = 0$ for all units other than *j* and *k*. Thus, the total difference is 200. That is why the sum of differences is divided by 2 to make the DI to range from 0 to 100.

The closer the DI is to 100, the more dissimilar or unequal the distribution of wealth between the units, and the closer the DI is to 0, the more similar or equal the distribution of wealth between units. However, which are the units that are more dissimilar and which are more similar can be inferred by sorting the data in the ascending or descending order of the values of $\lvert x_i - y_i \rvert$.

A Numerical Example

Table 15.4 gives the distribution of sample rural households (including landless households) and their total landholding by major states of India.

Dissimilarity index = 24.996/2 = 12.5. The inference is that the inter-state difference in the landholding pattern of households is only marginal. However, states such as Uttar Pradesh and Bihar have shown higher dissimilarity ($\lvert x - y \rvert$ is around 3), while many states have shown very less dissimilarity of $\lvert x - y \rvert < 1$.

HUMAN DEVELOPMENT INDEX (HDI)

The human development index (HDI) is a summary measure of human development in social and economic terms. It measures the average achievements in a country or in a territory in three basic dimensions of human development: a long and healthy life (life expectancy), access to knowledge (schooling) and a decent standard of living (income). The HDI is the geometric mean of normalised indices measuring achievements in each of these three dimensions. The HDI presented here

Table 15.4 Distribution of Sample Rural Households and Their Total Landholding by Major States of India, NFHS-3

State	Households	Landholding (acres)	Percent Households	Percent Landholding	Difference
	X	Y	x	y	|x−y|
Tamil Nadu	1,053	82,590.3	2.98	2.62	0.355
Haryana	1,127	135,972.6	3.19	4.32	1.130
Punjab	1,148	91,623.2	3.25	2.91	0.337
Andhra Pradesh	1,279	141,423.3	3.62	4.49	0.873
Gujarat	1,338	123,749.6	3.78	3.93	0.146
Assam	1,380	85,643.2	3.90	2.72	1.183
Bihar	1,441	222,203.1	4.07	7.05	2.979
Jharkhand	1,537	88,846.3	4.34	2.82	1.525
Uttaranchal	1,561	71,823.0	4.41	2.28	2.133
West Bengal	1,600	155,001.5	4.52	4.92	0.397
Maharashtra	1,642	119,509.3	4.64	3.79	0.848
Himachal Pradesh	1,899	85,201.6	5.37	2.70	2.664
Jammu and Kashmir	1,907	105,584.8	5.39	3.35	2.039
Chhattisgarh	1,960	130,017.9	5.54	4.13	1.414
Rajasthan	2,107	216,024.0	5.96	6.86	0.901
Madhya Pradesh	2,197	226,461.6	6.21	7.19	0.977
Odisha	2,209	215,953.5	6.24	6.85	0.610
Karnataka	2,475	258,519.9	7.00	8.21	1.209
Uttar Pradesh	5,515	594,364.3	15.59	18.87	3.276
Total	35,375	3,150,513.0	100.0	100.0	24.996

Note: Data are obtained by processing the unit level dataset of NFHS-3. The calculation of $|x−y|$ and total are very obvious, and hence, not discussed.

Figure 15.3 Specific Indicators Used in the HDI

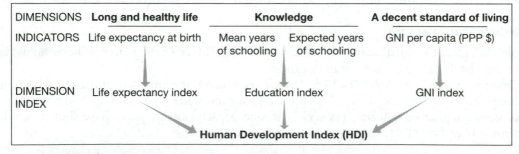

Source: UNDP (2011).

is a replica of HDI used in the Human Development Report 2011 of the UNDP. The specific indicators used in the HDI are depicted in Figure 15.3.

The first step is to create subindices for each dimension. For this, minimum and maximum values need to be set in order to transform the indicators into standard indices that will range from 0 to 1. Because the geometric mean is used for aggregation, the maximum value does not affect the relative comparison (in percentage terms) between any two countries or periods of time. The maximum values are set to the actual observed maximum values of the indicators from the countries in the time series, that is, 1980–2011. The minimum values will affect comparisons, so values that can be appropriately conceived of as subsistence values or 'natural' zeros are used. Progress is, thus, measured against minimum levels that a society needs to survive over time.

The minimum values are set at 20 years for life expectancy, at 0 years for education variables and at $100 for per capita GNI. The life expectancy of a minimum of 20 years is based on long-run historical evidence. Societies can subsist without formal education, and, hence, the minimum education is set at zero. The low value for income can be justified by a considerable amount of unmeasured subsistence and non-market production in economies close to the minimum, not captured in the official data. The maximum values are: for life expectancy 83.4 (Japan, 2011), mean years of schooling 13.1 (Czech Republic, 2005), expected years of schooling 18, combined education index 0.978 (New Zealand, 2010) and per capita income (PPP $) 107,721 (Qatar, 2011). Having defined the minimum and maximum values, the subindices are calculated as follows:

$$\text{Dimension index} = \frac{\text{Progress made so far}}{\text{Maximum range}}$$

$$= \frac{\text{Actual value} - \text{Minimum value}}{\text{Maximum value} - \text{Minimum value}}$$

For India, the calculations are made as follows. The values for India for the year 2010 as given in the Human Development Report are as follows.

India (2011)	Value
Life expectancy at birth	65.4
Mean years of schooling	4.4
Expected years of schooling	10.3
Gross national income (GNI) per capita	3,468

$$\text{Life expectancy index} = \frac{65.4 - 20}{83.4 - 20} = 0.7161$$

$$\text{Mean years of schooling index} = \frac{4.4 - 0}{13.1 - 0} = 0.3359$$

$$\text{Expected years of schooling index} = \frac{10.3 - 0}{18 - 0} = 0.5722$$

$$\text{Education index} = \frac{\sqrt{0.3359 \times 0.5722} - 0}{0.978 - 0} = 0.4483$$

$$\text{GNI index} = \frac{\text{Log}(3,468) - \text{Log}(100)}{\text{Log}(107,721) - \text{Log}(100)} = 0.5079$$

$$\text{Human Development Index} = \sqrt[3]{0.7161 * 0.4483 * 0.5079} = 0.5463$$

Note: The GNI index is calculated using adjusted GNI per capita measured in US$. Because achieving a respectable level of human development does not require unlimited income, so a higher level of income is attached with a lesser weightage for computing the index. This is done by considering the logarithm of the income. The following table gives the *ln* (natural logarithm) values for select numbers.

X	1	10	100	1,000	10,000	100,000
$\ln(X)$	0.00	2.30	4.61	6.91	9.21	11.51

It is clear from the table that the number 100 is 10 times the number 10 but $\ln(100)$ is just twice $\ln(10)$. Similarly, 10,000 is 100 times the number 100, but $\ln(10,000)$ is just twice $\ln(100)$, that is, when the values of X are multiplicative, the values of $\ln(X)$ are only additive. Hence, a higher income is given lesser weightage.

INEQUALITY-ADJUSTED HUMAN DEVELOPMENT INDEX (IHDI)

The IHDI adjusts the HDI for inequality in the distribution of each dimension of HDI across the population. It is computed as a 'geometric mean' of the 'geometric means' with the geometric means calculated based on the indices for the subgroups of the population. While HDI can be determined based on the overall indices of the three components of HDI (namely, life expectancy at birth, mean years of schooling, expected years of schooling and GNI per capita), the IHDI is calculated as an adjustment to the HDI. The calculation of adjustment factors requires information at an individual level, or at least the indices are available for the subgroups of the population (say, by state). The adjustment factor ensures that improvements or deteriorations in the distribution of human development within a particular group will be reflected in the changes in the overall measure of human development.

Let $X_1, X_2,..., X_n$ be n observations, then the arithmetic mean $\bar{X}$ is defined as the sum of all observations divided by the number of observations, that is,

$$\bar{X} = \frac{X_1 + X_2 + X_3 + \cdots + X_n}{n}.$$

And the geometric mean $\widehat{X}$ (X – cap) is defined as the nth root of the product of all the n observations. The measure is not discussed under 'Measures of Central Tendency and Dispersion' as it is rarely used in social sciences.

$$\widehat{X} = \sqrt[n]{X_1 * X_2 * X_3 *\cdots * X_n}.$$

The adjustment factor for X, say X_a, is defined as the geometric mean divided by the arithmetic mean, that is,

$$X_a = \frac{\widehat{X}}{\bar{X}}.$$

That is, the 'geometric mean' is the 'adjustment factor' times the 'arithmetic mean' of the variable, and, thus, the adjustment factor acts as a weight factor in the IHDI. It is clear that for determining the IHDI, we need adequate information about all the subgroups of the population.

The next step is to obtain the inequality-adjusted dimension index, which is the dimension index multiplied by the inequality-adjustment factor, and finally obtain the IHDI as a geometric mean of the inequality-adjusted dimension indices.

As deriving the IHDI requires subgroup-wise information and also it involves lengthy calculations, it is not demonstrated here. Furthermore, mathematically, if any one observation is zero, the geometric mean as a whole is zero and if some observations are negative, then the multiplicative value will be negative (if the negative value observations are in odd number) and geometric mean is indeterminate (undefined or cannot be determined). In order to avoid these problems, some adjustments are made (minimum values are set) in the original data before deriving the adjustment factors. Such a numerical example is beyond the scope of this book.

While the HDI can be viewed as an index of 'potential' human development that could be obtained if achievements were distributed equally, the IHDI is the actual level of human development (accounting for inequality in the distribution of achievements across subgroups in the population or society). The IHDI will be equal to the HDI when there is no inequality in the distribution of achievement across people in the society, but falls below the HDI as inequality rises. The loss in potential human development due to inequality is the difference between the HDI and IHDI, usually expressed as a percentage. Thus, HDI reflects the level of 'overall development', the difference between HDI and IHDI (often expressed as a percentage) reflects the 'inequality in the development between the subgroups of the population'.

Appendices

APPENDIX A: PERMUTATIONS AND COMBINATIONS

Factorial

Factorial is a simple way of writing the product of all positive whole numbers from 1 to a given number n. Accordingly, 'factorial n' (or 'n factorial' or symbolically $n!$) is defined as the product of all the integers from 1 to n, that is,

$$n! = 1 * 2 * 3 * \cdots * (n-2) * (n-1) * n$$

or

$$n! = (n) * (n-1) * (n-2) * \cdots * (3) * (2) * (1).$$

Examples:

$$5! = 5 \times 4 \times 3 \times 2 \times 1 = 120$$
$$2! = 1 \times 2 = 2$$
$$1! = 1$$
$$0! = 1 \text{ (always)}.$$

Permutations (Ordered Arrangements)

An arrangement (or ordering) of a set of objects is called a permutation. In a permutation, the order of arrangement of objects is important but repetitions are not allowed. For example, consider arranging three letters: A, B and C. These three letters can be arranged in six ways. ABC, ACB, BCA, BAC, CAB, CBA, CBA. Generally, the number of permutations of n distinct objects taken r at a time, denoted by P_r^n (or ^nP_r or $_nP_r$), is given by

$$P_r^n = n(n-1)(n-2)\cdots(n-\overline{r-1})$$
$$P_r^n = n(n-1)(n-2)\cdots(n-r+1)$$
$$P_r^n = \frac{n(n-1)(n-2)\cdots(n-r+1)(n-r)\cdots(2)(1)}{(n-r)(n-r-1)\cdots(2)(1)} = \frac{n!}{(n-r)!}.$$

Notes:

$$P_n^n = \frac{n!}{(n-n)!} = \frac{n!}{(0)!} = \frac{n!}{1} = n! \quad (\text{since } 0! = 1)$$

$$P_1^n = \frac{n!}{(n-1)!} = \frac{n(n-1)!}{(n-1)!} = n$$

$$P_0^n = \frac{n!}{(n-0)!} = \frac{n!}{n!} = 1.$$

Combinations (Unordered Selections)

A combination of n objects taken r at a time is a selection of r objects from n objects without considering the order or arrangement of the objects, that is, the order is not important.

For example, consider a combination of two letters from three letters: A, B and C. The combinations of two letters are AB, AC and BC. Note that AB or BA, AC or CA and BC or CB does not matter.

Generally, the number of combinations of n distinct objects taken r at a time is denoted by $\binom{n}{r}$ and sometimes as C_r^n, ^nC_r or $_nC_r$:

$$C_r^n = \frac{n!}{r!(n-r)!}.$$

Notes:

$$C_r^n = \frac{n!}{r!(n-r)!} = \frac{P_r^n}{r!}$$

$$C_n^n = \frac{n!}{n!(n-n)!} = \frac{n!}{n!(0)!} = \frac{n!}{n!} = 1$$

$$C_1^n = \frac{n!}{1!(n-1)!} = \frac{n(n-1)!}{(n-1)!} = n$$

$$C_0^n = \frac{n!}{0!(n-0)!} = \frac{n!}{n!} = 1.$$

APPENDIX B: ONE-WAY ANOVA TECHNICAL ASPECTS

If there is only one explanatory variable, then the analysis of variance (ANOVA) procedure is called one-way or one-factor ANOVA. Let us assume that we have a sample of n cases, and these cases are classified according to the categorical variable X (independent variable) having k groups. Let the number of cases in the first group be n_1, in the second group be n_2, in the kth group be n_k and so on, so that $n_1 + n_2 + \cdots + n_k = n$. Now, the n values of the dependent variable Y are distributed into the k groups of the independent variable X as follows.

Table B.1   Distribution of the Dependent Variable Y into the K Groups of the Independent Variable X

X (Groups) (1)	Cases (2)	Y (Values) (3)	Group Mean (4)	Group Sum of Squares (5)
1	n_1	$Y_{11}, Y_{12}, \ldots, Y_{1n}$	$\overline{Y}_1 = \sum_{j=1}^{n_1} Y_{1j}$	$SS_1 = \sum_{j=1}^{n_1}(Y_{1j} - \overline{Y}_1)^2$
2	n_2	$Y_{21}, Y_{22}, \ldots, Y_{2n_2}$	$\overline{Y}_2 = \sum_{j=1}^{n_2} Y_{2j}$	$SS_2 = \sum_{j=1}^{n_2}(Y_{2j} - \overline{Y}_2)^2$
...	...	...	...	...
k	n_k	$Y_{k1}, Y_{k2}, \ldots, Y_{kn_k}$	$\overline{Y}_k = \sum_{j=1}^{n_k} Y_{kj}$	$SS_k = \sum_{j=1}^{n_k}(Y_{kj} - \overline{Y}_k)^2$

From Column 2, the total sample size n is given by

$$n = n_1 + n_2 + \cdots + n_k = \sum_{i=1}^{k} n_i.$$

From Column 3, the mean of Y values is given by

$$\bar{Y} = \frac{1}{n}\{(Y_{11}, Y_{12}, \ldots, Y_{1n_1}) + (Y_{21}, Y_{22}, \ldots, Y_{2n_2}) + \cdots + (Y_{k1}, Y_{k2}, \ldots, Y_{kn_k})\}.$$

That is, we are summing the Y values in each group, then we add the summed values of each group and then divide the grand-sum value by n. This can be written using the summation notation as

$$\bar{Y} = \frac{1}{n}\sum_{i=1}^{k}\sum_{j=1}^{n_i} Y_{ij}.$$

Similarly, we can write the total sum of squares of Y's (deviation from overall mean $\bar{Y}$), termed SS_T, as

$$SS_T = \sum_{i=1}^{k}\sum_{j=1}^{n_i}(Y_{ij} - \bar{Y})^2.$$

Please note that the term $\frac{1}{n}$ or $\frac{1}{n-1}$ is missing in the equation because here we are considering sum of squares only and not variance (σ^2 or s^2). Now,

$$\sum_{i=1}^{k}\sum_{j=1}^{n_i}(Y_{ij} - \bar{Y})^2 = \sum_{i=1}^{k}\sum_{j=1}^{n_i}\{(Y_{ij} - \bar{Y}_i) + (\bar{Y}_i - \bar{Y})\}^2.$$

That is, we have just subtracted and added the term $\bar{Y}_i$ on the RHS so that the value of the RHS remains the same. We know that $(a+b)^2 = a^2 + b^2 + 2ab$ and when this formula is applied to the RHS, the equation becomes

$$\sum_{i=1}^{k}\sum_{j=1}^{n_i}(Y_{ij} - \bar{Y})^2 = \sum_{i=1}^{k}\sum_{j=1}^{n_i}\{(Y_{ij} - \bar{Y}_i)^2 + (\bar{Y}_i - \bar{Y})^2 + 2(Y_{ij} - \bar{Y}_i)(\bar{Y}_i - \bar{Y})\}$$

$$\sum_{i=1}^{k}\sum_{j=1}^{n_i}(Y_{ij} - \bar{Y})^2 = \sum_{i=1}^{k}\sum_{j=1}^{n_i}(Y_{ij} - \bar{Y}_i)^2 + \sum_{i=1}^{k}\sum_{j=1}^{n_i}(\bar{Y}_i - \bar{Y})^2 + 2\sum_{i=1}^{k}\sum_{j=1}^{n_i}(Y_{ij} - \bar{Y}_i)(\bar{Y}_i - \bar{Y})$$

$$\sum_{i=1}^{k}\sum_{j=1}^{n_i}(Y_{ij} - \bar{Y})^2 = \sum_{i=1}^{k}\sum_{j=1}^{n_i}(Y_{ij} - \bar{Y}_i)^2 + \sum_{i=1}^{k}\sum_{j=1}^{n_i}(\bar{Y}_i - \bar{Y})^2$$

It is to be noted that the rightmost $2ab$ term reduces to 0 (not solved here).

The LHS is the sum of squares of the deviation of individual observations from the overall mean and is called the total sum of squares (TSS) or total variation. The first term on the RHS is the sum of squares of the deviation of the individual observations from their respective group means and is called the within-group sum of squares (WSS) or within-group variation. The second term on the RHS is the sum of squares of deviation of the group means from the overall mean and is called between-group sum of squares (BSS) or between-group variation, that is, the total variation is the sum of within-group variation and between-group variation or TSS=WSS+BSS.

The quantity BSS is associated with $(k-1)$ degrees of freedom and the quantity WSS is associated with $(n-k)$ degrees of freedom.

The ratio $\dfrac{\text{BSS}/(k-1)}{\text{WSS}/(n-k)}$ follows the F-distribution with $(k-1, n-k)$ degrees of freedom.

The F-test is a simultaneous test of the hypothesis that confirms that all the group means are the same, that is, the null hypothesis is

$$H_0: \overline{Y_1} = \overline{Y_2} = \ldots = \overline{Y_k}.$$

Table B.2 shows ANOVA.

Correlation Ratio

Suppose that n observations of a numerical variable (often termed as dependent variable) Y are classified into k groups of a categorical variable (often termed as independent variable). Let the individual observations be $y_1, y_2,\ldots, y_n$ and the number of observations in each category be $n_1, n_2,\ldots, n_k$, so that $n_1+n_2+\cdots+n_k=n$. Let $\overline{Y}$ be the overall mean and $\overline{Y_1}, \overline{Y_2},\ldots,\overline{Y_k}$ be the group means. We have seen in one-way ANOVA that

$$\sum_{i=1}^{k}\sum_{j=1}^{n_i}(Y_{ij} - \overline{Y})^2 = \sum_{i=1}^{k}\sum_{j=1}^{n_i}(Y_{ij} - \overline{Y_i})^2 + \sum_{i=1}^{k}\sum_{j=1}^{n_i}(\overline{Y_i} - \overline{Y})^2$$

or TSS = WSS + BSS.
The correlation ratio η (eta) is obtained from

$$\eta^2 = \frac{\text{BSS}}{\text{TSS}} = \frac{\sum_{i=1}^{k}\sum_{j=1}^{n_i}(\overline{Y_i} - \overline{Y})^2}{\sum_{i=1}^{k}\sum_{j=1}^{n_i}(Y_{ij} - \overline{Y})^2}.$$

The term $(\overline{Y_i} - \overline{Y})^2$ on the numerator is free from the subscript j and so for the range $j=1$ to n_i, the sum of the term $(\overline{Y_i} - \overline{Y})^2$ is n_i times $(\overline{Y_i} - \overline{Y})^2$, that is, $\sum_{j=1}^{n_i}(\overline{Y_i} - \overline{Y})^2 = n_i(\overline{Y_i} - \overline{Y})^2$. Further in the denominator, the summation of the term $(Y_{ij} - \overline{Y})^2$ is for the whole range from 1 to n and so the term in the denominator can be written with only one subscript $j=1$ to n as $\sum_{j=1}^{n}(Y_j - \overline{Y})^2$. So, the equation for the correlation ratio can be written as

$$\eta^2 = \frac{\sum_{i=1}^{k}n_i(\overline{Y_i} - \overline{Y})^2}{\sum_{j=1}^{n}(Y_j - \overline{Y})^2}.$$

The denominator is the sum of squares of the deviation of the individual observations from the overall mean or *total variation* in Y. The numerator is the sum of squares of the deviation of group

Table B.2 Analysis of Variance

Source of Variation	Variation or Sum of Squares	Degrees of Freedom	Mean Sum of Squares or Variance	F-ratio
Between groups	$BSS = \sum_{i=1}^{k} \sum_{j=1}^{n_i} (\overline{Y_i} - \overline{Y})^2$	$k-1$	$MBSS = \dfrac{ESS}{k-1}$	
Within group	$WSS = \sum_{i=1}^{k} \sum_{j=1}^{n_i} (Y_{ij} - \overline{Y_i})^2$	$n-k$	$MWSS = \dfrac{USS}{n-k}$	$F = \dfrac{MBSS}{MWSS}$
Total	$TSS = \sum_{i=1}^{k} \sum_{j=1}^{n_i} (Y_{ij} - \overline{Y})^2$	$n-1$	NA	$(k-1, n-k)$ df

means from the overall mean or *between-group variation* (also called *group means variation*). So the correlation ratio is the ratio of between-group variation to total variation.

APPENDIX C

Table C.1 Random Number Table (5 Digits)

Column	1	2	3	4	5	6	7	8	9	10
1	13962	70992	65172	28053	02190	83634	66012	70305	66761	88344
2	43905	46941	72300	11641	43548	30455	07686	31840	03261	89139
3	00504	48658	38051	59408	16508	82979	92002	63606	41078	86326
4	61274	57238	47267	35303	29066	02140	60867	39847	50968	96719
5	43753	21159	16239	50595	62509	61207	86816	29902	23395	72640
6	83503	51662	21636	68192	84294	38754	84755	34053	94582	29215
7	36807	71420	35804	44862	23577	79551	42003	58684	09271	68396
8	19110	55680	18792	41487	16614	83053	00812	16749	45347	88199
9	82615	86984	93290	87971	60022	35415	20852	02909	99476	45568
10	05621	26584	36493	63013	68181	57702	49510	75304	38724	15712
11	06936	37293	55875	71213	83025	46063	74665	12178	10741	58362
12	84981	60458	16194	92403	80951	80068	47076	23310	74899	87929
13	66354	88441	96191	04794	14714	64749	43097	83976	83281	72038
14	49602	94109	36460	62353	00721	66980	82554	90270	12312	56299
15	78430	72391	96973	70437	97803	78683	04670	70667	58912	21883
16	33331	51803	15934	75807	46561	80188	78984	29317	27971	16440
17	62843	84445	56652	91797	45284	25842	96246	73504	21631	81223
18	19528	15445	77764	33446	41204	70067	33354	70680	66664	75486
19	16737	01887	50934	43306	75190	86997	56561	79018	34273	25196
20	99389	06685	45945	62000	76228	60645	87750	46329	46544	95665
21	36160	38196	77705	28891	12106	56281	86222	66116	39626	06080
22	05505	45420	44016	79662	92069	27628	50002	32540	19848	27319
23	85962	19758	92795	00458	71289	05884	37963	23322	73243	98185
24	28763	04900	54460	22083	89279	43492	00066	40857	86568	49336
25	42222	40446	82240	79159	44168	38213	46839	26598	29983	67645
26	43626	40039	51492	36488	70280	24218	14596	04744	89336	35630
27	97761	43444	95895	24102	07006	71923	04800	32062	41425	66862
28	49275	44270	52512	03951	21651	53867	73531	70073	45542	22831
29	15797	75134	39856	73527	78417	36208	59510	76913	22499	68467

30	04497	24853	43879	07613	26400	17180	18880	66083	02196	10638
31	95468	87411	30647	88711	01765	57688	60665	57636	36070	37285
32	01420	74218	71047	14401	74537	14820	45248	78007	65911	38583
33	74633	40171	97092	79137	30698	97915	36305	42613	87251	75608
34	46662	99688	59576	04887	02310	35508	69481	30300	94047	57096
35	10853	10393	03013	90372	89639	65800	88532	71789	59964	50681
36	68583	01032	67938	29733	71176	35699	10551	15091	52947	20134
37	75818	78982	24258	93051	02081	83890	66944	99856	87950	13952
38	16395	16837	00538	57133	89398	78205	72122	99655	25294	20941
39	53892	15105	40963	69267	85534	00533	27130	90420	72584	84576
40	66009	26869	91829	65078	89616	49016	14200	97469	88307	92282

Source: The Rand Corporation, *A Million Random Digits with 100,000 Normal Deviates* (New York: The Free Press, 1955).

Box C.1: Drawing Random Numbers from Random a Number Table

A random number table is a table of random numbers of fixed digits (say three, four or five digits) arranged in rows and columns (see Table C.1). These numbers are already generated at random and so there is no need to select numbers from it at random again, but just select numbers sequentially either row-wise or column-wise starting from a random location in the table. For this, first choose a random number table. Having the number of digits in the random numbers is the same or higher as that of the number of digits in the population size. For example, let the population size be 450. Since it is a three-digit number, choose a three or higher digit random number table. For our example, we have selected a random number table of five digits. Then, randomly choose a row (say 5), a column (say 3), a direction (right or down, say, down). First, read the random number given in the fifth row of third column (it is 16239) and note the last three digits of the number (it is 239). If the number is between 1 and the population size (here 450), then select the unit having that serial number in the population (239 is less than 450 and so 239th unit is selected). Then read the next number in the chosen direction (here downwards, and the number is 21636) and note the last three digits (it is 636) and if the number is between 1 and the population size (450) and if the number is not yet selected, then select the unit having that serial number in the population; otherwise, discard the number (here the number 636 is greater than 450 and so discarded). Continue the process until the required number of units is selected.

APPENDIX D

Table D.1 Cumulative Standard Normal Probability (−ve Values)

Z	−0.09	−0.08	−0.07	−0.06	−0.05	−0.04	−0.03	−0.02	−0.01	0.00
−3.9	0.00003	0.00003	0.00004	0.00004	0.00004	0.00004	0.00004	0.00004	0.00005	0.00005
−3.8	0.00005	0.00005	0.00005	0.00006	0.00006	0.00006	0.00006	0.00007	0.00007	0.00007
−3.7	0.00008	0.00008	0.00008	0.00008	0.00009	0.00009	0.00010	0.00010	0.00010	0.00011
−3.6	0.00011	0.00012	0.00012	0.00013	0.00013	0.00014	0.00014	0.00015	0.00015	0.00016
−3.5	0.00017	0.00017	0.00018	0.00019	0.00019	0.00020	0.00021	0.00022	0.00022	0.00023
−3.4	0.00024	0.00025	0.00026	0.00027	0.00028	0.00029	0.00030	0.00031	0.00032	0.00034
−3.3	0.00035	0.00036	0.00038	0.00039	0.00040	0.00042	0.00043	0.00045	0.00047	0.00048
−3.2	0.00050	0.00052	0.00054	0.00056	0.00058	0.00060	0.00062	0.00064	0.00066	0.00069
−3.1	0.00071	0.00074	0.00076	0.00079	0.00082	0.00084	0.00087	0.00090	0.00094	0.00097
−3.0	0.00100	0.00104	0.00107	0.00111	0.00114	0.00118	0.00122	0.00126	0.00131	0.00135
−2.9	0.00139	0.00144	0.00149	0.00154	0.00159	0.00164	0.00169	0.00175	0.00181	0.00187
−2.8	0.00193	0.00199	0.00205	0.00212	0.00219	0.00226	0.00233	0.00240	0.00248	0.00256
−2.7	0.00264	0.00272	0.00280	0.00289	0.00298	0.00307	0.00317	0.00326	0.00336	0.00347
−2.6	0.00357	0.00368	0.00379	0.00391	0.00402	0.00415	0.00427	0.00440	0.00453	0.00466
−2.5	0.00480	0.00494	0.00508	0.00523	0.00539	0.00554	0.00570	0.00587	0.00604	0.00621
−2.4	0.00639	0.00657	0.00676	0.00695	0.00714	0.00734	0.00755	0.00776	0.00798	0.00820
−2.3	0.00842	0.00866	0.00889	0.00914	0.00939	0.00964	0.00990	0.01017	0.01044	0.01072
−2.2	0.01101	0.01130	0.01160	0.01191	0.01222	0.01255	0.01287	0.01321	0.01355	0.01390
−2.1	0.01426	0.01463	0.01500	0.01539	0.01578	0.01618	0.01659	0.01700	0.01743	0.01786
−2.0	0.01831	0.01876	0.01923	0.01970	0.02018	0.02068	0.02118	0.02169	0.02222	0.02275
−1.9	0.02330	0.02385	0.02442	0.02500	0.02559	0.02619	0.02680	0.02743	0.02807	0.02872
−1.8	0.02938	0.03005	0.03074	0.03144	0.03216	0.03288	0.03362	0.03438	0.03515	0.03593
−1.7	0.03673	0.03754	0.03836	0.03920	0.04006	0.04093	0.04182	0.04272	0.04363	0.04457
−1.6	0.04551	0.04648	0.04746	0.04846	0.04947	0.05050	0.05155	0.05262	0.05370	0.05480
−1.5	0.05592	0.05705	0.05821	0.05938	0.06057	0.06178	0.06301	0.06426	0.06552	0.06681
−1.4	0.06811	0.06944	0.07078	0.07215	0.07353	0.07493	0.07636	0.07780	0.07927	0.08076
−1.3	0.08226	0.08379	0.08534	0.08691	0.08851	0.09012	0.09176	0.09342	0.09510	0.09680
−1.2	0.09853	0.10027	0.10204	0.10383	0.10565	0.10749	0.10935	0.11123	0.11314	0.11507
−1.1	0.11702	0.11900	0.12100	0.12302	0.12507	0.12714	0.12924	0.13136	0.13350	0.13567
−1.0	0.13786	0.14007	0.14231	0.14457	0.14686	0.14917	0.15151	0.15386	0.15625	0.15866
−0.9	0.16109	0.16354	0.16602	0.16853	0.17106	0.17361	0.17619	0.17879	0.18141	0.18406
−0.8	0.18673	0.18943	0.19215	0.19489	0.19766	0.20045	0.20327	0.20611	0.20897	0.21186
−0.7	0.21476	0.21770	0.22065	0.22363	0.22663	0.22965	0.23270	0.23576	0.23885	0.24196
−0.6	0.24510	0.24825	0.25143	0.25463	0.25785	0.26109	0.26435	0.26763	0.27093	0.27425
−0.5	0.27760	0.28096	0.28434	0.28774	0.29116	0.29460	0.29806	0.30153	0.30503	0.30854
−0.4	0.31207	0.31561	0.31918	0.32276	0.32636	0.32997	0.33360	0.33724	0.34090	0.34458
−0.3	0.34827	0.35197	0.35569	0.35942	0.36317	0.36693	0.37070	0.37448	0.37828	0.38209
−0.2	0.38591	0.38974	0.39358	0.39743	0.40129	0.40517	0.40905	0.41294	0.41683	0.42074
−0.1	0.42465	0.42858	0.43251	0.43644	0.44038	0.44433	0.44828	0.45224	0.45620	0.46017
0.0	0.46414	0.46812	0.47210	0.47608	0.48006	0.48405	0.48803	0.49202	0.49601	0.50000

Note: Example: Value Z=−2.64 is (−2.6)+(−0.04)=−2.64 and cumulative probability of (−2.64) is 0.00415.

Table D.2 Cumulative Standard Normal Probability (+ve Values)

Z	0.00	0.01	0.02	0.03	0.04	0.05	0.06	0.07	0.08	0.09
0.0	0.50000	0.50399	0.50798	0.51197	0.51595	0.51994	0.52392	0.52790	0.53188	0.53586
0.1	0.53983	0.54380	0.54776	0.55172	0.55567	0.55962	0.56356	0.56749	0.57142	0.57535
0.2	0.57926	0.58317	0.58706	0.59095	0.59483	0.59871	0.60257	0.60642	0.61026	0.61409
0.3	0.61791	0.62172	0.62552	0.62930	0.63307	0.63683	0.64058	0.64431	0.64803	0.65173
0.4	0.65542	0.65910	0.66276	0.66640	0.67003	0.67364	0.67724	0.68082	0.68439	0.68793
0.5	0.69146	0.69497	0.69847	0.70194	0.70540	0.70884	0.71226	0.71566	0.71904	0.72240
0.6	0.72575	0.72907	0.73237	0.73565	0.73891	0.74215	0.74537	0.74857	0.75175	0.75490
0.7	0.75804	0.76115	0.76424	0.76730	0.77035	0.77337	0.77637	0.77935	0.78230	0.78524
0.8	0.78814	0.79103	0.79389	0.79673	0.79955	0.80234	0.80511	0.80785	0.81057	0.81327
0.9	0.81594	0.81859	0.82121	0.82381	0.82639	0.82894	0.83147	0.83398	0.83646	0.83891
1.0	0.84134	0.84375	0.84614	0.84849	0.85083	0.85314	0.85543	0.85769	0.85993	0.86214
1.1	0.86433	0.86650	0.86864	0.87076	0.87286	0.87493	0.87698	0.87900	0.88100	0.88298
1.2	0.88493	0.88686	0.88877	0.89065	0.89251	0.89435	0.89617	0.89796	0.89973	0.90147
1.3	0.90320	0.90490	0.90658	0.90824	0.90988	0.91149	0.91309	0.91466	0.91621	0.91774
1.4	0.91924	0.92073	0.92220	0.92364	0.92507	0.92647	0.92785	0.92922	0.93056	0.93189
1.5	0.93319	0.93448	0.93574	0.93699	0.93822	0.93943	0.94062	0.94179	0.94295	0.94408
1.6	0.94520	0.94630	0.94738	0.94845	0.94950	0.95053	0.95154	0.95254	0.95352	0.95449
1.7	0.95543	0.95637	0.95728	0.95818	0.95907	0.95994	0.96080	0.96164	0.96246	0.96327
1.8	0.96407	0.96485	0.96562	0.96638	0.96712	0.96784	0.96856	0.96926	0.96995	0.97062
1.9	0.97128	0.97193	0.97257	0.97320	0.97381	0.97441	0.97500	0.97558	0.97615	0.97670
2.0	0.97725	0.97778	0.97831	0.97882	0.97932	0.97982	0.98030	0.98077	0.98124	0.98169
2.1	0.98214	0.98257	0.98300	0.98341	0.98382	0.98422	0.98461	0.98500	0.98537	0.98574
2.2	0.98610	0.98645	0.98679	0.98713	0.98745	0.98778	0.98809	0.98840	0.98870	0.98899
2.3	0.98928	0.98956	0.98983	0.99010	0.99036	0.99061	0.99086	0.99111	0.99134	0.99158
2.4	0.99180	0.99202	0.99224	0.99245	0.99266	0.99286	0.99305	0.99324	0.99343	0.99361
2.5	0.99379	0.99396	0.99413	0.99430	0.99446	0.99461	0.99477	0.99492	0.99506	0.99520
2.6	0.99534	0.99547	0.99560	0.99573	0.99585	0.99598	0.99609	0.99621	0.99632	0.99643
2.7	0.99653	0.99664	0.99674	0.99683	0.99693	0.99702	0.99711	0.99720	0.99728	0.99736
2.8	0.99744	0.99752	0.99760	0.99767	0.99774	0.99781	0.99788	0.99795	0.99801	0.99807
2.9	0.99813	0.99819	0.99825	0.99831	0.99836	0.99841	0.99846	0.99851	0.99856	0.99861
3.0	0.99865	0.99869	0.99874	0.99878	0.99882	0.99886	0.99889	0.99893	0.99896	0.99900
3.1	0.99903	0.99906	0.99910	0.99913	0.99916	0.99918	0.99921	0.99924	0.99926	0.99929
3.2	0.99931	0.99934	0.99936	0.99938	0.99940	0.99942	0.99944	0.99946	0.99948	0.99950
3.3	0.99952	0.99953	0.99955	0.99957	0.99958	0.99960	0.99961	0.99962	0.99964	0.99965
3.4	0.99966	0.99968	0.99969	0.99970	0.99971	0.99972	0.99973	0.99974	0.99975	0.99976
3.5	0.99977	0.99978	0.99978	0.99979	0.99980	0.99981	0.99981	0.99982	0.99983	0.99983
3.6	0.99984	0.99985	0.99985	0.99986	0.99986	0.99987	0.99987	0.99988	0.99988	0.99989
3.7	0.99989	0.99990	0.99990	0.99990	0.99991	0.99991	0.99992	0.99992	0.99992	0.99992
3.8	0.99993	0.99993	0.99993	0.99994	0.99994	0.99994	0.99994	0.99995	0.99995	0.99995
3.9	0.99995	0.99995	0.99996	0.99996	0.99996	0.99996	0.99996	0.99996	0.99997	0.99997

Note: Example: Value $Z = 2.64$ is $(2.6) + (0.04) = 2.64$ and cumulative probability of (2.64) is 0.99585.

APPENDIX E

Table E.1 't' Table (t Values for One-tailed and Two-tailed Tests)

One-tailed =>	0.25	0.2	0.15	0.1	0.05	0.025	0.02	0.01	0.005	0.0025	0.001	0.0005
Two-tailed =>	0.5	0.4	0.3	0.2	0.1	0.05	0.04	0.02	0.01	0.005	0.002	0.001
df												
1	1.000	1.376	1.963	3.078	6.310	12.700	15.900	31.820	63.650	127.300	318.300	636.619
2	0.817	1.061	1.386	1.886	2.920	4.303	4.849	6.965	9.925	14.080	22.330	31.599
3	0.765	0.979	1.250	1.638	2.353	3.182	3.482	4.541	5.841	7.453	10.220	12.924
4	0.741	0.941	1.190	1.533	2.132	2.776	2.999	3.747	4.604	5.598	7.173	8.610
5	0.727	0.920	1.156	1.476	2.015	2.571	2.757	3.365	4.032	4.773	5.893	6.869
6	0.718	0.906	1.134	1.440	1.943	2.447	2.612	3.143	3.707	4.317	5.208	5.959
7	0.711	0.896	1.119	1.415	1.895	2.365	2.517	2.998	3.499	4.029	4.785	5.408
8	0.706	0.889	1.108	1.397	1.860	2.306	2.449	2.896	3.355	3.833	4.501	5.041
9	0.703	0.883	1.100	1.383	1.833	2.262	2.398	2.821	3.250	3.690	4.297	4.781
10	0.700	0.879	1.093	1.372	1.812	2.228	2.359	2.764	3.169	3.581	4.144	4.587
11	0.697	0.876	1.088	1.363	1.796	2.201	2.328	2.718	3.106	3.497	4.025	4.437
12	0.696	0.873	1.083	1.356	1.782	2.179	2.303	2.681	3.055	3.428	3.930	4.318
13	0.694	0.870	1.079	1.350	1.771	2.160	2.282	2.650	3.012	3.372	3.852	4.221
14	0.692	0.868	1.076	1.345	1.761	2.145	2.264	2.624	2.977	3.326	3.787	4.140
15	0.691	0.866	1.074	1.341	1.753	2.131	2.249	2.602	2.947	3.286	3.733	4.073
16	0.690	0.865	1.071	1.337	1.746	2.120	2.235	2.583	2.921	3.252	3.686	4.015
17	0.689	0.863	1.069	1.333	1.740	2.110	2.224	2.567	2.898	3.222	3.646	3.965
18	0.688	0.862	1.067	1.330	1.734	2.101	2.214	2.552	2.878	3.197	3.610	3.922
19	0.688	0.861	1.066	1.328	1.729	2.093	2.205	2.539	2.861	3.174	3.579	3.883
20	0.687	0.860	1.064	1.325	1.725	2.086	2.197	2.528	2.845	3.153	3.552	3.850
21	0.686	0.859	1.063	1.323	1.721	2.080	2.189	2.518	2.831	3.135	3.527	3.819
22	0.686	0.858	1.061	1.321	1.717	2.074	2.183	2.508	2.819	3.119	3.505	3.792
23	0.685	0.858	1.060	1.319	1.714	2.069	2.177	2.500	2.807	3.104	3.485	3.768
24	0.685	0.857	1.059	1.318	1.711	2.064	2.172	2.492	2.797	3.091	3.467	3.745
25	0.684	0.856	1.058	1.316	1.708	2.060	2.167	2.485	2.787	3.078	3.450	3.725
26	0.684	0.856	1.058	1.315	1.706	2.056	2.162	2.479	2.779	3.067	3.435	3.707
27	0.684	0.855	1.057	1.314	1.703	2.052	2.158	2.473	2.771	3.057	3.421	3.690
28	0.683	0.855	1.056	1.313	1.701	2.048	2.154	2.467	2.763	3.047	3.408	3.674
29	0.683	0.854	1.055	1.311	1.699	2.045	2.150	2.462	2.756	3.038	3.396	3.659
30	0.683	0.854	1.055	1.310	1.697	2.042	2.147	2.457	2.750	3.030	3.385	3.646
40	0.681	0.851	1.050	1.303	1.684	2.021	2.123	2.423	2.704	2.971	3.307	3.551
50	0.679	0.849	1.047	1.299	1.676	2.009	2.109	2.403	2.678	2.937	3.261	3.496
60	0.679	0.848	1.045	1.296	1.671	2.000	2.099	2.390	2.660	2.915	3.232	3.460
80	0.678	0.846	1.043	1.292	1.664	1.990	2.088	2.374	2.639	2.887	3.195	3.416
100	0.677	0.845	1.042	1.290	1.660	1.984	2.081	2.364	2.626	2.871	3.174	3.390
1,000	0.675	0.842	1.037	1.282	1.646	1.962	2.056	2.330	2.581	2.813	3.098	3.300
Z	0.674	0.841	1.036	1.282	1.645	1.960	2.054	2.326	2.576	2.807	3.090	3.291
Conf. level	50%	60%	70%	80%	90%	95%	96%	98%	99%	99.5%	99.8%	99.9%

APPENDIX F

Table F.1 Significance Points of Chi-square Test

df	0.995	0.99	0.975	0.95	0.9	0.1	0.05	0.025	0.01	0.005
1	–	–	0.001	0.004	0.016	2.706	3.841	5.024	6.635	7.879
2	0.010	0.020	0.051	0.103	0.211	4.605	5.991	7.378	9.210	10.597
3	0.072	0.115	0.216	0.352	0.584	6.251	7.815	9.348	11.345	12.838
4	0.207	0.297	0.484	0.711	1.064	7.779	9.488	11.143	13.277	14.860
5	0.412	0.554	0.831	1.145	1.610	9.236	11.070	12.833	15.086	16.750
6	0.676	0.872	1.237	1.635	2.204	10.645	12.592	14.449	16.812	18.548
7	0.989	1.239	1.690	2.167	2.833	12.017	14.067	16.013	18.475	20.278
8	1.344	1.646	2.180	2.733	3.490	13.362	15.507	17.535	20.090	21.955
9	1.735	2.088	2.700	3.325	4.168	14.684	16.919	19.023	21.666	23.589
10	2.156	2.558	3.247	3.940	4.865	15.987	18.307	20.483	23.209	25.188
11	2.603	3.053	3.816	4.575	5.578	17.275	19.675	21.920	24.725	26.757
12	3.074	3.571	4.404	5.226	6.304	18.549	21.026	23.337	26.217	28.300
13	3.565	4.107	5.009	5.892	7.042	19.812	22.362	24.736	27.688	29.819
14	4.075	4.660	5.629	6.571	7.790	21.064	23.685	26.119	29.141	31.319
15	4.601	5.229	6.262	7.261	8.547	22.307	24.996	27.488	30.578	32.801
16	5.142	5.812	6.908	7.962	9.312	23.542	26.296	28.845	32.000	34.267
17	5.697	6.408	7.564	8.672	10.085	24.769	27.587	30.191	33.409	35.718
18	6.265	7.015	8.231	9.390	10.865	25.989	28.869	31.526	34.805	37.156
19	6.844	7.633	8.907	10.117	11.651	27.204	30.144	32.852	36.191	38.582
20	7.434	8.260	9.591	10.851	12.443	28.412	31.410	34.170	37.566	39.997
21	8.034	8.897	10.283	11.591	13.240	29.615	32.671	35.479	38.932	41.401
22	8.643	9.542	10.982	12.338	14.041	30.813	33.924	36.781	40.289	42.796
23	9.260	10.196	11.689	13.091	14.848	32.007	35.172	38.076	41.638	44.181
24	9.886	10.856	12.401	13.848	15.659	33.196	36.415	39.364	42.980	45.559
25	10.520	11.524	13.120	14.611	16.473	34.382	37.652	40.646	44.314	46.928
26	11.160	12.198	13.844	15.379	17.292	35.563	38.885	41.923	45.642	48.290
27	11.808	12.879	14.573	16.151	18.114	36.741	40.113	43.195	46.963	49.645
28	12.461	13.565	15.308	16.928	18.939	37.916	41.337	44.461	48.278	50.993
29	13.121	14.256	16.047	17.708	19.768	39.087	42.557	45.722	49.588	52.336
30	13.787	14.953	16.791	18.493	20.599	40.256	43.773	46.979	50.892	53.672
40	20.707	22.164	24.433	26.509	29.051	51.805	55.758	59.342	63.691	66.766
50	27.991	29.707	32.357	34.764	37.689	63.167	67.505	71.420	76.154	79.490
60	35.534	37.485	40.482	43.188	46.459	74.397	79.082	83.298	88.379	91.952
70	43.275	45.442	48.758	51.739	55.329	85.527	90.531	95.023	100.425	104.215
80	51.172	53.540	57.153	60.391	64.278	96.578	101.879	106.629	112.329	116.321
90	59.196	61.754	65.647	69.126	73.291	107.565	113.145	118.136	124.116	128.299
100	67.328	70.065	74.222	77.929	82.358	118.498	124.342	129.561	135.807	140.169

Notes: Chi-square value for intermediate degrees of freedom (df) is obtained by interpolation. For example, the chi-square value for df=32 at p=0.05 is $[(32-30) * 55.758+(40-32) * 43.773)]/(40-30)=46.17$.
Often 0.05 and sometimes 0.01 probability levels are used for chi-square tests.

APPENDIX G

Table G.1   Critical Values for the Wilcoxon/Mann–Whitney Test (U)

Non-directional (Two-sided) $\alpha = 0.05$ and Directional (One-sided) $\alpha = 0.2$

n_1	\ n_2 → 0	2	3	4	5	6	7	8	9	10	11	12	13	14	15	16	17	18	19	20
2		–	–	–	–	–	–	0	0	0	0	1	1	1	1	1	2	2	2	2
3		–	–	–	0	1	1	2	2	3	3	4	4	5	5	6	6	7	7	8
4		–	–	0	1	2	3	4	4	5	6	7	8	9	10	11	11	12	13	13
5		–	0	1	2	3	5	6	7	8	9	11	12	13	14	15	17	18	19	20
6		–	1	2	3	5	6	8	10	11	13	14	16	17	19	21	22	24	25	27
7		–	1	3	5	6	8	10	12	14	16	18	20	22	24	26	28	30	32	34
8		0	2	4	6	8	10	13	15	17	19	22	24	26	29	31	34	36	38	41
9		0	2	4	7	10	12	15	17	21	23	26	28	31	34	37	39	42	45	48
10		0	3	5	8	11	14	17	20	23	26	29	33	36	39	42	45	48	52	55
11		0	3	6	9	13	16	19	23	26	30	33	37	40	44	47	51	55	58	62
12		1	4	7	11	14	18	22	26	29	33	37	41	45	49	53	57	61	65	69
13		1	4	8	12	16	20	24	28	33	37	41	45	50	54	59	63	67	72	76
14		1	5	9	13	17	22	26	31	36	40	45	50	55	59	64	67	74	78	83
15		1	5	10	14	19	24	29	34	39	44	49	54	59	64	70	75	80	85	90
16		1	6	11	15	21	26	31	37	42	47	53	59	64	70	75	81	86	92	98
17		2	6	11	17	22	28	34	39	45	51	57	63	67	75	81	87	93	99	105
18		2	7	12	18	24	30	36	42	48	55	61	67	74	80	86	93	99	106	112
19		2	7	13	19	25	32	38	45	52	58	65	72	78	85	92	99	106	113	119
20		2	8	14	20	27	34	41	48	55	62	69	76	83	90	98	105	112	119	127

Non-directional (Two-sided) $\alpha = 0.01$ and Directional (One-sided) $\alpha = 0.005$

n_1	\ n_2 → 0	2	3	4	5	6	7	8	9	10	11	12	13	14	15	16	17	18	19	20
2		–	–	–	–	–	–	–	–	–	–	–	–	–	–	–	–	–	0	0
3		–	–	–	–	–	–	–	0	0	0	1	1	1	2	2	2	2	3	3
4		–	–	–	–	0	0	1	1	2	2	3	3	4	5	5	6	6	7	8
5		–	–	–	0	1	1	2	3	4	5	6	7	7	8	9	10	11	12	13
6		–	–	0	1	2	3	4	5	6	7	9	10	11	12	13	15	16	17	18
7		–	–	0	1	3	4	6	7	9	10	12	13	15	16	18	19	21	22	24
8		–	–	1	2	4	6	7	9	11	13	15	17	18	20	22	24	26	28	30
9		–	0	1	3	5	7	9	11	13	16	18	20	22	24	27	29	31	33	36
10		–	0	2	4	6	9	11	13	16	18	21	24	26	29	31	34	37	39	42
11		–	0	2	5	7	10	13	16	18	21	24	27	30	33	36	39	42	45	46
12		–	1	3	6	9	12	15	18	21	24	27	31	34	37	41	44	47	51	54
13		–	1	3	7	10	13	17	20	24	27	31	34	38	42	45	49	53	56	60
14		–	1	4	7	11	15	18	22	26	30	34	38	42	46	50	54	58	63	67
15		–	2	5	8	12	16	20	24	29	33	37	42	46	51	55	60	64	69	73
16		–	2	5	9	13	18	22	27	31	36	41	45	50	55	60	65	70	74	79
17		–	2	6	10	15	19	24	29	34	39	44	49	54	60	65	70	75	81	86
18		–	2	6	11	16	21	26	31	37	42	47	53	58	64	70	75	81	87	92
19		0	3	7	12	17	22	28	33	39	45	51	56	63	69	74	81	87	93	99
20		0	3	8	13	18	24	30	36	42	46	54	60	67	73	79	86	92	99	105

Bibliography

Blalock, H.M. (1979). *Social Statistics*. New York: McGraw Hill.

Champion, D.J. (1970). *Basic Statistics for Social Research*. New York: Harper and Row.

Croxton, F.E. and Cowden, D.J. (1967). *Applied General Statistics*. New Delhi: Prentice-Hall.

Hanushek, E.A. and Jackson, J.E. (1977). *Statistical Methods for Social Scientiststs*. New York: Academic Press.

Levin, J. and Foz, J.A. (2010). *Elementary Statistics in Social Research*. Boston, MA: Allyn & Bacon (in India by Dorling Kindersley Pvt Ltd, New Delhi).

Nachmias, C. and Nachmias, D. (1995). *Research Methods in the Social Sciences*. New York: St Martin's.

Nie, N.H., Hull, C., Jenkins, J.G., Steinbrenner, K. and Bent, D.H. (1975). *Statistical Package for the Social Sciences*. New York: McGraw Hill.

Norušis, M.J. (2008). *SPSS Guide to Data Analysis*. New York: Prentice Hall.

Rajaretnam, T. (2000). "Sociocultural Determinants of Contraceptive Method Choice in Goa and Kerala, India." *The Journal of Family Welfare* 46 (2): 1–11.

Rajaretnam, T. and Hallad, J.S. (2000). *Determinants of Nutritional Status of Young Children in India: An Analysis of 1992–93 NFHS Data*. Vol. 29.2 of *Demography India*, pp. 179–200. New Delhi: Indian Association for the Study of Population.

Retherford, R.D. and Choe, M.K. (1993). *Statistical Model for Casual Analysis*. New York: John Wiley & Sons, Inc.

Siegel, S. and Castellan, N.J. Jr. (1988). *Non-Parametric Statistics for the Behavioral Sciences*. New York: McGraw-Hill.

Sprinthall, R.C. (1987). *Basic Statistical Analysis*. Englewood-Cliffs, NJ: Prentice-Hall.

Tacq, J. (1996). *Multivariate Analysis Techniques in Social Science Research*. London: SAGE Publications.

UNDP (United Nations Development Programme) (2011). Human Development Report 2011.

Weiss, N.A. (2011). *Introductory Statistics*. Boston, MA: Addison Wesley (in India by Dorling Kindersley Pvt Ltd, New Delhi).

WHO (1994). *A User's Guide to the Self Reporting Questionnaire* (WHO/MNH/PSF/948). Geneva: Division of Mental Health, World Health organization.

Wonnacott, R.J. and Wonnacott, T.H. (1979). *Econometrics*. New York: John Wiley & Sons, Inc.

Wonnacott, R.J. and Wonnacott, T.H. (1990). *Introductory Statistics for Business and Economics*. New York: John Wiley & Sons, Inc.

Yamane, T. (1970). *Statistics: An Introductory Analysis*. New York: Harper and Row.

Index

About the Author

T. Rajaretnam is Program Management Specialist (Professor) at Tata Institute of Social Sciences, Mumbai. Earlier, he was Deputy Director at Population Research Centre, Institute of Economic Research, Dharwad, Karnataka. He has conducted many research studies in the fields of demography, reproductive health and nutrition, drinking water and sanitation, agriculture, rural livelihoods, monitoring and evaluation and socioeconomic studies spanning over a period of more than 35 years. He was involved in some of the nation-wide large-scale surveys such as National Family Health Surveys and District Level Household Surveys. He was also teaching Social Statistics to MA, MSc, MPhil and PhD students of different social science disciplines.